WORKS ISSUED BY
THE HAKLUYT SOCIETY

———

THE VOYAGE OF GEORGE VANCOUVER, 1791–1795

VOLUME II

SECOND SERIES
NO. 164

Plate 20. Zachary Mudge.

A Voyage of Discovery to the North Pacific Ocean and Round the World

1791–1795

With an Introduction and Appendices

VOLUME II

EDITED BY

W. KAYE LAMB

THE HAKLUYT SOCIETY
LONDON
1984

ISBN 0 904180 18 2
0 904180 16 6 (set of four volumes)

Printed in Great Britain by the
University Press, Cambridge

Published by the Hakluyt Society
c/o The Map Library,
British Library Reference Division
London WC1B 3DG

CONTENTS

v

ILLUSTRATIONS

† Indicates engravings reproduced from a set of the 1798 edition of *A Voyage of Discovery* in the British Library (1889 R 42), by permission of the Library. Original captions, where retained, are indicated by quotation marks.

PLATES

SKETCH MAPS

All base maps by Michael E. Leek

ix

BOOK THE SECOND.

VISIT THE SANDWICH ISLANDS; PROCEED TO SURVEY THE
COAST OF NEW ALBION; PASS THROUGH AN INLAND
NAVIGATION; TRANSACTIONS AT NOOTKA; ARRIVE AT
PORT ST. FRANCISCO.

CHAPTER I.

*Passage to the Sandwich Islands—Arrive off Owhyhee—Visit from Tianna and
other Chiefs—Leave Towereroo at Owhyhee—Proceed to Leeward—Anchor in
Whytete Bay in Waohoo—Arrival at Attowai.*

OUR friends having quitted us soon after noon on Tuesday the 24th, we
directed our course to the northward, and notwithstanding we had now been
nearly ten months absent from England, it was not until the present moment
that our voyage could be considered as commenced; having now for the first
time pointed our vessels' heads towards the grand object of the expedition.
I cannot help mentioning that I felt, on this occasion, very considerable regret
for the little progress we had hitherto made. It was now within a few days
of the time I had calculated, agreeably to the arrangements in England, that
we should be quitting the Sandwich islands which were yet at the remote
distance of nearly eight hundred leagues. One satisfactory reflection however
was, that we had not been retarded by any mispent time, or inexcusable
delays; and that although a month had been devoted to the examination of
the south-west part of New Holland, that period was, without doubt, not
unprofitably employed. Adverse winds, and the indifferent sailing of the
vessels had principally operated to prevent our being further advanced.

A light eastwardly breeze brought us in the afternoon within sight of
Titeroa,[1] and at sun-set that island bore by compass from N. by W. to N.
by E.; Otaheite S.E. to S.; and Morea S.S.W. to S.W. Our progress was so
slow that, at noon on Wednesday the 25th, we observed in latitude 17° 1′,

---

[1] Tetiaroa.

Morea bearing by compass from S. 24 W. to S. 8 W.; Otaheite from S. 11 E. to S. 41 E. and Titeroa from N. 85 E. to N. 45 E. about three or four miles distant. Some of the inhabitants visited us from this island, and brought a few fowls, fish, and cocoa nuts to barter.[1] The weather falling calm, and the ship drifting fast in with the land, we were employed until sun set in towing her from it. At this time a light breeze springing up from the south the boats were taken on board, and all sail made to the northward; but so tardily did we proceed that, on Friday the 27th, in the morning, Otaheite and Morea were still in sight astern. We continued moving at this gentle rate until Wednesday the 1st of February, at which time we had reached only the latitude of 13° 54', longitude 209° 53'. The wind had been variable, though chiefly from the eastern quarter, with tolerably fair weather. From this period our progress was somewhat accelerated. We were daily visited by numerous birds, which inhabit the low half drowned islands of this ocean, varying in their kinds as well as numbers, until Wednesday the 8th, when, in latitude 4° 36', and longitude 209° 15', they appeared to have intirely deserted us.[2] During this last week the weather had been clear, though very sultry, with a moderate breeze between the E.N.E. and N.N.E. The dead reckoning had hitherto varied about half a degree only to the westward of the chronometer; but as we now advanced, we found a very strong westwardly current,[3] which affected us so much, that when we reached the equator, which was about noon on Sunday, the 12th, our longitude by account was 210° 35', although by the chronometer we were then in 207° 38' only.[4] This afternoon, Wednesday the 15th, a few birds were again seen about the ship; the winds and weather continued nearly the same, attended with a heavy northwardly swell, which continued to be very unpleasant, and generally from the N.E. After crossing the line, the current seemed to set to the north-westward, until in latitude 4° 54' north,* longitude by the chronometer 204° 4', by the dead reckoning, 209° 22', which proved, that since we had entered the northern hemisphere, we had been set, in the course of three days, 81' to the westward, and 50' to the north. From this point the current ceased to set to the westward, but continued its northern

---

[1] 'The Chief of the Island whose name was *Modoc* came off with a trifling present – he was a relative of Otoo's – to whom this Island is subject.' – Bell, 24 January.

[2] Sharks offered the crew some sport and amusement: 'we could always kill what numbers of Sharks we pleased. All sailors have a natural antipathy to this Fish and often Hook them for no other purpose than to practice torments and cruelties on them.' – Manby, letters, 11 February.

[3] The South Equatorial Current. Mudge estimated that the current was 'Setting to the Westward at 50 Miles in 24 Hours.' – 13 February.

[4] 'If the Winds had admitted of our fetching Christmas Island Capt. Vancouver intended to have stopt a day for the purpose of catching Turtle but unfortunately we were now fully fifty Leagues to Leeward of it.' – Manby, 11 February. Vancouver was with Cook in December 1777 when the island was discovered. The first landing was made on Christmas Day.

* The latitude is hereafter to be considered as north latitude until it shall be otherwise indicated.

direction, inclining a little to the east, at the rate of four to five leagues per day. Several birds, which had been our constant attendants since the 12th, became very scarce after this evening. The trade wind between N.E. and E.N.E. blew a fresh gale. The weather in general was cloudy, with squalls, accompanied with a very heavy sea from the eastward.

The sky, on the morning of Thursday the 16th, being tolerably clear, I was enabled to obtain six sets of distances of ☾ a ☉, the mean result of which gave the longitude 204° 5′ 53″, the chronometer shewed 204° 6′ 15″; latitude 6° 14′. Very few birds were now to be seen; but in the morning one or two turtles were observed. The wind prevailing to the northward of N.E., rendered our reaching the Sandwich islands, without being first led a considerable distance beyond them, a very doubtful circumstance. This induced me to take advantage of the current, which still continued to set to the northward; and by standing to the eastward or northward as the wind veered, on Thursday the 23d we reached the latitude of 12° 18′, the longitude by the chronometer 203° 16′, and by the dead reckoning 207° 42′. The wind now blew a moderate breeze mostly from the eastward; which permitted us to make a course a little to the eastward of north.

On Sunday the 26th, the mean result of six sets of distances ☾ a ☉ gave the longitude at noon 203° 48′, the chronometer 203° 40′, by the dead reckoning 208° 23′, the latitude 15° 25′.

The wind, which was light, continued between the east and N.E. attended with a hollow rolling swell from the N.W. On Wednesday the 29th, in latitude 17° 22′, longitude 203° 30′, after a few hours calm, towards sun-set a breeze sprang up from the N.W. We now stood to the N.N.E.; which course, by day-light on Thursday the 1st of March, brought us in sight of Owhyhee, [1] bearing by compass from north to N. by E. about twenty-four leagues distant.

The order for prohibiting general trade with the Indians was again read to the ship's company. A particular attention to such regulations with persons circumstanced as we were, was not only of material importance, but was absolutely indispensable.

As the day advanced, which was delightfully pleasant, the wind gradually veered round to the north-eastward, which enabled us shortly after noon to steer for the south point of Owhyhee, [2] then bearing by compass N. 8 W. 14 leagues distant. Our latitude was now 18° 9′, longitude per dead reckoning 209° 33′; by the chronometer 204° 19′, which latter is to be received as the true longitude, notwithstanding the difference of 5° 14′; for so much had we been affected by western or lee currents, in performing this very long and tedious passage. About midnight, we passed to the westward of the south point of Owhyhee; and in the hope of procuring some provisions and refreshments, as we sailed past the west coast of this island we kept close in shore.

[1] The old spelling of Hawaii, the name of the largest island in the Sandwich (now the Hawaiian) Islands.

[2] Ka Lae (South Cape) in lat. 18° 55′ N, long. 155° 41′ W (204° 19′ E).

In the morning of Friday the 2d, with a light breeze from the land, at the distance of about three miles, we stood along shore to the northward. Several canoes came off with a supply of pigs,[1] and vegetables; amongst the latter were some very excellent water melons:[2] the natives, however, demanded a very exorbitant return for these refreshments, and seemed very indifferent about trading, or having any other communication with us.[3] At noon on Saturday the 3d, with very pleasant weather and light breezes, generally from off the land, Karakakooa[4] bore north about five miles distant; and we had now the satisfaction of finding our chronometer, allowing the Otaheitean rate, to agree within a few seconds of its longitude as settled by Captain Cook. The Portsmouth rate made it 1° 18' to the eastward. On board the Chatham, Mr. Arnold's chronometer erred 24' to the westward, according to its rate of going as settled at Otaheite.

The steep precipice which forms the north side of Karakakooa bay, renders its too remarkable to be easily mistaken, especially as the interior country rises thence more abruptly than from the coast to the north or south of the bay; which, although presenting both wood-land and cultivated country above the barren rocky shores where the habitations of the natives are chiefly situated, is, nevertheless, in a great degree destitute of the diversity of prospect which might have been expected here, and which is also the general character of all this side of the island.

Several canoes having stood to sea after us in the morning, we now brought to, for the purpose of trading with them; and were soon honored with a visit from *Tianna*,[5] the person mentioned in Mr. Meare's voyage. He was received in a manner agreeable to the distinguished character he had been represented to support, and which, from his grateful inquiries after his patron, he appeared to deserve. This complimentary conversation he seemed desirous of speedily putting an end to, being very anxious to acquaint us that, since his return from

[1] Pigs, dogs and fowl were brought to the Hawaiian Islands by the Polynesians when they migrated to them.

[2] Menzies noted that he had seen no melons when he visited Hawaii in 1787–88. – 2 March. Bell states that he was told that they had been planted first by Captain William Douglas of the *Iphigenia*, a trader that visited Kealakekua Bay in December 1788. – 3 March.

[3] Bell correctly suspected that this reluctance to trade was an attempt to force Vancouver to sell arms and ammunition: 'the Masters of the different Merchant Ships...have given the Natives Fire Arms and Ammunition in Barter for refreshments, and I have reason to suppose that the seeming scarcity was nothing more than a political scheme to endeavour to force us to offer the like articles for a larger & better supply.' – 2 March.

[4] Kealakekua Bay, where Cook was killed in a clash with the natives in February 1779. It is 40 miles N of Ka Lae.

[5] The name is now spelled Kaiana. Hawaiian was still an unwritten language in Vancouver's time; it was 'firmed in writing' by a committee of missionaries in 1826. 'They found difficulty in distinguishing between *l* and *r*, *k* and *t*, *w* and *v*, and, by vote, chose *l*, *k*, and *w* to represent these sounds.' – Dorothy Barrère, *Hawaii Aboriginal Culture* (Honolulu, 1962), p. 11. Hence the disappearance of *r*, *t* and *v* from the modern spelling of Hawaiian names.

China, he had resided on this island,[1] where many severe conflicts had taken place; in which he had taken part with *Tamaahmaah*,[2] against *Teamawheere*,[3] who, it seemed, had, since the death of *Tereeoboo*,[4] shared the government with *Tamaahmaah*. In one of these battles *Tianna* having shot *Teamawheere*, a complete victory was gained, and these two chiefs agreed to divide the island between them. *Tamaahmaah* becoming the sovereign over the three northern, and *Tianna* of the three southern districts.[5]

Understanding that I purposed going directly to the Leeward islands, *Tianna* requested he might be permitted to accompany us, and, with his wives and retinue, to sleep on board; with which request I thought proper to comply. From the character given of this chief,* I was not a little surprized to find him totally ignorant of our language, and unable to pronounce a single word articulately; but by our knowledge of his speech[6] we soon understood, that, since the preceding autumn, not any vessel had arrived; that about that time three of four American brigs, and one, in which was Mr. Colnett, belonging

---

[1] Kaiana, ambitious, restless and warlike, had been taken to China by Meares in the *Nootka* in 1787 and returned to Hawaii in December 1788, by way of the Northwest Coast, in the *Iphigenia*, another ship owned by Meares and his associates. Meares published a portrait of him in his *Voyages* that suggests his 'Herculean appearance' and he described him as 'a prince of the island of Atooi [Kauai], a chief of illustrious birth and high rank.' – John Meares, *Voyages...from China to the North West Coast of America* (London, 1790), p. 4. Meares assumed he was a prince of Kauai because it was there that he had joined the *Nootka*, but he was in fact a nephew of Kalaniopuu, king (or chief) of Hawaii at the time of Cook's visit. Dissatisfied with prospects in Hawaii, he threw in his lot with Kahekili, who controlled Maui, and took a prominent part in Kahekili's invasion of Oahu in 1783. Again dissatisfied, he broke with Kahekili and went to Kauai, where he was soon at loggerheads with Kaeo, Kahekili's half-brother, who ruled over much of the island. The voyage to China thus offered him both escape and adventure. On his return he settled in his native island of Hawaii and became a supporter of Kamehameha.

[2] Kamehameha, the warrior chief under whom the Sandwich Islands were eventually brought under one control.

[3] Also spelled Teewaroh; in modern Hawaiian, Kiwalao.

[4] Now spelled Kalaniopuu.

[5] This is very much Kaiana's version of events. Accounts are conflicting, but in summary the story appears to be as follows: Kalaniopuu, Chief of Hawaii, died in 1782, having made only two provisions for the succession: he named his son Kiwalao as his successor, but knowing that he was a weak character, he entrusted the war god to his warrior nephew, Kamehameha. A troubled decade followed, as dissatisfaction and ambition were rife amongst the chiefs who had not been recognized in the will. Eventually rival factions assembled around Kiwalao and Kamehameha. In a battle that followed, Kiwalao was killed (though Kaiana's claim that it was he who killed him is suspect) and Kamehameha gained control of much of the island of Hawaii. Kaiana exercised considerable authority under Kamehameha, but he was neither equal to him in status nor independent of him, as his statement to Vancouver implied.

* See Meares's Voyage. [pp. 4–9].

[6] The Hawaiian language, which shares about 85 per cent. of its basic vocabulary with Tahitian. Manby notes that 'the little English' Kaiana 'had learnt was intirely forgot, except the Name of Wine, which he instantly asked for on coming on board.' – letters, 3 March.

to Macao,[1] had visited the islands; and, that it was not possible for any vessels to touch at the other islands, without himself and the people of Owhyhee being informed of their arrival. This intelligence made me despair of meeting the storeship;[2] and the hope which I had so long indulged, as a compensation for the tardy progress which circumstances had hitherto compelled us to make, now seemed intirely to vanish.

Tianna viewed every transaction on board with attentive admiration, whilst our numbers seemed to create in his mind a degree of surprize he was unable to subdue. In the course of the evening he held frequent conversations with *Towereroo*, and during the night he was several times on deck, endeavouring to ascertain the number of men on duty in the different parts of the ship.[3]

The retinue of *Tianna* on this occasion was to consist of a considerable number; part were to attend him on board the Discovery, and the remainder was to proceed in the Chatham. His residence was a little to the north of Karakakooa; and as it was proposed his suite should be taken on board the next afternoon, we kept off that station. A messenger, apparently of some consequence, was dispatched to the shore with directions for this purpose the preceding evening; in the forenoon of Sunday the 4th, however, several consultations took place with those about him, which finally ended in his declining to accompany us to Attowai.[4] The conversation he had held with *Towereroo* had induced him to believe that the services of this lad might be of great importance to him; and as he promised *Towereroo* a very handsome establishment of house, land, and other advantages, I thought it adviseable to fix him with *Tianna* for the present, that, on my return in the winter, I might be enabled to form some judgment of his treatment. Morotoi,[5] the native island of *Towereroo*, was in a state of great confusion, in consequence of its being the general rendezvous of *Titeere* and *Taio*, the sovereigns of Woahoo and Attowai,[6] who were then meditating a war against this island. This was

---

[1] Colnett and his ship, the *Argonaut*, had been seized at Nootka by the Spaniards in July 1789 and taken to Mexico. They were released a year later, and after visiting Nootka Sound Colnett sailed for China by way of Hawaii. He was at the islands from 27 March to 18 April 1791.

[2] Vancouver had hoped to find the storeship *Daedalus* awaiting him. She did not arrive until 9 May, after his departure.

[3] Vancouver was suspicious of Kaiana's motives, and with good reason. He was undoubtedly gauging the possibility of seizing one or both of Vancouver's ships and gaining possession of their guns, arms and ammunition. Vancouver's remarks are paralleled in an entry in the journal of Joseph Ingraham, commander of the trading ship *Hope*. Kaiana had spent the night of 23 May 1791 on board: 'During the night it was observed by the officers and seamen that Tiana slept but little, frequently going on deck. He called me twice to have the ship run nearer shore, but each time I gave orders to the contrary. He likewise enquired of Opye [Opai] the number of men, guns, and quantity of powder on board, etc., which it seems Opye exaggerated.' – M. K. Kaplanoff (ed.), *Joseph Ingraham's Journal of the Brigantine 'Hope'*...(Barre, Mass., 1971), p. 73.

[4] Kauai.   [5] Molokai.

[6] Kahekili, chief of Maui, who also controlled Oahu (Woahoo), and his half-brother Kaeo, who, under his overlordship, controlled much of Kauai.

an additional reason for consenting to the arrangement. *Towereroo*, though exceedingly anxious to accept *Tianna*'s offer, seemed to entertain great doubts as to the future safety of himself and his property; to the last moment he had his choice of remaining on board, or departing with *Tianna*; and, notwithstanding he did not hesitate to prefer the latter, yet he earnestly requested the few clothes he had left, and the articles I had given him, since our leaving Otaheite, might be taken care of on board, until our return; and he would take with him a very small assortment of the different articles of traffic only, to supply his present necessities.[1]

As *Tianna* had several goats, I did not present him with any of these animals, but made him very happy by giving him some vine and orange plants, some almonds, and an assortment of garden seeds, to all of which he promised the most particular care and attention. After receiving some acceptable valuables in return for ten small hogs, he took his leave of us with *Towereroo* about five in the afternoon; and though he affected to be pretty well satisfied with his reception, and flattered with being saluted with four guns on his departure, yet it was very evident he was extremely disappointed and chagrined in not having been able to procure any fire arms or ammunition; which were anxiously solicited, not only by himself but by all his countrymen, and by us as uniformly refused.[2]

To the care of *Towereroo* I intrusted a letter, addressed to the officer commanding the vessel charged with stores and provisions for our service,[3] acquainting him with our departure from Owhyhee, and of my intention to call at the Leeward islands to recruit our water, after which, we should proceed immediately to the coast of America: and I directed him to follow us thither without loss of time, agreeably to the arrangements I had previously made with the Secretary of State's office.

As we stood along shore with a light breeze, we were in the evening greatly surprized on being hailed from a large canoe, which was meeting us, in broken English, demanding who we were, and to what country we belonged, and very civilly requesting to be admitted on board. This being granted, the

[1] Some were highly critical of Vancouver's treatment of Towereroo. Manby states that when the proposal to leave him with Kaiana was made, he 'with joy agreed to the plan, no doubt happy in the idea of parting with a set of Men who had treated him with the utmost barbarity by tearing him from the object of his affections at Otahite.' – letters, 3 March. 'Poor fellow I pity'd him when I thought how much happier he wou'd have been had he been suffered to remain at Otaheite which he wish'd so much for, – ...he seem'd low spirited & dejected.' He was 'put ashore like a Convict to his place of transportation.' – Bell, March.

[2] 'It was but too evident...that the attention of *Tianna* & his followers were wholly directed to warlike preparations, for nothing was now held in greater estimation or more eagerly sought after than fire arms & powder by those very people who but a few years back shudderd at the report of a musquet, but which they could now handle with a degree of ease & dexterity that equalld the most expert veteran.' – Menzies, 3 March. Menzies had visited the islands in the *Prince of Wales* in 1787–8.

[3] Neither this letter nor a copy is known to have survived.

speaker proved to be a young man named *Tarehooa*, a native of Attowai,[1] who had accompanied a Mr. John Ingram commanding an American ship laden with furs, from North West America, bound to Boston in New England by the way of China. *Tarehooa* had been with Mr. Ingram in North America about seven months, and had returned in a brig with him some months before.[2]

His present master, he informed me, was a chief named *Kahowmotoo*;[3] of great importance, and nearly equal in consequence with *Tianna*; and who like him had been very instrumental in gaining for *Tamaahmaah* the sovereignty of the whole island. We were instantly made known to this chief, who presented me with a letter written in Spanish, dated 'Sloop Princess Royal, March 28, 1791,' (probably the same vessel that was captured at Nootka) attended by an English translation of the same date, and both signed 'Emanuel Kimper;'[4] recommending in the strongest terms *Tamaahmaah*, *Tianna*, and this chief *Kahowmotoo*, for their having, on all occasions, shewn Mr. Kimper and his people every mark of friendly attention and hospitality. *Kahowmotoo* presented me with three fine hogs, for which in return he received ample compensation; but, like *Tianna*, was much mortified that it had not been made in arms or ammunition. He requested to sleep on board, and that his canoe might be taken in tow, in both of which he was indulged. Much conversation took place in the evening. He confirmed the account given by *Tianna* of the non-arrival of any vessels for some months past, and the wars which had taken place; but it was excessively difficult to reconcile the story he told of *Tianna*, with that which *Tianna* had related of himself. *Tianna*'s atchievements he readily admitted, and candidly allowed him great merit for his military exploits; but denied his having equal power with *Tamaahmaah*; saying, there was but one *aree de hoi* over all Owhyhee, and he was *Tamaahmaah*; and that if *Tianna* was an *aree de hoi*,[5] so also must he be, and other chiefs of equal consequence with *Tianna* and himself.

[1] Kalehua, a native of Kauai.

[2] Joseph Ingraham was mate of the Boston trader *Columbia*. She arrived at the Sandwich Islands from the Northwest Coast late in August 1789 and left on 17 September for Boston, where she arrived on 9 August 1790. Kalehua, whom Ingraham knew as Opye (Opai), was only six weeks in America, not seven months, as Ingraham was given command of the brigantine *Hope*, which sailed from Boston for the Northwest Coast on 16 September. She arrived at Hawaii on 20 May 1791. There Opye left the ship, having been with Ingraham twenty months.   [3] Keeaumoku.

[4] The *Princess Royal* was, as Vancouver surmised, the ship seized at Nootka; the Spaniards were taking her to Macao, where she was to be handed back to her owners. She was commanded by Manuel Quimper, who had been instructed to visit the Sandwich Islands and establish friendly relations with the natives. Colnett believed the Spaniards intended to establish a settlement there. Colnett in the *Argonaut* met up with Quimper in the *Princess Royal* in Kailua Bay, and a near clash occurred, as Colnett at one time had it in mind 'to retake the Vessel by force of arms, which the Ship's Crew Joyfully agreed to.' – F. W. Howay (ed.), *The Journal of Captain James Colnett* (Toronto, 1940), pp. 213–19.

[5] This is not a Hawaiian expression; Vancouver was repeating the term he had heard in Tahiti. The correct expression would be alii-nui, meaning a great or principal chief, the head of an aupuni, a term meaning both kingdom and government.

This instance will serve to illustrate how very difficult it is, according to our comprehension of their language, to obtain matter of fact from these people; and that nothing short of indefatigable labour can obtain the ʼruth, and correct information, from man in so early a state of civilization.

The next morning we were abreast of the south point of Toca-yah-ha bay,[1] near which is *Kahowmotoo's* residence. It was a great pleasure to observe the avidity with which all the chiefs who had visited the ship sought after the vegetable productions we had brought; which, if attended to, will in future add to their present abundant production. *Kahowmotoo* was very anxious to obtain every acquisition of this sort, and was made very happy by receiving some fine orange plants, and a packet of different garden seeds; and likewise a goat and kid. With these valuables he appeared to be highly delighted, and promised to give them his greatest care and attention.

Tareehooa, who preferred the name of Jack, had been with Mr. Ingram in the capacity of a servant; but was now promoted to the office of interpreter in the service of this chief, which he by no means badly executed. Jack was extremely solicitous to remain on board, and to accompany us on our voyage. As he appeared to be a very shrewd active fellow, and there was a probability of his being made useful, I accepted of his services on Monday the 5th, to which the chief consented, though with a mixture of regret, and a friendly regard for Jack's future advantage and success. After being saluted with four guns, a compliment which *Tianna* had received, and taking a very affectionate leave of his interpreter, *Kahowmotoo* departed with the most friendly assurance, that whenever we should think proper to visit his district, we should be abundantly supplied with refreshments.

A light breeze, chiefly from the south, advanced us slowly towards the north point of Owhyhee, until the trade wind at E.N.E. no longer intercepted by the high mountains which compose the island, met us; when we directed our course towards Woahoo.[2] Early in the morning of Tuesday the 6th, being well in with the island of Tahoorowa,[3] the Chatham's signal was made to denote our situation in bearing up along the south side of that island; but as neither this nor some previous signals had been acknowledged, I concluded the Chatham had remained becalmed under the high land of Owhyhee; whilst we had benefited by a very fine gale, owing to our being a little further advanced; and Woahoo being our next appointed rendezvous, a long separation could not be apprehended. The trade wind blew strong from the N.E. until we were under the lee of Ranai,[4] when light and variable winds succeeded. At noon Tahoorowa by compass bore S. 88 E.; the S.W. part of Mowee[5] N. 79 E.; the east part of Ranai N. 60 E.; south point N. 20 E.; north west point N. 18 W.; and the western part of Morotoi indistinctly seen,

---

[1] Kawaihae Bay, on the N side of the W coast of Hawaii.
[2] Oahu, now much the most populous island in the group, on which Honolulu is situated.
[3] Kahoolawe, an island off the SW corner of Maui.
[4] Lanai.   [5] Maui.

bore N.N.W. In this situation the latitude was observed to be 20° 41′, longitude by the chronometer 203° 2′. The south point of Ranai being the nearest land, was about four miles distant, and was placed by our observations 1′ south, and 5½ to the west of the situation assigned to it by Captain King. In the afternoon some few of the natives visited us from Ranai, merely, I believe, to satisfy their curiosity, as they brought with them scarcely any thing for barter. Indeed, the dreary and desolate appearance of their island, seemed a sufficient apology for their coming empty handed. The apparent sterility of the country, and a few scattered miserable habitations which we were able with our glasses to discern, indicated the part of it now presented to our view to be very thinly inhabited, and incapable of affording any of its productions to strangers. During the afternoon we proceeded to the north along the west side of Ranai; and, towards sun-set again met the trade wind, which about midnight brought us in sight of Woahoo, bearing by compass west six or seven miles distant. We plied until day light of Wednesday the 7th, when we directed our course along the south side of that island, whose eastern shores bear a similar desolate appearance to those of Ranai, and are principally composed of barren rocks and high precipices, which fall perpendicularly into the sea. We did not pass at a greater distance than a league, yet verdure or cultivation was not any where to be seen. From its east point the north east side of Woahoo takes a direction N. 35 W. off which are scattered some detached islets and rocks; the northernmost of these which we saw, is a low flat rock, lying from the east point N. 22 W. three or four leagues distant; and near the shore was a hill whose summit bears the appearance of a volcanic crater.[1] The land to the north of the east point seemed much indented, but whether capable of affording any shelter or not, we were too far off to discern. On the south east part of this island are two remarkable promontories, which lie from each other S. 81 W. and N. 81 E. about seven miles asunder; the first or easternmost of these is formed of barren rocky cliffs, rising so suddenly from the sea,[2] that to all appearance vessels might brush their sides in passing them; whence the land falls a little back, and forms a shallow bay in a northern direction,[3] where the different colours in the water indicated a rocky bottom; on the beach the surf broke very violently, behind which a lagoon extended some distance to the northward. Should the bottom be found good, vessels might ride in this bay tolerably well protected against the general trade wind; but as our place of rendezvous was round the second promontory, we did not examine it in a more particular manner. Continuing our course about nine we hauled round the reef which lies about a quarter of a mile from that point, and had soundings from 22 to 10 fathoms; in which latter depth of water we anchored about ten o'clock, the bottom sand and pieces of small coral. This promontory, which is the south point of the island, has also on its top the appearance of a crater,[4]

[1] Koko Crater, a sharp cone 1204 feet high.
[2] Koko Head.   [3] Maunalua Bay.
[4] Diamond Head, an extinct volcano. The crater, now occupied by a military installation, may be seen clearly from the air.

formed by volcanic eruptions; this bore by compass N. 82 E.; the outward part of the reef S. 81 E.; the westernmost part of the land in sight N. 82 W. a break in the reef, which extends at irregular distances along the shore, N. 20 W.; a low sandy point, near the west end of a large Indian village N. 7 W.; and the middle of the village (where, the natives informed us, we might land in perfect safety with our boats) N.N.E. about two miles distant. We examined a considerable space around the ship, and found in shore the same description of bottom, though the coral which principally composed it was of so soft a nature, as to cause little apprehension for the safety of our cables. The depth of water within us gradually decreased to six fathoms, and without, to the distance of nearly a mile, as gradually increased to 25 and 30 fathoms, where the bottom was found to be a fine grey sand.

As our quarter deck required caulking, the carpenters were immediately employed on this business. Some few of the natives visited us from the shore, who brought in their canoes a very sparing supply of refreshments, amongst which, the musk and water melons made no inconsiderable part, and were very excellent of their kinds.[1] The situation occupied by us in this bay, which the natives call Whyteete,[2] seemed nearly as eligible as most of the anchoring places these islands are generally found to afford. The inhabitants were excessively orderly and docile, although there was not a chief or any person of distinction amongst them to enforce their good behaviour; neither man nor woman attempted to come on board, without first obtaining permission; and when this was refused, they remained perfectly quiet in their canoes alongside.

The information obtained at Owhyhee, that *Titeere* and *Taio*, with most of the principal chiefs and warriors of this island, and those to leeward, were on a hostile expedition at Morotoi and Mowee, was here confirmed; but differed as to the immediate cause of their absence, which was now represented to be for the purpose of repelling an invasion likely to take place from Owhyhee, by *Tamaahmaah*, *Kohowmotoo*, and *Tianna*. This, in a great measure, seemed to account for the small number of inhabitants who visited us, the wretched condition of their canoes, and the scanty supply of their country's produce which they brought to market. On the shores, the villages appeared numerous, large, and in good repair; and the surrounding country pleasingly

---

[1] Vancouver does not mention two other items of trade: salt and pearls. As the ships had expended all their salt at Tahiti, a new supply was most welcome. The *Chatham* was offered 'a large quantity of excellent Salt, this Salt was brought off in small neat Bundles of about 15 & 20 lbs Wt. – two of which were purchased for a Small Knife or half a dozen Small nails, and in the course of a few hours we fill'd Seven Barrels with this commodity.' Later Bell adds that they 'purchased a large quantity of excellent Salt fish which was well cured, and wou'd no doubt keep very well...' – Bell, 8 and 12 March. Beaglehole states that 'The Hawaiians, alone among Polynesians, produced salt from sea-water by means of properly-constructed salt pans.' – Cook, *Journals*, III, 276n. Cook secured some salt at Niihau in 1778. In his account of his next visit to the islands, Vancouver describes how the salt was harvested. 'They also brought some Pearls to dispose of, but they were for the most part small badly shapd & ill colord, so consequently of little value.' – Menzies, 8 March.   [2] Waikiki.

interspersed with deep, though not extensive valleys; which, with the plains near the sea-side, presented a high degree of cultivation and fertility. The apparent docility of these people, who have been represented by former visitors as the most daring and unmanageable of any who belong to the Sandwich islands, might probably, be attributed in a great measure to the absence of their fighting men, and to our manifest superiority in numbers, regularity in point of order, and military government; which seemed to make a wonderful impression on all who were permitted to come on board, and who, to a man, appeared very much afraid of fire-arms. This was evinced, on our mounting guard to post the centinels round the ship. On this occasion they all hastily paddled towards the shore, and it was not without much persuasion that they were induced to return.[1]

It appeared very singular, that the war of which we had heard so much, was not yet begun; and *Kahowmotoo*, who had frequently mentioned the subject, said they were not to begin the combat until after the expiration of fifteen months. If this information be correct, designs so long premeditated, or preparations delayed so long from being carried into execution, were hard to account for. *Taio* and *Titeere* had now been several months from their respective governments.[2]

Our new ship-mate Jack became very useful; he took upon him to represent us in the most formidable point of view to all his countrymen; magnifying our powers, and augmenting our numbers, and proclaiming that we were not traders, such as they had been accustomed to see; but that we were belonging to King George, and were all mighty warriors. This being his constant discourse, it is not to be wondered that his countrymen became much intimidated; and as this could be productive of no ill consequences, we permitted Jack to proceed in his encomiums, and unanimously agreed it would not be his fault if we were not in high repute amongst the islanders.

After caulking the decks I purposed to execute such trivial repairs, at this place, as might be found necessary to the rigging, &c. &c. provided that water, for which I was alone solicitous, could be procured; as the abundant and excellent refreshments we had obtained at Otaheite, and the high state of health which we had enjoyed since our leaving Dusky bay, rendered supplies of any other nature a secondary consideration.

For this purpose, attended by two armed boats, and a guard of seven marines, I landed, accompanied by Mr. Mudge, Mr. Whidbey, and Mr. Menzies. Our boats remained perfectly quiet on the beach, having passed to the shore between some rocks, which completely protected it from the surf. The natives, who were present, received us in a very orderly manner. Two

---

[1] The relatively large, well armed and well disciplined crews of the *Discovery* and *Chatham* offered a sharp contrast to those of the trading ships with which the islanders were familiar. To attempt to seize them would obviously be a hazardous undertaking.

[2] The anticipated war did not in fact break out in earnest until after the death of Kahekili, chief of Maui, in July 1794. This was after Vancouver's third and last visit to the islands.

bustling men with large sticks, kept the few spectators at a respectful distance: to these I made some presents; and, on inquiring for water, they directed us to some stagnant brackish ponds near the beach. This being rejected, we were given to understand that good water was to be had in abundance at some distance, to which they readily undertook to conduct us: and as they all appeared friendly and pacific, the boats were left in charge of Mr. Swaine and Mr. Manby; and we proceeded, with our guard, in search of the promised supply. Our guides led us to the northward through the village, to an exceedingly well-made causeway, about twelve feet broad, with a ditch on each side.

This opened to our view a spacious plain, which, in the immediate vicinity of the village, had the appearance of the open common fields in England; but, on advancing, the major part appeared divided into fields of irregular shape and figure, which were separated from each other by low stone walls, and were in a very high state of cultivation. These several portions of land were planted with the eddo or *taro* root, [1] in different stages of inundation; none being perfectly dry, and some from three to six or seven inches under water. The causeway led us near a mile from the beach, at the end of which was the water we were in quest of. It was a rivulet five or six feet wide, and about two or three feet deep, well banked up, and nearly motionless; some small rills only, finding a passage through the dams that checked the sluggish stream, by which a constant supply was afforded to the *taro* plantations. The water was excellent, but the road was too rough and hard for rolling our casks such a distance, without exposing them to great damage. This induced me to make our guides understand, that, if the inhabitants would collect, and carry this water on board in gourds, they should be well rewarded for their trouble. The offer was instantly communicated to their neighbours about us, who immediately replied, we should have an ample supply the next day. At the termination of the causeway, the paths of communication with the different fields or plantations were on these narrow stone walls; very rugged, and where one person only could pass at a time. The gentleness and civility of the natives tempted us to extend our walk through the plantations, which we found very pleasant. A fine refreshing breeze prevailed, and the Indians kept at a sufficient distance to prevent their company being incommodious. In this excursion we found the land in a high state of cultivation, mostly under immediate crops of *taro*; and abounding with a variety of wild fowl, chiefly of the duck kind, some of which our sportsmen shot, and they were very fine eating. The sides of the hills, which were at some distance, seemed rocky and barren; the intermediate vallies, which were all inhabited, produced some large trees, and made a pleasing appearance. The plains, however, if we may judge from the labour bestowed on their cultivation, seem to afford the principal proportion of the different vegetable productions on which the inhabitants depend for

[1] Kalo, the most widely cultivated food plant. Poi, the staple food of the islanders, was made from its tubers.

their subsistence. The soil, though tolerably rich, and producing rather a luxuriant abundance, differs very materially from that of Matavai, or the other parts of Otaheite. At Woahoo, Nature seems only to have acted a common part in her dispensations of vegetable food for the service of man; and to have almost confined them to the *taro* plant,[1] the raising of which is attended with much care, ingenuity, and manual labour. In the several parts of its culture, the inhabitants, whether planting, weeding, or gathering, must, during the whole of these operations, be up to their middle in mud, and exposed to the rays of a vertical sun: whereas, on the plains of Otaheite, the surface teems, as it were, spontaneously with the most abundant produce of esculent vegetables, without the help of industry to sow, plant, or rear them, or the assistance of the aqueducts which these people construct with great labour and ingenuity to insure them a crop. There, the continued groves of the lofty and umbrageous bread fruit, apple, palm, and other trees, afford a delightful cool retreat to those favored islanders; here the inhabitants know not the luxury of such retirement. Nor did it appear in the vegetable kingdom alone that Nature here had been less[2] favorable; the human species, though without doubt originally of the same nation, differ excessively; and it would seem that the comparative benevolence of the Otaheiteans and these people was about equal to the natural fertility of the soil on which they respectively lived. It may however appear rather uncharitable to form any decided opinion on so short an acquaintance; yet first impressions will ever have their influence on visiting different countries under circumstances similar, or nearly so. On such occasions it is scarcely possible to avoid comparisons, in which one must necessarily suffer. On our landing at Otaheite, the effusions of friendship and hospitality were evident in the countenances of every one we met. Each endeavoured to anticipate our wants or our wishes by the most fascinating attention, and by sedulously striving to be first in performing any little service we required; inviting us to take refreshments at every house we approached, and manifesting a degree of kindness that would justly be extolled amongst the most polished nations. At Woahoo we were regarded with an unwelcome austerity, and our wants treated by the generality with a negligent indifference. In the course of our walk they exhibited no assiduity to please, nor did they appear apprehensive lest offence should be given; no refreshments were offered, nor had we invitation to any of their houses. Their general behaviour was distantly civil, apparently directed by a desire to establish a peaceable intercourse with strangers, from whom there was a prospect of deriving many valuable acquisitions, which would be unattainable by any other mode of conduct; as they must have been convinced immediately on our landing, that

[1] Menzies' account differs. He states that the plantation 'was nearly level & very extensive & laid out with great neatness into little fields planted with Taro Yams Sweet Potatoes & the Cloth plant [wauke].' – 7 March.

[2] 'more' in the first edition, a mistake one would have expected to find noted in the errata.

we were too powerful to be conquered, and too much upon our guard to suffer the least indignity by surprize.[1] I must, however, do justice to the hospitality of our two guides, who on our reaching the shore took upon them the office of constables; and who had also each caused a hog and a quantity of vegetables to be prepared for our entertainment. On our return this repast was ready, and we were much intreated by them to partake of it; but as it was now past sun set, we were under the necessity of declining their civility; on which they very obligingly put our intended supper into the boats. I presented each of our guides with an acceptable acknowledgment, and earnestly renewing my request of a supply from the brook, which they promised should be complied with the next day, we returned on board.

Towards midnight the Chatham arrived, and anchored a little to the westward of the Discovery. I soon learned from Mr. Broughton that as I had suspected, his vessel had been becalmed the evening we parted until near one the next morning, when they stood towards Mowee; but on his not being able to see the Discovery at day light, he steered to the north-west along the southern side of that island, and found an eligible anchoring place off its western part, with soundings regular and good;[2] and as the natives brought

[1] Johnstone, who had been with Colnett in the *Prince of Wales* in 1787-8, when she wintered in the Sandwich Islands, noted a marked difference in the attitude of the natives. Whereas on the first visit 'we found the Natives behave so very audacious and apparently hostile, their conduct was now the reverse for they were docile and orderly trading fairly, without once seeking to visit on board after being denied. I do not conceive that this amicable change had arisen from any change of disposition, but from the great superiority which they must have observed in the Ships and the regulations in their government, for with us it was an order and positive followed, not to admit any native whatever, except the chiefs within the Ship or out of their Canoes, and since those orders had been followed, not the smallest theft had happened nor had their once been the slightest interruption to the most perfect harmony that subsisted through all our dealings.' – 8 March. Johnstone was in the *Chatham*; isolation from the shore was not so complete in the *Discovery*, which was longer at Waikiki: 'whoever might be inclined to censure the conduct of the ladies for with-holding their company from us on the preceeding day, had now no cause to complain for they came off in large groups not only in the Canoes but on swimming boards with no other intention than that of tendering their persons to any one that would choose to have them, & those who were unsuccessful in their aim went away chiding us for our want of gallantry.' – Menzies, 8 March.
[2] This was the Lahaina anchorage, in later years much frequented by whalers. Bell describes their approach to it and their brief visit to the bay: 'as we got towards the Western Extreme of Mowee we were crowded with Canoes – and being about half way between it and Ranai [Lanai], we had Canoes not only from these two, but from all the other Islands – I reckoned at one time upwards of a hundred & twenty round us – each of which *upon an average* contained 5 people, – they brought with them a large supply of Roots, some fish, Wood & fresh Water, and a very considerable quantity of good Water Melons, and a few Musk Melons – but did not bring off a Single Pig, – the People behaved very quietly and dealt very fairly with us.' Two chiefs came on board who 'told us there were plenty of Hogs on Shore and wanted us much to go into a Bay under the Western Extreme of Mowee, – towards Noon we got a fresh trade Wind with which we made a Stretch into this Bay. We found it to be much more pleasantly situated than any Bay we had yet seen; and though not very deep, had the appearance of being tolerably well shelter'd from the

off a considerable quantity of water, he had great reason to believe that article could there be readily procured.

The few natives in our immediate neighbourhood, though they conducted themselves in a very civil and submissive manner, yet brought us so little water in the course of the next day, Tuesday the 8th, that I was induced to give up the idea of obtaining a supply by their means,[1] and to proceed immediately to Attowai; where I was assured we should have that necessary article completely within our own reach and power. After employing the forenoon in setting up our rigging, and in other useful occupations, we weighed anchor, and steered to the westward.

Anxious to communicate the intelligence of our progress to the officer commanding the storeship, (this being one of the appointed rendezvous) I entrusted a letter to one of the natives, a very active sensible fellow, who promised to take great care of it, and to deliver it on the vessel's arrival in this bay; and for the faithful discharge of this trust, he was assured of receiving a very handsome present, to which I promised him an addition on my return.

Whyteete bay is formed, by the land falling a little back round the south point of Woahoo; and although open above half the compass in the southern quarters, it is unquestionably the most eligible anchoring place in the island. We found the latitude of the ship's station by four good meridional altitudes to be 21° 16′, 47″; its longitude by the chronometer 202° 9′ 37″; and the variation of the compass to be 7° 50′ eastwardly. Mr. Arnold's chronometer on board the Chatham gave the longitude 201° 45′ 30″, allowing the rate as settled at Otaheite; our chronometer by the Portsmouth rate, shewed the longitude to be 203° 29′ 50″; but 202° 9′ 37″ is to be received as its true longitude.[2]

A fine breeze between five and six brought us round the south-west part of Woahoo, which lies from the south point N. 82 W. five leagues distant.[3] This point is low flat land, with a reef round it, extending about a quarter of a mile from the shore. The reef and low land continue some distance to the eastward towards Whyteete bay, and form, between the south and south-west points, a large open shallow bay,[4] with high land rising very irregularly at some distance from the beach; which, towards the south-west

prevailing Winds: – the Country about the Bay had a very charming appearance...After satisfying our Curiosity in looking at this place & getting no Hogs off, we hove away between the Islands of Morotai [Molokai] & Ranai, for Woahoo.' – 7 March 1792. A year later the *Chatham* made a longer stay in the anchorage, this time in company with the *Discovery*.

[1] There was more than slow delivery to complain of; the natives 'attempted many impositions on us – by filling the Empty Calabashes with salt water. the buyers sometimes paid the Nails without tasting, which gave them an opportunity to exult in their roguery as the Cheat would sneak off laughiing at the Joke.' – Manby, letters, March 8.

[2] Honolulu Harbor Entrance Light is in lat. 21° 17′ 9″ N, long. 157° 52′ 3″ W (202° 07′ 57″ E). The Waikiki anchorage is about 3 miles to the E.

[3] Barbers Point, 17 miles W of Diamond Head.
   Mamala Bay.

458

point, appeared to be broken in two places,[1] and to form lagoons that seemed capable of receiving boats and small craft. One of the natives, who was accompanying us to Attowai, informed me, that all along the shore off these openings the bottom was rocky, and would cut our cables. This, with some other circumstances, induced me to believe, that there was not any where in this spacious bay such good anchorage as at our last station.

At eight in the evening, the west point of Woahoo bore N. $\frac{1}{2}$ E. three leagues distant. The Chatham being under the land becalmed, we soon lost sight of her. We continued our course under all sail, and to our great surprize came within sight of Attowai, by half past four the next morning, Friday the 9th. The east end,[2] by compass, bore N. by W. at a trifling distance, having gained almost six leagues in the night's run from land to land, more than the log ascertained; which I concluded must have been effected by a very strong north-west-current.

At day-break, we bore away along the south side of Attowai for Whymea bay,[3] where about nine o'clock we anchored, and moored a cable each way; the depth of water was 24 fathoms, with a bottom of dark grey sand and mud. The east point of the bay bearing, by compass, S. 67 E. the west point N. 70 W.; and the river N. 31 E. about two miles distant.

[1] Keehi Lagoon and the entrance to Pearl Harbor.
[2] Makahuena Point, the SE point of Kauai.
[3] Waimea Bay, where Cook, the discoverer of the Sandwich Islands, made his first landing in January 1778.

CHAPTER II.

Transactions at Attowai—The Prince and Regent visit the Ships—Fidelity of the Natives—Observations on the Change in the several Governments of the Sandwich Islands—Commercial Pursuits of the Americans.

BY the time we had anchored, several of the natives visited us in the same submissive and orderly manner as at Woahoo, and appeared better provided. Towards noon of Friday the 9th, the Chatham arrived; but the wind shifting about prevented her coming to anchor until sun-set, when she moored a little to the westward of the station we had taken.

Our boats, guard, &c. being in readiness, about one o'clock we proceeded to the shore. Mr. Menzies accompanied me in the yawl, and Mr. Puget followed with the cutter and launch. The surf was not so high as to prevent our landing with ease and safety; and we were received by the few natives present, with nearly the same sort of distant civility which we experienced at Woahoo.

A man, named *Rehooa*,[1] immediately undertook to preserve good order, and understanding we purposed to remain some days, caused two excellent houses to be *tabooed* for our service; one for the officers, the other for the working people, and for the guard, consisting of a serjeant and six marines. Stakes were driven into the ground from the river to the houses, and thence across the beach, giving us an allotment of as much space as we could possibly have occasion for; within which few encroachments were attempted.[2] This business was executed by two men, whose authority the people present seemed to acknowledge and respect, although they did not appear to us to be chiefs of any particular consequence. I made them some very acceptable presents; and a trade for provisions and fuel was soon established. Certain of the natives, who had permission to come within our lines, were employed in filling and rolling our water-casks to and from the boats; for which service they seemed highly gratified by the reward of a few beads or small nails.

Having no reason to be apprehensive of any interruption to the harmony

---

[1] Presumably Lehua in modern Hawaiian.

[2] The restrictions were not universally popular: 'The party on shore complaind much that the Taboo on the part they occupied was so strict as to deprive them of the society of the ladies, for no inducement could get any of them to enter either of the houses or come within the lines.' – Menzies, 10 March.

and good understanding that seemed to exist, and the afternoon being invitingly pleasant, with Mr. Menzies, our new ship-mate Jack, and *Rehooa*, I proceeded along the river-side and found the low country which stretches from the foot of the mountains towards the sea, occupied principally with the *taro* plant, cultivated much in the same manner as at Woahoo; interspersed with a few sugar canes of luxuriant growth, and some sweet potatoes. The latter are planted on dry ground, the former on the borders and partitions of the *taro* grounds, which here, as well as at Woahoo, would be infinitely more commodious were they a little broader, being at present scarcely of sufficient width to walk upon. This inconvenience may possibly arise from a principle of œconomy, and the scarcity of naturally good land. The sides of the hills extending from these plantations to the commencement of the forest, a space comprehending at least one half of the island, appeared to produce nothing but a coarse spiry grass from an argillaceous soil, which had the appearance of having undergone the action of fire, and much resembled that called the red dirt in Jamaica, and there considered little better than a *caput mortuum*.[1] Most of the cultivated lands being considerably above the level of the river, made it very difficult to account for their being so uniformly well watered. The sides of the hills afforded no running streams; and admitting there had been a collection of water on their tops, they were all so extremely perforated, that there was little chance of water finding any passage to the *taro* plantations. These perforations, which were numerous, were visible at the termination of the mountains, in perpendicular cliffs abruptly descending to the cultivated land; and had the appearance of being the effect of volcanic eruptions, though I should suppose of very ancient date. As we proceeded, our attention was arrested by an object that greatly excited our admiration, and at once put an end to all conjecture on the means to which the natives resorted for the watering of their plantations. A lofty perpendicular cliff now presented itself, which, by rising immediately from the river, would effectually have stopped our further progress into the country, had it not been for an exceedingly well constructed wall of stones and clay about twenty-four feet high, raised from the bottom by the side of the cliff, which not only served as a pass into the country, but also as an aqueduct, to convey the water brought thither by great labour from a considerable distance; the place where the river descends from the mountains affording the planters an abundant stream, for the purpose to which it is so advantageously applied. This wall, which did no less credit to the mind of the projector than to the skill of the builder,[2] terminated the extent of our walk; from whence we returned through the

[1] A worthless residue.

[2] It was built 'in so neat & artful a manner as would do no discredit to more scientific builders.' – Menzies, 9 March. A stretch of wall about 200 feet long still exists. Known as the Menehune Ditch, Hawaiian legend maintains that it was built by the Menehunes, a race of incredibly strong and active little people who are said to have inhabited Kauai before the coming of the Polynesians. The same origin is ascribed to the much larger 900-foot wall that cuts off a bend in the Huleia Stream and forms Alekoko Fish Pond, also on Kauai.

plantations, whose highly improved state impressed us with a very favorable opinion of the industry and ingenuity of the inhabitants.

On our arrival at the beach, I had the comfort of finding all things in perfectly good order. As the trading and working party were extremely well lodged, it was reasonable to believe that our business would not only be much facilitated, but that a more plentiful supply of refreshments would, probably, be procured, by allowing them to remain on shore.[1] This induced me to leave Mr. Puget in charge of the party, and I returned on board perfectly satisfied with the safety of their situation.

Like our treatment at Woahoo, our reception here was not of that hearty, friendly nature, I had been accustomed to experience from our southern friends. The eagerness, nay even avidity, with which the men here assisted in the prostitution of the women; and the readiness of the whole sex, without any exception, to surrender their persons without the least importunity, could not fail, at the moment, to incur our censure and dislike; and, on reflection, our disgust and aversion. I have read much, and seen something in my several visits to this ocean, of the obscenity attributed to the inhabitants of Otaheite and the Society islands; but no indecency that ever came under my observation, could be compared with the excessive wantonness presented in this excursion. Had this levity, now so offensively conspicuous, been exhibited in my former visits to these islands, its impressions could not have been effaced, and it must have been recollected at this time with all the abhorrence which it would at first have naturally created; but as no remembrance of such behaviour occurred, I was induced to consider this licentiousness as a perfectly new acquirement, taught, perhaps, by the different civilized voluptuaries, who, for some years past, have been their constant visitors.

At Woahoo, and also on our arrival here, we were given to understand that there were Englishmen resident on this island.

One of them, a young man about seventeen years of age, whose name was Rowbottom, on Saturday the 10th came on board in a large double canoe, who said he was of Derbyshire, that he had sailed from England about five years since in an Indiaman to China, which ship he had quitted in order to engage with some of the vessels in the fur trade between North-West America and China; and that he had ever since been thus employed in the American service. He informed me, that himself, John Williams a Welchman, and James Coleman an Irishman, had been left at Onehow,[2] in order that they might

---

[1] Items given in trade included 'pieces of Iron Nails Knives Beads looking Glasses & Scissars, the last article was in great estimation particularly among the Women for cutting their hair, with which they were very particular.' – Menzies, 10 March. In addition to the usual refreshments, the natives offered 'what surprized us much – Cabbage. This last vegetable was planted here by Captain Cook, and they seem to have taken some care of it, for during our stay we got sufficient every day to supply the Officers Mess and boil in the Ship's Company's Soup, but they have not much of it, for as they Boil none of their food, they cannot use it themselves.' – Bell, 10 March.

[2] Niihau, which is about 19 miles W of Kauai.

return to this island for the purpose of collecting sandal-wood, and pearls, for their master John Kendrick, an American, commanding the brig Lady Washington,[1] in whose service they still remained at the wages of eight dollars per month. The Lady Washington had quitted these islands the preceding October, bound to New England,[2] with a cargo of furs to dispose of in her way thither at China; she was immediately to return from Boston, and having spent the next winter in North-West America, was, in the autumn of the ensuing year, to call for these men at Attowai, and take in a cargo of sandal-wood for the Indian market, with such pearls as they might have collected.

With Rowbottom came two chiefs, the one named *No-ma-tee-he-tee*,[3] the other *Too*;[4] both of whom he said would be useful at Attowai and Onehow. On making these chiefs each a present, with which they were greatly pleased, they said they were directed by the king, or rather the prince *Ta-moo-eree*,[5] (who is a boy, and the eldest son of *Taio* the sovereign of this and the neighbouring islands) to say, that *Enemoh*,[6] the regent in *Taio's* absence, and *Tamooeree*, would be with us in a day or two; giving me to understand that *Enemoh* was the principal acting officer. A messenger was immediately dispatched to request of his highness, that, as my stay would be very short, he would do me the favor to lose no time in giving us the honor of his company; and, as a pledge of our friendly disposition, I sent him a large axe as a present.

Our young countryman said it was highly important to have the strictest

---

[1] Kendrick commanded the first trading expedition to sail from New England to the Northwest Coast. It consisted of the ship *Columbia Rediviva*, usually referred to as the *Columbia*, and the sloop *Lady Washington*; Vancouver was to encounter both vessels several times. They left Boston on 30 September 1787, but Kendrick was subject to spells of inactivity, and they did not reach Nootka Sound until September 1788. The following summer Kendrick exchanged commands with Gray and embarked upon a somewhat erratic trading career in the *Lady Washington*. This was his second attempt to trade in sandalwood. Late in 1789 he had left three men in the islands to collect a cargo. According to Ingraham, two of them soon tired of the assignment and joined a ship bound for China; the third man was reported to be in Oahu. Rowbottom told Menzies that he and his companions 'were almost starvd & very ill treated by the Natives for some time after they landed', but the chiefs came to realize the advantage of having someone in their service who had a good knowledge of English and of trading practices; 'they now livd with the young King & his Guardian on very good terms & were no ways tird of their situation.' – 10 March. But the sandalwood project was again falling by the wayside; Bell gained the impression that the men 'had not made much progress in the business they were employ'd in, nor did they seem to think it wou'd answer.' – 10 March.

[2] Kendrick did not return to Boston; he spent a year in China and returned to the Northwest Coast in 1793.

[3] Laamaikahiki.

[4] Ku, a friendly and obliging chief: 'the principal business here [Kauai] was entrusted to *Too* the same Chief which Mr. Meers named Friday, whose authority over the Natives & obliging disposition we on many occasions found extremely usefull.' – Menzies, 14 March. Meares made grateful acknowledgement to his help in his *Voyages*, p. 280.

[5] Vancouver's spelling of the names varies; Kaumualii in modern Hawaiian.

[6] Also spelled Enemoo and Enomoo.

watch over the behaviour of these people; for although he conceived our force was too great for them to attempt any thing hostile with the least prospect of success, yet he could not determine how far their ambitious views might lead them, as, since their success in taking a schooner at Owhyhee,[1] they had become so elated, that they had attempted to take a brig at Mowee.

The schooner belonged to a Mr. Metcalf, an American trader, who having been successful in the fur trade, equipped and entrusted her to the command of his son, who sailed with eight men from Macao, in order to prosecute that branch of commerce. This vessel was captured at Owhyhee; but as Rowbottom's narrative of the facts was afterwards found erroneous, the particulars of the enterprize, from better authority, will be given in a future chapter.

Nomateehetee and *Too*, with other natives present, confirmed the intelligence of this atrocious act, and, at the same time, highly reprobated the inhuman murder of the crew, who were all put to death excepting one man.[2] *Tianna* was accused by them of having projected this wicked scheme, and of having perpetrated the horrible massacre; but they positively denied that *Taio*, who had been suspected of meditating the capture of the brig at Mowee, had any knowledge of that business; saying, that it was intirely the act of the people of Mowee. On becoming acquainted with these daring and ambitious designs, I inquired what reception *Tianna* would have experienced had he accompanied us from Owhyhee? Every one present seemed to be astonished at his entertaining such an idea, and agreed that he would have been put to death the instant he had landed, as they all considered him as their most inveterate enemy. These reports, and the observations that were made by the natives in consequence of their being related to me, gave me great reason to apprehend that *Tianna*'s intentions of accompanying us hither, which on reflection he had thought proper to decline, were not dictated by motives of the most friendly and disinterested nature.[3]

These unwelcome tidings being concluded, Mr. Broughton attended me on shore with the two chiefs and the young Englishman, who was extremely serviceable to us as an interpreter; and pointed out to the natives our friendly intentions towards them, and the manner in which they should conduct themselves, not only to insure our good opinion, but to obtain the advantages that would eventually result to themselves from our visit. On landing, I understood from Mr. Puget that every thing was, and had been, conducted with the greatest propriety and good order by all parties. Trade for provisions, wood, &c. was going on very briskly, and our supply of water was equal to our wishes.

[1] The schooner was the *Fair American*, purchased at Macao by Captain Simon Metcalfe of the American brig *Eleanora*, and commanded by his son, Thomas Metcalfe.

[2] In February 1793, as he records later, Vancouver met Isaac Davis, the sole survivor of the attack on the *Fair American*, who described the massacre to him.

[3] Vancouver was right to be on his guard when dealing with Kaiana, but Kameeiamoku (Tamaahmotoo), chief of the district of Kohala (Koarra) in the N extremity of the island of Hawaii, was the prime instigator of the attack on the *Fair American*.

Matters thus pleasantly circumstanced, we embarked with Mr. Menzies and Mr. Whidbey, who had accompanied us on shore in a double canoe to examine the river, which, at the distance of about half a league from the entrance, divides into two branches, one stretching towards the E.N.E.; the other, seemingly the furthest navigable, took a northerly direction,[1] in which however we were not able to advance more than five hundred yards beyond the wall we had visited the preceding evening. Here we landed, and considered ourselves about three miles from the sea-side, to which we now returned by a path somewhat nearer the foot of the mountains than before, through a similar country; and were on this occasion, more pestered and disgusted, if possible, with the obscene importunities of the women, than on our former excursion.

Nomateehetee returned with us to dinner; *Too* remains with *Rehooa* to assist our party on shore. The next morning, Sunday the 11th, *Nomateehetee* produced a list of certificates from four different commanders of trading vessels who had lately visited these islands. The first, dated in April 1791, signed by J. Colnett of the Argnonaut, recommended this chief to the notice of future visitors; but the others signed by J. Ingram[2] of the Hope, Thomas Barnet of the Gustavus,[3] and John Kendrick of the Lady Washington, the two former without dates, the latter dated 27th of October, 1791, all direct that the greatest circumspection should be observed in the intercourse of strangers with these islanders, notwithstanding the good opinion entertained of their fidelity, or the recommendation given, by Mr. Colnett. I told *Nomateehetee* the paper spoke much in his praise and favor, and desired that he would not omit shewing it to the commander of the next and every other vessel that might arrive at Attowai, which he promised to do, and requested it might remain on board until our departure.

The caulkers having finished the quarter deck of the Discovery, they were sent on board the Chatham to execute a similar service.

Another of the party left by the Lady Washington now made his appearance, which did not speak much in his favor. This man's name was Coleman, and Rowbottom had said he was of Ireland, which the man himself positively denied, and declared he was an American, born at New York. He had in most respects adopted the customs of the natives, particularly in dress, or rather in nakedness; for, excepting the *maro*,[4] which he wore with much less decency than the generality of the inhabitants, he was perfectly naked, and the colour of his skin was little whiter than the fairest of these people. I asked him what he had done with his former clothes; to which he answered with a sneer, that 'they were hanging up in a house for the admiration of

---

[1] The main river is the Waimea, leading to the spectacular Waimea Canyon; the tributary (here referred to as the E.N.E. branch) is the Makaweli River.

[2] Joseph Ingraham.

[3] Thomas Barnett, in command of the *Gustavus III*, formerly the *Mercury*. A journal by John Bartlett, printed in *The Sea, The Ship, and The Sailor* (Salem, Mass., 1925), gives an account of the voyage.   [4] A loin cloth.

the natives;' and seemed greatly to exult in having degenerated into a savage way of life. He acquainted me, that he was charged with a message from the prince, to ask what stay I intended to make, and to inquire if we were friendly and peaceably disposed. I desired he would inform the prince, that we should depart the instant a supply of water was obtained; that I was very desirous of having an interview both with him and *Enemoh*, but that I could not be detained for this purpose; and that, as a further pledge of the favorable disposition we bore towards him and his people, I desired he would present to the prince a piece of scarlet cloth in my name. With this embassy he immediately set off, after assuring me that the prince and regent, with many other chiefs, would pay us their respects by noon the next day.

The afternoon being delightfully pleasant, I made a small excursion to the westward along the beach; and on returning, observed the hills to the eastward of the river to be on fire from a considerable height, in particular directions, down towards the water's edge. I was by no means pleased with this appearance, well knowing that fires are generally resorted to by these and other rude nations as the signal for collecting the distant inhabitants, when an enterprize or scheme is meditated to be carried into effect.

I desired Rowbottom to attend to the conversation of the Indians who were near; but he collected nothing from them in our walk that could give rise to suspicion. On joining the shore party, I asked *Nomateehetee* and some other chiefs, what was the cause of this extensive conflagration. Some replied, it was to announce the arrival of the prince, the regent, and other great chiefs in this neighbourhood on the morrow; whilst others contended it was for no other purpose than that of burning the weeds. This disagreement in opinion concerning the cause of so unusual an appearance, was far from being satisfactory.[1] The surf ran very high, and other circumstances concurred to render the embarkation of our working party very inconvenient;[2] in addition

[1] The fires greatly alarmed Vancouver, who, Menzies records, 'supposed that it might be a signal for commencing hostilities on the part of the Inhabitants, & so firm was he in this opinion that on our joining the party he could not help expressing his mind to the surrounding multitude with such menacing threats that they became alarmd in their turn by a general desertion from our Encampment, excepting the chiefs...who still remain with us & to do them justice used every means in their power to convince him to the contrary, saying that the fire had been kindled to burn down the old shrivelld grass & low vegetables & for no other purpose whatever, which I believe was literally the case, as I recollected well that the same fields were burnt down in the same manner when I was here a few years ago'. – Menzies, March 11. Bell had seen similar fires a few days before, as the *Chatham* was sailing along the coast of Maui: 'as we passed Tahoorowa [Kahloolawe], we observed large fires made on the side of the Hills running in different directions that had the effect of a grand illumination, and was either intended as a compliment to us, or for the purpose of clearing away the ground for a new Crop of the grass used by the natives for covering their Houses with.' – March 6. No doubt the latter suggestion was made by Johnstone, who had been with Menzies on his previous voyage.

[2] The embarkation was more than 'very inconvenient' and very nearly resulted in tragedy: 'When we were afterwards going on board it was necessary to send into the village for two of the affrighted natives to carry us in one of their Canoes through the surf to

to which, I did not think it prudent to manifest our apprehensions by a sudden and hasty retreat. The party on shore amounting to twenty armed persons was tolerably strong. Mr. Puget had directions to be vigilantly on his guard; and he was informed that the two launches, armed and provided with false fires to make signals in case of alarm, would be stationed as close to the beach as the surf would permit during the night, in case he should need further assistance. Having taken these precautions I returned on board, with the hope, that in the event of any tumult little danger was to be apprehended. During the night, the chiefs who had taken up their lodgings near our party, frequently visited the beach near where our boats rode, and seemed inquisitive as to the cause of the precautions which they beheld. The night however passed without the least interruption; and in the morning the natives were again trading in their usually civil and friendly manner. [1]

Our supply of water was completed on Monday the 12th, [2] and the few hogs and vegetables we were able to purchase were received from the shore. As the market no longer afforded provisions, [3] and as our business was now finished, directions were given for the embarkation of the party in the afternoon, it being my intention the next day to sail for Onehow. The surf having prodigiously increased, Mr. Puget, on these orders being delivered to him, represented to me, that he was fearful our people would not be able to reach the boats with their arms without exposing themselves to some danger. Conceiving that with the assistance of a canoe, which hitherto had been the general mode of conveyance between our boats and the shore, there would be little hazard, I desired he would use his utmost endeavours to get off; as the re-appearance of the fires on the hills, and the non-appearance of either prince or regent, indicated a possibility that the natives might have thought proper to discontinue their former services and good behaviour.

In the evening our boats returned; they had been some time detained by

the Pinnace which lay off at a grappling, & by some accident or other this Canoe upset in going with Captain Vancouver & two of the young gentlemen, who owed their safety in great measure to the strength of the surf driving them back again upon the beach. Captain Vancouver would not trust himself again in the Canoe as he suspected [the natives] had upset it designedly, he therefore swam off to the Boat attended by two of our own people who in going afterwards with one of the gentlemen lost hold of him in a violent surf which broke over their heads so that he was nearly drownd.' – Menzies, March 11. Robert Pigot, a midshipman, was the 'gentleman' endangered; he could not swim.

[1] Menzies was so convinced that the natives were friendly that 'to secure that confidence which they placd in us I went into the village where I was kindly treated & slept in Nahometee-eete's house all night.' – 11 March.

[2] Vancouver does not mention that Baker was seriously ill at this time: 'On my coming back again about breakfast time to the Encampment I found a messenger had come on shore for me requesting my attendance on Lieutenant Baker who had been very ill since we came among these Islands of a rheumatic fever; I therefore hastend on board to see him.' – Menzies, 12 March. There is no further mention of his illness.

[3] Purchases included 'a quantity of Rope, both of two & three Strands and of all sizes to as large as three Inches. It answered many purposes on board, as well as the best Tarr'd Rope, and of this we had reason to be extremely careful.' – Bell, 12 March.

the absence of a man belonging to the Chatham, who had strayed from the party, and whom at length they had been obliged to leave behind. To effect the embarkation, Mr. Puget had procured a large double canoe, which unfortunately was stove and swamped the first trip; but by the exertions of those in the boats every person had happily been saved, though amongst them were some who could not swim. By this accident two muskets, three axes, a cross cut saw, and a set of accoutrements went to the bottom, but they had recovered one of the muskets. Several articles belonging to the officers who had been on shore on duty could not be taken without imminent danger of being lost, as those on shore after the loss of the canoe, had to swim to the boats through the surf. Amongst these were some arms, and a valuable double barrelled fowling-piece, which were left in the charge of *Nomateehetee*, who *tabooed* them; and, with John Williams, (the Welchman left by the Lady Washington) gave every assurance of their security; to insure which, they both proposed to sleep in the house where the valuables were deposited. Mr. Puget seemed to entertain great confidence of the safety of the articles and of their being all forthcoming; but I must own, I expected that this confidence [1] would put their fidelity severely to the test, [2] and might eventually be the means of preventing our interview with the prince and regent; especially as Williams had returned with an apology for their having broken their engagement, which he said had been occasioned by excessive fatigue; but that we might rely on seeing them the next morning. This unpleasant state of suspense occasioned me some anxiety; but at day-break I was agreeably relieved by receiving a message that the prince and regent were arrived at Whymea.

On Tuesday the 13th Mr. Puget was dispatched to the shore for the purpose of obtaining the things which had been left behind, and with directions to use every possible means to impress the prince and regent with our friendly disposition, and to prevail on them to visit the ships. In these respects he had the good fortune to succeed, and communicated to me the following particulars of his reception.

On landing, he was received with great marks of friendship and cordiality by *Enemoh*, who is an elderly chief; guardian to the children of *Taio*, king of the island, and regent during his absence. At some distance the young prince was seated in a man's lap, to whom Mr. Puget hastened to pay his respects, and had the satisfaction of seeing him well pleased with the presents he made him on this occasion. Having settled the business of their visiting the ships, to which *Enemoh* had consented, he was extremely anxious to become acquainted with the fate of the several articles which he had intrusted to the care of Williams and *Nomateehetee* the preceding evening. Much to their credit

[1] 'this necessity' in the first edition.
[2] Manby was less apprehensive than Vancouver: 'I was so impressed with the goodness of Heart of these people that I left my valuable Gun and every thing belonging to myself, to their protection promising to come for it in the Morning.' – letters, 13 March.

and honor, he not only found every thing he had consigned to their protection and integrity, but also the musket with its bayonet, and cross cut saw, which had been lost out of the canoe, but which in the course of the night had been recovered by the natives; who promised, that the axes which were not yet obtained should likewise be restored, the instant they were recovered. The several articles being collected and sent down to the boat, with the man belonging to the Chatham who had been left on shore the preceding evening, Mr. Puget acquainted *Enemoh* that he was ready to attend them on board. *Enemoh* replied that, with respect to himself, he had not the least objection to accompany Mr. Puget with the young prince and *Tipoone*,[1] a young chief about the prince's age, who seemed his principal companion; but that he was now prevented following his own inclinations by the chiefs who were present, and some women apparently of great consequence, who collectively demanded an hostage to be left with them on shore, whilst we on board were honored with the company of these illustrious personages. On Mr. Puget's receiving and making known my orders, that Mr. Manby and Mr. Sheriff should remain behind in compliance with their desires, a general approbation was expressed by all present, and the regent with some attendants embarked;[2] saying, that on his return the prince and his young friend should go on board, but that the island could not be left without either the prince or the regent.

On *Enemoh*'s coming on board he affected to recollect me,[3] and said we had been acquainted when I was at Attowai with Captain Cook; and, to recall himself to my remembrance added, that he was present when I gave a lock of my hair to *Taio*, which *Taio* had ever since preserved, and always carried about him; and that he, *Enemoh*, had on that occasion requested a similar pledge of friendship, which, however, I thought proper to decline. These circumstances

---

[1] Kapuni.

[2] Vancouver was doubtless kept in ignorance of the way in which Manby spent his time on shore: 'Some apprehension hung heavily on the Mind of the regent, as on taking leave of the young King, he wept for some Minutes over him, and assured me, before he enter'd the Boat, that if any thing happened to him, his subjects would retaliate by taking my life. I begg'd him, to eradicate fear from his Breast, by being perfectly at ease, promising at the same time I would amuse his little charge and divert his Queens to the utmost of my abilities. Good natured Souls, without reluctance they yielded to the encircling Arms of Youth so far superior to the loathsome embrace their situation obliges them [to] bear from the feeble and infirm Enemoo. Two hours I reveld in extatic enjoyment and was then call'd off by a summons from the young King to attend him in a neighbouring House.' There was a sequel: 'I was surpris'd after dark by a Canoe paddling under the stern of the Ship inquiring for me by the name of Mappee. I happened to be on Deck and instantly knew the voice of the Stranger to be [that of a] Royal female that I had pass'd some happy moments with in the early part of the day. She had deserted from the residence of Enemoo to say again farewell, bringing me some handsome mats and a few pieces of Cloth. after staying with me two hours she again took a sorrowful adieu and left the Ship with a heavy heart.' – 13 and 14 March.

[3] Menzies also noted that Enemoo 'instantly recollected me & I had a friendly embrace from all of them, for the old chief & his family attached themselves very much to the Vessel [the *Prince of Wales*] I was on board at these Islands a few years ago...' – 13 March.

were very likely to have taken place, although at the moment they did not recur to my memory.

A dozen hogs, and a quantity of mats and cloth, being presented by *Enemoh*, I made no delay in offering a suitable return, with which, however, he did not seem either delighted or satisfied. This produced an inquiry on my part; on which he frankly acknowledged, that the present I made him was a very liberal one, but that he would gladly give up the whole for a musket, or even for a pistol. These engines of destruction had been uniformly solicited with the greatest ardency, by every native of the least consequence with whom we had any dealings; and I had frequently been much perplexed how, without offence, to refuse complying with requests so importunate, and, at the same time, in my humble opinion, so repugnant to the cause of humanity. On this occasion I availed myself of our peculiar situation, as it had respect to the trading vessels which he had been accustomed to visit; and informed him, that the ship, and every thing she contained, belonged to His Majesty King George, who had *tabooed* muskets, pistols, and various other articles. On this gunpowder and balls were immediately solicited; but, on being told that these were under similar restrictions, he remained silent, and seemed very thoughtful. At length, conceiving no importunities would avail, he recovered himself, and became as suddenly cheerful, as on the refusal of his favorite weapons he had seemed dejected. He now shook me very heartily by the hand, and said, since arms and ammunition were *tabooed*, he must acknowledge that the presents he and his friends had received were very ample, and that they had reason to be highly satisfied. *Enemoh* recommended in the strongest terms the attendance of *Nomateehetee* and *Too* on our passage to Onehow, where they would be very serviceable in procuring us the different productions, and would prevent any disorderly behaviour on the part of the inhabitants. His opinion of his own importance was greatly flattered by our saluting him with four guns on his departure; and he took leave with every appearance of being extremely gratified with his visit.

Mr. Puget, who had to execute the remaining part of his embassy, attended the venerable old chief and his suite on board the Chatham, where they paid their respects to Mr. Broughton; and, having received some presents from that gentleman, they proceeded to the shore. On landing, *Enemoh* exposed the several articles which had been given to him, and recounted the treatment he had received.

Although Mr. Puget was much pleased with the satisfaction and happiness which the visit had afforded all present, he was much disappointed on understanding that the embarkation of the prince and his young friend would not take place. On his searching for the cause of this sudden alteration, and pointing out to *Enemoh* the reception he had met, the presents he had received, and assuring him, that we had no wish or desire but to shew the same marks of respect and friendship to *Tamooere*, which he had given us an opportunity of paying to him (all of which were readily admitted) *Enemoh*, with some hestitation, explained; and at length the reason was discovered to have proceeded from their having observed, that the two gentlemen who had been left as hostages, were down on the beach near the boats, and they supposed were going on board without waiting the return of the prince to the shore. Mr. Puget instantly removed their apprehensions, when all objections ceased; and the prince and his young companion were now as eager to get to the boat, as they before had been willing to return on the demur of the regent; from whom Mr. Puget understood, that some hogs and vegetables were every minute expected to arrive. But not thinking it adviseable to wait, lest any other objection might arise and detain the prince on shore, he immediately put off, leaving Mr. Manby and Mr. Sheriff in their former situation as hostages.

I was much pleased with the appearance and behaviour of this young prince, who seemed to be about twelve years of age. In his countenance was exhibited much affability and cheerfulness; and, on closely observing his features, they had infinitely more the resemblance of an European than of those which generally characterize these islanders; being destitute of that natural ferocity so conspicuous in the persons about him. In these respects, and in the quickness of his comprehension and ideas, he greatly surpassed his young friend and companion *Tipoone*.[1] At first, he was not without considerable agitation, marked as evidently by the sensibility of his countenance, as by his actions; in constantly clinging to me, and repeatedly saluting me according to their custom, by touching noses. I soon dissipated his fears by a few trifling presents, and encouraged him to visit every part of the ship. His inquiries and observations, on this occasion, were not, as might have been expected from his age, directed to trivial matters; which either escaped his notice, or were by him deemed unworthy of it; but to such circumstances alone, as would have authorized questions from persons of matured years and some experience. He conducted himself with a great degree of good breeding, and applied to Rowbottom or Williams, who were with him, to know if he might be permitted, or if it were proper, to make this, or that inquiry; and never moved forward, or sat down, without first inquiring, if, by so doing, he should incur any displeasure. It was now about our dinner-time. His young friend *Tipoone* did not fail to partake of our repast, whilst the prince seemed infinitely more entertained with the several new objects that surrounded him, and, I believe, would have returned to the shore perfectly satisfied with his visit, had I offered him nothing more. Considering, however, that some acknowledgment was due for their care and honesty in restoring not only the articles, which through necessity had been committed to their charge, but such as were recovered from the sea; when dinner was ended I presented *Tamooere* with

[1] 'He was about 13 years of age, well made, with a fine handsome manly countenance, – I did not see so fine a Boy at all the Islands, – he possess'd all that native dignity in his appearance that (in this Country at least) distinguishes those of high rank from the lower Class of people, – indeed this remark we found to hold good both at Otaheite and these Islands, and we could always distinguish the men of rank from the other Classes of people by their appearance, they are in general finer made men, and handsomer.' – Bell, 13 March.

nearly a duplicate assortment of the valuables I had in the forenoon given to *Enemoh*, with some few other things that seemed particularly to attract his attention. Amongst these was a quantity of wine and rum, for which these islanders, like our southern friends, have acquired no inconsiderable relish. I presented likewise to his friend a collection of valuables; and gave to each of his attendants some trivial article, with which they seemed agreeably surprized, as this compliment was expected by none of them. Our countrymen who were in the habit of living with the prince, were instructed to impress on the minds of the royal party and the inhabitants in general, that the liberality they had experienced was wholly to be ascribed to their own civil, orderly, and honest behaviour; and, that, (in addition to what they had received) as a particular testimony of my approbation of their conduct, if they would remain on board until it was dark they should be entertained with a display of fire-works. *Tamooere*, though well satisfied that our intentions were pacific and friendly, and though perfectly reconciled to his situation on board, yet requested he might be permitted to go on shore, and, if *Enemoh* had no objection, he would return. He intreated us to remain a few days, to enable him to make us some return for our civilities, in hogs and vegetables; a supply of which he expected were already at the beach; but as we had accomplished all the business for which we had stopped at this island, and being desirous of obtaining from Onehow a stock of yams, (a vegetable that Attowai did not at that time afford) I gave the young prince to understand, that if the wind should prove favorable in the course of the night, we should, on a certainty, depart for Onehow.

After visiting the Chatham with the prince, Mr. Puget returned with his charge to the shore, where the party was received with the greatest cordiality by a large concourse of the natives, who, under the restrictions of the *taboo*, were kept in excellent order. The prince was carried on a man's shoulders and seated in the house which our officers occupied. There he was soon joined by *Enemoh*, with a large train of attendants, who unanimously expressed their satisfaction and gratitude for the treatment their young chief had experienced; of which, the valuable presents brought from the ships bore undeniable testimony.

Not seeing, nor hearing any tidings of, the promised supply of provisions, nor discovering any inclination in the royal party to return for the purpose of attending the fire-works, Mr. Puget took his leave and repaired on board. Previously to his quitting the shore, the prince found out that the exhibition could be equally well seen from the beach, and therefore requested he might be indulged.

As our young friend was anxiously waiting, with a large crowd of his countrymen, in expectation of something new, as soon as it became dark I ordered some sky and water rockets to be displayed. *Nomateehetee* and *Too*, who, with several of the natives, male and female, had begged a passage to Onehow, observed the rockets with infinite surprize and admiration, as did the concourse of people assembled on shore; which was announced to us by their repeated bursts of acclamation, distinctly heard, though at the distance of nearly two miles.

I should be guilty of an unpardonable injustice to these people, were I to neglect this opportunity of observing, that the faithful performance of their engagement with Mr. Puget, combined with those principles of honesty that directed the restoration of the articles recovered from the sea, produced in our minds opinions very contrary to those which we had, perhaps too hastily, formed of Attowai, on the report of the recent visitors to this country; and which, on the prejudice of our first impressions, were confirmed greatly to the disadvantage of the general character, to which, it now appeared, these islanders were entitled. The reports, however, ought not to be considered as having originated without cause; though, in all likelihood, transgressions may have been committed by strangers as well as by the natives, and the want of a sufficient knowledge of each other's language, may have provoked mutual aggression, which otherways would not, so repeatedly, have produced misunderstandings. That the natives had not been faithfully dealt with on all occasions, seemed evident, from the prince or regent demanding an hostage for their safe return, on their consenting to venture themselves amongst us; a circumstance that had never before occurred in any of my visits to the islands in this ocean. That they are capable of being taught by proper lessons and examples how to respect the property of others, is placed out of doubt by the exercise of those principles of rectitude that directed the honorable restoration of the musket and tools which they recovered from the sea; and this also affords reasonable grounds to believe, that, on their being convinced that irregularities and frauds are not to be committed with impunity, all the inhabitants of these islands would soon be induced to avoid disgrace and punishment, and secure the advantages resulting from the friendship of the more civilized world.[1] We might possibly be in some measure indebted for the good behaviour of the natives, to the confidence that the chiefs had reason to suppose was placed in their integrity. This, when reposed in their chiefs or responsible persons, I have, in former instances, seen attended with the most happy effect.

The people of the several nations who have visited these islands, are well known and distinguished by the inhabitants. I was extremely well pleased to understand that the three resident men, though at present in the service of an American, had used every endeavour to impress on the minds of the natives the most favorable opinion of the English; and I was made very happy on being convinced of the strong predilection and attachment which the young

[1] The following sentence on p. 184 of the first edition was omitted in the second, presumably because it is repetitious: 'Nothing could manifest more powerfully their being already extremely conscious of this important interest, than the faithful discharge of the trust reposed in them by Mr. Puget, and the delivery of the valuables recovered out of the water, which might have been secreted and with-held without fear of detection, and for which they were not requested to search; nor was any reward offered to those who might exert themselves to procure them.'

prince had conceived for the subjects of Great-Britain. This prepossession, if properly cherished, may eventually be highly important to the British traders; for, if conclusions may be permitted to be drawn from the general deportment and manners of his early years, the riper ones of this young prince must be attended with a very considerable degree of consequence in this part of the world. This presumption appears the more warrantable, by the splendid achievements, and the example he will have had exhibited by his father, who has raised himself to the high station he at present fills by his perseverance and prowess in military exploits.

The predilection of the prince was not only conspicuous in the attention shewn to Rowbottom and his comrades, whose persons and property he had made sacred by their constantly residing with him, and by his making them his companions in all his diversions and amusements, but in his having assumed the title of King George; not suffering his domestics to address him by any other name, and being much displeased with us, as well as his countrymen, if we called him *Tamooere*.

Besides the different articles of traffic with which I presented this promising youth, were a male and female goat, and two geese; Mr. Broughton added a third; and we had hopes they were of different sexes. He had likewise an ewe and a ram in most excellent condition, left by Mr. Colnett; these had bred, but their progeny had been unfortunately killed by a dog. Notwithstanding this accident, there was every prospect of their future propagation and success.

From Mr. Puget I learned, that there appeared in none of his transactions with the royal party any marks of external respect towards them, either from the subordinate chiefs, or the common people. When I was at these islands with Captain Cook, prostration was very usually observed, [1] and seemed then

---

[1] On a number of occasions Hawaiians had prostrated themselves before Cook himself as well as before influential chiefs, who were regarded (in Beaglehole's words) as 'beings in whom there was a tinge of the god'. 'The conclusion seems inescapable,' in his opinion, that Cook 'was being treated as a god'. – Cook, *Journals*, III, cxliii. Briefly, the reasons appear to have been three. First, Cook and his men were the first Europeans the Hawaiians had seen, and it was evident from their ships and extraordinary possessions that they were superior beings of some sort. Secondly, Cook arrived at Kealakekua Bay during the winter season known as *makahiti*, and Lono, one of the four great gods of the Hawaiian pantheon, was the god of that season. As it happened, the presence of Lono was 'symbolized by a long staff bearing a banner of *tapa* in form much like the square sail of a ship'. The sails of Cook's ships thus suggested some identification with Lono, and Cook was referred to by that name. In January 1779, less than a month before his death, Cook was the subject of an elaborate religious ceremony that some believe was intended to acknowledge him as an incarnation of Lono. King (who found the ceremony both puzzling as to meaning and 'long & rather tiresome') describes it in considerable detail. – *Ibid.*, 505–6. Burney noted that 'All the people, except those of the Priesthood, laying prostrate or rather on their Hands and Knees with their Heads bowed down to the Ground.' – *Ibid.*, 504n. Beaglehole notes that some, Sir Peter Buck for one, have interpreted the deference paid to Cook differently. Buck's view is that although 'it is certain that Captain Cook was elevated to the highest rank of chieftainship' he points out that the 'Hawaiian custom of

to be demanded even by chiefs, though not of the highest rank. On this occasion, the only circumstance which proclaimed the prince's superior rank, was a guard consisting of about thirty men, armed with iron pahooas,[1] who attended him and the royal personages on all excursions, carrying thirteen muskets made up into three bundles, with some callibashes containing ammunition, of which it was thought expedient we should be apprized previous to their visit, lest such formidable appearances should create in us distrust or suspicion. During the time our party was employed on shore, an armed man was scarcely ever seen; and such of the natives who appeared so provided, brought their weapons for the purpose of sale only.

About three in the morning of Wednesday the 14th, we sailed[2] with a fine northerly breeze for Onehow,[3] in order, whilst the decks of the Chatham were caulking, to take on board such yams and other vegetables as we might be able to procure.

On our arrival at Onehow, we anchored in 14 fathom water off the south part of the island, about ¾ of a mile from the shore; its south-east point[4] bearing by compass S. 77 E. its west point N. 48 W. and the island of Tahoora S. 58 W. Finding the bottom here soft, sandy, regular, and good, I was induced to prefer this anchorage to a situation I had been in, further to the N.N.W. as the surf broke with great violence on the N.W. side of the island, though here we rode very smoothly. *Nomateehetee* wished we had proceeded further west; saying, the natives would have a great way to bring us their yams and other productions. The station we had taken was not however attended with any such inconvenience; as, by Friday the 16th, in the afternoon, we had purchased a very ample supply:[6] and the Chatham's

---

deification of selected high chiefs was a post mortem event, not an ante mortem one.' – *Ibid.*, cxliv, n. By the time Vancouver arrived, 12 years later, frequent encounters with trading ships whose captains and crews were often anything but godlike, would have destroyed their reverence for the white man.

[1] pahoa, a dagger.

[2] 'this early hour of moving created no little confusion among the Ladies upwards of a hundred being on board and only three Single Canoes along side some of them Swam to Shore but the major part made up their minds to go with good spirits to Onchow as the distance was only a few Leagues they trusted to chance their again getting back.' – Manby, letters, 14 March.

[3] Niihau.

[4] Kawaihoa Point.

[5] Kaula, a small island 19 miles SW of Niihau.

[6] 'We compute the quantity of yams which we [in the *Chatham*] have taken in here to be about eight tons and the Discovery to have taken a good deal more...' – Johnstone, 16 March. Yams would keep at sea for two or three months and were therefore a very welcome item. Hewett as usual strikes a sour note and is critical of Vancouver: 'Two Pounds of Yams more than one half of which were waste and the remainder not sufficient for dinner were served instead of a pound of Bread so that the People complained of being half starved having no Breakfast or Supper. I have seen them instead of Breakfast tying each others Hair to pass away the time. One Hundred pounds of Bread per day was saved by this means the Captn. received the Emolument of.'

deck being now finished, about six in the evening we proceeded together towards the coast of America.

On our departure, the two Englishmen with our other friends took their leave, who, for the good services they had rendered us, received acknowledgments far beyond their most sanguine expectations.[1]

The supply of refreshments which the Sandwich islands on this occasion had afforded us, was undeniably a very scanty one. This, however, I did not solely attribute to scarcity, as I had frequently great reason to believe an abundant stock might have been procured, had we been inclined to have purchased them with arms and ammunition; with which, through the unpardonable conduct of the various traders, who have visited these islands, the inhabitants have become very familiar, and use these weapons with an adroitness that would not disgrace the generality of European soldiers. Their great avidity for procuring these destructive engines may possibly have been increased by the successes of *Tianna*, who, it should seem, is principally indebted for his present exaltation to the fire-arms he imported from China, and those he has since procured from the different traders. His example has produced in every chief of consequence an inordinate thirst for power; and a spirit of enterprize and ambition seems generally diffused amongst them. If reliance is to be placed on the information which I received, the flame of these unwarrantable desires has been raised by the practice of every species of artifice and address in their European and American visitors; who have thereby enhanced the value of such destructive articles of commerce.[2] For these alone the natives now seem inclined to exchange the valuable refreshments, with which there can be little doubt these islands still abound. The evil of this trade will be materially felt by vessels that may have occasion to resort to this country, unequipped with military stores for the inhuman purpose of barter with these people; and it is much to be apprehended the mischief will

[1] Johnstone commented on the good relations enjoyed with the natives: 'This is the evident good effect of not suffering any but the Chiefs or principal friends to come on board. I belive [sic] during the whole time which we were at Atooi [Kauai] and this Island that we had not above four or six men altogether on the ship, nor was it solicited, they made their traffick contentedly in their Canoes. The duty of the Vessel was carried on with as much quietness and regularity as if they had been laying in the most civilized port.' – 17 March.

[2] Colnett was amongst those who had contributed to the increase of arms in the island, in his case allegedly for political reasons. He charged that Quimper and the Spaniards had 'expected to gain great credit with the Indians by acquainting them...what a pitiful nation we were' but that he 'arrived unexpectedly and Just [in] time enough to undeceive them...By a little well timed liberality, I wiped out every impression of their superiority...and by a Present of a three Pound swivel, a few muquetes [muskets], and two or three Blunderbusses, I stood well with the great, and got well supplied with hogs, and other articles when they could not get an individual thing.... My supply of Powder came very apropos, they being at war with the other Isles.' – *The Journal of Captain James Colnett*, pp. 219–20. Colnett was in Kailua Bay, Hawaii, and the arms and ammunition would be used by Kamehameha in his efforts to conquer Maui.

extend considerably further, as we have been acquainted, by the late adventurers in the fur trade, that these islanders have tried various schemes to destroy the crews, and to gain possession of some of the trading vessels, in which they succeeded too well with Mr. Medcalf's schooner at Owhyhee. These ambitious designs however, had been rendered in most instances ineffectual, by the superiority alone which the traders possessed in fire-arms; and yet, neither the conviction of their own security being wholly dependant on these powerful means of defence, nor the common principles of humanity, seem to have had sufficient influence to restrain a traffic, encouraged by avaricious pursuits in defiance of all moral obligation.

The alteration which has taken place in the several governments of these islands since their first discovery by Captain Cook, has arisen from incessant war, instigated both at home and abroad by ambitious and enterprizing chieftains; which the commerce for European arms and ammunition cannot fail of encouraging to the most deplorable extent.

If we may be allowed to decide by comparing the numerous throngs that appeared on the first visits of the Resolution and Discovery, and which were then constantly attendant on all our motions, with the very few we have seen on the present occasion, the mortality must have been very considerable. It may however be objected, that the novelty of such visitors having, at this time, greatly abated, is sufficient to account for the apparent depopulation. But when it is considered how essential our different implements and manufactures are now become to their common comforts, that reason will not apply; as every individual is eager to bring forth all his superfluous wealth, on the arrival of European commodities in the market.

At Whyteeta I had occasion to observe that, although the town was extensive, and the houses numerous, yet they were thinly inhabited, and many appeared to be intirely abandoned. The village of Whymea is reduced at least two-thirds of its size, since the years 1778 and 1779. In those places where, on my former visits, the houses were most numerous, was now a clear space, occupied by grass and weeds. That external wars and internal commotions had been the cause of this devastation, was further confirmed by the result of my inquiries off Owhyhee, when it did not appear that any of the chiefs, with whom I had been formerly acquainted, excepting *Tamaahmaah*, was then living; nor did we understand that many had died a natural death, most of them having been killed in these deplorable contests.[1]

The short time we remained among these people, did not allow of my obtaining the satisfactory information I sought, and which was so very

---

[1] Hewett states that depopulation was a 'Favorite Theme' of Vancouver's. Johnstone saw little sign of it, at least in the Waikiki area, where cultivation seemed to him to be just as extensive as it had been at the time of his previous visit, 'and the extent and number of habitations were nothing diminished.' If there were any depopulation, he believed it 'was merely the temporary emigration of the King and his followers' owing to military activity. – 8 March.

desirable on this, as well as on other important topics. This has induced me to reserve the subject matter I had collected, until I should have an opportunity of going into a more correct investigation: for the present, therefore, I shall take leave of the Sandwich islands, by stating the advantages which the Americans promise themselves by the commerical interests they are endeavouring to establish in these seas.

Previously to the departure of Rowbottom and Williams, they informed me, that their captain had conceived a valuable branch of commerce might be created, by the importation of the sandal-wood of this country into India, where it sells at an exorbitant price; that, in the fur trade, immense profits had been gained, insomuch that it was expected not less than twenty vessels would, on these pursuits, sail with their captain (Kendrick) from New England, and that they were desired to engage the natives to provide several cargoes of this wood, which is easily procured, as the mountains of Attowai as well as those of Owhyhee, abound with the trees from which it is produced; though we were not able to procure any of their leaves, to determine its particular class or species. The wood seemed but slightly to answer the description given of the yellow sandal wood of India, which is there a very valuable commodity, and is sold by weight.[1]

The pearls I saw were but few, and consisted of three sorts, the white, yellow, and lead colour. The white were very indifferent, being small, irregular in shape, and possessing little beauty; the yellow, and those of a lead colour, were better formed, and, in point of appearance, of superior quality. Mr. Kendrick must, undoubtedly, flatter himself with great emoluments from these branches of commerce, or he would not thus have retained three men in constant pay for such a considerable length of time, with a promise of further reward if they conducted themselves with fidelity towards his interest. This proceeding, however, appears to have been the effect of a sudden thought, as it was not until his brig was weighing anchor at Onehow that he came to this determination, and landed the three men; who, in consequence of such short notice, had no means of equipping themselves, and were left almost destitute of apparel. The few clothes they had were nearly worn out; these I replaced with a sufficient stock to serve them some time; and, to add as much as possible to their comforts in their present situation, and to make them respectable in the eyes of the people with whom they were yet to remain for several months, they received such tools and articles of traffic as would best answer their purpose, and some books, pens, ink, and paper, for their

[1] This was not the first attempt to develop a trade in sandalwood. In August 1790 William Douglas, captain and owner of the schooner *Grace*, left two men in Kauai with instructions to gather a cargo. Kendrick's men arrived more than a year later, in October 1791. Ralph S. Kuykendall states that 'it does not appear that either the men left by Douglas or those left by Kendrick actually collected any sandalwood.' And he adds: 'these early projects were not followed up and the sandalwood trade did not become important in Hawaii until some time after 1800.' – *The Hawaiian Kingdom*, vol. I, 1778–1854 (Honolulu, 1938), appendix C, p. 434.

amusement, with an assortment of garden seeds, and some orange and lemon plants that were in a very flourishing state.[1]

To the care of Rowbottom, who seemed the most qualified, I intrusted a letter of instructions to the commanding officer of the store-ship, whose arrival we daily expected; as also one to the Lords of the Admiralty,[2] acquainting them with the time we had quitted these islands, the state and condition of the vessels, and health of their crews, the route I had taken to this station, and the discoveries we had made.

Kendall's chronometer, agreeably to its error and rate of going as ascertained at Otaheite, agreed so well on our arrival at Owhyhee, that I was not at all solicitous for any further investigation. Our observations in Whymea road made its latitude 21° 57½′, and its longitude, by the chronometer, 200° 18′ 15″, varying 5′ 15″ to the eastward of Captain Cook's, and 1′ 45″ to the westward of Captain King's assigned true longitude of the roadsted; whence I concluded its rate of going very correct. The Portsmouth rate shewed 201° 40′ 45″.[3] Mr. Arnold's chronometer, on board the Chatham, made the longitude of Whymea, according to its Otaheitean rate, 199° 58′ 30″. Our anchorage at Onehow, by observation, was in latitude 21° 46′ 30″, the longitude, by the chronometer, 199° 40′.[4] This station is to the E.S.E. of the spot where the Resolution anchored, and which is laid down by Captain Cook in latitude 21° 50′, longitude 199° 45′; consequently, our observations place the south point of Onehow nearly in the same latitude, though 8′ further to the westward, and two leagues further distant from Whymea. The Portsmouth rate shewed the longitude to be 201° 5′; but Mr. Arnold's chronometer made a much greater difference, as it placed the anchorage at Onehow in longitude 199° 12′ 15″. At this island, we found the tides regular, as noticed by Captain Cook; but at Attowai and Woahoo, there was a current which generally set to the eastward.

[1] 'upwards of a hundred young Orange Plants were sent on shore before our departure under the care of the Lady Washington's people to be planted in different places through the Island.' – Menzies, 13 March

[2] No copy of either of these letters has come to light.

[3] The position of Waimea Bay is lat. 21° 57′ N, long. 159° 40′ W (200° 20′ E).

[4] The anchorage seems to have been in Kaumuhonu Bay, W of Kawaihoa Point; its position is lat. 21° 47′ N, long. 160° 13′ W (199° 47′ E).

CHAPTER III.

Passage to the coast of America—Find the main-mast sprung—See the land of New Albion—Proceed along the coast—Fall in with an American Vessel— Enter the supposed straits of De Fuca—Anchor there.

HAVING put to sea from Onehow, as before related, we stood to the N.W. close hauled, with a moderate breeze at N.N.E. attended by a heavy swell from the N.W. until Saturday morning the 17th March, 1792, when the wind having veered to that quarter, we made sail to the N.E. in order that we might pass to the north of the Sandwich islands, and be enabled to steer to the eastward, should the wind continue its northern direction, from whence it had lately prevailed. By noon the wind blew a fresh gale from N.N.W. attended with some trifling squalls; our latitude was now 22° 16', longitude 199° 17'; the west point of Onehow bearing by compass S. 57 E. eight leagues distant. About two in the afternoon we discovered a spring in the main mast on the larboard side, about six feet below the hounds. This part of the mast had occupied much of our attention since our departure from Teneriffe, in consequence of a suspicious appearance near a rugged knot, opposite to the place where the defect now became evident. We were under an immediate necessity of getting down the top-gallant-mast, with every moveable out of the top; close reefing the topsail, and lightening the head of the mast as much as possible, until a fish should be prepared; which the carpenters lost no time in getting ready. A defect was also discovered in the head of the foremast, above the rigging, which was of less importance, and did not require any additional security for the present.

At sun-set Attowai bore by compass from S. 80 E. to S. 45 E. and Onehow from S. 4 W. to S. 14 W. The wind remaining in the N.W. we stood on, and about midnight passed the north point of Attowai at no great distance; though the weather being very dark and hazy, prevented our seeing the land.

On Sunday the 18th in the morning, we took our departure from the Sandwich islands: Attowai bearing by compass from S. 5 E. to S. 30 W. 10 or 11 leagues distant. In the afternoon all the sails were furled on the main-mast, and we were employed until six in the evening in fixing the fish, and securing the head of the mast; when the sails were again set, and we proceeded to the E.N.E.[1] The wind was generally to the westward of north, with cool and

[1] Vancouver makes no mention of an incident recorded by Menzies: 'This morning the 19th [March] our foretop gallant Yard which had been complaining for some time

pleasant, though generally cloudy weather, attended by a great swell from the N.W. which indicated the wind having blown with much violence in that direction. The main-mast, after a trial of some days in a fresh gale with a heavy sea, not seeming to complain, the top-gallant-mast was on Friday the 23d got up, and the usual quantity of sail carried.[1] The N.W. swell had now almost subsided, and the wind veered round to N.E. with which we stood to the N.N.W. The weather continuing dark and gloomy prevented our making any observations on the solar eclipse this morning; but at noon our observed latitude was 24° 43', longitude 209° 6'; and in the afternoon the variation was found to be 11° 5' eastwardly.

Our course was directed to the eastward or northward as the wind veered, which was mostly on the northern board, blowing a moderate breeze with pleasant weather. On Thursday the 29th, in latitude 27°, I got five sets of distances of the moon and sun; the mean result gave the longitude 214° 21' 15"; by the chronometer it was 213° 46' 30"; and by the dead reckoning, 211° 44'. This error in the dead reckoning seemed gradually to have taken place since our departure from Attowai; and many of the officers having lately made several lunar observations with great accuracy, whose mean result gave from 25' to 40' east of the chronometer, I was led to believe, that our change of climate (the thermometer having fallen from about 80 to about 66 since leaving the Sandwich islands,)[2] had caused some acceleration in its rate of going. From hence our progress was attended by a very smooth sea, and in general by cloudy and gloomy weather. The wind between N. by W. and N.N.E. blew so gently, that on the 7th of April[3] we had only reached the

was carried away in the slings, it was immediately got down & the carpenter set about making another to supply in its place; but not finishing it agreeable to Capt. Vancouvers particular directions, Mr. Philips the Carpenter of the Discovery was in the afternoon confined prisoner in his Cabin for that & his insolent & disrespectful behaviour to him on the occasion, and...Lathwood [Thomas Laithwood] Carpenters Mate received orders to act in his room.' – 19 March. Phillips was sent home in the Daedalus and a court martial was held over three and a half years later, in November 1795. Vancouver had charged him with inattention to duty, neglect of the stores in his keeping, disobedience and contemptuous behaviour. The court ruled that the first three charges were not proved, but found Phillips guilty of 'disrespectful behaviour' to Vancouver and sentenced him to be 'broke as Carpenter' of the Discovery and 'to serve during the remainder of the present War' in whatever ship should be designated. Phillips' statement in his own defence is printed in the appendix.

[1] The Chatham had a problem of her own: 'We still find that the Vessel makes a good deal of water, when pressed for Sail on the starboard tack whilst on the other tack under the same circumstances she is tight may not this be owing to the larbd side having been exposed to the Sun and weather for a long run across the North and South Atlantic trades and not being caulked since, the Starboard side being there heeled in the shade and water.' – Johnstone, 28 March.

[2] Both man and beast felt the 'very considerable change in the weather, and from the thin Linen Cloathes that we were used to wear at the Islands, we were oblig'd to change to our warmest dresses. The Sandwich Island Fowls though fed on their own Country food all died.' – Bell, 23 March.

[3] Vancouver makes no mention of 1 April, the anniversary of his departure from England, but it was noticed in the Chatham if not in the Discovery: 'double allowance of

latitude of 35° 25'; longitude 217° 24', by the dead reckoning 214° 42'; when we found ourselves in the midst of immense numbers of the sea blubber of the species of the Medusa Villilia;[1] so that the surface of the ocean as far as the eye could reach, was covered with these animals in such abundance, that even a pea could hardly be dropped clear of them. The largest did not exceed four inches in circumference; and adhering to them was found a worm of a beautiful blue colour, much resembling a caterpillar. This worm is about an inch and a half long, thickest toward the head, forming a three-sided figure, its back being the broadest; its belly, or under part was provided with a festooned membrane, with which it attached itself to the medusa villilia. Along the ridge connecting the sides and back from the shoulders to the tail, on each side, are numberless small fibres, about the eighth of an inch in length, like the downy hair of insects, but much more substantial; probably intended to assist the animal in its progress through the water. This worm or caterpillar Mr. Menzies considered to be a new genus.[2] We saw also in the forenoon a bird, which I took to be of the duck or awke kind, flying to the N.W. but at too great a distance to discover its character.

Since our leaving the land we had been daily visited by one or two large birds, but not more at a time, which we sometimes took for the quebrantahuessos,[3] and at others for a species of albatross. On Sunday the 8th, the weather being perfectly calm, Mr. Menzies was so fortunate as to determine this point, by killing a brown albatross; of the same sort, I believe, as are found in abundance about Tierra del Fuego, distinguished vulgarly by the name of Mother Cary's geese, on account of the white rump, shape of the tail, &c. which resemble the storm-petrel, commonly called Mother Cary's chicken.[4] This albatross had also a white mark, about the eighth of an inch wide, and two inches long, extending in a diagonal direction from the inner corner of its eye towards the neck. From tip to tip of each wing it measured

Grog was served to the Ships Company to commemorate the day and drink the health of their old friends at home.' – Bell, 1 April.

[1] 'A bucket was lowerd down in the water in which several of them were pickd up & I found them to agree very nearly with the Medusa velella of Linnaeus – a kind of sea blubber.' – Menzies, April 7.

[2] The following day 'as the Jolly Boat was lowerd down in the water to go on board the Chatham I took that opportunity to examine farther the large extended patches of *Medusa vellela* which still covered the surface of the sea all around us, & to many of these I found adhering in clusters another kind of vermes of the same natural order but to what genus it belongs to I am really at a loss to determine.' Menzies' description, in somewhat more scientific terms than Vancouver's, then follows. – April 8. In C. F. Newcombe (ed.), *Menzies' Journal of Vancouver's Voyage, April to October 1792* (Archives of British Columbia, memoir 5, Victoria, 1923) Newcombe concluded that this was 'Probably a mullusk of the Nudibranch division.' p. 2n.

[3] The giant petrel.

[4] Mother Carey's chickens and Mother Carey's geese were the sailors' names for the stormy petrel and the giant petrel. Menzies gives a description of the bird he shot from which Newcombe concludes that it was a black-footed albatross. *Menzies' Journal of Vancouver's Voyage*, p. 3n.

seven feet; and, from the extremity of the beak to that of the tail, three feet.

The weather continued pleasant, nearly calm or with light variable breezes until Tuesday the 10th, when in latitude 36°, longitude 219° 34′, the wind blew a moderate gale, and seemed settled in the southern quarter; with which we made all sail, steering to the eastward. Notwithstanding I had, in case of separation with the Chatham, appointed our next rendezvous in Berkley's sound,[1] yet whilst we were so fortunate as to keep together, it was my fixed determination to fall in with the coast of New Albion as far to the southward of that station as circumstances would permit.

Several small whales and grampusses had lately been observed about the ship; and this afternoon we passed within a few yards of about twenty whales of the anvil-headed or spermaceti kind,[2] that were playing in the water. The immense number of the medusa with which this region abounds, may probably induce the spermaceti whale to resort hither in quest of food. We now advanced very pleasantly to the eastward, and gradually lost sight of the medusa villilia, which had attended us in the greatest abundance over a space of seven degrees of longitude; and, as Mr. Johnstone of the Chatham paid particular attention to these extraordinary creatures, I shall insert his description of them.

'These small blubbers are of an oval form, quite flat, and measuring about an inch and an half the longest way; their under side is somewhat concave; the edges, for near a quarter of an inch in width, are of a deep blue colour, changing inwardly to a pale green; the substance being much thinner and more transparent there than on the upper side. Perpendicularly to the plain of their surface stands a very thin membrane, extending nearly the whole length of its longest diameter in a diagonal direction; it is about an inch in height, and forms a segment of a circle. This membrane, which seemed to serve all the purposes of a fin and a sail, was sometimes observed to be erect; at others lying flat, which was generally the case in the morning; but as the day advanced, it became extended. Whether this was voluntary, or the effect of the sun's influence, was a question not easily to be decided. When the membrane was down, these little animals were collected into compact clusters, were apparently destitute of any motion, and their colour at that time seemed of a dark green.'[3]

The wind gradually veered round to the S.E. and E.S.E. increasing in its force, attended generally with a very smooth sea; though sometimes with a

[1] Barkley Sound, on the W coast of Vancouver Island. Named after captain Charles William Barkley, who discovered and named it in 1787. He made a sketch plan of the sound that Meares published in his *Voyages* in 1790.

[2] The sperm whale or cachelot. The spermaceti is a waxy substance found in a reservoir in the whale's head. In Vancouver's day was used to make church candles. At one time whalers thought it was the whale's seminal fluid, hence the name.

[3] Partly quoted and partly paraphrased from Johnstone's log, 11 April 1792. Menzies included a shorter description in his journal for 8 April.

little swell from the westward and S.W. accompanied by cloudy and gloomy weather. On Sunday morning the 15th, I got one set of lunar distances, which at noon gave the longitude 232° 56½′; by the chronometer 232° 7¾′; and by the dead reckoning 229° 39′: the latitude 37° 55′.

The wind at E.S.E. by two the next morning, increased with such violence as to make it necessary that the topsails should be close-reefed; the squalls were very heavy, with an appearance of an approaching storm. No soundings were to be had with 120 fathoms of line; and as I could not depend upon the longitude of the coast of New Albion under this parallel, we stood on a wind until day-light, when we again resumed our course to the N.E. with an increasing gale, attended by thick rainy weather; which, by two in the afternoon, obliged us to strike our top-gallant-masts, and stand to the southward under the foresail and storm staysails. At ten that night the wind veered round to the south, blew a moderate gale, and brought with it fair and pleasant weather. Our upper canvas was again spread; and the necessary signals made to the Chatham not being answered, and not seeing her at day-break on Tuesday the 17th, we abandoned our course to the eastward to go in search of her. About five she was seen from the mast-head to the N.W.; upon which we bore down to her, and having joined company, we again directed our route to the eastward.[1] The sky being tolerably clear, although the wind had again put us under double-reefed topsails, enabled me to obtain six sets of lunar distances, whose mean result at noon gave the longitude 50′ to the eastward of the chronometer, the true longitude being 236° 8′, and the dead reckoning 231° 30′; the observed latitude was 39° 20′.

Soon after mid-day we passed considerable quantities of drift wood, grass, sea weed, &c. Many shags, ducks, puffins, and other aquatic birds were flying about; and the colour of the water announced our approach to soundings. These circumstances indicated land not far off, although we were prevented seeing any object more than three or four miles distant, by the weather, which had become very thick and rainy. Being anxious to get sight of the land before night if possible, we stood to the eastward with as much sail as we could carry, and at four in the afternoon reached soundings at the depth of 53 fathoms, soft brown sandy bottom. The land was now discovered[2] bearing by compass

[1] Johnstone had been chagrined to find that when 'The Discovery from the injury her mainmast had received could not carry her top gallt mast yet without it she outsailed us.' – March 20. A month later he mentioned one reason: 'In this [stormy] weather our worn sails suffered much. We had been obliged to shift every one of the small sails, and this forenoon the foresail being the one which we had got so much mildewed at Otaheite and was breaking out in holes all over.' – 17 April.

[2] Vancouver's chart indicates that his landfall was near lat. 39° 20′ N, in the vicinity of Point Cabrillo, California. The point is about 115 miles N of the entrance to San Francisco Bay. Johnstone's comment was: 'Got to our station after a passage of one year and eighteen days.' – 18 April. Baker's log shows that by ship time land was sighted on 18 April at 4 p.m., which was 4 p.m. on 17 April by civil time. Vancouver had made no time adjustment for the fact that he was sailing eastward around the world, and by local time (used by the Spaniards he was soon to meet) the sighting was made on 16 April. Vancouver, using unadjusted civil time, dated it 17 April.

from E.N.E. to E. by S. at the distance of about two leagues, on which the surf broke with great violence. We stood in for the shore under our topsails for about an hour, and perceived the coast to extend from N. to S.E. The nearest shore was about two miles distant. The rain and fog with which the atmosphere was now loaded, precluded our seeing much of this part of the coast of New Albion. The shore appeared straight and unbroken, of a moderate height, with mountainous land behind, covered with stately forest trees; excepting in some spots, which had the appearance of having been cleared by manual labour; and exhibited a verdant, agreeable aspect. During the night we plied under an easy sail, in order to be near the land next morning, Wednesday the 18th;[1] when, in consequence of a thick haze, it remained obscured until a light breeze from the eastward about ten o'clock gave us a view of the shore to the north eastward, for which we immediately steered. The northern extremity of the land bore by compass at noon N.N.W. the nearest shore east about six leagues, the land I considered we were off the preceding night S. 72 E. about eight leagues; and the southernmost land in sight S. 60 E. about ten leagues distant. The observed latitude was at this time 39° 27'; longitude 235° 41' 30"; by the chronometer 235°. The former was deduced from the mean result of eighty-five sets of lunar distances, taken by the several persons as under, and reduced at noon by the chronometer since the 27th of March, according to its *Otaheitean rate*, (viz.)

Nine sets taken by Mr. Puget gave	235° 36' 0"
Eighteen sets by Mr. Whidbey	235 49
Nineteen by Mr. Orchard	235 35
Ten by Mr. John Stewart	235 44
Seventeen by Mr. Ballard	235 46
Twelve by myself	235 39
The mean result of the above eighty-five sets	235 41 30

This made the chronometer 41' 30" to the west of that which I supposed to be nearest the true longitude; and from the general result of these observations it evidently appeared, that the chronometer had materially altered in its rate since we had reached these northern regions. The longitude of the respective points, headlands, &c. as hereafter stated, will therefore be corrected and affixed, by subsequent observations, agreeably to the explanation contained in the following chapter; whence, by allowing a different rate to the chronometer, the true longitude this day at noon was ascertained to be 236° 25'.[2]

---

[1] Bell explains: 'As we had now entered upon our Station and the Survey of the Coast, we were obliged to haul off at dark & spend the night in short boards, that we might take up the Land in the Morning where we left off the Evening before.' – April 17.

[2] The *Discovery* was in lat. 39° 27' (the lat. of Fort Bragg) and Mudge noted that she was 4 leagues from land. Her true position must therefore have been approximately long. 235° 56' E (124° 04' W). Vancouver's longitudes along the coast are almost all too far E and this is a notable example: 236° 25' E would place the ship a dozen miles inland. Vancouver's

The gentle breeze of wind that now prevailed appearing to be settled in the southern quarter, favoured my wish to pursue a northern course; for which purpose we bore away along the coast at the distance of three or four leagues. The weather was delightfully pleasant; and as we drew nearer the land, the shore seemed to be perfectly compact, formed, generally speaking, by cliffs of a moderate height and nearly perpendicular. The inland country, which rises in a pleasing diversity of hills and dales, was completely clothed with forest trees of considerable magnitude; and those spots which, on our first view, had the appearance of having been cleared of their wood by art, were now seen to extend, generally, along the sea-side; and their being destitute of wood, was evidently to be ascribed to some natural cause. They were beautifully green, with a luxuriant herbage, interrupted by streaks of red earth. At sun-set, the southern-most land in sight bore by compass, S. 45 E.; a small white rock, not unlike a vessel under sail, close to the shore, east; the nearest shore E.N.E. four leagues; and the northernmost land in sight, which I considered to be cape Mendocino, N. 36 W. about ten leagues distant. In this situation, the variation by the surveying compass was observed to be 16° eastwardly.

The night was spent in making short trips. The next morning, Thursday the 19th, brought with it a return of calm or light baffling winds, a very heavy swell from the S.W. and so thick a haze over the land, that the shores were scarcely perceptible. Immense numbers of whales were playing about us during the morning. Most of them were of that tribe which, in Greenland, are called finners.[1] Towards noon, we had again from the southward a moderate breeze; but the weather still remained extremely gloomy.

In directing our course along the coast to the northward, we observed in latitude 40° 3′ longitude 235° 51′. The mean variation of the surveying compass, by observations made before and after noon, was 15° eastwardly. In this situation, the northernmost land in sight bore, by compass, N. 10 W.; cape Mendocino, N. 2 W.; the easternmost land in sight, S. 60 E.; and the nearest shore N.E. about four leagues distant. In the afternoon we passed cape Mendocino. It is formed by two high promontories, about ten miles apart;[2] the southernmost, which is the highest, and when seen either from the north or the south much resembles Dunnoze,[3] is situated in latitude 40° 19′, longitude 235° 53′.[4] Off the Cape lie some rocky islets and sunken rocks, near

earlier calculation – 235° 41′ 30″ (124° 29′ 30″ W), based on the observations of himself, Mudge, Whidbey and others – was much nearer the mark, but was unusual in that instead of being eastward the error (about 12 miles) was westward.

[1] The finback whale, or common rorqual, which has a dorsal fin.

[2] At this time Vancouver considered that Cape Mendocino extended from the cape proper to Punta Gorda, a 900-foot promontory 11 miles to the S. On his chart, however, the name is confined to the northern cape. Cape Mendocino was a famous landmark for the old Spanish navigators. The name can be traced back as far as an Ortelius map of 1587.

[3] Dunnose, on the S coast of the Isle of Wight.

[4] The position of Punta Gorda is approximately lat. 40° 15′ N, long. 235° 38′ 30″ E (124° 21′ 30″ W).

a league from the shore. The southernmost of these from the northernmost promontory, lies S. 61 W. about a league distant; and within it are two rocky islets in shape much resembling hay-cocks. The northernmost of them lies N. 3 W. distant five or six miles, nearly of the same shape and size with the other to which it is apparently connected by a ledge of rocks, whose outermost part lies from the above promontory N. 38 W. about two leagues distant, having a smaller islet, about midway, between them. On some parts of this ledge the sea constantly breaks with great violence; on others, at intervals only. The broken water appeared from the mast-head to extend along the coast, as far north as could be discerned; which, however, was at no great distance, owing to the weather being still thick and hazy. The whole of this Cape, though by no means a very projecting head land, is doubtless very remarkable, from being the highest on the sea-shore of this part of New Albion. The mountains at its back are considerably elevated, and form altogether a high steep mass, which does not break into perpendicular cliffs, but is composed of various hills that rise abruptly, and are divided by many deep chasms. In some of these, as well as on some of the ridges of the hills, grew a few dwarf trees. The general surface was covered with vegetables of a dull green colour, interspersed in some places with perpendicular strata of red earth or clay. South of the Cape the coast is nearly straight, forming only a trifling bend, to the southernmost part we had seen. Its elevation is regular, it may be considered as high land, and is apparently steep to, as we sounded without gaining bottom with 120 fathoms of line at distances from two to five leagues from the shore. This had been uniformly the case since the evening we first saw the coast, having no where else gained any soundings, nor seen any drift wood, sea-weed, or aquatic birds, nor noticed any difference in the colour of the water. These circumstances induced some of us to suspect, that an opening or river existed to the southward of our then station.[1] To the northward of cape Mendocino, the elevation of the country appeared suddenly to decrease beyond the rocky islets, where it seemed to assume a moderate height. As the day advanced, the weather becoming unpleasant, and adverse to our pursuit, about five o'clock we hauled off the shore. The outermost of the sunken rocks on a line with the middle islet, bore by compass E. by N. at the distance of about a league; the main land, then indistinctly seen, from N.E. by N. to E.S.E. In this situation, we had soundings at the depth of 49 fathoms; dark brown sand. As we stood into the offing, we tried, at the distances of two, three, and four leagues S.W. from the rocks, but gained no bottom at the depth of 80 and 90 fathoms.[2]

The gale had so much increased by midnight from the S.E. as to render close-reefing the topsails necessary; under which we again stood in for the land, in the hope of the wind abating the next morning, Friday the 20th.

[1] The nearest river of any considerable size is the Eel River 12½ miles N of Cape Mendocino.

[2] At no great distance from the coast there are water depths of well over 1000 fathoms.

Instead of which it became more violent, attended with such very heavy squalls of rain and thick weather, that we were obliged to strike the top-gallant yards, and stand to sea under our courses. In the afternoon the head-railing on the starboard side was entirely carried away. This obliged us to reef the foresail, and bring the tack to the cat-head; by which means, the sail stood so indifferently, that the consequences attendant on this accident might have been very alarming, had we had a lee shore instead of a weather shore to contend with.

The gale, accompanied by torrents of rain, continued until midnight; when it veered to the south, moderated, and permitted us to steer again for the land under close-reefed topsails. On Saturday morning the 21st, our top-gallant sails were again set, but the weather was very unpleasant, being thick, with heavy rain; which, towards noon, terminated in a calm and fog.[1] By our reckoning, the south promontory of cape Mendocino bore, by compass, S. 60 E., 11 miles distant. In this situation, no bottom could be reached with 120 fathoms of line.

The fog, with calms, or light variable winds, continued until about ten the next forenoon, Sunday the 22d, when the weather suddenly altered, and brought with it a fine pleasant gale from the south. All sail was now made for the land; at noon the south promontory of cape Mendocino bore, by compass, S. 64 E., distant nine leagues; its north part, N. 88 E. six leagues; the northernmost of the rocky islets, N. 71 E., five or six leagues; and the northernmost land in sight, N.E.; the observed latitude 40° 32′; longitude 235° 28′, and the variation of the compass 16° eastwardly.

From cape Mendocino the coast takes a direction N. 13 E.; along which we ranged at the distance of about two leagues. After passing the above islets, the shores became straight and compact, not affording the smallest shelter; and, although rising gradually from the water's edge to a moderate height only, yet the distant interior country was composed of mountains of great elevation; before which were presented a great variety of hills and dales, agreeably interspersed with wood-land, and clear spots, as if in a state of cultivation; but we could discern neither houses, huts, smokes, nor other signs of its being inhabited. The coast we had passed this afternoon, seemed to be generally defended by a sandy beach;[2] but the evening brought us to a country of a very different description, whose shores were composed of rocky precipices, with numberless small rocks and rocky islets extending about a mile

---

[1] 'Saw some Whales, the spoutings of these afterwards in the hazy horizon loomd so as to be taken for strange vessels under sail & it was even some time before the deception was clearly detected.' – Menzies, April 21.

[2] Much of the coastline consists of low sandy spits, two of which shelter Humboldt Bay, but this would not be apparent to Vancouver, as the *Discovery* was some distance off shore. The bay is now a busy commercial port. Dredging and modern aids to navigation have greatly reduced the dangers of the bar at its narrow mouth, the cause of many disasters in earlier days.

into the sea: the most projecting part, which is situated in latitude 41° 8',
longitude 236° 5', obtained the name of ROCKY POINT.[1] This, at seven in the
evening, bore by compass N. 18 e. six miles distant; the nearest shore east
four miles; and the northernmost land in sight N. 6 E. We spent the night
in preserving our situation with the land, and the next morning, Monday the
23d, again pursued our course along the coast, which from Rocky Point takes
a direction N. 9 W. The wind at south was light, the weather was cloudy,
with some little rain. At eight o'clock Rocky Point bore by compass S. 40
E., five or six miles; the nearest shore, N.E. by E. three miles distant; and
a detached rocky islet N. 18 W.; within which we afterwards passed in 35
to 50 fathoms water, black sandy bottom. This rock is a high round lump
about half a mile in circuit, apparently steep to, and lies from Rocky Point
N. 11 W. distant 13 miles, and about half a league from the shore.[2] When
abreast of Rocky Point, the colour of the sea suddenly changed from the
oceanic hue to a very light river-coloured water, extending as far a-head as
could be discerned. This gave us reason to suppose some considerable river
or rivers were in the neighbourhood.[3]

A fresh gale from the south permitted our sailing along the coast within
a league of the shore, which appeared to be destitute of any opening, and
similar to that which we had passed the preceding evening, bounded by
innumerable small rocks and rocky islets. The face of the country may be
considered as mountainous, and did not appear so pleasing as that lying to
the south of Rocky Point. In this respect, however, we were able to say but
little, as the land was nearly obscured by the haziness of the weather, excepting
immediately on the sea-shore; which being composed of steep rocky precipices
broken by deep gullies, at a distance would put on the appearance of harbours,
or breaks in the land. At noon, we were again in oceanic-coloured water;
the observed latitude 41° 36'; longitude 235° 58'; and variation of the compass
16° eastwardly. In this situation, the southernmost land in sight bore by
compass S.S.E.; the nearest shore N.E. four miles distant; and the northernmost
extremity in sight, (being a cluster of remarkable, rocky hummocks at the
termination of a considerable tract of low level land, that at a distance seemed
to be an island,) bore N. 15 W. At the junction of the low level land with

[1] Vancouver's chart indicates that this was Trinidad Head, in lat. 41° 03' N, not the
present Rocky Point, which is 5½ miles farther N, although the latter happens to be in
lat. 41° 08' N.
[2] Redding Rock. Vancouver must have intended to write 'a league and a half from the
shore'. Baker noted that the *Discovery* passed 'between the detached Rock and the Main,
the distance between them is about 5 Miles.' – April 23. Redding Rock is 4½ miles offshore.
[3] The only large river in this part of the coast is the Klamath, 30 miles N of Trinidad
Head. The change in colour caused some uneasiness: 'we came into exceeding pale &
muddy water forming a defined line with the other as if it rushd out of some considerable
river or Inlet. At first we were a little alarmd thinking it might be shallow water & tryd
Soundings but with no ground with 50 fathoms line, & it appeard of the same colour all
along the shore to the Northward & Southward of us.' – Menzies, April 23.

the high rocky coast, a shallow bay is formed; at the bottom of which was an appearance of a small harbour or opening, which bore N. 5 E. Here I entertained hopes of finding shelter;[1] but the number of breakers along the shore of the low level land, some of which were detached, and lie at a considerable distance from the coast, together with a ledge of rocks and rocky islets seen from the mast-head, extending as far to the westward as N.W., and a sky bearing the same dull and gloomy aspect as that which preceded the former gale, induced me to consider it most prudent to decline the attempt; and to embrace the opportunity of the favorable gale at S.S.W. to continue my examination of the coast, in the confidence of soon finding a more convenient shelter.

We stood off W.N.W. in order to sail round the outwardmost of the rocks, which we passed at the distance of about three or four miles, about four o'clock; and again hauled in for the north side of the low level land. This land forms a very conspicuous point, which I named POINT ST. GEORGE, and the very dangerous cluster of rocks extending from thence, the DRAGON ROCKS.[2] The outwardmost of these lies from Point St. George, which is situated in latitude 41° 46½, and longitude 235° 57'½,[3] N. 52 W., three leagues distant. The rocks above water are four in number, with many sunken ones, and numerous breakers stretching from the outermost, (southward of point St. George) towards the opening mentioned at noon. This point forms a bay on each side; that into which we stood from the north side is perfectly open to the N.W., yet apparently sheltered from the W.S.W. and southwardly winds by the Dragon rocks; the soundings we found regularly from 35 to 45 fathoms, black sand and muddy bottom: when at the former depth, Point St. George bore by compass S. 33 E. 10 miles; the northernmost of the Dragon rocks S. 7 W. four miles; and the north point of the bay, which I called ST. GEORGE'S BAY,[4] N. 24 W. six or seven miles distant.

The surf broke with great violence all round the bay; and although we were again in whitish water, there was not any opening on this side of the point: the shores of the northernmost part of the bay, like the coast of the bay on the south side of Point St. George, rise very abruptly from the sea, forming numberless gullies and chasms, which were covered with a dull brownish herbage, and produced little or no wood. North of the bay the shores were again bounded with numberless small rocks and rocky islets, similar to those already mentioned; but the low land of Point St. George terminates in a sandy beach, from whence the coast takes a direction N. 15 W.

Not finding a situation here likely to answer our purpose, we directed our

[1] The bay a few miles SE of Point St. George, the N part of which now forms the harbour of Crescent City. Both ships were in need of wood and water.

[2] 'Capt. Vancouver [on April 23] named the Southern Point St. George & the Outer Rocks Dragon Rocks, it being St. George's Day.' – Puget, April 24. The name Point St. George survives, but the Dragon Rocks are now called St. George Reef. A Dragon Channel runs through some of them.

[3] The true position is lat. 41° 48' N, long. 235° 45' E (124° 15' W).

[4] Now Pelican Bay.

route along the coast until it was dark, when we hauled off shore, and spent the night in the offing. The next morning, Tuesday the 24th, the north point of St. George's bay bore by compass east two leagues distant. With a favorable breeze at S.E. and less hazy weather, our survey was continued to the northward along the shores,[1] which are composed of high steep precipices and deep chasms, falling very abruptly into the sea. The inland mountains were much elevated, and appeared, by the help of our glasses, to be tolerably well clothed with a variety of trees, the generality of which were of the pine tribe; yet amongst them were observed some spreading trees of considerable magnitude. Although some of these mountains appeared quite barren, they were destitute of snow; but on those at the back of cape Mendocino, which were further to the south, and apparently inferior in point of height, some small patches of snow were noticed. The shores were still bounded by innumerable rocky islets, and in the course of the forenoon we passed a cluster of them,[2] with several sunken rocks in their vicinity, lying a league from the land; which, by falling a little back to the eastward, forms a shallow bay, into which we steered. As the breeze that had been so favorable to our pursuit since the preceding Sunday died away, and as a tide or current set us fast in shore, we were under the necessity of coming to an anchor in 39 fathoms water, black sand and mud. The latitude of this station, was found to be 42° 38′, longitude 235° 44′. In this situation, the outermost rock of the cluster before mentioned bore by compass S. 16 E. six miles distant; a remarkable black rock, the nearest shore being N. 64 E. 3½ miles; a very high black cliff resembling the gable end of a house, N. 1 E.; the northernmost extremity of the main land, which is formed by low land projecting from the high rocky coast a considerable way into the sea, and terminating in a wedge-like low perpendicular cliff, N. 27 W. This I distinguished by the name of CAPE ORFORD,[3] in honor of my much respected friend the noble Earl (George) of that title: off it lie several rocky islets, the outwardmost of which bore N. 38 W.

Soon after we had anchored, a canoe was seen paddling towards the ship; and with the greatest confidence, and without any sort of invitation, came immediately alongside. During the afternoon two others visited the Discovery, and some repaired to the Chatham, from different parts of the coast in sight; by which it appeared, that the inhabitants who are settled along the shores of this country, may probably have their residence in the small nooks that are protected from the violence of the westwardly swell by some of the larger rocky islets, so abundantly scattered along the coast.[4]

[1] In the course of the morning Vancouver crossed lat. 42° N, now the boundary line between the states of California and Oregon.

[2] Rogue River Reef, just N of the mouth of the Rogue River.

[3] Now Cape Blanco. The name Orford survives in Port Orford, a bay 6½ miles S of Cape Blanco, and in Orford Reef, SW of the cape. Baker states that the latter, 'a Cluster of Small Rocks...obtain'd the Name of Walpole Rocks.' – April 25. The proposal is not mentioned elsewhere. Walpole was the family name of the Earls of Orford.

[4] These were Tututni Indians, a tribe that inhabited the lower valley of the Rogue River and the coast N and S of it. They are also referred to as the Rogue River Indians.

A pleasing and courteous deportment distinguished these people. Their countenances indicated nothing ferocious; their features partook rather of the general European character; their colour a light olive; and besides being punctuated in the fashion of the South-Sea islanders, their skin had many other marks, apparently from injuries in their excursions through the forests, possibly, with little or no cloathing that could protect them; though some of us were of opinion these marks were purely ornamental, as is the fashion with the inhabitants of Van Dieman's land.* Their stature was under the middle size; none that we saw exceeding five feet six inches in height. They were tolerably well limbed, though slender in their persons; bore little or no resemblance to the people of Nootka; nor did they seem to have the least knowledge of that language. They seemed to prefer the comforts of cleanliness to the painting of their bodies; in their ears and noses they had small ornaments of bone; their hair, which was long and black, was clean and neatly combed,[1] and generally tied in a club behind; though some amongst them had their hair in a club in front also. They were dressed in garments that nearly covered them, made principally of the skins of deer, bear, fox, and river otter; one or two cub skins of the sea otter were also observed amongst them. Their canoes, calculated to carry about eight people, were rudely wrought out of a single tree; their shape much resembled that of a butcher's tray, and seemed very unfit for a sea voyage or any distant expedition.[2] They brought but a few trifling articles to barter, and they anxiously solicited in exchange iron and beads. In this traffic they were scrupulously honest, particularly in fixing their bargain with the first bidder; for, if a second offered a more valuable commodity for what they had to sell, they would not consent, but made signs (which could not be mistaken,) that the first should pay the price offered by the second, on which the bargain would be closed. They did not entertain the least idea of accepting presents; for on my giving them some beads, medals, iron, &c. they instantly offered their garments in return, and seemed much astonished, and I believe not less pleased, that I chose to decline them. The

---

*   Vide Cook's last Voyage. ['They were quite naked & wore no ornaments, except the large punctures or ridges raised on the skin, some in straight and others in curved lines, might be reckoned as such...' – Cook, *Journals*, III, 52. Beaglehole adds that 'they came from cuts incised with a flint or other sharp stone knife, which were often rubbed with ashes or clay to enlarge the effect.']

[1]   Opinion as to the cleanliness of the natives varied sharply: 'they were of a copper colour but cleanly, as we observd no vestige of greasy paint or ochre about their faces or among their hair'. – Menzies, April 24. 'their Colour was not easily to be found out from the quantity of dirt and paint with which they were besmeared, but were they clean I suppose they were something of an Olive Colour'. – Bell, April 24. 'In stature small and in person filthy and stinking, we considered them the nastyest race of people under the Sun.' – Manby, letters, April 24.

[2]   Menzies described a canoe as being 'about 18 feet long 4 feet & ½ broad in the middle but a little narrower towards the end, & it was about 2 feet deep, formed of one piece of Pine Tree dug out tolerably well finishd, so that the wood on this part of the Coast must be pretty large.' – 24 April.

first man, in particular, gave me some trouble to persuade him that he was to retain both the trinkets and his garment.

We remained in this situation until near midnight, when a light breeze springing up from the S.S.E. attended with some rain and dark gloomy weather, we weighed and stood to and fro until day-light, Wednesday the 25th; when we directed our course round the group of rocks lying off cape Orford, comprehending four detached rocky islets, with several dangerous sunken rocks about them, on which the sea broke with great violence: the outermost of these lies from the Cape S. 38 W., distant about four miles; we passed close to the breakers in soundings of 45 fathoms, black sandy bottom. Cape Orford, which is situated in latitude 42° 52', longitude 235° 35',[1] at the extremity of a low projecting tract of land, forms a very conspicuous point, and bears the same appearance whether approached from the north or the south. It is covered with wood as low down as the surf will permit it to grow. The space between the woods and the wash of the sea, seemed composed of black craggy rocks, and may from the mast head be seen at the distance of seven or eight leagues; but I should suppose not much further. Some of us were of opinion that this was the cape Blanco of Martin D'Aguilar; its latitude, however, differed greatly from that in which cape Blanco is placed by that navigator;[2] and its dark appearance, which might possibly be occasioned by the haziness of weather, did not seem to intitle it to the appellation of cape Blanco. North of this cape, the coast takes a direction about N. 13 E.; and south of it towards Point St. George, S. 18 E.

The rocky islets which we had seen in such numbers along the shore, ceased to exist about a league to the north of cape Orford; and in their stead, an almost straight sandy beach presented itself, with land behind gradually rising to a moderate height near the coast; but the interior was considerably elevated, and much diversified both by its eminences and productions, being generally well wooded, though frequently interrupted with intervals of clear spots, which gave it some resemblance to a country in an advanced state of cultivation.

The weather having become more clear and pleasant at noon, cape Orford was visible astern nearly in the horizon, bearing by compass S. 11 E. five leagues distant; the nearest shore about a league distant east; a small projecting point, forming the north point of a small cove off which lie five detached rocks, N. 23 E., distance seven miles; and the northernmost land in sight, which I

---

[1] The position of Cape Blanco is lat. 42° 50' N, long. 124° 29' W (235° 31' E). Vancouver's error in longitude here was small.

[2] Martin de Aguilar was first pilot of the *Tres Reyes*, part of Sebastian Vizcaino's expedition of 1602–3. The expedition named a Cabo Blanco de San Sebastian which Wagner thinks may have been the present Point St George. Cape Blanco, as he remarks, was 'a favorite name in the imaginary geography of the northwest coast'. It seems first to have appeared on the Ortelius *Maris Pacifici* of 1589, where it was placed in lat. 33° N. On other maps its position varied all the way from 30° to 58° N. See H. R. Wagner, *The Cartography of the Northwest Coast of America to the Year 1800* (Berkeley, 1937), II, 432–3.

considered to be cape Blanco,[1] N. 2 E.; the observed latitude was 43° 6′; longitude 235° 42′; and the variation 16° eastwardly.

Having now a fine gale from the S.S.W. with serene and pleasant weather, we ranged along the coast at the distance of about a league, in hopes of determining the existence or non-existence of the extensive river or straits, asserted to have been discovered by Martin D'Aguilar.[2] About three in the afternoon we passed within a league of the cape above-mentioned; and at about half that distance from some breakers that lie to the westward of it. This cape, though not so projecting a point as cape Orford, is nevertheless a conspicuous one, particularly when seen from the north, being formed by a round hill on high perpendicular cliffs, some of which are white, a considerable height from the level of the sea. Above these cliffs it is tolerably well wooded, and is connected to the main land, by land considerably lower. In this respect it seemed exactly to answer Captain Cook's description of cape Gregory; though its situation did not appear to correspond with that assigned to cape Gregory by that navigator; our observations placing it in latitude 43° 23′; longitude 235° 50′;[3] whence the coast tends N. 21 E. About a league north of the pitch of the cape, the rocky cliffs composing it terminate, and a compact white sandy beach commences, which extends along the coast eight leagues, without forming any visible projecting point or head land. We sailed along this beach at a distance of from three to five miles, and had there been any projecting point or inlet in it, neither could have escaped our observation. This induced me to consider the above point as the cape Gregory of Captain Cook, with a probability of its being also the cape Blanco of D'Aguilar, if the latter ever saw land hereabouts. The difference in latitude between our computation and that of Captain Cook was 7′; our observations placing the cape that distance farther south. This might possibly have been occasioned by the tempestuous weather with which the Resolution and Discovery contended when off this coast, preventing the position of the several head lands being then ascertained with that accuracy which the fair winds and pleasant weather have enabled us to assign to them. The land seen to the south of cape Gregory by Captain Cook, and by him considered as answering nearly to the situation of cape Blanco, must have been some of the inland mountains, which to the south of cape Gregory rise to a great height; whilst the land near the sea shore,

[1] Now Cape Arago.

[2] Aguilar was not the discoverer of the river; he was one of the 48 members of the Vizcaino expedition who died on the voyage. Estéban López, who succeeded him in command of the *Tres Reyes*, claimed that a storm drove him N as far as lat. 43° and that he discovered large rivers at 39° 15′ and 40° 30′ N. The larger of these he named Rio de Martin Aguilar. Later its supposed location migrated N to 43° (where Vancouver was watching for it) and some thought it might be the entrance to the Strait of Juan de Fuca.

[3] Beaglehole 'suspects' that the cape that Cook named Cape Gregory was the present Cape Arago; there would seem to be little room for doubt, as there is no other prominent feature on the coast for a considerable distance either N or S of it. Cook gave its lat. as 43° 30′ N; its true position is 43° 18′ N. The name was changed from Cape Gregory to Cape Arago in 1850 by the U.S. Coast Survey to honour a French physicist of that name.

particularly in the neighbourhood of cape Orford, was much too low to have been seen at the distance which Captain Cook was at that time from it; and it is fair to presume, that the excessive bad weather led Captain Cook and his officers to consider the extremely white sand on the sea shore and on the hills to be snow. With us it put on the same appearance, excepting where it was interrupted by the clumps of trees, and until it was intirely lost in the forest. There could be no doubt of its being mistaken in winter for snow; but as the general temperature of the thermometer since our arrival on the coast had been at 59 and 60, the error of such conclusion was sufficiently manifested.[1]

The night was spent as before; and in the morning of Thursday the 26th, we sailed along the coast, which extended from S.E. by S. to N. ½ E.; the land we hauled off from the preceding evening, S. 40 E. four or five leagues; and the nearest shore east, six or seven miles distant. A considerable increase in the wind from the S.W. with appearances of a threatening nature, made me consider it not prudent to venture nearer than within two or three leagues of the shore; which being greatly obscured by the haziness of the atmosphere, prevented our seeing much of the inland country. We lost sight again of the sandy beaches and low shores, and in lieu of them we were presented with a straight and compact coast, composed of steep craggy rocky cliffs, nearly perpendicular to the sea, with a retired mountainous country much broken, and forming a great variety of deep chasms; the whole but thinly covered with wood. At eight we passed the only projecting point from cape Gregory. It is a high rocky bluff, nearly perpendicular to the sea; against it the billows, that now ran very high, broke with immense violence. This promontory I considered to be that which Captain Cook calls cape Perpetua; our observations placing it in latitude 44° 12′, longitude 236° 5′.[2] From hence the coast takes a north direction, which we ranged along at the distance of about three leagues from the shore, until towards noon; when having nearly reached the northern extent of the coast hereabout seen by Captain Cook, and the gale still increasing, we close-reefed the topstails and hauled off shore, until the weather should prove more favorable to the examination of an unknown coast. Cape Foulweather at this time bore by compass N. 42 E. three or four leagues distant,

[1] There is no mention of snow in Cook's own journal; his description agrees with Vancouver's: 'In general the land here is not very high, but it is hilly and covered with wood, with white sand banks next to the Sea.' – *Journals*, III, 290. The reference to snow was evidently added by the editor of the printed version, perhaps on the authority of Samwell's journal, which refers to the coast of America as being 'high and Craggy & mostly covered with Snow.' – *ibid.*, III, 1088. The virtually apologetic tone of Vancouver's mild criticism of Cook, his hero, is typical.

[2] It seems probable that the promontory seen by both Cook and Vancouver was Hecata Head, in lat. 44° 08′ N, rather than the present Cape Perpetua in lat. 44° 17′ N. This would reduce the error in Cook's latitude, on which Beaglehole comments, from 11′ to 2′. *Journals*, III, 290n. Vancouver's latitude for Cape Gregory (now Cape Arago) was 5′ too far N; if the cape he identified as Cape Perpetua was Heceta Head, his error would have been a fairly consistent 4′ N; for Cape Perpetua the error would have been an unlikely 5′ S.

and the coast indistinctly seen, from N. by E. to S.E. by S. The observed latitude 44° 42′, longitude 235° 53′, and the variation 18° eastwardly.

The gale having a little abated, veered to the south; and the haze clearing away from the land, we again pursued our route, and in the afternoon passed cape Foulweather, which is a conspicuous promontory, almost as singular in its appearance as any we had seen along the coast. A high round bluff point projects abruptly into the sea; a remarkable table hill is situated to the north, and a lower round bluff to the south of it. Our observations placed this cape in latitude 44° 49′, longitude 236° 4′.[1]

From cape Foulweather the coast takes a direction a little to the eastward of north, and is nearly a straight and compact shore, considerably elevated, and in general steep to the sea. The face of the country is much chequered, in some places covered with a pleasing verdure, in others occupied by barren rocks and sand; but in none very thickly wooded.

Sun-set brought us in sight of that part of the coast which had been seen by Mr. Meares;[2] its northern extremity in sight bore by compass N. ½ W.; cape Look-out[3] N. 10 E.; the nearest shore N. 34 E. about a league distant. This, being a remarkably steep bluff cliff, flattered us for some time with an appearance like the entrance of an harbour; but on a nearer approach the deception was found to have been occasioned by the low land to the north of the bluff forming a very shallow open bay;[4] the southernmost land in sight bore S.S.E.; in this situation we had 50 fathoms of water, black sandy bottom.

The night, which was tolerably fair, was spent as usual in preserving our station until day-light, Friday the 27th, when we pursued our examination along the coast with a favourable breeze, attended with some passing showers. Cape Look-out then bore by compass east, about two leagues distant. This Cape forms only a small projecting point, yet it is remarkable for the four rocks which lie off from it: one of which is perforated, as described by Mr. Meares;[5] and excepting a rock passed the preceding afternoon, these were the first we had seen north of cape Gregory.

From cape Look-out, which is situated in latitude 45° 32′, longitude

[1] The true position is lat. 44° 46′ N, long. 124° 04′ W (235° 56′ E). Once again Vancouver's latitude is too far N, 3′ in this instance. Cook named 'Cape Foul Weather from the very bad weather we soon after met with'. – *Journals*, III, 289.

[2] Wrongly spelled Mears here and in several other places in the first edition.

[3] Now Cape Meares. The cape was named Cape Lookout by Meares on 6 July 1788, but in the period 1850–3 the name was moved on U.S. charts to the more prominent cape 8 miles to the S. The original Cape Lookout was named Cape Meares a few years later. It marked the southern limit of Meares' exploration of the coast: 'As we had met with nothing but discouragement, we here gave up all further pursuit, and closed our progress to the Southward'. – *Voyages*, p. 169.

[4] Tillamook Bay, the Quicksand Bay of Meares.

[5] Now called Three Arch Rocks. Meares had named them The Three Brothers. 'The middle one has an archway, perforated, as it were, in its centre, through which we very plainly discovered the distant sea.' – Meares, *Voyages*, p. 169.

236° 11′,[1] the coast takes a direction about N. 8 W. and is pleasingly diversified with eminences and small hills near the sea shore, in which are some shallow sandy bays, with a few detached rocks lying about a mile from the land. The more inland country is considerably elevated; the mountains stretch towards the sea, and at a distance appeared to form many inlets and projecting points; but the sandy beach that continued along the coast renders it a compact shore, now and then interrupted by perpendicular rocky cliffs, on which the surf breaks violently. This mountainous inland country extends about 10 leagues to the north from cape Look-out, where it descends suddenly to a moderate height; and had it been destitute of its timber, which seemed of considerable magnitude and to compose an intire forest, it might be deemed low land. Noon brought us up with a very conspicuous point of land composed of a cluster of hummocks, moderately high, and projecting into the sea from the low land before mentioned. These hummocks are barren, and steep near the sea, but their tops are thinly covered with wood. On the south side of this promontory was the appearance of an inlet, or small river, the land behind not indicating it to be of any great extent; nor did it seem accessible for vessels of our burthen, as the breakers extended from the above point two or three miles into the ocean, until they joined those on the beach nearly four leagues further south. On reference to Mr. Meares's description of the coast south of this promontory, I was first induced to believe it to be cape Shoalwater, but on ascertaining its latitude, I presumed it to be that which he calls cape Disappointment; and the opening to the south of it, Deception bay.[2] This cape was found to be in latitude 46° 19′, longitude 236° 6′.[3]

The sea had now changed from its natural, to river coloured water; the probable consequence of some streams falling into the bay, or into the ocean

---

[1] The position of Cape Meares is lat. 45° 29′ N; that of the present Cape Lookout is 45° 20′ N.

[2] Meares' name for the estuary of the Columbia River, which he did not recognize as being the outlet of a major river. The relevant part of his account of the events of 6 July 1788 reads: 'After we rounded the promontory [Cape Disappointment], a large bay, as we had imagined, opened to our view, that bore a very promising appearance, and into which we steered with encouraging expectation...As we steered in, the water shoaled to nine, eight, and seven fathoms, when the breakers were seen from the deck, right a-head; and, from the mast-head, they were observed to extend across the bay. We therefore hauled out...The name of Cape Disappointment was given to the promontory, and the bay obtained the title of Deception Bay....We can now with safety assert, that there is no such river as that of Saint Roc exists, as laid down in the Spanish charts'. – Voyages, p. 167. The reference is to the discovery of the estuary by Bruno de Hezeta on 17 August 1775. He attempted to enter, but was defeated by an outflowing current that was so strong that he concluded that he was off 'the mouth of some great river, or of some passage to another sea.' Quoted by Warren Cook, Flood Tide of Empire (New Haven, 1973), p. 176. Thereafter on Spanish charts the Columbia estuary was noted either as the Estrada de Hezeta or the Rio de San Rogue. Hezeta had named Cape Disappointment Cabo San Roque.

[3] The position of the cape is lat. 46° 16′ N, long. 124° 04′ W (235° 56′ E). Vancouver's position is thus 10′ too far E.

to the north of it, through the low land. Not considering this opening worthy of more attention, I continued our pursuit to the N.W. being desirous to embrace the advantages of the prevailing breeze and pleasant weather, so favourable to our examination of the coast,[1] which now took a direction N. 12 W.; the latitude at this time was 46° 14′; longitude 236° 1½′; and the variation of the compass 18° eastwardly. In this situation we had soundings at the depth of 33 fathoms, black sandy bottom; the northernmost land seen from the deck bore by compass north; the promontory of cape Disappointment, from N. 14 E. to N. 32 E.; this, the nearest shore, was about two leagues distant; and the southernmost land in sight bore S.E. by S.

The country before us presented a most luxuriant landscape, and was probably not a little heightened in beauty by the weather that prevailed. The more interior parts were somewhat elevated, and agreeably diversified with hills, from which it gradually descended to the shore, and terminated in a sandy beach. The whole had the appearance of a continued forest extending as far north as the eye could reach, which made me very solicitous to find a port in the vicinity of a country presenting so delightful a prospect of fertility; our attention was therefore earnestly directed to this object, but the sandy beach bounded by breakers extending three or four miles into the sea, seemed to be completely inaccessible until about four in the afternoon, when the appearance of a tolerably good bay presented itself. For this we steered, in the hope of finding a division in the reef, through which, should admittance be gained, there was great reason to expect a well sheltered anchorage; but on approaching within two or three miles of the breakers, we found them produced by a compact reef, extending from a low projecting point of land along the shores to the southward, until they joined the beach to the north of cape Disappointment. This projecting point is somewhat more elevated than the rest of the coast, and is situated in latitude 46° 40′;[2] longitude 236°. Not a little disappointed, we resumed our route along the shores of this pleasant

[1] Vancouver has been much criticized for his failure to recognize that he was off the mouth of a major river, the Columbia, but it is evident that the existence of the river was suspected. Lack of time and the famous Columbia River bar were what discouraged any detailed examination at this time. Bell noted that 'there was every appearance of an opening there, but to us the Sea seem'd to break entirely across it.' – April 27. Menzies was more specific: 'About noon seeing some whitish water ahead induced us to haul the wind...to avoid the apparent danger of getting into shoal water. The exterior edge of this water like the former we met with made a defined line with the other & appeard muddy like the over flowings of a considerable river...I could see at this time from the Mast head the appearance of a river or inlet going in on the South side of this rocky point which I took to be what Mr Mears named Cape Disappointment'. – April 27. In a narrative probably written soon after the event Manby wrote: 'When we observed a considerable breach in the Land, we approached it, as near as safety would permit, as a continued roll of tremendous breakers lay right across its entrance, it may [be] from a River and perhaps admissable at certain periods. We had it not in our power to loiter away any time on it at present, intending to inspect it farther on a Future day.' – Manby, letters, April 28.

[2] Meares placed Cape Shoalwater in lat. 46° 47′ N; its true position is 46° 44′ N.

country. The projecting point, at six, bore compass N. 10 E.; the centre of the bay, and the nearest part of the reef in a line N. 69 E.; distant from the former about seven, and from the latter, about three miles. Immediately within the point, the interior country is more elevated than to the north or south of it; rising in gradual ascent to land of a moderate height. In respect of latitude, this point answered nearly to Mr. Meares's cape Shoalwater; but, from his description of the adjacent country, it should rather appear to be his Low Point; and the bay we endeavoured to enter to the south of it, Shoalwater bay;[1] as in it there appeared two openings, the one taking a northerly, and the other an eastwardly direction. Mr. Meares likewise states, 'that, with their glasses, they traced the line of the coast to the south of cape Shoalwater, which presented no opening that promised like an harbour;'[2] those to the south of both these points flattered our expectations, until the breakers, extending across each of them, gave us reason to consider them inaccessible, and unworthy any loss of time whilst accompanied by so favorable a breeze. At sun-set we again shortened sail, and as usual hauled our wind to preserve our station until morning. Our soundings were from 24 to 43 fathoms, dark brown sandy bottom. It was calm for a few hours during the evening and night, attended with a heavy fall of rain.

The next morning, Saturday 28th, at 4 o'clock, with a light breeze at E.S.E. we again steered in for the land, and found that we had been materially affected by a northern current. The land we had been abreast of the preceding evening, now bore by compass S.E. six or seven leagues distant; and the coast to the north of it still continuing to appear a straight and compact shore, I did not attempt gaining a nearer view, but passed on to the northward, keeping at about a league from the land[3] which now took an almost north direction, to a point that, after the Right Honorable Lord Grenville, I named POINT GRENVILLE, situated in latitude 47° 22', longitude 235° 58½';[4] whence the coast tends N.N.W. Lying off point Grenville are three small rocky islets, one of which, like that at cape Look-out, is perforated.[5]

From hence, as we proceeded to the north, the coast began to increase regularly in height, and the inland country, behind the low land bordering on the sea shore, acquired a considerable degree of elevation. The shores we passed this morning, differed in some respects from those we had hitherto seen.

[1] The name Cape Shoalwater has been retained, but Shoalwater Bay is now Willapa Bay. The cape is the N point of the entrance; Meares' Low Point, the S point of entrance, is now Point Leadbetter.

[2] As usual, Vancouver has taken small but unimportant liberties with the quotation, which is from Meares, *Voyages*, p. 167.

[3] This swing out to sea prevented Vancouver from seeing Grays Harbor, which Whidbey would survey later.

[4] Point Grenville is in lat. 47° 20' N. long. 124° 16' W (235° 44' E). Baron Grenville married Anne Pitt, sister of the Hon. Thomas Pitt, heir of Lord Camelford, the troublesome young man who was a midshipman in the *Discovery*. The point had been named Punta de Martires by the Hezeta expedition in 1775.

[5] This island has been named Grenville Arch.

They were composed of low cliffs rising perpendicularly from a beach of sand or small stones; had many detached rocks of various romantic forms, lying at the distance of about a mile, with regular soundings, between 16 and 19 fathoms, soft sandy bottom. Noon brought us in sight of land, which was considered to be that named by Mr. Barclay, Destruction island;[1] bearing by compass from N. 14 W. to N. 17 W.; the southernmost land in sight, S. 53 E.; the northernmost N. 36 W.; and the nearest shore N. 65 E. at the distance of about four miles; in this situation our observed latitude was 47° 30', longitude 235° 49', and the variation of the compass 18° eastwardly.

In the afternoon the wind we had been so happily favored with died away, and was succeeded by calms and light variable breezes. These, with a current or tide setting rapidly in shore, obliged us to anchor in 21 fathoms, on a bottom of soft sand and mud: the coast, which now formed a straight and compact shore, bore by compass from N. 30 W. to S. 49 E.; the nearest part of the main land, east, about five miles; Destruction island being the nearest land N. 5 E. to N. 5 W. about a league distant, some breakers extending from its north point N. 8 W.

This island is situated in latitude 47° 37'; longitude 235° 49';[2] and is, by far, the largest detached land yet observed on the coast. It is about a league in circuit, low, and nearly flat on the top, presenting a very barren aspect, and producing only one or two dwarf trees at each end.[3] A canoe or two were seen paddling near the island. It was a fact not less singular than worthy observation, that, on the whole extensive coast of New Albion, and more particularly in the vicinity of those fertile and delightful shores we had lately passed, we had not, excepting to the southward of cape Orford and at this place, seen any inhabitants, or met with any circumstances, that in the most distant manner indicated a probability of the country being inhabited.

Notwithstanding the serenity and pleasantness of the weather, our voyage was rendered excessively irksome by the want of wind; our progress was slow, and our curiosity was much excited to explore the promised expansive mediterranean ocean, which, by various accounts, is said to have existence in these regions. The several large rivers and capacious inlets that have been described as discharing their contents into the pacific, between the 40th and 48th degree of north latitude, were reduced to brooks insufficient for our vessels to navigate, or to bays, inapplicable as harbours, for refitting; excepting that one of which Mr. Dalrymple informs us, that 'it is alledged that the Spaniards have recently found an entrance in the latitude of 47° 45' north,

[1] The island appears on Quadra's map of 1775 as Isla Dolores. The second mate and five crewmen from Barkley's ship were massacred by the Indians when they entered a river near the island, which Barkley called Destruction River. Vancouver extended the name to the island.
[2] The true position is lat. 47° 41' N, long. 124° 28' W (235° 32' E).
[3] Vancouver's description would still apply: 'It is flat-topped and covered with brush, with a few clumps of trees.' – United States Coast Pilot 7 (12th ed., Washington, 1976), p. 265.

which in 27 days course brought them to the vicinity of Hudson's bay; this latitude exactly corresponds to the ancient relation of John De Fuca, the Greek pilot, in 1592.'* This inlet could be now only ten miles from us; and another that had been visited by Mr. Meares and other traders on the coast, was not more than 20 leagues distant. We had been extremely fortunate in the favorable winds that had attended us along this coast, and their absence at this juncture made us impatient for their return. Our anxiety was, however, of no long duration; as by three o'clock on Sunday morning the 29th, we were indulged with a pleasant breeze, with which at day-light we weighed and stood along the shore to the N.W. Whilst at anchor we found a constant current, without intermission, setting in the line of the coast to the northward, at an uniform rate of near half a league per hour. Since we had passed cape Orford, we had been regularly thus affected, and carried further to the north by ten or twelve miles per day than we expected.

At four o'clock, a sail was discovered to the westward standing in shore. This was a very great novelty, not having seen any vessel but our consort, during the last eight months. She soon hoisted American colours, and fired a gun to leeward. At six we spoke her. She proved to be the ship Columbia, commanded by Mr. Robert Gray, belonging to Boston, whence she had been absent nineteen months. Having little doubt of his being the same person who had formerly commanded the sloop Washington, I desired he would bring to, and sent Mr. Puget and Mr. Menzies on board to acquire such information as might be serviceable in our future operations.

The most remarkable mountain we had seen on the coast of New Albion, now presented itself. Its summit, covered with eternal snow, was divided into a very elegant double fork, and rose conspicuously from a base of lofty mountains clothed in the same manner, which descended gradually to hills of a moderate height, and terminated like that we had seen the preceding day, in low cliffs falling perpendicularly on a sandy beach; off which were scattered many rocks and rocky islets of various forms and sizes. This was generally considered, though it was not confirmed by its latitude, to be the mount Olympus of Mr. Meares; it being the only conspicuous mountain we had observed on the part of the coast he had visited. Mount Olympus is placed in latitude 47° 10'; whereas our latitude now was 47° 38'; and as this mountain bore N. 55 E. it must consequently be to the north of us; although we were unable to determine its precise situation, by the thick hazy weather which shortly succeeded.[1]

On the return of the boat, we found our conjectures had not been ill grounded, that this was the same gentleman who had commanded the sloop

---

* Vide Mr. Dalrymple's plan for promoting the fur trade, &c. p. 21, 1789. [Alexander Dalrymple, *Plan for Promoting the Fur Trade, and securing it to this Country, by uniting the Operations of the East India and Hudson's Bay Companys*, London, 1789.]

[1] Mount Olympus (7,915 ft.) was seen and named Cerro Nevado de Santa Rosalia by Pérez in 1774. The present name was bestowed by Meares in July 1788.

Washington at the time, we are informed, she had made a very singular voyage behind Nootka. It was not a little remarkable that, on our approach to the entrance of this inland sea, we should fall in with the identical person who, it had been stated, had sailed through it. His relation, however, differed very materially from that published in England. It is not possible to conceive any one to be more astonished than was Mr. Gray, on his being made acquainted, that his authority had been quoted, and the track pointed out that he had been said to have made in the sloop Washington. In contradiction to which, he assured the officers, that he had penetrated only 50 miles into the straits in question, in an E.S.E. direction; that he found the passage five leagues wide; and that he understood from the natives, that the opening extended a considerable distance to the northward; that this was all the information he had acquired respecting this inland sea, and that he returned into the ocean by the same way he had entered. The inlet he supposed to be the same that De Fuca had discovered, which opinion seemed to be universally received by all the modern visitors.[1] He likewise informed them of his having been off the mouth of a river in the latitude of 46° 10′, where the outset, or reflux, was so strong as to prevent his entering for nine days. This was, probably, the opening passed by us on the forenoon of the 27th; and was, apparently,

---

[1] Menzies gives us the only first-hand account of the historic interview with Gray: 'Mr. Gray informd us that in his former Voyage [in 1789] he had gone up the Streights of Juan de Fuca in the Sloop Washington about 17 leagues in an East by South Direction & finding he did not meet with encouragement as a Trader to pursue it further he returnd back & came out to Sea again the very same way he had enterd it – he was therefore struck with astonishment when we informd him of the sweeping tract of several degrees which Mr. Mears had given him credit for in his chart and publication.' – 29 April. The relevant passage in Meares, in which he credits Gray with having established the insularity of Vancouver Island, reads: 'The Washington entered the Straits of John de Fuca, the knowledge of which she had received from us; and, penetrating up them, entered into an extensive sea, where she steered to the Northward and Eastward, and had communication with the various tribes who inhabit the shores of the numerous islands that are situated at the back of Nootka Sound, and speak, with some little variation, the language of the Nootkan people. The track of this vessel is marked on the map, and is of great moment. as it now completely ascertains that Nootka Sound, and the parts adjacent, are islands, and comprehended within the Great Northern Archipelago.' – Voyages, p. lvi. The map in question, which has been referred to derisively as the 'butter pat' map, is opp. p. 1 of the Voyages. Manby, who did not go on board the Columbia, gives an interesting comment: 'The return of our Officer [Puget] made known the whole to be an egregious falsehood, as Mr. Grey had never penetrated ten leagues up the strait, this Gentleman related many other absurdities practiced by Mr Meares, and candidly made known what most likely produced, this imprudent humbug. These two Navigators [Meares and Gray] both engaged in the same pursuit, met by accident in Nootka Sound, the Jealousies of trade, taught them to play off their artful deceptions, and as Quissing was the order of the Day, Captain Meares boasted of ideal successes in having procured many Hundred Sea Otter Skins. The cunning Yanky in retaliation knowing the North West passage, to be the Hobby horse of his opponent in Commerce, reports his discovery of it – which is believed with greedy avidity, and given to the deluded public factum factorum, dressed up in language with a Chart annexed to it, of this imaginary Ocean, that points out the track of the Vessell with fanciful precision.' – Manby, letters, 29 April.

inaccessible, not from the current, but from the breakers that extended across it.[1] He had also entered another inlet to the northward, in latitude $54\frac{1}{2}°$; in which he had sailed to the latitude of 56°, without discovering its termination.[2] The south point of entrance into De Fuca's straits he stated to be in 48° 24',[3] and conceived our distance from it to be about eight leagues. The last winter he had spent in port Cox, or, as the natives call it, Clayoquot,[4] from whence he had sailed but a few days. During the winter he had built a small vessel,[5] in which he had dispatched a mate and ten men to barter for furs on Queen Charlotte's islands, and was himself now commencing his summer's trade along the coast to the southward. Whilst he remained at Clayoquot, *Wicananish*, the chief of that district, had concerted a plan to capture his ship, by bribing a native of Owhyhee, whom Mr. Gray had with him, to wet the priming of all the fire-arms on board, which were constantly kept loaded; upon which the chief would easily have overpowered the ship's crew, by a number of daring Indians who were assembled for that purpose. This project was happily discovered, and the Americans being on their guard the fatal effects of the enterprize were prevented.[6]

Having obtained this information, our course was again directed along the coast to the northward. It continued to increase in height as we advanced, with numberless detached rocky islets, amongst which were many sunken rocks, extending in some places a league from the shore. As we passed the outermost of these rocks at the distance of a mile, we plainly distinguished the south point of entrance into De Fuca's straits, bearing by compass N. 8 W.: the opposite side of the straits, though indistinctly seen in consequence of the haze, plainly indicated an opening of considerable extent. The thick rainy weather permitted us to see little of the country, yet we were enabled to ascertain that this coast, like that which we had hitherto explored from cape Mendocino, was firm and compact, without any opening into the mediterranean sea, as stated in latitude 47° 45'; or the least appearance of a safe or secure harbour, either in that latitude, or, from it southward to cape Mendocino; notwithstanding that, in that space, geographers have thought it

[1] The mouth of the Columbia River, which Gray was to enter on 12 May and name after his ship on the 18th.

[2] Clarence Strait, between Prince of Wales Island and the mainland of Alaska, which the *Columbia* had visited in August 1791.

[3] This is within a minute of the correct lat. of Cape Flattery. In spite of the account given by Gray, Hewett contends that Vancouver was still sceptical that the strait existed: 'At this time Captn. Vancouver continued to laugh at a Opening having been discovered by a Merchant Vessel which he said Captn. Cook could not have missed had such a one existed.'

[4] Clayoquot Sound, on the W coast of Vancouver Island, S of Nootka.

[5] The *Adventure*, a sloop of about 45 tons, built to act as a tender to the *Columbia*.

[6] See John Boit's log, in F. W. Howay (ed.), *Voyages of the 'Columbia' to the Northwest Coast* (*Collections*, Massachusetts Historical Society, 79, Boston, 1941), pp. 387–91. On Gray's orders Boit burned the Indians' village – 'a Command I was in no ways tenacious off'. 'This fine Village, the Work of Ages, was in a short time totally destroy'd.'

expedient to furnish many. Those, however, who from such ideal reports may be induced to navigate, in the confidence of meeting such resorts for shelter or refreshment, will, it is greatly to be apprehended, be led into considerable error, and experience like myself no small degree of mortification.

We now saw several villages scattered along the shore, whose inhabitants came off for the purpose, as we supposed, of trading; as the Columbia brought to for a short time, and again made all the sail she could after us; which led us to conjecture, that Mr. Gray had not been perfectly satisfied with the account given by our officers, and suspected that our object was of a commercial nature like his own, as he had informed our gentlemen that he was immediately going a considerable way to the southward. [1] We were, at this time, within two or three miles of the shore; the wind blew a fresh gale, attended with thick rainy weather from the E.S.E. But as it was favourable for entering this inlet, we were eager to embrace the opportunity it afforded, and shortened sail that the Chatham might take the lead. About noon, we reached its south entrance, which I understand the natives distinguish by the name of Classet[*]; it is a projecting and conspicuous promontory; and bore, by compass, from N. 56 E. to N. 39 E. distant from its nearest part about two miles. Tatooche's island, [2] united to the promontory by a ledge of rocks over which the sea violently breaks, bore from N. 17 E. to N. 30 E.; and the rock lying off the island, as described by Mr. Duncan in his excellent sketch of the entrance into this inlet, N. 14 E. [3] In the latitude, however, there appears to be an error of ten miles; which, from Mr. Duncan's accuracy in other respects, I was induced to attribute to the press. The south entrance is by him stated to be in 48° 37′; whereas, by our run, and making every allowance, we could not place it so far north as Mr. Gray. No great violence of tide was experienced; nor did we observe the Pinnacle rock, as represented by Mr. Meares and Mr. Dalrymple, in order to identify these as De Fuca's straits, [4]

[1] Menzies also thought that Gray 'had probably taken us for rivals in trade & followd us into the Streights to have his share in the gleanings of those Villages at the entrance.' – 30 April.

[*] Cape Flattery.

[2] Now spelled Tatoosh Island. Duncan had named it Green Island in 1788.

[3] Charles Duncan, in command of the *Princess Royal*, prepared a 'Sketch of the Entrance of the Strait of Juan de Fuca' at the time of his visit, in August 1788; it was published by Dalrymple in 1790. It is supplemented by a drawing of the entrance showing Cape Claaset (Cape Flattery), Pinnacle Rock (Fuca Pillar) and Green Island (Tatoosh Island).

[4] Pinnacle Rock, now Fuca Pillar, is S of the W point of Cape Flattery and is seen more clearly from the N than from the S, as Vancouver first saw it. It is of interest because its existence has been regarded by many as tangible evidence that there was some truth in Juan de Fuca's story, which reads in part: 'at the entrance of this said Strait, there is on the North-west coast thereof, a great Hedland or Island, with an exceeding high Pinnacle, or spired Rocke, like a pillar thereupon.' The rock was seen from the N from the *Chatham*: 'What we took for pinnacle rock...we saw after we got within the Island – and instead of lying in the entrance of the straits [as suggested by Duncan's drawing] it is close on the shore of Classat [Cape Flattery], by no means answering the idea which I had been led to form of its situation...' – Johnstone, 30 April. 'At One O'Clock we hauld round Green

or any other rock more conspicuous than thousands along the coast, varying in form and size; some conical, others with flat sides, flat tops, and almost every other shape that can be figured by the imagination.

We followed the Chatham between Tatooche's island and the rock, hauling to the eastward along the southern shore of the supposed straits of De Fuca. This rock, which rises just above the surface of the water, and over which the surf breaks with great violence, I called ROCK DUNCAN,[1] in commemoration of that gentleman's discovery. It is situated, as he represents, about N. 20 E. nearly half a league from Tatooche's island; forming a passage, to all appearance, perfectly clear. The island of Tatooche is of an oblong shape, lying nearly in a N.W. and S.E. direction, about half a league in circuit, bearing a verdant and fertile appearance, without any trees. On the east side is a cove which nearly divides the island into two parts; the upper part of the cliff in the centre of the cove, had the appearance of having been separated by art for the protection or conveniency of the village there situated; and has a communication from cliff to cliff above the houses of the village by a bridge or causeway, over which the inhabitants were seen passing and repassing. On the beach were seen several canoes, and some of them would most probably have visited us, had we thought proper to shorten sail. This promontory, though not greatly elevated, rises very abruptly from the sea in steep barren cliffs; above these it seems well wooded; but the badness of the weather that obscured the adjacent country, prevented also our ascertaining its situation. From the north-west part of Tatooche's island, which bears from the north point of the promontory of Classet N. 79 W. distant about two miles, the exterior coast takes a direction nearly south about ten leagues; where, as we passed, I anxiously looked out for the point which Captain Cook had distinguished by the name of Cape Flattery, of which I could not be completely satisfied, on account of the difference in latitude. A shallow bay, however, does extend about three leagues to the southward of Classet, which falls some distance back from the general line of the coast;[2] and the base of the inland mountains which project there, and form deep ravines, present at a distance the appearance of a safe and secure port; but, on a nearer approach, the whole was found firmly connected by a sandy beach. This, most probably, is the bay which the Resolution and Discovery stood into; and Classet is the point, with an island lying off it, which Captain Cook called cape Flattery. The difference in latitude, (if Mr. Gray is correct, who has passed it several times,

[Tatoosh] Island, and as we pass'd had a view of the Spiral Rock which is remarkable.' – Bell, 30 April. It was also sighted from the *Discovery*: 'no distinguishable Spiral Rock or Pillar made its appearance to my knowledge, however Mr. Baker & Menzies say, that after rounding Green Island a Rock of that Description came in Sight for a Minute or two.' – Puget, remarks. In *Flood Tide of Empire* (New Haven, 1973) Warren Cook reproduced Duncan's drawing alongside photographs taken from the N and S which show that the rock stands out almost as prominently as the drawing suggests. Its height is 157 feet and diameter 60 feet.

[1] Now Duncan Rock.   [2] Mukkaw Bay.

and always made it nearly the same,) may have been occasioned by a current similar to that which we had lately experienced along the coast; affecting the Resolution in the same manner, between noon, when their latitude was observed, and late in the evening, when Captain Cook hauled off the coast.[1]

As we proceeded along the shore, we passed the village of Classet, which is situated about two miles within the Cape, and has the appearance of being extensive and populous. As the fresh southwardly wind became much moderated by the intervention of the high land we were now under, some of the inhabitants found no difficulty in visiting us; this they did in a very civil, orderly, and friendly manner, requesting permission before they attempted to enter the ship; and on receiving some presents, with assurances of our friendship, they very politely and earnestly solicited us to stop at their village.[2] The situation of the anchorage however being much exposed, and wishing for some snug port where, with ease and convenience, the various necessary services we now required might be performed, I declined their very cordial invitation, and directed our course up the inlet, entertaining no doubt that we should soon be enabled to accommodate ourselves with a more advantageous station.

The few natives who came off resembled, in most respect, the people of Nootka. Their persons, garments, and behaviour, are very similar; some difference was observed in their ornaments, particularly in those worn at the nose; for instead of the crescent, generally adopted by the inhabitants of Nootka, these wore straight pieces of bone. Their canoes, arms, and implements, were exactly the same. They spoke the same language, but did not approach us with the formality observed by those people on visiting the Resolution and Discovery; which may probably be owing to their having become more familiar with strangers. The wind veering to the S.E. obliged us to turn up along shore on the southern side of the straits, which, from cape Classet, takes a direction S. 70 E. About two miles within the village we passed a small open bay, with a little island lying off its eastern side,[3] apparently too insignificant to answer our purpose of refitting. The weather becoming more unpleasant as the day advanced, at seven in the evening we came to anchor in 23 fathoms water, on a bottom of black sand and mud, about a mile from the shore.

I now became acquainted that after we had passed within Tatooche's island

---

[1] The promontory was, of course, Cook's Cape Flattery, which he had placed in lat. 48° 15′ N; its true position is 48° 23′ N. Once again Vancouver's reluctance to criticize Cook is evident. Recording the discovery of the cape in his journal, Cook added: 'It is in the very latitude we were now in where geographers have placed the pretended *Strait of Juan de Fuca*, but we saw nothing like it, nor is there the least probability that iver such thing exhisted.' – 22 March 1778. *Journals*, III, 293.

[2] These were Makah Indians, who claimed the coast for some distance S of Cape Flattery, and the S. coast of the Strait of Juan de Fuca eastward as far as the Hoko River. They were affiliated with the Nootka and closely resembled them, as Vancouver notes in the next paragraph.

[3] Neah Bay. The island was Waadah Island.

a rock was noticed, and supposed to be that represented as De Fuca's pinnacle rock; this however was visible only for a few minutes, from its being close to the shore of the main land, instead of lying in the entrance of the straits; nor did it correspond with that which has been so described.

It was somewhat remarkable, that although we rode all night by the wind, the Chatham, though anchored not a quarter of a mile in shore of us, rode to a regular six hours tide, running near half a league per hour; and, by the appearance of the shores, the ebb and flow seemed to have been very considerable.

CHAPTER IV.

Proceed up the Straits—Anchor under New Dungeness—Remarks on the Coast of New Albion—Arrive in Port Discovery—Transactions there—Boat excursion—Quit Port Discovery—Astronomical and nautical Observations.

THE evening of the 29th brought us to an anchor in very thick rainy weather, about eight miles within the entrance on the southern shore of the supposed straits of De Fuca. The following morning, Monday the 30th, a gentle breeze sprang up from the N.W. attended with clear and pleasant weather, which presented to our view this renowned inlet. Its southern shores were seen to extend, by compass, from N. 83 W. to E.; the former being the small island we had passed the preceding afternoon, which, lying about half a mile from the main land, was about four miles distant from us:[1] its northern shore extends from N. 68 W. to N. 73 E.; the nearest point of it,[2] distant about three leagues, bore N. 15 W. We weighed anchor with a favorable wind, and steered to the east along the southern shore, at the distance of about two miles, having an uninterrupted horizon between east and N. 73 E. The shores on each side the straits are of a moderate height; and the delightful serenity of the weather permitted our seeing this inlet to great advantage.[3] The shores on the south side are composed of low sandy cliffs, falling perpendicularly on beaches of sand or stones. From the top of these eminences, the land appeared to take a further gentle moderate ascent, and was intirely covered with trees chiefly of the pine tribe, until the forest reached a range of high craggy mountains, which seemed to rise from the wood-land country in a very abrupt manner, with a few scattered trees on their steril sides, and their summits covered with

[1] Many of Vancouver's anchorages are marked on his charts, but the positions indicated are only approximate. In a study entitled 'Vancouver's Anchorages in Puget Sound' (*Pacific Northwest Quarterly*, XLIV (1953), 115–128) Robert B. Whitebrook has endeavoured to pinpoint them precisely. His findings would place this first anchorage about 3 miles W of Waadah Island rather than the 4 miles Vancouver suggests.

[2] San Juan Point, on Vancouver Island.

[3] Manby was moved to eloquence: 'Never was contrast greater, in this days sailing than with that we had long been accustomed too. It had more the aspect of enchantment than reality, with silent admiration each discerned the beauties of Nature, and nought was heard on board but expressions of delight murmured from every tongue. Imperceptibly our Bark skimmed over the glassy surface of the deep, about three Miles an hour, a gentle Breeze swelled the lofty Canvass whilst all was calm below.' – Manby, letters, 30 April.

snow. The northern shore did not appear quite so high: it rose more gradually from the sea-side to the tops of the mountains, which had the appearance of a compact range, infinitely more uniform, and much less covered with snow than those on the southern side.

Our latitude at noon was 48° 19′; longitude 236° 19′; and the variation of the compass 18° eastwardly. In this situation, the northern shore extended by compass from N. 82 W. to N. 51 E.; between the latter, and the eastern extremity of the southern shore, bearing N. 88 E., we had still an unbounded horizon; whilst the island before mentioned, continuing to form the west extremity of the southern shore, bore S. 84 W. By these observations, which I have great reason to believe were correctly taken, the north promontory of Classet is situated in latitude 48° 23½′; longitude 235° 38′.[1] The smoothness of the sea, and clearness of the sky, enabled us to take several sets of lunar distances, which gave the longitude to the eastward of the chronometer, and served to confirm our former observations, that it was gaining very materially on the rate as settled at Otaheite. As the day advanced, the wind, which as well as the weather was delightfully pleasant, accelerated our progress along the shore. This seemed to indicate a speedy termination to the inlet; as high land now began to appear just rising from that horizon, which, a few hours before, we had considered to be unlimited. Every new appearance, as we proceeded, furnished new conjectures; the whole was not visibly connected; it might form a cluster of islands separated by large arms of the sea, or be united by land not sufficiently high to be yet discernible. About five in the afternoon, a long, low, sandy point of land was observed projecting from the craggy shores into the sea, behind which was seen the appearance of a well-sheltered bay,[2] and, a little to the S.E. of it, an opening in the land, promising a safe and extensive port. About this time a very high conspicuous craggy mountain, bearing by compass N. 50 E. presented itself, towering above the clouds: as low down as they allowed it to be visible, it was covered with snow; and south of it, was a long ridge of very rugged snowy mountains, much less elevated, which seemed to stretch to a considerable distance.

As my intention was to anchor for the night under the low point, the necessary signals were made to the Chatham; and at seven we hauled round it, at the distance of about a mile. This was, however, too near, as we soon found ourselves in three fathoms water; but, on steering about half a mile to the north, the depth increased to ten fathoms, and we rounded the shallow spit, which, though not very conspicuous, is shewn by the tide causing a considerable rippling over it. Having turned up a little way into the bay, we anchored on a bottom of soft sand and mud in 14 fathoms water. The low

---

[1] A very accurate latitude observation: the position of Cape Flattery is lat. 48° 23′ N, long. 124° 44′ W (235° 16′ E). The 'north promontory' would be a fraction of a minute N of this.

[2] Dungeness Spit (considerably shorter in 1792 than at present) and Dungeness Bay.

sandy point of land, which from its great resemblance to Dungeness in the British channel, I called NEW DUNGENESS, [1] bore by compass N. 41 W. about three miles distant, from whence the low projecting land extends until it reaches a bluff cliff of a moderate height, bearing from us S. 60 W. about a league distant. From this station the shores bore the same appearance as those we had passed in the morning, composing one intire forest. The snowy mountains of the inland country were, however, neither so high nor so rugged, and were further removed from the sea shore. The nearest parts bore by compass from us, south about half a league off; the apparent port S. 50 E. about two leagues; and the south point of an inlet, seemingly very capacious, S. 85 E.; with land appearing like an island, moderately elevated, lying before its entrance, from S. 85 E. to N. 87 E.; and the S.E. extremity of that which now appeared to be the southern shore, N. 71 E. From this direction round by the N. and N.W. the high distant land formed, as already observed, like detached islands, amongst which the lofty mountain, discovered in the afternoon by the third lieutenant, and in compliment to him called by me MOUNT BAKER, [2] rose a very conspicuous object, bearing by compass N. 43 E. apparently at a very remote distance. A small Indian village was near us on the south side of the bay, but we had not yet been visited by any of the inhabitants. We had now advanced further up this inlet than Mr. Gray, or (to our knowledge) any other person from the civilized world; [3] although it should hereafter be proved to be the same which is said to have been entered by De Fuca, in support of which oral testimony is the only authority produced; a tradition rendered still more doubtful by its entrance differing at least 40′ in latitude.

Considering ourselves now on the point of commencing an examination of an entirely new region, I cannot take leave of the coast already known, without obtruding a short remark on that part of the continent, comprehending a space of nearly 215 leagues, on which our inquiries had been lately employed under the most fortunate and favorable circumstances of wind and weather. So minutely had this extensive coast been inspected, that the surf had been constantly seen to break on its shores from the mast-head; and it was but in a few small intervals only, where our distance precluded its being visibile from the deck. Whenever the weather prevented our making free with the shore, or on our hauling off for the night, the return of fine weather and of day-light

[1] Dungeness is the most southerly point in Kent. This was one of the points at which Manuel Quimper had taken formal possession for Spain in 1790 and had named the bay Puerto y Bahia de Quimper, after himself.

[2] Mount Baker (10,750 ft.) is about 90 miles NE of Dungeness Bay. Quimper does not mention it in his journal, but it is named Gran Montaña del Carmelo on the map of his discoveries made by López de Haro.

[3] Gray evidently confined the information he gave to Puget and Menzies to some details of his own movements. He must have been aware that Quimper had explored the strait in 1790 and that Francisco de Eliza had extended the survey in 1791. Vancouver had no inkling of this until he met Spanish vessels near Point Grey in June.

uniformly brought us, if not to the identical spot we had departed from, at least within a few miles of it, and never beyond the northern limits of the coast which we had previously seen. An examination so directed, and circumstances happily concurring to permit its being so executed, afforded the most complete opportunity of determining its various turnings and windings; as also the position of all its conspicuous points, ascertained by meridional altitudes for the latitude, and observations for the chronometer, which we had the good fortune to make constantly once, and in general twice every day, the preceding one only excepted.

It must be considered as a very singular circumstance that, in so great an extent of sea-coast, we should not until now have seen the appearance of any opening in its shores, which presented any certain prospect of affording shelter; the whole coast forming one compact, solid, and nearly straight barrier against the sea.

The river Mr. Gray mentioned should, from the latitude he assigned to it, have existence in the bay, south of cape Disappointment.[1] This we passed on the forenoon of the 27th; and, as I then observed, if any inlet or river should be found, it must be a very intricate one, and inaccessible to vessels of our burthen, owing to the reefs and broken water which then appeared in its neighbourhood. Mr. Gray stated that he had been several days attempting to enter it, which at length he was unable to effect, in consequence of a very strong outset. This is a phenomenon difficult to account for, as, in most cases where there are outsets of such strength on a sea coast, there are corresponding tides setting in.[2] Be that however as it may, I was thoroughly convinced, as were also most persons of observation on board, that we could not possibly have passed any safe navigable opening, harbour, or place of security for shipping on this coast, from cape Mendocino to the promontory of Classet;[3] nor had we any reason to alter our opinions, notwithstanding that theoretical geographers have thought proper to assert, in that space, the existence of arms of the ocean, communicating with a mediterranean sea, and extensive rivers, with safe and convenient ports. These ideas, not derived from any source of substantial information, have, it is much to be feared, been adopted for the sole purpose of giving unlimited credit to the traditionary exploits of ancient foreigners, and to undervalue the laborious and enterprizing exertions of our own countrymen, in the noble science of discovery.

Since the vision of the southern continent, (from which the Incas of Peru are said to have originated,) has vanished; the pretended discoveries of De Fuca and De Fonte have been revived, in order to prove the existence of a north-west

[1] The Columbia River.
[2] This would be true of an inlet, as Vancouver was to find later on many occasions, but it is less true of the mouth of a large river, where the incoming tide will be opposed by the river's current.
[3] Given the then state of bars and breakers at the various openings along the coast, and the fact that all ships of the time were propelled by sails, this was a reasonable opinion.

passage. These have been supported by the recent concurring opinions of modern traders, one of whom is said to conceive, that an opening still further to the north is that which De Fuca entered. Under this assertion, should any opening further to the northward be discovered leading to a N.W. passage, the merit of such discovery will necessarily be ascribed to De Fuca, De Fonte, or some other favorite voyager of these closet philosophers.

The preceding evening brought us to an anchor under New Dungeness. Our May-day, Tuesday, was ushered in by a morning of the most delightfully pleasant weather, affording us, from the broken appearance of the coast before us, the prospect of soon reaching a safe and commodious harbour. Indeed, our present situation was far from ineligible, as it promised to admit us as near the shore as we might think proper to take our station. Mr. Whidbey was therefore dispatched in the cutter, to sound, and search for fresh water.

The appearance of the huts we now saw, indicated the residence of the natives in them to be of a temporary nature only; as we could perceive with our glasses, that they differed very materially from the habitations of any of the American Indians we had before seen, being composed of nothing more than a few mats thrown over cross sticks; whereas those we had passed the preceding day, in two or three small villages to the eastward of Classet, were built exactly after the fashion of the houses erected at Nootka.* The inhabitants[1] seemed to view us with the utmost indifference and unconcern; they continued to fish before their huts as regardless of our being present, as if such vessels had been familiar to them, and unworthy of their attention.[2] On the low land of New Dungeness were erected perpendicularly, and seemingly with much regularity, a number of very tall straight poles, like flag-staves or beacons, supported from the ground by spurs. Their first

---

* Vide Cook's last Voyage. [The reference would be to Cook's *Voyages*, II, 288–312 and/or 313–24. For the account in Cook's own words see *Journals*, III, 317–18; additional details are given by Clerke, 1327–8, and King, 1408–9.]

[1] These were Clallam Indians, who lived along the S shore of the Strait of Juan de Fuca from the Hoko River (the E boundary of Makah territory) to Discovery Bay (named Port Discovery by Vancouver and known by that name until recently). This was the expedition's first contact with the Coast Salish, whose tribes occupied much of the area Vancouver would be exploring in the next two months. They were linked by language affinity, and comprised the Salishan linguistic group, which was divided into a coastal division and the Nisqually dialectic division. The former included the Clallam, the Twana Indians in Hood Canal, and the tribes inhabiting the SE coast of Vancouver Island and both sides of the Strait of Georgia. Almost all the Puget Sound Indians belonged to the Nisqually group.

[2] Menzies soon suspected that other ships had visited the strait. When natives visited the ships he noted that they had 'seemingly little curiosity to gratify, our appearance affording them no degree of novelty [which] lead us to suppose that ours was not the first European Vessel with which they had had intercourse...' And he soon found evidence to confirm his supposition: 'we saw several stumps of small trees as if they had been cut down with an Axe not many months ago, from this it was thought probable that some other Vessel might have been here before us, as I never observd the Natives on any part of this Coast make use of an Axe in felling of Timber...' – 5 May.

appearance induced an opinion of their being intended as the uprights for stages on which they might dry their fish; but this, on a nearer view seemed improbable, as their height and distance from each other would have required spars of a greater size to reach from one to the other, than the substance of the poles was capable of sustaining. They were, undoubtedly, intended to answer some particular purpose; but whether of a religious, civil, or military nature, must be left to some future investigation.[1]

Mr. Whidbey found from ten to three fathoms water close to the shore. He landed at the upper part of the bay, but could not find any water; nor did he see the appearance of any along the shore near the habitations of the Indians, who remained as before described, or fishing on the water, without paying any more attention to the cutter, than if she had been one of their own canoes.

On receiving this report, the Chatham's cutter, with the Discovery's yawl and cutter, were ordered to be armed and supplied with a day's provision; with which we set off to examine the two apparent openings nearest to us. We found the surface of the sea almost covered with aquatic birds of various kinds, but all so extremely shy that our sportsmen were unable to reach them with their guns, although they made many attempts. The first opening to the S.E. appeared to be formed by two high bluffs; the elevated land within them seemingly at a considerable distance. It proved, however, to be a close and compact shore, the apparent vacant space being occupied by a very low sandy beach, off which extended a flat of very shallow soundings.[2] From hence we made the best of our way for land, appearing like an island, off the other supposed opening;[3] from whose summit, which seemed easy of access, there was little doubt of our ascertaining whether the coast afforded any port within reach of the day's excursion. On landing on the west end of the supposed island, and ascending its eminence which was nearly a perpendicular cliff, our attention was immediately called to a landscape, almost as enchantingly beautiful as the most elegantly finished pleasure grounds in Europe. From the height we were now upon, our conjectures of this land being an island situated before the entrance of an opening in the main land were confirmed. The summit of this island presented nearly a horizontal surface, interspersed with some inequalities of ground, which produced a beautiful variety on an

---

[1] More poles of the kind were seen elsewhwere, notably in Port Townsend. Their purpose remained a mystery; actually they were for catching birds; Indians at Discovery Bay so informed Dr. John Scouler in 1825. E. S. Meany was given a detailed explanation in 1905: Between the poles the Indians 'stretched nets woven of willow twigs. At night or in hazy weather the ducks would strike these nets when the watchers would pull a rope of twisted roots or twigs fastened to a loop of the net and down would come a flap, holding in the strong meshes of willow the entire flock of birds. It was practically a fish net made to work on land.' – Meany, *Vancouver's Discovery of Puget Sound* (New York, 1907), p. 85n.

[2] Sequim Bay, which is almost landlocked, and the sandspit across its N End.

[3] Protection Island.

extensive lawn covered with luxuriant grass, and diversified with an abundance of flowers. To the northwestward was a coppice of pine trees and shrubs of various sorts, that seemed as if it had been planted for the sole purpose of protecting from the N.W. winds this delightful meadow, over which were promiscuously scattered a few clumps of trees, that would have puzzled the most ingenious designer of pleasure grounds to have arranged more agreeably. Whilst we stopped to contemplate these several beauties of nature, in a prospect no less pleasing than unexpected, we gathered some gooseberries and roses in a state of considerable forwardness. Casting our eyes along the shore, we had the satisfaction of seeing it much broken, and forming to all appearance many navigable inlets. The inlet now before us[1] did not seem so extensive as we had reason to believe it to be from the ships; yet there was little doubt of its proving sufficiently secure and convenient for all our purposes. We therefore proceeded to its examination, and found its entrance to be about a league wide, having regular good soundings from 10 fathoms close to the shores, to 30, 35, and 38 fathoms in the middle, without any apparent danger from rocks or shoals. Fresh water, however, seemed hitherto a scarce commodity, and yet, from the general face of the country, a deficiency in this respect was not to be apprehended. The shores of the harbour were of a moderate height; its western side, bounded at no very great distance by a ridge of high craggy mountains covered with snow, were, as I conceived, connected with the mountain we took for mount Olympus. In quest of the only great object necessary for constituting this one of the finest harbours in the world, we prosecuted our researches; until almost despairing of success, I suddenly fell in with an excellent stream of very fine water. The design of our excursion was thus happily accomplished; and, after taking some little refreshment, we returned towards the ships, and arrived on board about midnight, perfectly satisfied with the success of our expedition, and amply rewarded for our labour.[2]

During my absence, some of the natives had been trading with the vessels in a very civil and friendly manner. They did not appear to understand the Nootka language; as those of our people who had some knowledge of it were by no means able to make themselves understood.

A light pleasant breeze springing up, we weighed on Wednesday morning the 2d, and steered for the port we had discovered the preceding day, whose entrance about four leagues distant bore S.E. by E. The delightful serenity of the weather greatly aided the beautiful scenery that was now presented;

---

[1] Discovery Bay.

[2] This day some of the party had their first encounter with a skunk, shot by Manby: 'After firing I approached him with all speed, and was saluted by a discharge from him the most nauseous and fetid, my sense of smelling ever experienced; My Gun and Cloathes were so impregnated with the stench, that tho boiled in many waters the cursed effluvia could never be eradicated.' – letters, 1 May. Menzies 'was anxious to take it on board for examination & made it fast to the bow of the Cutter, but the stink it emitted was so intolerable that I was obliged to relinquish my prize. I took it to be the Skunk or Polecat.' – 1 May.

the surface of the sea was perfectly smooth, and the country before us exhibited every thing that bounteous nature could be expected to draw into one point of view. As we had no reason to imagine that this country had ever been indebted for any of its decorations to the hand of man, I could not possibly believe that any uncultivated country had ever been discovered exhibiting so rich a picture. The land which interrupted the horizon between the N.W. and the northern quarters, seemed, as already mentioned, to be much broken; from whence its eastern extent round to the S.E. was bounded by a ridge of snowy mountains, appearing to lie nearly in a north and south direction, on which mount Baker rose conspicuously; remarkable for its height, and the snowy mountains that stretch from its base to the north and south. Between us and this snowy range, the land, which on the sea shore terminated like that we had lately passed, in low perpendicular cliffs, or on beaches of sand or stone, rose here in a very gentle ascent, and was well covered with a variety of stately forest trees. These, however, did not conceal the whole face of the country in one uninterrupted wilderness, but pleasingly clothed its eminences, and chequered the vallies; presenting, in many directions, extensive spaces that wore the appearance of having been cleared by art, like the beautiful island we had visited the day before. As we passed along the shore near one of these charming spots, the tracks of deer, or of some such animal, were very numerous, and flattered us with the hope of not wanting refreshments of that nature, whilst we remained in this quarter.

A picture so pleasing could not fail to call to our remembrance certain delightful and beloved situations in Old England. Thus we proceeded without meeting any obstruction to our progress; which, though not rapid, brought us before noon abreast of the stream that discharges its water from the western shore near five miles within the entrance of the harbour; which I distinguished by the name of PORT DISCOVERY, after the ship.[1] There we moored, in 34 fathoms, muddy bottom, about a quarter of a mile from the shore.[2]

The entrance of this harbour is formed by low projecting points, extending, on each side, from the high woodland cliffs which in general bound the coast; bearing by compass from N. 18 W. to N. 54 W. in a line with two corresponding points from the island already described, lying off this harbour. Had this insular production of nature been designed by the most able engineer, it could not have been placed more happily for the protection of the port, not only from the N.W. winds to the violence of which it would otherwise be greatly exposed, but against all attempts of an enemy, when properly fortified; and hence I called it PROTECTION ISLAND.[3]

[1] Now Discovery Bay. Quimper had named it Puerto de la Bodega y Quadra (shortened on some maps to Puerta de Quadra). When this became known, Menzies felt that the Spanish name should have been retained: 'having then anchored in it, surely gives their name a prior right of continuing, to prevent that confusion of names which are but too common in new discovered countries.' – 16 May. The inlet is named Port Quadra on Baker's MS map, but Port Discovery on the engraved chart.

[2] The anchorage was off what is now Carr Point, half way down the inlet.

[3] Quimper had named it Isla de Carrasco after Juan Carrasco, his second pilot.

The stream of water, near which we had taken a very convenient station, appeared to have its source at some distance from its outfal, through one of those low spits of sand already mentioned, which constitute most of the projecting points we had seen ever since our having entered this inlet. These usually acquire a form somewhat circular, though irregular; and, in general, are nearly steep to, extending from the cliffy woodland country, from one to six hundred yards towards the water's edge, and are composed of a loose sandy soil. The surface of some was almost intirely occupied by a lagoon of salt water, or brackish swamp; others were perfectly dry; no one of them produced any trees; but were mostly covered with a coarse spiry grass, interspersed with strawberries, two or three species of clover, samphire, and a great variety of other small plants; some of which bore very beautiful flowers. On a few of the points were some shrubs that seemed to thrive excessively; such as roses, a species of sweet briar, gooseberries, raspberries, currants, and several other smaller bushes, which, in their respective seasons, produce most probably the several fruits common to this and the opposite side of America. These all appeared to grow very luxuriantly; and, from the quantity of blossoms with which they were loaded, there was great reason to believe them very productive.

We had little trouble in clearing a sufficient space for our encampment, which was very commodiously situated close to the north side of the stream or brook. The tents, observatory, chronometers and instruments, guarded by a party of marines, were sent on shore after dinner; and, whilst they were properly arranging, I made a short excursion up the harbour.[1] It extended nearly in a south direction, about four miles from the ship, and then terminated in a muddy flat across its head, about a quarter of a mile from the shore. The water, which was seven fathoms deep close to the flat, gradually deepened to 10, 20, and 30 fathoms, good holding ground. On this bank were found some small indifferent oysters. The shores beyond it are low and thickly wooded, and through them there appeared to run a very considerable stream of water, with several smaller ones, emptying themselves into the harbour. The back country had the appearance of a swampy fen for a considerable distance. We landed not far from the largest rivulet, where we found a deserted village capable of containing an hundred inhabitants. The houses were built after the Nootka fashion, but did not seem to have been lately the residence of the Indians.

The habitations had now fallen into decay; their inside, as well as a small surrounding space that appeared to have been formerly occupied, were over-run

[1] Menzies accompanied Vancouver, and it was in the course of this excursion that he first saw small specimens of the beautiful arbutus tree – *Arbutus Menziesii* – the botanical discovery with which his name is still closely associated on the Northwest Coast. He called it the Oriental Strawberry Tree: 'this last grows to a small Tree & was at this time a peculiar ornament to the Forest by its large clusters of whitish flowers & ever green leaves, but its peculiar smooth bark of a reddish brown colour will at all times attract the Notice of the most superficial observer.' – 2 May.

Plate 21. 'View of a Boat Encampment, Pugets Sound.'

John Sykes

Plate 22. 'View of Observatory Point, Port Quadra [now Discovery Bay], Straits de Fuca.'

FOUR remarkable supported POLES, in PORT TOWNSEND, GULPH of GEORGIA.

Plate 23. 'Four remarkable supported Poles, in Port Townshend, Gulph of Georgia.'

MOUNT RAINIER, from the South part of ADMIRALTY INLET.

Plate 24. 'Mount Rainier, from the South part of Admiralty Inlet.'

with weeds; amongst which were found several human sculls, and other bones, promiscuously scattered about.

On Thursday morning the 3d we sat seriously to work on board, and on shore where the sail-makers were repairing and altering the sails; coopers inspecting the casks; gunners airing the powder; and parties cutting wood, brewing spruce beer, and filling water: whilst those on board were as busily employed in necessary repairs about the rigging; getting the provisions to hand; clearing the main and after holds for the reception of shingle ballast, of which we had for some time stood in much need; some of our carpenters were stopping leaks about the bows, and the rest assisted in caulking the Chatham's sides. The serenity of the climate and season was extremely favorable to the execution of their several duties, as also to our astronomical inquiries. The part of the coast that we had now reached being nearly destitute of inhabitants, few circumstances occurred to divert our attention, or interfere with the pursuits in which we were all engaged.

So little leisure or rest had been afforded in the several ports we had hitherto visited since we left the Cape of Good Hope, that it was not until this morning, Sunday the 6th, that our people could be indulged with a holiday, for the purpose of taking some recreation and exercise on shore.

A few of the natives in two or three canoes favored us with their company, and brought with them some fish and venison for sale. The latter was extremely good, and very acceptable, as we had not hitherto obtained any; though on our first arrival we had entertained hopes of procuring a supply, from the numerous tracks of deer which appeared fresh, and in all directions.[1]

These people, in their persons, canoes, arms, implements, &c. seemed to resemble chiefly the inhabitants of Nootka; though less bedaubed with paint, and less filthy in their external appearance. They wore ornaments in their ears, but none were observed in their noses; some of them understood a few words of the Nootka language; they were clothed in the skins of deer, bear, and some other animals, but principally in a woollen garment of their own manufacture, extremely well wrought. They did not appear to possess any furs. Their bows and implements they freely bartered for knives, trinkets, copper, &c;[2] and, what was very extraordinary, they offered for sale two children, each about six or seven years of age, and, being shewn some copper, were very anxious

[1] Having failed to make contact with his supply ship, the *Daedalus*, as he had expected to do, Vancouver now thought it prudent to conserve his supplies, lest she should fail him entirely, 'in which case,' Bell records, 'we should have been somewhat distress'd for Provisions, particularly Bread & Flour...The Ships Company was therefore on the 5th put to *two-thirds* allowance of *Bread only*. This on the Coast of America cou'd be no hardship, as Fish is always to be got...' – May.

[2] It was here that Menzies, Hewett and Swaine began to collect the Indian artifacts that eventually found their way to the British Museum and Cambridge University Museum. Manby also acquired many items, but the present whereabouts of his collections seems not to be known.

that the bargain should be closed. This, however, I peremptorily prohibited, expressing, as well as I was able, our great abhorrence of such traffic.[1]

As our several employments, on board and on shore, would still require some time before they could be fully completed; and as I was desirous of obtaining some further knowledge of this inlet, in order that, when the vessels should be ready, we might extend our researches without fear of interruption; I directed the Discovery's yawl and launch, with the Chatham's cutter, properly armed, and supplied with stores for five days, to be in readiness early the next morning. I committed to Mr. Broughton the charge of the ships, and to Mr. Whidbey that of the observatory and encampment, with directions to make a survey of the port, and such further necessary observations as circumstances would admit during my absence.

Mr. Menzies, with two of the young gentlemen, accompanied me in the yawl, Mr. Puget commanded the launch, and Mr. Johnstone the Chatham's cutter. With this arrangement, about five o'clock on Monday morning the 7th, we took our departure for the purpose of becoming more intimately acquainted with the region in which we had so very unexpectedly arrived.[2] The day did not promise to be very auspicious to the commencement of our examination. That uninterrupted serenity of weather that we had experienced the last seven days, seemed now to be materially changed; the wind which, in the day-time, had constantly blown from the N.W. with light southwardly airs, or calms, from sun-set until eight or ten o'clock in the forenoon, had now blown, since the preceding evening, a moderate gale from the S.E.; and, before we had proceeded a mile from the ship, brought with

[1] Unknown to Vancouver there was at this time a considerable traffic in Indian children, who were purchased by the Spaniards in the belief that they were either rescuing them from slavery or preventing them from being killed and eaten. As noted in a later comment, several of the priests were convinced that Maquinna, amongst others, made a practice of eating children. In July 1790, while Quimper was in Neah Bay, five miles E of Cape Flattery, Chief Tatooch's brother sold Quimper's first pilot 'an Indian girl of eight or nine years of age, his daughter, for a little copper and a small cutlass.' Quimper suspected that the transaction was dishonest and that the intention was that the girl should escape, but she was prevented from doing so. – H. R. Wagner's translation of Quimper's diary in his *Spanish Explorations of the Strait of Juan de Fuca* (Santa Ana, Calif., 1933), pp. 125–26. Malaspina states that when his ships left Nootka for San Blas in August 1791 they had on board 'no fewer than twenty-two children of both sexes, sold indiscriminately by Macuina [Maquinna] or lesser chieftains'; and in '1792 Eliza would report with satisfaction that during his three-year stay at Nootka no fewer than fifty-six children had been purchased there, at Clayoquot, or at Fuca.' – Warren L. Cook, *Flood Tide of Empire* (New Haven, 1973) pp. 313–14.

[2] Menzies, Puget and Johnstone all describe this expedition in considerable detail. It was to be the first of many, as Vancouver found that they were the only practicable means of surveying the continental shore in any detail. For Menzies' account of this expedition and others in which he participated in the spring and summer of 1792 see C. F. Newcombe (ed.), *Menzies' Journal...April to October 1792* (Victoria, 1923). Puget's account of this and his later explorations in the Puget Sound area were edited and published by his biographer: Bern Anderson (ed.), 'The Vancouver Expedition: Peter Puget's Journal of the Exploration of Puget Sound May 7 – June 11, 1792', *Pacific Northwest Quarterly* xxx (1939), 177–217.

it a very thick fog, through which we steered, keeping the starboard, or continental shore, on board, trusting that towards noon the fog would disperse itself and clear away.

On our arrival in port Discovery, we passed to the S.W. of Protection island; another channel, equally as safe and convenient, we now found to the S.E. of it. Having rowed against a strong tide along the shore about two or three leagues to the N.E. from the entrance of port Discovery, we rounded a low projecting point,[1] and though the fog prevented our seeing about us, yet there was no doubt of our having entered some other harbour or arm in the inlet that took a southwardly direction.[2] Here I proposed to wait until the weather should be more favorable, and in the mean time to haul the seine; which was done, along the beach to the southward, with little success.

Prosecuting our labours as fishermen along the beach, we were led near a point similar to that we had passed, and distant from it about two miles; here the fog intirely dispersing, afforded an opporunity of ascertaining its latitude to be 48° 7′ 30″, its longitude 237° 31½′.[3] A very spacious inlet now presented itself, whose N.E. point, in a line with its S.W. being the point from which we had last departed, bore by compass N. 25 W. and seemed about a league asunder:[4] mount Baker bore N. 26 E.; a steep bluff point opposite to us, appearing to form the west point of another arm of this inlet,[5] S. 87 E. about four miles distant; the nearest eastern shore S. 50 E. about two miles; and a very remarkable high round mountain, covered with snow, apparently at the southern extremity of the distant range of snowy mountains before noticed, bore S. 45 E.:[6] the shores of this inlet, like those in port Discovery, shoot out into several low, sandy, projecting points, the southernmost of which bore S. 9 E. distant about two leagues, where this branch of the inlet seemed to terminate, or take some other direction. Here we dined, and having taken the necessary angles, I directed Mr. Puget to sound the mid-channel, and Mr. Johnstone to examine the larboard or eastern shore, whilst I continued my researches on the continental shore, appointing the southernmost low point for our next rendezvous. As we advanced, the country seemed gradually to improve in beauty. The cleared spots were more numerous, and of larger extent; and the remote lofty mountains covered with snow, reflected greater

[1] Point Wilson.
[2] Admiralty Inlet.
[3] Point Hudson, 1·7 miles SSE of Point Wilson. The name is not mentioned in Vancouver's narrative but appears on his chart. Wagner suggests that it was named after Capt. Thomas Hudson, commander of the *Princess Royal*, companion ship of Colnett's *Argonaut*, and like her seized by the Spaniards at Nootka in 1789. The position of the point is lat. 48° 07′ N, long. 122° 48′ W (237° 12′ E).
[4] Partridge Point, Whidbey Island. It is 5 miles from Point Wilsoin, not 3 miles, as Vancouver estimated.
[5] Vancouver was about to explore Port Townsend, which branches off to the SW from Admiralty Inlet. He was looking across at Marrowstone Point, the W point of entrance to the southward continuation of Admiralty Inlet (which he refers to as 'another arm').
[6] Mount Rainier.

lustre on the fertile productions of the less elevated country. On arriving near our place of rendezvous, an opening was seen, which gave to the whole of the eastern shore under the examination of Mr. Johnstone, the appearance of being an island.[1] For this we steered, but found it closed by a low sandy neck of land, about two hundred yards in width, whose opposite shore was washed by an extensive salt lake, or more probably by an arm of the sea[2] stretching to the S.E. and directing its main branch towards the high round snowy mountain we had discovered at noon: but where its entrance was situated we could not determine, though conjecture led to suppose it would be found round the bluff point of land we had observed from our dinner station.[3]

In the western corner of this isthmus was situated a deserted Indian village, much in the same state of decay as that which we had examined at the head of port Discovery. No signs of any inhabitants were discernible; nor did we visit it, it being expedient we should hasten to our appointed station, as night was fast approaching, during which Mr. Johnstone did not join us; this led us to suppose he had found some entrance into the above lake or inlet that had escaped my notice; and which afterwards proved to have been the cause of his absence. Having determined the extent of this inlet, whose south extremity is situated in latitude 47° 59′, longitude 237° 31′;[4] at day-break the next morning, Tuesday the 8th, we embarked in pursuit of the entrance into the lake or inlet that we had discovered the preceding evening. About this time we heard and answered the report of a swivel gun. A very strong run of water was now observed, but being brackish, we were under the necessity of carrying our kegs near a mile into the country to replenish them, not having found any fresh water since we left the ships. Whilst we were thus engaged, Mr. Johnstone came up. He had found a narrow channel into the inlet, which had flattered him with returning by the isthmus that had opposed our progress; but to his great mortification he found it closed, and was obliged to keep rowing the greater part of the night, in order that he might join us by the same passage he had entered, which he had now just effected. Its southern entrance was found to be navigable for small boats only, from half flood to half ebb, and was dry at low water; but as its northern part formed a snug little port, and, with its tide, seemed likely to be made useful in careening; Mr. Johnstone was induced to prosecute its examination.[5] The survey of this inlet, which had occupied our time since the preceding day at noon, having been finally accomplished by the joining of the boats, it proved to be a very safe and more

[1] Indian Island.
[2] Oak Bay, which, as Vancouver surmised, is a cove on the W side of Admiralty Inlet. The isthmus between the bottom of Port Townsend and Oak Bay is now pierced by the Port Townsend Canal.
[3] Marrowstone Point.
[4] The correct position would be about lat. 48° 01′ 30″ N, long. 122° 45′ W (237° 15′ E).
[5] Johnstone had explored Kilisut Harbor, between Indian Island and Marrowstone Island, only to find it closed at the S end by a sand bank; 'as he had been so deceived in this Passage,' Puget notes, 'we called it Johnstones Decoy.' – 8 May.

capacious harbour than port Discovery; and rendered more pleasant by the high land being at a greater distance from the water-side. Its soundings also give it a further advantage, being very regular from side to side, from 10 to 20 fathoms depth of water, good holding ground: but, with respect to fresh water, so far as we could determine by our transitory visit, it was very deficient, as has been already observed. To this port I gave the name of PORT TOWNSHEND, in honor of the noble Marquis of that name.[1]

Mr. Johnstone, who had a much better opportunity than I had of seeing the above lake or inlet, represented it as appearing very extensive and divided into two or three branches; but he had not been able to determine its communication either with the ocean or the main inlet, although he had great reason to believe it did communicate by the way of the bluff point already mentioned; which about noon was confirmed. In our way thither, we found on one of the low points projecting from the eastern shore, two upright poles set in the ground, about fifteen feet high, and rudely carved. On the top of each was stuck a human head, recently placed there. The hair and flesh were nearly perfect; and the heads appeared to carry the evidence of fury or revenge, as, in driving the stakes through the throat to the cranium, the sagittal, with part of the scalp, was borne on their points some inches above the rest of the skull. Between the stakes a fire had been made, and near it some calcined bones were observed, but none of these appearances enabled us to satisfy ourselves, concerning the manner in which the bodies had been disposed of.

The situation of this point is a little to the southward of the narrow passage Mr. Johnstone had gone through; the north extremity of which is formed by a very long sandy spit, where seventeen of the long supported poles were seen[2] like those before described on New Dungeness. These poles had frequently presented themselves, though in less numbers than on the present occasion; but though these afforded us an opportunity of examining them, they did not contribute the least instruction concerning the purpose for which they were intended. They were uniformly placed in the center of the low sandy spit, at the distance of about eighty yards from each other; and it should seem that they were required to be of certain definite heights, although not all equally high. They were, in general, about six inches in diameter at the bottom,

---

[1] Townshend was one of Wolfe's brigadiers in the Quebec campaign of 1759 and assumed command of the British forces after Wolfe's death. He succeeded his father as 4th Viscount Townshend in 1764 and was created Marquis Townshend in 1786. A kinsman, John Thomas Townshend, later Viscount Sydney, was one of the Lords of the Admiralty who signed Vancouver's instructions. Manby was a friend of the family and records the naming of the port: 'On a green fertile bank we landed to dine, where Captain Vancouver named it Port Townshend in Honor of the Marquis my sincere and long known friend.' On one of the 'prodigious Cypress trees' he carved 'Anne Marie Townshend and under it T.M. 1792 – and whoever thou art Traveller, know that she possesses every beauty as a Woman, this unequaled Cypress possesses as a Tree, without fault or blemish.' – letters, May 8. The name is now spelled Port Townsend.

[2] Johnstone gives the number of poles as seven, not seventeen, and Menzies states that there were 'nine or ten'.

and perfectly straight; and, when too short, a piece was added, which was very neatly scarfed on; the top of each terminating in two points like a crescent, or rather like the straight spreading horns of an ox. The tallest of these poles I should suppose to be about one hundred feet, the shortest not so high by ten or fifteen feet. Between several of them large holes were dug in the ground, in which were many stones that had been burnt, which gave these holes the resemblance of the cooking places in the South-Sea islands. There was, however, no appearance of any recent operations of that kind.

In most of my excursions I met with an indurated clay, much resembling fuller's earth. The high steep cliff, forming the point of land we were now upon, seemed to be principally composed of this matter; which, on a more close examination, appeared to be a rich species of the marrow stone, from whence it obtained the name of MARROW-STONE POINT.[1] East of this cliff, the shore is extended about a quarter of a mile by one of those sandy projecting points we had so frequently met with. Here we dined, and had an excellent view of this inlet, which appeared to be of no inconsiderable extent. The eastern shore stretched by compass from N. 41 W. to S. 51 E.; the south extremity of the western shore bore S. 26 E.; and, between these latter bearings, the horizon was occupied by islands, or land appearing much broken. The weather was serene and pleasant, and the country continued to exhibit, between us and the eastern snowy range, the same luxuriant appearance. At its northern extremity, mount Baker bore by compass N. 22 E.; the round snowy mountain, now forming its southern extremity, and which, after my friend Rear Admiral Rainier, I distinguished by the name of MOUNT RAINIER,[2] bore N. 42 E. Having finished all our business at this station, the boats received the same directions as before; and having appointed the western part of some land appearing like a long island, and bearing S.E. by S. four leagues distant, for our evening's rendezvous, we left Marrow-Stone point with a pleasant gale, and every prospect of accomplishing our several tasks. The favorable breeze availed us but little; for we had not advanced a league before we found the influence of so strong an ebb tide that, with all the exertions of our oars in addition to our sails, we could scarcely make any progress along the coast. Towards sun-set, both the wind and the weather materially changed; the former became light and variable, from the southern quarter, and brought with it incessant torrents of rain. We persevered, however, in our endeavours to gain our destined point, but without success, until about eleven at night; when, having collected the boats by signal, we bore up for the western, which was nearest the shore, and landed about one in the morning, completely drenched. With some difficulty we got a fire, and found a tolerable place for

[1] Now spelled Marrowstone Point. The name has been extended to Marrowstone Island, of which the point is the NE extremity.

[2] Peter Rainier. The only time his path and Vancouver's seem to have crossed was in 1790, when both served in the Channel Fleet. Rainier did not attain the rank of Rear Admiral until June 1795, three years after Vancouver named the mountain.

our tents. This, though uncomfortable, protected us in some degree from the inclemency of the weather, which detained us all the next day. On Wednesday morning the 9th, we found ourselves near the south extremity of the narrow shoal passage through which Mr. Johnstone had passed from port Townshend, in a very fine cove, affording good anchorage from 10 to 25 fathoms, excellent holding ground, and sufficiently capacious to accommodate many vessels. We traversed its northern shores, but could not find any water, except such as dripped in small quantities from the rocks. Whilst detained by this unfavorable weather, some of the young gentlemen in their excursions found several oak-trees, of which they produced specimens; but stated that they had not seen any exceeding three or four feet in circumference. In consequence of this valuable discovery, the place obtained the name of OAK COVE.[1]

The weather in some measure clearing up soon after day-break on Thursday the 10th, we again embarked, and continued on the same western or continental shore, making a very slow progress, owing to a strong ebb tide, and a fresh S.E. wind, against us.

We had not been long out of Oak Cove, when we descried some Indians paddling slowly under the lee of a rocky point, with an apparent intention of waiting our approach. In this they were soon gratified, and on our arrival, they did not seem to express the least doubt of our friendly disposition towards them. They courteously offered such things as they possessed, and cordially accepted some medals, beads, knives, and other trinkets, which I presented to them, and with which they appeared to be highly pleased.[2] We were now employed in taking such necessary angles as the weather permitted us to obtain,

---

[1] Now Oak Bay.

[2] This encounter took place in what is now Port Ludlow, which Menzies states 'was named Indian Cove'. The natives would be Chimakum Indians – the only non-Salish tribe in Puget Sound – which claimed the coast all the way from Port Townsend to Port Ludlow. They were 'constantly at war with the Clallam and other Salish tribes, and, being inferior in numbers, suffered very much at their hands.' – John R. Swanton, *The Indian Tribes of North America* (Bureau of American Ethnology, bulletin 145, Washington, 1952), p. 417. Puget described the visitors: 'The People in their Persons were Low & Ill made with broad faces & Small Eyes. Their Foreheads appear to be Deformed or out of Shape comparatively speaking with those of Europeans. The Head has something of a Conical Shape. They wear the Hair Long with Quantities of Red Ochre intermixed with whale Oil or some other Greasy Substance that has a Similar disagreeable Smell. Only One Man had a thick Beard, the others wore a Small Tuft of Hair on the Point of the Chin & on the Upper lip like Mustachios & on other parts of the Body they suffered Nature to have its Course, which were as well supplied as in the Common Run of Men except the Breast, which was all totally destitute of Hair. Square pieces of ear Shells were hung to small perforations in their Ears with small Rolls of Copper. Necklaces of the same Materials as the Latter were used as also round the Ancles & wrists. Their Garments consisted of the Skin of an Animal tied at the two Corners over one Shoulder the upper Edge coming under the Opposite Arm – by which both Hands were free. The Rest of the Body was perfectly naked. They had no other Arms but Bows and Arrows pointed with barbed Flints & long Spears in their Canoes. The last consisted only of a Log hollowed out Sharp at both End & tolerably well constructed for paddling. The Paddles were Short & pointed at the Ends.' – 10 May.

and in acquiring some further information of this inlet. It appeared to be divided into two branches; the most extensive one took its direction to the south-eastward[1] of land appearing like a long, low island; the other, apparently much less, stretched to the south-westward of the same land;[2] the shores of which terminating in a high perpendicular bluff point, was, in consequence of the change we experienced in its neighbourhood, called FOULWEATHER BLUFF.[3]

As my intentions were not to depart from the continental boundary, the western arm was the first object of our examination; and we directed our course towards a high lump of land that had the appearance of an island, entertaining little doubt of finding a way into the south eastern, or main arm, south of the supposed long low island. Off this point lie some rocks above water, with others visible only at low tide, extending at the distance of three fourths of a mile, and nearly a mile along the shore. The country thereabouts presented a very different aspect from that which we had been accustomed to see. Instead of the sandy cliffs that form the shores within the straits, these were composed of solid rocks. On them the herbage and shrubs seemed to flourish with less luxuriance, though the trees appeared to form a much greater variety. Having landed about nine o'clock to breakfast, and to take the advantage of the sun and wind to dry some of our clothes, our friends the Indians, seventeen in number, landed also from six canoes about half a mile a-head of us, and then walked towards our party, attended by a single canoe along the shore; they having hauled up all the others. They now approached us with the utmost confidence, without being armed, and behaved in the most respectful and orderly manner. On a line being drawn with a stick on the sand between the two parties, they immediately sat down, and no one attempted to pass it, without previously making signs, requesting permission for so doing.

In their persons, dress, canoes, &c. they much resembled the Indians of port Discovery; they had not the most distant knowledge of the Nootka language, and it was with some difficulty that any of their numerals were acquired. They had not any thing to dispose of excepting their bows, arrows, and some few of their woollen and skin garments; amongst the latter appeared to be the skin of a young lioness.[4] These they exchanged for trinkets, and other things

---

[1] Puget Sound. The application of this name varies and is confusing. On his chart, Vancouver applied the name Admiralty Inlet southward to the vicinity of Elliott Bay and Seattle; Puget Sound applied to the waters farther S. On modern U.S. charts Admiralty Inlet ends and Puget Sound begins in the vicinity of Foulweather bluff, but in its general description the *United States Coast Pilot* 7 lumps these and other waterways together and defines Puget Sound as 'a bay with numerous channels and branches' extending 'about 90 miles S from the Strait of Juan de Fuca to Olympia.'

[2] Hood Canal.

[3] The tip of the peninsula that separates the Hood Canal from Puget Sound.

[4] The skin of a cougar or puma, which Menzies identified correctly as *Felis concolor*. – 10 May.

of little value, and in the traffic conducted themselves in a very fair and honest manner.

After we had embarked they examined the place where we had been sitting, and then paddled towards their village, which was situated in a very pleasant cove a little to the S.W. and built with wood, after the fashion of the deserted ones we had before seen. The wind blowing strong from the southward so much retarded our progress, that at noon we had only reached the N.W. point of the arm we had been steering for,[1] and which was not more than five miles from our station in Oak cove, in a direction S. 14 E.; its observed latitude was 47° 53′, longitude 237° 30′, Foulweather bluff forming the opposite point of entrance into the arm, bore east about half a league distant. The strength of the ebb tide obliged us to stop near two hours, and from its rapidity we were induced to believe, as we had before suspected, that either the eastern shore was an island, or that the tide had extensive inland communication.

On the flood returning, we resumed our route, and found our supposed high round island connected with the main by a low sandy neck of land, nearly occupied by a salt-water swamp.[2] Into the bay, formed between this point and that we had departed from, descended a few small streams of fresh water; with which, so far as we were enabled to judge, the country did not abound. This opinion was sanctioned by the Indians who visited us this morning, bringing with them small square boxes filled with fresh water, which we could not tempt them to dispose of. Hence this branch of the inlet takes a direction about S.W. ½ S. near 13 miles, and is in general about half a league wide. Its shores exhibited by no means the luxuriant appearance we had left behind, being nearly destitute of the open verdant spots, and alternately composed of sandy or rocky cliffs falling abruptly into the sea, or terminating on a beach; whilst in some places the even land extended from the water side, with little or no elevation. The low projecting points cause the coast to be somewhat indented with small bays, where, near the shore, we had soundings from five to twelve fathoms; but in the middle of the channel, though not more than two miles in width, no bottom could be reached with 110 fathoms of line.

We had not advanced more than two or three miles before we lost the advantage of the flood tide, and met a stream that ran constantly down. This, with a very fresh S.W. wind, so retarded our progress, that it was not until Friday the 11th at noon that we reached the extent above mentioned, which we found to be situated due south of our observatory in port Discovery, in the latitude of 47° 39′. From this station, which I called HAZEL POINT in consequence of its producing many of those trees,[3] the channel divides into two branches, one taking a direction nearly due north, the other S.W.[4] We

[1] Tala Point.

[2] Hood Head, 220 feet high, which is connected with the W shore by a narrow strip of sand.

[3] The name still applies. Its location is about lat. 47° 41′ 30″ N.

[4] Dabob Bay to the N and the continuation of Hood Canal to the SW. Dabob Bay is 9 miles long.

still continued on the right hand, or continental shore, and found the northern arm terminate at the distance of about seven miles in a spacious bason, where bottom could not be found with 70 fathoms of line. As we returned to take up our abode for the night at the S.W. point of this arm, we observed some smoke on shore, and saw a canoe hauled up into a small creek; but none of the inhabitants could be discovered, nor did we hear or see any thing of them during the night.

The next morning, Saturday the 12th, at four o'clock, we again embarked. Having been supplied for five days only, our provisions were greatly exhausted, and the commencement of this, which was the sixth, threatened us with short allowance. Our sportsmen had been unable to assist our stock; and the prospect of obtaining any supplies from the natives was equally uncertain. The region we had lately passed seemed nearly destitute of human beings. The brute creation also had deserted the shores; the tracks of deer were no longer to be seen; nor was there an aquatic bird on the whole extent of the canal; animated nature seemed nearly exhausted; and her awful silence was only now and then interrupted by the croaking of a raven, the breathing of a seal, or the scream of an eagle. Even these solitary sounds were so seldom heard, that the rustling of the breeze along the shore, assisted by the solemn stillness that prevailed, gave rise to ridiculous suspicions in our seamen of hearing rattlesnakes, and other hideous monsters, in the wilderness, which was composed of the productions already mentioned, but which appeared to grow with infinitely less vigour than we had been accustomed to witness.

To the westward and N.W. lay that range of snowy mountains, noticed the morning we spoke with the Columbia. These gradually descended in a southern direction, whilst the summit of the eastern range now and then appearing, seemed to give bounds to this low country on that side. Between the S.E. and S.W. a country of a very moderate height seemed to extend as far as the eye could reach; and, from its eminences and vallies, there was reason to believe that this inlet continued to meander a very considerable distance, which made me much regret that we were not provided for a longer excursion. Yet, having proceeded thus far, I resolved to continue our researches, though at the expence of a little hunger, until the inlet should either terminate, or so extensively open, as to render it expedient that the vessels should be brought up; which would be a very tedious and disagreeable operation, in consequence of the narrowness of the channel, and the great depth of the water. Soundings in some places only could be gained close to the shore; and in the middle no bottom had any where been found with 100 fathoms of line, although the shores were in general low, and not half a league asunder.

Having very pleasant weather, and a gentle favorable breeze, we proceeded, [1] and passed several runs of fresh water. Near one of the largest we observed

---

[1] Travel was not always as comfortable as Vancouver seems to imply: 'After being greatly tormented by Musquito's Sand Flies &c we left our Quarters early & continued the further Investigation of this Branch.' – Puget, 12 May.

our latitude at noon to be 47° 27′; and once again had the pleasure of approaching an inhabited country. A canoe, in which there were three men, went alongside the launch, and bartered a few trifles for beads, iron, and copper, but declined every invitation from us[1] to come on shore. From Mr. Puget I learned, that they appeared to be very honest in their dealings, and had used their utmost endeavours to prevail on the party in the launch to attend them home, which he understood to be at the distance of about a league, and for which they seemed to make the best of their way, probably to acquaint their friends with the approach of strangers. Soon after we had dined, a smoke was observed near the supposed place of their residence; made, as we concluded, for the purpose of directing us to their habitations, for which we immediately set off, agreeably to their very civil invitation.[2]

An idea during this excursion had occurred to us, that part of the brute creation have an aversion to the absence of the human race; this opinion seemed now in some measure confirmed, by the appearance for the first time during the last three days, of several species of ducks, and other aquatic birds. I do not, however, mean absolutely to infer, that it is the affection of the lower orders of the creation to man, that draws them to the same spots which human beings prefer, since it is highly probable that such places as afford the most eligible residence in point of sustenance to the human race, in an uncivilized state, may be, by the brute creation, resorted to for the same purpose.

The habitations of our new friends appeared to be situated nearly at the extremity of this inlet, or where it appeared to take a very sharp turn to the S.E. still favoring our hopes of returning by the great eastern arm. These, however, vanished on landing, as we found its S.W. direction terminate in land, apparently low and swampy, with a shoal extending some distance from its shores,[3] formimg a narrow passage to the south-eastward into a cove or bason, which seemed its termination also in that direction.[4]

Here we found the finest stream of fresh water we had yet seen; from the size, clearness, and rapidity of which, little doubt could be entertained of its having its source in perpetual springs. Near it were two miserable huts with mats thrown carelessly over them, protecting their tenants neither from the heat nor severity of the weather,[5] these huts seemed calculated to contain only

[1] The words 'from us', added in the second edition, refer to Puget, who was in charge of the launch.
[2] These would be Twana Indians, who inhabited both shores of Hood Canal. They belonged to the coastal linguistic division of the Coast Salish.
[3] Annas Bay, at the S end of Hood Canal.
[4] Vancouver had reached The Great Bend, where the canal turns sharply to the E. The 'cove or bason' was the continuation of the canal. From the beginning of the bend the canal would appear to end at a narrows about 3 miles to the E, but it then swings to the NE and continues on for about 10 miles.
[5] 'The Stench of this Place,' Puget noted, 'was intolerable, though Close to a fine fresh Water Run, yet the Indolence of the Inhabitants appears so great that the filth is left close to the Habitations, which if carried but a few Yards would be swept away in the Stream.' – 12 May.

the five or six men then present, though previously to our quitting the boats we supposed a greater number of persons had been seen; those were probably their women, who on our approach had retired to the woods.

These good people conducted themselves in the most friendly manner. They had little to dispose of, yet they bartered away their bows and arrows without the least hesitation, together with some small fish, cockles, and clams; of the latter we purchased a large quantity, a supply of which was very acceptable in the low condition of our stock. They made us clearly to understand, that in the cove to the S.E. we should find a number of their countrymen, who had the like commodities to dispose of; and being anxious to leave no doubt concerning a further inland navigation by this arm of the sea, and wishing to establish, as far as possible, a friendly intercourse with the inhabitants of the country, which, from the docile and inoffensive manners of those we had seen, appeared a task of no great difficulty, we proceeded to a low point of land that forms the north entrance into the cove.[1] There we beheld a number of the natives, who did not betray the smallest apprehension at our approach; the whole assembly remained quietly seated on the grass, excepting two or three whose particular office seemed to be that of making us welcome to their country. These presented us with some fish, and received in return trinkets of various kinds, which delighted them excessively. They attended us to their companions, who amounted in number to about sixty, including the women and children. We were received by them with equal cordiality, and treated with marks of great friendship and hospitality. A short time was here employed in exchanges of mutual civilities. The females on this occasion took a very active part. They presented us with fish, arrows, and other trifles, in a way that convinced us they had much pleasure in so doing. They did not appear to differ in any respect from the inhabitants we had before seen; and some of our gentlemen were of opinion that they recognized the persons of one or two who had visited us on the preceding Thursday morning; particularly one man, who had suffered very much from the small pox. This deplorable disease is not only common, but it is greatly to be apprehended is very fatal amongst them, as its indelible marks were seen on many; and several had lost the sight of one eye, which was remarked to be generally the left, owing most likely to the virulent effects of this baneful disorder. The residence of these people here was doubtless of a temporary nature; few had taken the trouble of erecting their usual miserable huts, being content to lodge on the ground, with loose mats only for their covering.

From this point, which is situated nearly at the south extremity of the channel in latitude 47° 21′, longitude 237° 6½′,[2] little doubt existed of the cove terminating its navigation. To ascertain this, whilst I remained with these civil people, Mr. Johnstone was directed to row round the projection that had obstructed our view of the whole circumference of the cove, which is about

[1] Ayres Point.
[2] Its position is lat. 47° 22′ 30″ N, long. 123° 06′ 30″ W (236° 53′ 30″ E).

two miles; and, if it were not closed, to pursue its examination. Our former conjectures being confirmed,[1] on his return we prepared to depart; and, as we were putting off from the shore, a cloak of inferior sea otter skins was brought down, which I purchased for a small piece of copper. Upon this they made signs that if we would remain, more, and of a superior quality, should be produced; but as this was not our object,[2] and as we had finished our proposed task sooner than was expected this morning, to the no small satisfaction of our whole party, we directed our course back towards port Discovery, from which we were now about 70 miles distant.

A fresh northwardly wind, and the approach of night, obliged us to take up our abode about two miles from the Indians, some of whom had followed us along the beach until we landed, when they posted themselves at the distance of about half a mile, to observe our different employments; at dark they all retired, and we neither heard nor saw any thing more of them. The rise and fall of the tide, although the current constantly ran down without any great degree of rapidity, appeared to have been nearly ten feet, and it was high water 3^h $50'$ after the moon passed the meridian.

Early on Sunday morning the 13th, we again embarked; directing our route down the inlet, which, after the Right Honorable Lord Hood, I called HOOD'S CHANNEL;[3] but our progress homeward was so very slow, that it was Monday afternoon, the 14th, before we reached Foulweather bluff. This promontory is not ill named, for we had scarcely landed, when a heavy rain commenced, which continuing the rest of the day, obliged us to remain stationary. This detention I endeavoured to reconcile with the hope that the next morning would permit some examination, or at least afford us a view of the great eastern arm, before we returned to the ships; but in this I was disappointed. After waiting until ten o'clock in the forenoon of Tuesday the 15th, without the least prospect of an alteration for the better, we again set out with a fresh breeze at S.S.E. attended with heavy squalls and torrents of rain; and about four in the afternoon arrived on board, much to the satisfaction I believe of

[1] On Vancouver's chart Hood Canal ends at the so-called cove that is part of The Great Bend. From this it must be assumed that Johnstone did not proceed far enough to see the part of the canal beyond the narrows at the E end of the bend.

[2] There was more trading for furs than Vancouver's account suggests: 'Beaver are plentiful, if we may Judge from the furs seen at the Village, many of these we bought, and one very fine Panther skin, that had not long been taken from the Animal...' – Manby, letters, May. Menzies noted a surprising fact: 'They had also Iron Chinese Cashes (a kind of base Money piercd with a hole) & beads which clearly showed that they had had either a direct or indirect communication with the Traders on the exterior part of the Coast.' – 12 May.

[3] 'Hood's Canal' in the first edition. When editing the text for the second edition, John Vancouver substituted 'channel' for 'canal' in almost every instance; the reason for this is not known. The name appears as Hood's Canal on Vancouver's chart. Hood was promoted Vice-Admiral of the Blue in 1787 and the next year became a member of the Board of Admiralty. In that capacity he had signed Vancouver's official instructions in March 1791.

all parties, as great anxiety had been entertained for our safety, in consequence of the unexpected length of our absence. The swivels fired from our boat and that of the Chatham's the morning after our departure, were heard on board, and were the cause of much alarm after the expiration of the time appointed for our return. Such attention had been paid to the several common occupations going forward when I left the ships, that I had the satisfaction to find every thing accomplished.[1] But from Mr. Whidbey I understood, that the weather had been so unfavorable to our astronomical pursuits, that he had not been able to obtain any lunar distances, though he had succeeded in ascertaining the rate of the chronometers. Having, however, acquired sufficient authority of this nature for correcting our survey, and carrying it further into execution, I determined to depart as soon as the weather should break up. This did not happen until Thursday afternoon the 17th; when the tents and observatory were re-embarked, and every thing got in readiness for sailing the next morning, Friday the 18th. A light air from the S.E. and pleasant weather, favored our departure; and about breakfast time, the ship arriving at the entrance of the port, I landed on the east end of Protection island, in order, from its eminence, to take a more accurate view of the surrounding shores. In most directions, they seemed much broken, particularly in the northern quarter, being there occupied by an archipelago of islands of various sizes.[2] On my return on board, I directed Mr. Broughton to use his endeavours, in the Chatham, to acquire some information in that line, whilst I continued my examination with the Discovery up the inlet which we had discovered in the boats, to the eastward of Foulweather bluff; appointing the first inlet to the south-eastward of that point on the starboard, or continental shore, as our place of rendezvous. We parted about noon in pleasant weather, and with a fine breeze directed our vessels agreeably to our respective pursuits.

As a more particular description of port Discovery and the surrounding country would have interfered with our primary object of ascertaining the boundary of this coast, I shall reserve it for the subject of the following short chapter; and shall conclude this with such astronomical and nautical observations as circumstances permitted us to make whilst in port, as well as those made previous to our arrival and after our departure; which have assisted in fixing its longitude, as well as that of the exterior coast of New Albion southward to cape Mendocino.

A part of this coast, prior to our visit, had been seen by different navigators, and the position of certain head lands, capes, &c. given to the world. Several of these I have found myself under the necessity of placing in different latitudes and longitudes, as well those seen by Captain Cook, as others laid down by the different visitors who have followed him. This, however, I have not

---

[1] 'The ship [the *Discovery*] being found crank 20 Tons of shingle ballast was got on board & Lieut Broughton & Mr Whidbey employed themselves in making an accurate survey of the Harbour & settling its exact situation...' – Menzies, 16 May. Whidbey's chart of Port Discovery appears as an inset on one of Vancouver's engraved charts.

[2] The San Juan Islands.

presumed to do, from a consciousness of superior abilities as an astronomer, or integrity as an historian; but from the conviction, that no one of my predecessors had the good fortune to meet so favorable an opportunity for the examination: under the happy circumstances of which I have been induced to assign, to the several conspicuous head lands, points, &c. the positions ascertained by the result of our several observations; from which, as it evidently appeared that our chronometer had materially accelerated on its Otaheitean rate, it may not be unacceptable to state the mode I adopted for the correction of that error.

In our passage towards, and during our stay amongst, the Sandwich islands, the chronometer, agreeably to its Otaheitean rate, seemed to have been accurate to a scrupulous degree of nicety; but, by some observations made prior to the 26th of March, it appeared to have deviated manifestly from the truth. The observations made on that day were the most remote ones I made use of on this occasion; and, by the mean result of all made since in port Discovery, instead of the chronometer gaining at the rate of 4″ 3‴ per day only, it was found to be gaining 11″ 55‴ per day; and therefore, instead of the allowance of the former rate, from the 26th of March to our arrival on the coast, it was increased to 8″ per day; and from the 17th of April, 11″ 30‴ were allowed as the rate of the chronometer, for the purpose of reducing all our observations from that period to our arrival in port Discovery; which medium, I trust, will hereafter be found fully to answer my expectations. The following will serve to exhibit the different observations made to establish this point, comprehending two hundred and twenty sets of lunar distances, each set containing six observations, taken by the several officers and gentlemen on board, as follow:

Mr. Puget, nine sets taken between the 28th March and 9th of April	237°	19′	5″
Mr. Whidbey, fifty-eight ditto, the 26th March and 12th of June	237	23	38
Mr. Orchard, fifty-three ditto, ditto	237	22	
Mr. J. Stewart, twenty-four ditto, the 27th of March and 29th of April	237	25	50
Mr. Ballard, thirty-eight ditto, ditto	237	22	13
Myelf thirty-eight ditto, the 28th of March and 5th of May	237	21	9
Hence, the longitude of the observatory deduced from the mean result of the above observed distances of the ☽ a ☉ and stars, was	237	22	19[1]
On our arrival in port Discovery, the chronometer, by the Portsmouth rate, on the 4th of May, shewed	237	51	
By the Otaheitean rate	235	59	

[1] The correct long. would be about 122° 52′ 30″ W (237° 07′ 30″ E), assuming that the observatory was near Carr Point.

Mr. Arnold's chronometer on board the Chatham,
   by the Otaheitean rate   235° 27′
   _____

From the above observations, and nine days corresponding altitudes, Kendal's chronometer was found, on the 13th of May at noon, to be fast of mean time at Greenwich 45′ 46″, and to be gaining on mean time at the rate of 11″ 55‴ per day. By the same observations, Mr. Arnold's, on the 13th of May at noon, was fast of mean time at Greenwich 2ʰ 56′ 49″, and was gaining on mean time at the rate of 27″ per day.

The latitude of the observatory, by the mean result
   of nine meridian altitudes, was   48° 2′ 30″ [1]
   _____

The variation, by all our compasses, in eleven sets
   of azimuths, differing from 20° to 26°, gave their
   mean result   21° 30′
   _____

The vertical inclination of the magnetic needle.

Marked end North face East		73° 50′
Ditto	West	75 57
Ditto South face East		72 17
Ditto	West	75 55
   _____

Mean vertical inclination of the North point of the
   marine dipping needle   74° 30′
   _____

In port Discovery, the tide was observed to flow on the full of the moon, about ten feet; and was high water 3ʰ 50′ after the moon passed the meridian.

[1] Probably very close to the correct location.

CHAPTER V.

Description of Port Discovery and the adjacent Country—Its Inhabitants—Method of depositing the Dead—Conjectures relative to the apparent Depopulation of the Country.

I SHALL now proceed to relate such matters respecting the country of New Albion as appeared intitled to notice, and which are not inserted in the preceding narrative.

Port Discovery, already mentioned as a perfectly safe and convenient harbour, has its outer points $1\frac{3}{4}$ miles asunder, bearing from each other S. 63 W. and N. 63 E.; its entrance is situated in latitude 48° 7′, longitude 237° $20\frac{1}{2}$,[1] whence the port first takes a direction S. 30 E. about eight miles, and then terminates S.W. by W. about a league further.[2] If it lies under any disadvantage, it is in its great depth of water; in which respect, however, we found no inconvenience, as the bottom was exceedingly good holding ground, and free from rocks. Towards the upper part of the harbour it is of less depth; but I saw no situation more eligible than that in which the vessels rode, off the first low sandy point on the western shore, about $4\frac{1}{2}$ miles within the entrance.[3] Here our wooding, watering, brewing, and all other operations were carried on with the utmost facility and convenience. The shores of Protection island form on its south side, which is about two miles long, a most excellent roadstead, and a channel into port Discovery, near two miles wide on either side, without any interruption, which, with other nautical particulars, are exhibited in the chart.

The country in the neighbourhood of this port may generally be considered of a moderate height, although bounded on the west side by mountains covered with snow, to which the land from the water's edge rises in a pleasing diversity by hills of gradual ascent. The snow on these hills probably dissolves as the summer advances, for pine trees were produced on their very summits. On the sea shore the land generally terminated in low sandy cliffs; though in some spaces of considerable extent it ran nearly level from high water mark. The soil for the most part is a light sandy loam, in several places of very considerable depth, and abundantly mixed with decayed vegetables. The vigour and luxuriance of its productions proved it to be a rich fertile mould, which possibly might be considerably improved by the addition of the

[1] The middle of the entrance is in lat. 48° 06′ N, long. 122° 54′ W (237° 06′ E).
[2] The total length of the bay is about 8 miles.   [3] Carr Point.

calcareous matter contained in the marrow stone that presented itself in many places. In respect to its mineral productions no great variety was observed. Iron ore, in its various forms, was generally found; and from the weight and magnetic qualities of some specimens, appeared tolerably rich, particularly a kind that much resembled the blood stone. These, with quartz, agate, the common flint, and a great intermixture of other silicious matter, (most of the stones we met with being of that class) with some variety of calcareous, magnesian, and argilaceous earths, were the mineral productions generally found.

The parts of the vegetable kingdom applicable to useful purposes appeared to grow very luxuriantly, and consisted of the Canadian and Norwegian hemlock, silver pines, the Tacamahac and Canadian poplar, arbor-vitæ, common yew, black and common dwarf oak, American ash, common hazel, sycamore, sugar, mountain, and Pensylvanian maple, oriental arbutus, American alder, and common willow; these, with the Canadian alder, small fruited crab, and Pensylvanian cherry trees, constituted the forests, which may be considered rather as encumbered, than adorned, with underwood; although there were several places where, in its present state, the traveller might pass without being in the least incommoded, excepting by the undecayed trunks of trees which had fallen. Of esculent vegetables we found but few; the white or dead nettle, and samphire, were most common; the wild orache, vulgarly called fat-hen, with the vetch. Two or three sorts of wild peas, and the common hedge mustard, were frequently though not always met with, and were considered by us as excellent of their kinds, and served to relish our salt provisions, on which, with a very scanty supply of fish, all hands subsisted. Amongst the more minute productions, Mr. Menzies found constant amusement; and, I believe, was enabled to make some addition to the catalogue of plants.[1]

The knowledge we acquired of the animal kingdom was very imperfect. The skins of the animals already noticed were such as are commonly found amongst the inhabitants on the sea coasts under the same parallel, and towards Nootka; these were mostly of the coarser and more common sorts. Garments of sea otter skins were not worn, nor did many such skins appear amongst the inhabitants. The only living quadrupeds we saw, were a black bear, two or three wild dogs, about as many rabbits, several small brown squirrels, rats, mice, and the skunk, whose effluvia were the most intolerable and offensive I ever experienced.

Few of the feathered tribe were procured, although, on our first arrival, the aquatic birds were so numerous, that we expected a profuse supply of wild

[1] See C. F. Newcombe (ed.), *Menzies' Journal of Vancouver's Voyage, April to October 1792* (Archives of British Columbia, Memoir V, Victoria, 1923). The journal naturally abounds in references to flora and to Menzies' botanizing activities. In an appendix the editor, himself a distinguished botanist and ethnologist, lists the ferns, flowering plants, mosses, lichens, and marine algae that Menzies mentioned.

fowl; but these were all so extremely shy and watchful, that our guns seldom reached them; and, on being fired at, they disappeared. About the shores and on the rocks, we found some species of the tern, the common gull, sea pigeon of Newfoundland, curlews, sand-larks, shags, and the black sea pye, like those in New Holland and New Zealand; these were however not so abundant as the others. Nor did the woods appear to be much resorted to by the feathered race; two or three spruce partridges had been seen; with few in point of number, and little variety, of small birds: amongst which the humming birds bore a great proportion. At the outskirts of the woods, and about the water side, the white headed and brown eagle; ravens, carrion crows, American king's fisher, and a very handsome woodpecker, were seen in numbers; and in addition to these on the low projecting points, and open places in the woods, we frequently saw a bird with which we were wholly unacquainted, though we considered it to be a species of the crane or heron; some of their eggs were found of a bluish cast, considerably larger than that of a turkey, and well tasted. These birds have remarkably long legs and necks, and their bodies seemed to equal in size the largest turkey. Their plumage is uniformly of a light brown, and when erect, their height, on a moderate computation could not be less than four feet.[1] They seemed to prefer open situations, and used no endeavours to hide or screen themselves from our sight, but were too vigilant to allow our sportsmen taking them by surprise. Some blue, and some nearly white herons of the common size were also seen.

The sea was not much more bountiful to us of its animal productions than was its shores. The scanty supply of fish we were enabled to procure, consisted in general of the common sorts of small flat-fish, elephant fish, sea bream, sea perch, a large sort of sculpin, some weighing six or eight pounds, with a greenish colour about their throat, belly, and gills; these were very coarse, but no ill effects were consequent on eating them.[2] The above, with a few trout, a small sort of eel extremely well tasted, of a yellowish green colour, were the fishes we most generally caught. A small common black snake, a few lizards and frogs, together with a variety of common insects, none of which could be considered as very troublesome, were the only creatures of the reptile tribe we observed.

This country, regarded in an agricultural point of view, I should conceive is capable of high improvement, notwithstanding the soil in general may be considered to be light and sandy. Its spontaneous productions in the vicinity of the woods are nearly the same, and grow in equal luxuriance with those under a similar parallel in Europe; favoring the hope, that if nutritious exotics

[1] The description suggests a young sandhill crane (which becomes gray later in life, with a red crown), but the eggs of the crane are olive coloured. Menzies refers to 'a few gigantic Cranes of between three & four feet high who strided over the Lawn with a lordly step.' – 7 May. Newcombe thought they were probably sandhill cranes.

[2] Hewett (a surgeon's mate) differs; he states that he reported to Vancouver 'the Names of Persons' who had 'been made Ill by having eaten this Fish... they were attacked with giddiness and Nausea in proportion to the Quantity they had eaten.'

were introduced and carefully attended to, they would succeed in the highest degree. The mildness of the climate, and the forwardness of every species of plants, afforded strong grounds in support of this opinion.

The interruptions we experienced in the general serenity of the weather, were probably no more than were absolutely requisite in the spring of the year to bring forward the annual productions. These were attended with no violence of wind, and the rain which fell, although disagreeable to travellers, was not so heavy as to beat down and destroy the first efforts of vegetation. Under all these favourable circumstances, the country yet labours under one material disadvantage in the scarcity of fresh water. The streams however that we met with appeared sufficient to answer all purposes, in the domestic œconomy of life, to a very numerous body of inhabitants: and, were the country cleared and searched, there can be little doubt that a variety of eligible situations might be found for establishments, where, with proper exertions, wholesome water might be procured.

What the low country before us toward the range of snowy mountains may produce, remains for future investigation; but judging from what we had seen, it seemed more than probable, that those natural channels [1] of the sea wind in various directions; and that they are capable of affording great advantages to commercial pursuits, by opening communications with parts of the interior country commodiously and delightfully situated. The great depth of water may be offered as an insuperable objection; yet, on a more minute examination, it is likely that many eligible and convenient stopping places might be found for the security of such vessels as would necessarily be employed in those occupations.

Having considered with impartiality the excellencies and defects of this country, as far as came under our observation, it now remains to add a few words on the character of its inhabitants.

None being resident in port Discovery, and our intercourse with them having been very confined, the knowledge we may have acquired of them, their manners, and customs, must necessarily be very limited, and our conclusions drawn chiefly from comparison. [2] From New Dungeness we traversed nearly one hundred and fifty miles of their shores without seeing that number of inhabitants. Those who came within our notice so nearly resembled the people of Nootka, that the best delineation I can offer is a reference to the description of those people, which has before been so ably

---

[1] 'Canals' in the first edition.

[2] Bell noted one contrast: 'The women being the first we had seen since leaving the Sandwich Islands, had not a few attacks of Gallantry made on them by the Sailors, though they were by no means inviting. But however great the difference between them, and the Sandwich Islanders in point of Beauty, much greater was it in point of behaviour, for here the smallest degree of indelicacy towards one of these Ladies, shocked their modesty to such a degree, and had such an effect on them, that I have seen many of them burst into Tears, they wou'd endeavour to hide themselves in the bottom of their Canoes – and discover the most extreme degree of uneasiness & distress.' – May.

and with so much justice given to the public.* The only difference I observed was, that in their stature they did not generally appear quite so stout; and in their habits were less filthy; for though these people adorn their persons with the same sort of paint, yet it is not laid on in that abundance, nor do they load their hair with that immense quantity of oil and colouring matter, which is so customary amongst the people of Nootka; their hair, as before mentioned, being in general neatly combed and tied behind.

In their weapons, implements, canoes, and dress, they vary little. Their native woollen garment was most in fashion, next to it the skins of deer, bear, &c.; a few wore dresses manufactured from bark, which, like their woollen ones, were very neatly wrought.

Their spears, arrows, fishgigs, and other weapons, were shaped exactly like those of Nootka; but none were pointed with copper, or with muscle shell. The three former were generally barbed, and those pointed with common flint, agate, and bone, seemed of their original workmanship. Yet more of their arrows were observed to be pointed with thin flat iron, than with bone or flint, and it was very singular that they should prefer exchanging those pointed with iron to any of the others.[1] Their bows were of a superior construction: these in general were from two and a half to three feet in length; the broadest part in the middle was about an inch and a half, and about three quarters of an inch thick, neatly made, gradually tapering to each end, which terminated in a shoulder and a hook, for the security of the bow string. They were all made of yew, and chosen with a naturally inverted curve suited to the method of using them. From end to end of the concave side, which when strung became the convex part, a very strong strip of an elastic hide is attached to some, and the skins of serpents to others, exactly the shape and length of the bow, neatly and firmly affixed to the wood by means of a cement, the adhesive property of which I never saw, or heard of being, equalled. It is not to be affected by either dry or damp weather, and forms so strong a connection with the wood, as to prevent a separation without destroying the component parts of both. The bow string is made of the sinew of some marine animal laid loose, in order to be twisted at pleasure, as the temperature of the atmosphere may require to preserve it at a proper length. Thus is this very neat little weapon rendered portable, elastic, and effective in the highest degree, if we

* Vide Captain Cook's last voyage. [For Cook's own account of the Indians at Nootka Sound see *Journals*, III, 311–30.]

[1] Puget, referring to Indians along the Hood Canal, wrote: 'They willingly disposed of the Bows and Arrows, some of which were barbed with Iron – This gave rise to various Conjectures, but it was generally supposed that either Europeans had before visited the Tribe or they must have some Mercantile Communication with those situated near the Sea.' – May 11. The latter surmise was the correct one. Hewett states that few of the arrows were pointed with iron. Of the 60 arrows in the Hewett Collection in the British Museum described by Gunther, only one is iron-tipped, and it is stated to be from Grays Harbor, on the ocean coast. – Erna Gunther, *Indian Life on the Northwest Coast* (Chicago, 1972), p. 236.

may be allowed to judge by the dexterity with which it was used by one of the natives at port Discovery.

We had little opportunity of acquiring any satisfactory information with regard to the public regulations, or private œconomy, of these people. The situation and appearance of the places we found them generally inhabiting, indicated their being much accustomed to a change of residence; the deserted villages tended to strengthen the conjecture of their being wanderers. Territorial property appeared to be of little importance; there was plenty of room for their fixed habitations, and those of a temporary nature, which we now found them mostly to occupy, being principally composed of cross sticks, covered with a few mats, as easily found a spot for their erection, as they were removed from one station to another, either as inclination might lead, or necessity compel: and having a very extensive range of domain, they were not liable to interruption or opposition from their few surrounding neighbours.

From these circumstances alone, it may be somewhat premature to conclude that this delightful country has always been thus thinly inhabited; on the contrary, there are reasons to believe it has been infinitely more populous. Each of the deserted villages was nearly, if not quite, equal to contain all the scattered inhabitants we saw, according to the custom of the Nootka people; to whom these have great affinity in their persons, fashions, wants, comforts, construction of these their fixed habitations, and in their general character. It is also possible, that most of the clear spaces may have been indebted, for the removal of their timber and underwood, to manual labour. Their general appearance furnished this opinion, and their situation on the most pleasant and commanding eminences, protected by the forest on every side, except that which would have precluded a view of the sea, seemed to encourage the idea. Not many years since, each of these vacant places might have been allotted to the habitations of different societies, and the variation observed in their extent might have been conformable to the size of each village; on the scite of which, since their abdication, or extermination, nothing but the smaller shrubs and plants had yet been able to rear their heads.

In our different excursions, particularly those in the neighbourhood of port Discovery, the scull, limbs, ribs, and back bones, or some other vestiges of the human body, were found in many places promiscuously scattered about the beach, in great numbers. Similar relics were also frequently met with during our survey in the boats; and I was informed by the officers, that in their several perambulations, the like appearances had presented themselves so repeatedly, and in such abundance, as to produce an idea that the environs of port Discovery were a general cemetery for the whole of the surrounding country. Notwithstanding these circumstances do not amount to a direct proof of the extensive population they indicate, yet, when combined with other appearances, they warranted an opinion, that at no very remote period this country had been far more populous than at present. Some of the human bodies were found disposed of in a very singular manner. Canoes were suspended between two or more trees about twelve feet from the ground, in which were the skeletons of two or three persons; others of a larger size were hauled up into the outskirts of the woods, which contained from four to seven skeletons covered over with a broad plank. In some of these broken bows and arrows were found, which at first gave rise to a conjecture, that these might have been warriors, who after being mortally wounded, had, whilst their strength remained, hauled up their canoes for the purpose of expiring quietly in them. But on a further examination this became improbable, as it would hardly have been possible to have preserved the regularity of position in the agonies of death, or to have defended their sepulchres with the broad plank with which each was covered.

The few skeletons we saw so carefully deposited in the canoes, were probably the chiefs, priests, or leaders of particular tribes, whose followers most likely continue to possess the highest respect for their memory and remains: and the general knowledge I had obtained from experience of the regard which all savage nations pay to their funeral solemnities, made me particularly solicitous to prevent any indignity from being wantonly offered to their departed friends.[1] Baskets were also found suspended on high trees, each containing the skeleton of a young child; in some of which were also small square boxes filled with a kind of white paste, resembling such as I had seen the natives eat, supposed to be made of the saranne root; some of these boxes were quite full, others were nearly empty, eaten probably by the mice, squirrels, or birds. On the next low point, south of our encampment, where the gunners were airing the powder, they met with several holes in which human bodies were interred slightly covered over, and in different states of decay, some appearing to have been very recently deposited. About half a mile to the northward of our tents, where the land is nearly level with high water mark, a few paces within the skirting of the wood, a canoe was found suspended between two trees, in which were three human skeletons; and a few paces to the right was a cleared place of nearly forty yards round; where, from the fresh appearance of the burnt stumps, most of its vegetable productions had very lately been consumed by fire. Amongst the ashes we found the sculls, and other bones, of near twenty persons in different stages of calcination; the fire, however, had not reached the suspended canoe, nor did it appear to have been intended that it should. The skeletons found thus disposed, in canoes, or in baskets, bore a very small proportion to the number of sculls and other human bones indiscriminately scattered about the shores. Such are the effects; but of the

---

[1] Some desecration did occur, probably unknown to Vancouver. Hewett states that 'one of the Canoes [containing remains] was emptied Sawed in half carried to the Tents and Set up for a Sentry Box.' Another instance: 'The Bones round the Fire Place were left undisturbed but the Curiosity of some of our People had induced them to cut the Canoe and Basket down & instead of replacing them in their former Situation they were left on the Beach.' – Puget, May.

cause or causes that have operated to produce them, we remained totally unacquainted; whether, occasioned by epidemic disease, or recent wars.[1] The character and general deportment of the few inhabitants we occasionally saw, by no means countenanced the latter opinion; they were uniformly civil and friendly, without manifesting the least sign of fear or suspicion at our approach; nor did their appearance indicate their having been much inured to hostilities. Several of their stoutest men had been seen perfectly naked, and contrary to what might have been expected of rude nations habituated to warfare their skins were mostly unblemished by scars, excepting such as the small pox seemed to have occasioned; a disease which there is great reason to believe is very fatal amongst them. It is not, however, very easy to draw any just conclusions on the true cause from which this havoc of the human race proceeded: this must remain for the investigation of others who may have more leisure, and a better opportunity, to direct such an inquiry: yet it may not be unreasonable to conjecture, that the present apparent depopulation may have arisen in some measure from the inhabitants of this interior part having been induced to quit their former abode, and to have moved nearer the exterior coast for the convenience of obtaining in the immediate mart, with more ease and at a cheaper rate, those valuable articles of commerce, that within these late years have been brought to the sea coasts of this continent by Europeans and the citizens of America, and which are in great estimation amongst these people, being possessed by all in a greater or less degree.

[1] Not only here but elsewhere Vancouver seems to have been mildly obsessed by the idea of depopulation. The burials in small canoes and boxes were normal practice, and the white man may well have been responsible for many of the skulls and bones that were found scattered about in many places. Gunther comments: 'There were many epidemics of new diseases like measles and smallpox that were not recorded, and a small community could be so reduced in numbers that the survivors fled, leaving the dead unburied.' – *Indian Life on the Northwest Coast* (Chicago, 1972), p. 76.

CHAPTER VI.

Enter Admiralty Inlet—Anchor off Restoration Point—Visit an Indian Village—
Account of several boat Excursions—Proceed to another Part of the Inlet—Take
Possession of the Country.

AGREEABLY to the proposed destination of each vessel, the Discovery and
Chatham, at noon, on Friday the 18th of May, directed their course towards the
objects of their respective pursuits; and as I had already traced the western
shore in the boats, we now kept the eastern side on board, which, like the
other, abounds with those verdant open places that have been so repeatedly
noticed. On one of these beautiful lawns, nearly a league within the entrance
of the inlet, about thirty of the natives came from the surrounding woods,
and attentively noticed us as we sailed along. We did not discover any
habitations near them, nor did we see any canoes on the beach. On the south
side of the lawn, were many uprights in the ground, which had the appearance
of having formerly been the supporters of their large wooden houses. We used
our endeavours to invite these good people on board, but without effect. After
advancing about four leagues up the inlet, the pleasant gale, which had
attended us from the N.W. died away, and a strong ebb making against us,
we were compelled to anchor for the night, in 18 fathoms water, about half
a mile from the eastern shore: Marrow-Stone point bearing by compass N.
56 W.; the N.E. point of Oak-cove S. 48 W.; and Foulweather bluff S.
51 E.[1]

During the night, we had a gentle southerly breeze, attended by a fog which
continued until nine o'clock on Saturday morning the 19th, when it was
dispersed by a return of the N.W. wind, with which we pursued our route
up the inlet; our progress was, however, soon retarded by the fore-topsail yard
giving way in the slings; on examination it appeared to have been in a defective
state some time. The spare fore-topsail yard was also very imperfect; which
obliged us to get the spare main-topsail yard up in its room; and it was a
very fortunate circumstance, that these defects were discovered in a country
abounding with materials to which we could resort; having only to make our
choice from amongst thousands of the finest spars the world produces.

To describe the beauties of this region, will, on some future occasion, be
a very grateful task to the pen of a skilful panegyrist. The serenity of the

[1] The anchorage was off Bush Point, Whidbey Island.

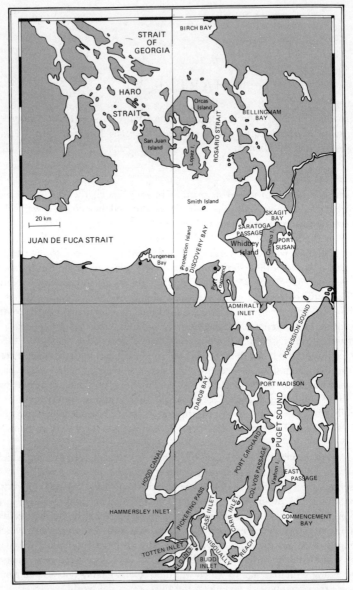

Figure 1. Puget Sound to Birch Bay. *Base map by Michael E. Leek.*

climate, the innumerable pleasing landscapes, and the abundant fertility that unassisted nature puts forth, require only to be enriched by the industry of man with villages, mansions, cottages, and other buildings, to render it the most lovely country that can be imagined; whilst the labour of the inhabitants would be amply rewarded, in the bounties which nature seems ready to bestow on cultivation.

About noon, we passed an inlet on the larboard or eastern shore, which seemed to stretch far to the northward,[1] but, as it was out of the line of our intended pursuit of keeping the continental shore on board, I continued our course up the main inlet, which now extended as far as, from the deck, the eye could reach, though, from the mast-head, intervening land appeared, beyond which another high round mountain covered with snow was discovered,[2] apparently situated several leagues to the south of mount Rainier, and bearing by compass S. 22 E. This I considered as a further extension of the eastern snowy range;[3] but the intermediate mountains, connecting it with mount Rainier, were not sufficiently high to be seen at that distance. Having advanced about eight leagues from our last night's station, we arrived off a projecting point of land, not formed by a low sandy spit, but rising abruptly in a low cliff about ten or twelve feet from the water side.[4] Its surface was a beautiful meadow covered with luxuriant herbage; on its western extreme, bordering on the woods, was an Indian village, consisting of temporary habitations, from whence several of the natives assembled to view the ship as we passed by; but none of them ventured off, though several of their canoes were seen on the beach. Here the inlet divided into two extensive branches, one taking a south-eastwardly,[5] the other a south-western direction.[6] Near this place was our appointed rendezvous with the Chatham; and under a small island to the S.W. of us,[7] appeared an eligible spot, in which, with security, we might wait her arrival; but, on approaching it, we found the depth of water no where less than 60 fathoms, within a cable's length of the shore. This obliged us to turn up towards the village point,[8] where we found a commodious roadstead; and about seven o'clock in the evening, anchored about a mile from the shore in 38 fathoms water, black sand and muddy bottom. The village point bore by compass N. 4. E.; the nearest opposite shore[9] of the main inlet N. 52 E. about a league distant; and the direction of its southern extent S.E.; the above island lying before the branch leading to the south-westward, bore from S. 36 E. to south, about half a league distant; and the appearance of a small inlet or cove, west, about the same distance.[10]

[1] Possession Sound.
[2] Mount St. Helens (9,671 ft.), a volcano long dormant that erupted suddenly, with great violence, in May 1980.
[3] The Cascade Range.   [4] Restoration Point, on the W shore.
[5] East Passage.   [6] Colvos Passage.
[7] Blake Island.   [8] Restoration Point.
[9] Alki Point.
[10] Rich Passage, the entrance to Port Orchard.

We had no sooner anchored than a canoe in which were two men, paddled round the ship. We attempted to induce them, but they were not to be prevailed upon, to enter the vessel; and having satisfied their curiosity, they hastily returned to the shore. Before the evening closed in, I proceeded to acquire some information respecting the small opening to the westward. It was nearly dark before I reached the shore, which seemed to form a small cove about half a mile in width, encircled by compact shores, with a cluster of rocks above water, nearly in its centre,[1] and little worthy of further notice.[2] On my return on board, I directed that a party, under the command of Lieutenant Puget and Mr. Whidbey, should, in the launch and cutter, proceed, with a supply of provisions for a week, to the examination of that branch of the inlet leading to the south-westward; keeping always the starboard or continental shore on board; which was accordingly carried into execution, at four o'clock the next morning.[3]

Our situation being somewhat incommoded by the meeting of different tides, we moved nearer in, and anchored in the same depth, and on the same bottom as before, very conveniently to the shore. Our eastern view was now bounded by the range of snowy mountains from mount Baker, bearing by compass north to mount Rainier, bearing N. 54 E. The new mountain was hid by the more elevated parts of the low land; and the intermediate snowy mountains in various rugged and grotesque shapes, were seen just to rear their heads above the lofty pine trees, which appearing to compose one uninterrupted forest, between us and the snowy range, presented a most pleasing landscape; nor was our western view destitute of similar diversification. The ridge of mountains on which mount Olympus is situated, whose rugged summits were seen no less fancifully towering over the forest than those on the eastern side, bounded to a considerable extent our western horizon;[4] on these however, not one conspicuous eminence arose, nor could we now distinguish that which on the sea coast appeared to be centrally situated, and forming an elegant bi-forked-mountain. From the southern extremity of these ridges of mountains, there seemed to be an extensive tract of land moderately elevated and beautifully diversified by pleasing inequalities of surface, enriched with every appearance of fertility.

On Sunday the 20th, in the meadow and about the village many of the

[1] Orchard Rocks.

[2] Owing to the darkness Vancouver did not discover at this time that Rich Passage led to Port Orchard.

[3] Puget notes that 'the two Boats [were] well armed, the Launch carried two Swivels besides Wall pieces Musquetoons & Musquetts.' – May 20. Menzies joined the party and made a comment that would be applicable to almost all the later expeditions in which he participated: 'though their mode of procedure in these surveying Cruizes was not very favorable for my [botanical] pursuits as it afforded me so little time on shore at the different places we landed at, yet it was the most eligible I could at this time adopt for obtaining a general knowledge of the produce of the Country.' – May 20.

[4] The Olympic Mountains.

natives were seen moving about,[1] whose curiosity seemed little excited on our account. One canoe only had been near us, from which was thrown on board the skin of some small animal, and then it returned instantly to the shore.

Our carpenters were busily engaged in replacing the topsail yards with proper spars, which were conveniently found for that purpose. Some beer was brewed from the spruce, which was here very excellent, and the rest of the crew were employed in a variety of other essential services. The gentle N.W. wind generally prevailed in the day, and calms, or light southerly breezes during the night.

Towards noon I went on shore to the village point, for the purpose of observing the latitude; on which occasion I visited the village, if it may be so dignified, as it appeared the most lowly and meanest of its kind. The best of the huts were poor and miserable, constructed something after the fashion of a soldier's tent, by two cross sticks about five feet high, connected at each end by a ridge-pole from one to the other, over some of which was thrown a coarse kind of mat, over others a few loose branches of trees, shrubs, or grass; none however appeared to be constructed for protecting them, either against the heat of summer, or the inclemency of winter. In them were hung up to be cured by the smoke of the fire they kept constantly burning, clams, muscles, and a few other kinds of fish, seemingly intended for their winter's subsistence. The clams perhaps were not all reserved for that purpose, as we frequently saw them strung and worn about the neck, which, as inclination directed, were eaten, two, three, or half a dozen at a time. This station did not appear to have been preferred for the purpose of fishing, as we saw few of the people so employed; nearly the whole of the inhabitants belonging to the village, which consisted of about eighty or an hundred men, women, and children, were busily engaged like swine, rooting up this beautiful verdant meadow in quest of a species of wild onion, and two other roots, which in appearance and taste greatly resembled the saranne, particularly the largest; the size of the smallest did not much exceed a large pea: this Mr. Menzies considered to be a new genus.[2] The collecting of these roots was most likely the object which attached them to this spot; they all seemed to gather them with much avidity, and to preserve them with great care, most probably for the purpose of making the paste I have already mentioned.

[1] These were Suquamish Indians, who occupied most of the W shore of Puget Sound S from Appletree Cove, which is about a dozen miles N of Restoration Point. At times they had settlements on the E shore as well. Elliott Bay, on the E shore opposite Restoration Point, around which the city of Seattle has grown up, was occupied by the Duwamish Indians, who were closely related to the Suquamish. Indeed, Chief Seattle, the Duwamish chief after whom the city was named, was also a chief of the Suquamish.

[2] 'Several of the women were digging on the Point which excited my curiosity to know what they were digging for & found it to be a little bulbous root of a liliaceous plant which on searching about for the flower of it I discovered to be a new *Genus* of the Triandria monogina.' – Menzies, May 28. Newcombe identifies it as some species of *Brodiaea* (wild hyacinth).

These people varied in no essential point from the natives we had seen since our entering the straits. Their persons were equally ill made, and as much besmered with oil and different coloured paints, particularly with red ochre, and a sort of shining chaffy mica, very ponderous, and in colour much resembling black lead; they likewise possessed more ornaments, especially such as were made of copper, the article most valued and esteemed amongst them. They seemed not wanting in offers of friendship and hospitality; as on our joining their party, we were presented with such things as they had to dispose of: and they immediately prepared a few of the roots, and some shell fish for our refreshment, which were very palatable. In these civil offices, two men who appeared the most active, and to be regarded by their countrymen as the most important persons of the party, were particularly assiduous to please. To each of them I made presents, which were received very thankfully; and on my returning towards the boat, they gave me to understand by signs, the only means we had of conversing with each other, that it would not be long ere they returned our visit on board the ship. This they accordingly did in the afternoon, with no small degree of ceremony. Beside the canoes which brought these two superior people five others attended, seemingly as an appendage to the consequence of these chiefs, who would not repair immediately on board, but agreeably to the custom of Nootka, advanced within about two hundred yards of the ship, and there resting on their paddles a conference was held, followed by a song principally sung by one man, who at stated times was joined in chorus by several others, whilst some in each canoe kept time with the handles of their paddles, by striking them against the gunwale or side of the canoe, forming a sort of accompanyment, which though expressed by simple notes only, was by no means destitute of an agreeable effect. This performance took place whilst they were paddling slowly round the ship, and on its being concluded, they came alongside with the greatest confidence, and without fear or suspicion immediately entered into a commercial intercourse with our people. The two chiefs however required some little intreaty before they could be induced to venture on board. I again presented them with some valuables, amongst which was a garment for each of blue cloth, some copper, iron in various shapes, and such trinkets as I thought would prove most acceptable. In this respect either my judgment failed, or their passion for traffick and exchange is irresistible; for no sooner had they quitted the cabin, than, excepting the copper, they bartered away on deck nearly every article I had given them, for others of infinitely less utility or real value, consisting of such things as they could best appropriate to the decoration of their persons, and other ornamental purposes, giving uniformly a decided preference to copper.

In the morning of Monday the 21st, fell a few showers of rain, which were neither so heavy as to retard our business on shore, nor to prevent the friendly Indians paying us a visit on board. Convinced of our amicable disposition towards them, near the whole of the inhabitants, men, women and children, gratified their curiosity in the course of the day by paddling round the ship; for neither the ladies nor the children ventured on board. This was the case also with the generality of the men, who contentedly remained in their canoes, rowing from side to side, bartering their bows and arrows; which, with their woollen and skin garments, and a very few indifferent sea-otter skins, composed the whole of their assortment for trading; these they exchanged, in a very fair and honest manner, for copper, hawk's bells, and buttons, articles that greatly attracted their attention. Their merchandize would have been infinitely more valuable to us, had it been comprised of eatables, such as venison, wild fowl or fish, as our sportsmen and fishermen had little success in either of these pursuits. All the natives we had as yet seen, uniformly preferred offering such articles as composed their dress, arms, and implements for sale, rather than any kind of food, which might probably arise either from the country not affording them a super-abundance of provisions, or from their having early discovered that we were more curious than hungry.

In the evening, some of the canoes were observed passing from the village to the opposite shore, for the purpose, as we supposed, of inviting their neighbours to partake of the advantages of our commerce. This was confirmed the next morning, Tuesday the 22d, by the return of our friends, accompanied by several large canoes, containing near eighty persons, who after ceremoniously paddling round the ship, came alongside without the least hesitation, and conducted themselves with the utmost propriety. The principal number of these evidently belonged to the other side of the inlet; they were infinitely more cleanly than our neighbours; and their canoes were of a very different form. Those of our friends at the village, exactly corresponded with the canoes at Nootka, whilst those of our new visitors were cut off square at each end; and were, in shape, precisely like the canoes seen to the southward of cape Orford, though of greater length, and considerably larger. The commodities they brought for sale were trifles of a similar description to those offered by the other society: in all other respects, they corresponded with the generality of the few inhabitants of the country with whom we had become acquainted.

On Wednesday the 23d, we had some lightning, thunder, and rain, from the S.E.; this continued a few hours, after which the day was very serene and pleasant. Some of our gentlemen having extended their walk to the cove I had visited the first evening of our arrival, found it to communicate by a very narrow passage with an opening apparently of some extent. In consequence of this information, accompanied by Mr. Baker in the yawl, I set out the next morning, Thursday the 24th, to examine it, and found the entrance of the opening situated in the western corner of the cove, formed by two interlocking points, about a quarter of a mile from each other; these formed a channel about half a mile long, free from rocks or shoals, in which there was not less than five fathoms water. From the west end of this narrow channel the inlet is divided into two branches, one extending to the S.W. about five or six miles, the other to the north about the same distance, constituting a most complete and excellent port,[1] to all appearance perfectly free from danger, with regular soundings from four fathoms near the shores, to nine and ten fathoms in the middle, good holding ground. It occupied us the whole day to row round it, in doing which we met a few straggling Indians, whose condition seemed excessively wretched and miserable.[2] The country that surrounds this harbour varies in its elevation; in some places the shores are low level land, in others of a moderate height, falling in steep low cliffs on the sandy beach, which in most places binds the shores. It produces some small rivulets of water, is thickly wooded with trees, mostly of the pine tribe, and with some variety of shrubs. This harbour, after the gentleman who discovered it, obtained the name of PORT ORCHARD.[3] The best passage into it is found by steering from the village point for the south point of the cove, which is easily distinguished, lying from the former S. 62 W. at the distance of about 2½ miles, then hauling to the N.W. into the cove, keeping on the larboard or S.W. shore, and passing between it and the rocks in the cove; in this channel the depth of water is from nine to fifteen fathoms, gradually decreasing to five fathoms in the entrance into the port. There is also another passage round to the north of these rocks, in which there is seven fathoms water; this is narrow, and by no means so commodious to navigate as the southern channel.

On my return to the ship I understood that few of our friendly neighbours had visited the vessel. The party was evidently reduced, and those who still remained having satisfied their curiosity, or being compelled by their mode of life, were preparing to depart with all their stock and effects. These it required little labour to remove, consisting chiefly of the mats for covering their habitations, wherever it may be convenient to pitch them; their skin and woollen garments, their arms, implements, and such articles of food as they had acquired during their residence; which, with their family and dogs, all find accommodation in a single canoe; and thus the party is easily conveyed to any station, which fancy, convenience, or necessity, may direct. The dogs belonging to this tribe of Indians were numerous, and much resembled those of Pomerania, though in general somewhat larger. They were all shorn as close to the skin as sheep are in England; and so compact were their fleeces, that large portions could be lifted up by a corner without causing any separation. They were composed of a mixture of a coarse kind of wool, with very fine long hair, capable of being spun into yarn. This gave me reason to believe that their woollen clothing might in part be composed of this material mixed

[1] Port Orchard, which is about 15 miles in length. Vancouver's examination was not complete, although sufficient for his immediate purpose. At the N end he missed Liberty Bay, which branches off to the NW, and Agate Passage, a narrow water way to the NE that provides an outlet to Puget Sound. In the S he did not note the narrows leading to Dyes Inlet. The S end of Port Orchard, now named Sinclair Inlet, is the site of the major U.S. Bremerton Naval Base.

[2] Two tribes of Suquamish Indians had villages in Port Orchard and the inlets that branch off from it.

[3] H. M. Orchard, clerk of the *Discovery*.

with a finer kind of wool from some other animal, as their garments were all too fine to be manufactured from the coarse coating of the dog alone. The abundance of these garments amongst the few people we met with, indicates the animal from whence the raw material is procured, to be very common in this neighbourhood; but as they have no one domesticated excepting the dog, their supply of wool for their clothing can only be obtained by hunting the wild creature that produces it; of which we could not obtain the least information.[1]

The weather continued delightfully serene and pleasant; the carpenters had executed their task, and the topsail yards were replaced.

In the course of the forenoon of Friday the 25th, some of our Indian friends brought us a whole deer, which was the first intire animal that had been offered to us. This they had killed on the island, and from the number of persons that came from thence, the major part of the remaining inhabitants of the village, with a great number of their dogs, seemed to have been engaged in the chase. This and another deer, parts of which remained in one of their canoes, had cost all these good people nearly a day's labour, as they went over to the island for this purpose the preceding evening; yet they were amply rewarded for their exertions by a small piece of copper not a foot square. This they gladly accepted as a full compensation for their venison, on which the whole party could have made two or three good meals; such is the esteem and value with which this metal is regarded!

About four in the afternoon, agreeably to our expectations, the Chatham was seen from the mast head over the land, and about sun-set she arrived and anchored near us. Mr. Broughton informed me, that the part of the coast he had been directed to explore, consisted of an archipelago of islands[2] lying before an extensive arm of the sea stretching in a variety of branches between the N.W. north, and N.N.E. Its extent in the first direction was the most capacious, and presented an unbounded horizon.

On due consideration of all the circumstances that had fallen under my own observation, and the intelligence now imparted by Mr. Broughton, I became thoroughly convinced, that our boats alone could enable us to acquire any correct or satisfactory information respecting this broken country; and although the execution of such a service in open boats would necessarily be

---

[1] 'This was the area where the wool dog was bred, and its fleece was mixed with mountain goat wool, the down of ducks, and the cotton of fireweed to create an unusual blanket for clothing and bedding.' 'These dogs were especially domesticated for wool bearing. They were sheared like sheep'. – Gunther, *Indian Life on the Northwest Coast* (Chicago, 1972), pp. 76, 259. Vancouver notes on a later page that Whidbey walked along the shore of Whidbey Island with Indians 'attended by about forty dogs in a drove, shorn close to the skin like sheep.' When commercial cloth became readily available, late in the 19th century, there was no longer any point in maintaining any purity in the race, and the dogs soon disappeared in the mongrel packs that were characteristic of Indian villages.

[2] The San Juan Islands. Broughton's account of his explorations is printed in the appendix, to supplement Vancouver's very brief mention of them.

extremely laborious, and expose those so employed to numberless dangers and unpleasant situations, that might occasionally produce great fatigue, and protract their return to the ships; yet that mode was undoubtedly the most accurate, the most ready, and indeed the only one in our power to pursue for ascertaining the continental boundary.

The main arm of the inlet leading towards mount Rainier still remained unexplored. It became evident from the length of time Mr. Puget and Mr. Whidbey had been absent, that the inlet they had been sent to examine, had led them to a considerable distance. We had no time to spare, and as it was equally evident none ought to be lost, I directed that Mr. Johnstone, in the Chatham's cutter, should accompany me in the morning, in the Discovery's yawl, for the purpose of examining the main arm;[1] and that Mr. Broughton, on the return of our boats, which were now hourly expected, should take Mr. Whidbey in one of them, and proceed immediately to the investigation of that arm of this inlet, which we had passed on the eastern shore, stretching to the N.N.E.;[2] and I desired that the Chatham might be anchored within its entrance in some conspicuous place on the starboard side, where the Discovery or the boats would easily find her, in case the result of my inquiries should render it expedient for the vessels to proceed further in that direction.

On Saturday morning the 26th, accompanied by Mr. Baker in the yawl, and favored by pleasant weather and a fine northwardly gale, we departed, and made considerable progress. Leaving to the right the opening which had been the object of Mr. Puget and Mr. Whidbey's expedition, we directed our route along the western shore of the main inlet, which is about a league in width; and as we proceeded the smoke of several fires were seen on its eastern shore. When about four leagues on a southwardly direction from the ships, we found the course of the inlet take a south-westerly inclination, which we pursued about six miles with some little increase of width. Towards noon we landed on a point on the eastern shore, whose latitude I observed to be 47° 21',[3] round which we flattered ourselves we should find the inlet take an extensive eastwardly course. This conjecture was supported by the appearance of a very abrupt division in the snowy range of mountains immediately to the south of mount Rainier, which was very conspicuous from the ship, and the main arm of the inlet appearing to stretch in that direction from the point we were then upon. We here dined, and although our repast was soon concluded, the delay was irksome, as we were excessively anxious to ascertain the truth, of which we were not long held in suspense. For having passed round the point, we found the inlet to terminate here in an extensive circular compact bay,[4] whose waters washed the base of mount Rainier, though its elevated summit was yet at a very considerable distance from the

[1] The East Passage of Puget Sound.
[2] Possession Sound.
[3] Browns Point, in lat. 47° 18' N.
[4] Commencement Bay. The city of Tacoma now occupies its S and SW shores.

shore,[1] with which it was connected by several ridges of hills rising towards it with gradual ascent and much regularity. The forest trees, and the several shades of verdure that covered the hills, gradually decreased in point of beauty, until they became invisible; when the perpetual clothing of snow commenced, which seemed to form a horizontal line from north to south along this range of rugged mountains, from whose summit mount Rainier rose conspicuously, and seemed as much elevated above them as they were above the level of the sea; the whole producing a most grand, picturesque effect. The lower mountains as they descended to the right and left, became gradually relieved of their frigid garment; and as they approached the fertile woodland region that binds the shores of this inlet in every direction, produced a pleasing variety. We now proceeded to the N.W. in which direction the inlet from hence extended, and afforded us some reason to believe that it communicated with that under the survey of our other party.[2] This opinion was further corroborated by a few Indians, who had in a very civil manner accompanied us some time, and who gave us to understand that in the north western direction this inlet was very wide and extensive; this they expressed before we quitted our dinner station, by opening their arms, and making other signs that we should be led a long way by pursuing that route; whereas, by bending their arm, or spreading out their hand, and pointing to the space contained in the curve of the arm, or between the fore-finger and thumb, that we should find our progress soon stopped in the direction which led towards mount Rainier. The little respect which most Indians bear to truth, and their readiness to assert what they think is most agreeable for the moment, or to answer their own particular wishes and inclinations, induced me to place little dependance on this information, although they could have no motive for deceiving us.

About a dozen of these friendly people had attended at our dinner, one part of which was a venison party. Two of them, expressing a desire to pass the line of separation drawn between us, were permitted to do so. They sat down by us, and ate of the bread and fish that we gave them without the least hesitation; but on being offered some of the venison, though they saw us eat it with great relish, they could not be induced to taste it. They received it from us with great disgust, and presented it round to the rest of the party, by whom it underwent a very strict examination. Their conduct on this occasion left no doubt in our minds that they believed it to be human flesh, an impression which it was highly expedient should be done away. To satisfy them that it was the flesh of the deer, we pointed to the skins of the animal they had about them. In reply to this they pointed to each other, and made signs that could not be misunderstood, that it was the flesh of human beings,

---

[1] In spite of appearing to be relatively close at hand, Mount Rainier is about 45 miles from Tacoma.

[2] This assumption was correct. Vancouver had entered Dalco Passage, which links the S ends of East Passage and Colvos Passage. Between them lies Vachon Island, 11 miles long. Puget had surveyed its W side; Vancouver had travelled down its E side.

and threw it down in the dirt, with gestures of great aversion and displeasure. At length we happily convinced them of their mistake by shewing them a haunch we had in the boat, by which means they were undeceived, and some of them ate of the remainder of the pye with a good appetite.

This behaviour, whilst in some measure tending to substantiate their knowledge or suspicions that such barbarities have existence, led us to conclude, that the character given of the natives of North-West America does not attach to every tribe. These people have been represented not only as accustomed inhumanly to devour the flesh of their conquered enemies; but also to keep certain servants, or rather slaves, of their own nation, for the sole purpose of making the principal part of the banquet, to satisfy the unnatural savage gluttony of the chiefs of this country, on their visits to each other. Were such barbarities practised once a month, as is stated, it would be natural to suppose these people, so inured, would not have shewn the least aversion to eating flesh of any description; on the contrary, it is not possible to conceive a greater degree of abhorrence than was manifested by these good people, until their minds were made perfectly easy that it was not human flesh we offered them to eat. This instance must necessarily exonerate at least this particular tribe from so barbarous a practice; and, as their affinity to the inhabitants of Nootka, and of the sea-coast, to the south of that place, in their manners and customs, admits of little difference, it is but charitable to hope those also, on a more minute inquiry, may be found not altogether deserving such a character.[1] They are not, however, free from the general failing attendant on

[1] In 1941 F. W. Howay stated that 'The established opinion today is that the Indians of the Northwest Coast were not cannibals', and took the view that 'not one well authenticated instance of cannibalism had been produced'. – *Voyages of the 'Columbia'*, 66n. But doubts persisted, and in 1973 Warren Cook could still refer to it as 'the touchiest [topic] in Northwest Coast ethnography'. – *Flood Tide of Empire*, p. 190. Christon Archer has now refuted the charge of cannibalism conclusively and explained the circumstances that gave rise to it in a paper entitled 'Cannibalism in the Early History of the Northwest Coast: Enduring Myths and Neglected Realities' (*Canadian Historical Review* LXI (1980), 453–79). It sprang initially from statements made in the published journals of Cook and Meares. Archer points out that the records of the first three Spanish expeditions, which visited the coast in 1774–9, contain no suggestions that their leaders either found, or expected to find, any evidence that the Indians were cannibals. Cook, by contrast, 'began his explorations in New Zealand and the South Pacific, [and] he and his men were accustomed to witnessing and reporting cannibalism'. He had come to regard it as a characteristic of primitive peoples, and readily believed that 'the horrid practice of devouring their enemies' existed amongst the Indians at Nootka 'as much as at New Zealand, and other South Seas Islands'. – *Journals*, III, 297. Some members of the expedition were not convinced; Clerke, King and Samwell all reserved judgement in their journals, and it is evident that Vancouver shared their doubts. But many years were to pass before those journals were published, whereas Cook's account appeared fairly promptly. Thanks to his great personal prestige his opinion prevailed, and his journal 'became the authoritative handbook for all who would navigate the North Pacific and contact the Northwest Coast inhabitants'. John Ledyard had already added a grisly detail to the charge of cannibalism in his unauthorized account of Cook's third voyage, published in 1783, in which he claimed that he had been offered 'a human arm roasted', had tasted it himself

a savage life. One of them having taken a knife and fork to imitate our manner of eating, found means to secrete them under his garment; but, on his being detected, gave up his plunder with the utmost good humour and unconcern.

They accompanied us from three or four miserable huts, near the place where we had dined, for about four miles; during which time they exchanged the only things they had to dispose of, their bows, arrows, and spears, in the most fair and honest manner, for hawk's bells, buttons, beads, and such useless commodities.

The first information of the natives we found perfectly correct; and it was not long before we had every reason to give credit to the second, by finding the inlet divided into two branches, one taking a northwardly direction towards the ships,[1] giving that which, in the morning, we had considered to be the western shore of the main inlet, the appearance of an island, eight or nine leagues in circuit;[2] the other stretched to the southwestward;[3] and into which ran a very strong tide. Although there was little doubt of our having been preceded in the examination of this branch, yet, as the strength of the

and found it 'very odious'. Cook's opinion was accepted as gospel by the maritime fur traders, and in particular by John Meares, who was at Nootka in September 1788. His journal, published in 1790, attracted wide attention because of his involvement in the Nootka Sound controversy. Meares stated repeatedly that the Indians were cannibals, and that Chief Maquinna 'was so much attached to this detestable banquet, as to kill a slave every moon, to gratify his unnatural appetite'. – *Voyages*, p. 225. He claimed, moreover, that Maquinna 'had avowed the practice'. – *ibid*, p. 256. Archer notes that the trading captains found the conviction that they were dealing with cannibals useful in some respects. It helped with crew discipline; Meares noted that 'the idea of being eaten by the Americans [Indians] haunted the imaginations and preyed upon the spirits of many of our people'. – *Voyages*, p. 191. And when they came to write an account of their adventures, at a time when books on exploration and primitive peoples were popular, cannibalism 'added spice to a travel narrative and sold books'. Archer aptly characterizes the fur traders' narratives as 'an interesting blend of fact, fiction and misunderstanding', and comments further: 'Although Meares warped the truth in almost every respect, no one bothered to question his material on cannibalism.' Cook's opinion was accepted by many later Spanish visitors as well as by the fur traders. For example, Martínez, who had sailed with the first Spanish voyage in 1774, returned to Nootka in 1789 and after spending some months there wrote in his diary that the Indian chiefs were 'accustomed, when there is a scarcity of fish, to eat the boys whom they take as prisoners'. – Quoted in Iris Wilson (ed.), *Noticias de Nutka*, by José Mariano Moziño (Seattle, 1970), p. 22n. He added that Maquinna and his brother 'have been the most addicted to this use of human flesh'. Caamaño blackened Maquinna's reputation further by describing the grim game of blindman's-buff by which it was alleged that Maquinna selected his victims – a story repeated by one of the Franciscan fathers who was at Nootka in 1792. – For translations of these statements see Cook, *Flood Tide of Empire*, pp. 190, 296. Upon a good many occasions traders and others were undoubtedly shown or offered human hands which appeared to be cooked, and which were taken as proof of cannibalism; but it is reasonably certain that these were in fact war trophies – the dried, shrunken and preserved (rather than cooked) hands of defeated enemies. It is notable that neither of the white men who lived for a considerable time with the Nootka Indians – John McKay in 1786–7, and John Jewitt in 1803–5 – makes any mention of cannibalism.

[1] Colvos Passage.
[2] Vachon Island.   [3] The Narrows.

influx indicated its extremity to be at some distance, I determined, as we were well supplied for the excursion, to embrace the advantage of so favourable an opportunity of keeping the larboard shore on board, and of examining such inlets as might be found leading to the left; that, in the event of Mr. Puget having been unable to accomplish the task assigned him, our survey might be completed without another expedition into this region. With the assistance of the strong tide, we rapidly passed through a fair navigable channel, near half a league wide, with soundings from 24 to 30 fathoms, free from any appearance of shoals, rocks, or other interruptions. The eastern shore was found nearly straight and compact; but on the western, three wide openings were seen,[1] whose terminations were not distinguishable; and the strength with which the tide flowed into the two northernmost, induced us to consider them as very extensive.

Having advanced in a direction S. 32 W. about three leagues from the south, or inner point of entrance, into an opening, situated in latitude 47° 19½', longitude 237° 42',[2] we halted about eight in the evening for the night, on a small island, lying about a mile from the eastern shore.[3] The general character of the situation in which we had now arrived, indicated it to be a continuation of the main branch of the inlet, we had been thus long navigating. The insular appearance of its western side, the rapidity of the flood tide, and its increasing width, gave us reason to suppose we should find it still more extensive. Whilst employed in arranging our matters for the night, we discovered, coming out of the southernmost opening, two small vessels, which, at first, were taken for Indian canoes, but, on using our glasses, they were considered to be our two boats.[4] The evening was cloudy; and, closing in very soon, prevented a positive decision. The original idea was, however, somewhat confirmed on firing two muskets, which were not answered.

During the night, we had some rain, with a fresh gale from the S.E. which abated by the morning; the rain still continued, but not so violently as to prevent our proceeding. At four o'clock on Sunday morning, the 27th, we again embarked, and steered about S.W. by S.; in which direction the inlet seemed to stretch to some distance; and the appearance of the southern land gave rise to an opinion of its terminating in a river. The space we had so considered was, by seven o'clock, proved to be a low swampy compact shore, forming the southern extremity of the inlet in this direction, about two leagues from our last resting place. The inlet here terminated in an expansive though

[1] Hale Passage, Carr Inlet and Balch Passage.

[2] Point Evans, in The Narrows, seems to be the point meant. Its position is lat. 47° 17' N, long. 122° 34' W (237° 26' E).

[3] Ketron Island.

[4] The two parties very nearly met, as Puget sighted Vancouver's campfire: 'In the Evening we reached the Southern Branch [Nisqually Reach], from whence we saw a Fire on Long Island [Ketron Island] where we had landed on Tuesday last, but supposing it to be Indians & having a fair Wind & Tide, we proceeded down towards the Ships'. – Puget, May 26.

shallow bay,[1] across which a flat of sand extended upwards of a mile from its shores;[2] on which was lying an immense quantity of drift wood, consisting chiefly of very large trees. The country behind for some distance, was low, then rose gradually to a moderate height; and, like the eastern shores of the inlet, was covered with wood, and diversified with pleasant inequalities of hill and dale, though not enriched with those imaginary parks and pleasure grounds we had been accustomed to behold nearer to the sea coast; the whole presenting one uninterrupted wilderness.

From hence the direction of the inlet was about N.W. by N. still preserving a considerable width;[3] the western shore appearing to be formed by a group of islands. Our progress was a little retarded by the rain in the forenoon; but, about mid-day the clouds dispersed, though not sufficiently early to procure an observation for the latitude. We had now reached a point on the larboard shore, where the inlet was again divided into two other large branches, one leading to the south-westward, the other towards the north.[4] As my plan was to pursue the examination of the larboard shore, the south-west branch became our first object. This we found divided into two narrow channels, leading to the southward,[5] with the appearance of two small coves to the northward.[6] Up the westernmost of the former,[7] about six miles, we took up our abode for the night, which was serene and pleasant.

Early in the morning, Monday 28th, we again started, and soon found the channel[8] to terminate about a league from the place where we had slept the night before, as the rest had done, in low swampy ground, with a shallow sandy bank extending to some distance into the channel. Here we met, as had been frequently the case, a few miserable Indians in their temporary habitations; these either had nothing to dispose of, or were not inclined to have intercourse with us; the latter seemed most probable, as our visit was not attended with that cordial reception we had generally experienced. This however might have been occasioned by our having disturbed them unusually early from their rest,[9] we made them some presents which they accepted very

[1] Nisqually Reach.

[2] Nisqually Flats, at the mouth of the Nisqually River.

[3] The continuation of Nisqually Reach to the NW.

[4] The point was Johnson Point; the branch to the SW was Dana Passage; the larger branch to the N, Case Inlet. Neither Vancouver nor Puget mentions Henderson Inlet, which runs southward from Johnson Point.

[5] Eld Inlet and Budd Inlet. Olympia, capital of the State of Washington, is at the S end of Budd Inlet, which Vancouver did not explore himself.

[6] Peale Passage and Squaxin Passage.

[7] Eld Inlet.

[8] Here and later in the sentence 'channel' has replaced the word 'canal' in the first edition.

[9] This welcome contrasted sharply with that accorded to Puget, who had been in Eld Inlet (which he refers to as 'Friendly Inlet') only two days before: 'In our Way down we landed for a Short time & were received by the Inhabitants with all the Friendship and Hospitality we could have expected. These people I should suppose were about Sixty in Number of all Ages and Descriptions they lived under a Kind of Shed open at the Front

coolly, and having satisfied ourselves with the extent of the inlet in this direction we returned, and about nine o'clock landed to breakfast about two miles within the main entrance of the south-west branch.[1] We left behind us to the westward the appearance of two or three small islands or points, that might form similar inlets to those we had already examined, leading to the south. These could be of little extent, as scarcely any visible tide was found in the narrowest parts.

From the length of time also that the other boats had been absent previous to our departure from the ships, together with the appearance and direction of the inlet, I entertained little doubt that the greater part of what we had seen, as also that which we were now leaving unexplored, had undergone the examination of Mr. Puget and Mr. Whidbey.[2] This induced me to return on board, considering we were now passing our time to little purpose; and as the branch of the main inlet before us stretching to the northward,[3] presented every prospect of communicating with some of those we had passed on Saturday evening, we pursued that route. The situation we quitted this morning, according to my survey, was in latitude 47° 3′, longitude 237° 18′, about 17 leagues from the sea coast of New Albion, towards which, from the moderate height of the country, there could be little doubt of an easy intercourse by land. About noon we landed on a point of the eastern shore, whose latitude is 47° 15$\frac{1}{2}$′, longitude 237° 17$\frac{1}{2}$′. From hence we proceeded with

and Sides.... Though it was perfectly Curiosity which had induced us to land, yet that was the sooner satisfied, by the horrid Stench which came from all parts of these Habitations, & glad were we to return to the Boats, having previously distributed Medals Trinkets & other Articles among the different Families, with which they were highly delighted. The Natives had but Two Sea Otter Skins which were purchased & a Variety of Marmot, Rabbit Racoon Deer & Bear Skins were also procured. The Men had a War Garment on, it consisted of a very thick Hide supposed made from the Moose Deer, & well prepared. I have no doubt but it is a Sufficient Shield against Arrows, though not against Fire Arms. The Garment reaches from the Shoulders down to the Knees, this however was got in exchange for a small piece of Copper, from which we may suppose that they are not of much Value, they likewise disposed of some well constructed Bows and Arrows, in Short it was only to ask, & have your Wish gratified. the only Difference, I perceived between our present Companions and former Visitors, were the Extravagance with Which their Faces were Ornamented, Streaks of Red Ochre & Black Glimmer were on some, others entirely with the Former, & a few that gave the Preference to the Latter – every Person had a fashion of his own, & to us who were Strangers to Indians, this Sight conveyed a Stronger Idea of the Savageness of the Native Inhabitants, than any other Circumstance we had hitherto met with; not but their Conduct, friendly & inoffensive, had already merited our warmest Approbation, but their Appearance was absolutely terrific... Though we could not behold these Ornaments with the same satisfactory Eye as themselves, yet on receiving the looking Glasses, each appeared well Satisfied with his own Fashion, at least the Paint was not at all altered.' – May 26. Eld Inlet and the other inlets at the S end of Puget Sound were the home of the Sahehwamish, Salishan Indians who belonged to the Nisqually dialectic group.

[1] Vancouver was back near Johnson Point, where Nisqually Reach and the S end of Case Inlet meet.

[2] This assumption proved to be correct.   [3] Case Inlet.

a pleasant southerly gale, to ascertain if any communication existed, as we had before conjectured. The further we advanced the more doubtful it became, until at length, about three leagues north of the above point, it terminated like all the other channels in a shallow flat before a low swampy bog. Here we dined, and about four in the afternoon set out on our return by the way we had come, purposing to stop for the night at a cove a little to the south of the point we were upon at noon, where we arrived about nine in the evening. Mr. Johnstone, who had kept along the western shore in order to look into a small opening we had passed in sailing down,[1] had the advantage by being on the weather shore, and had arrived a short time before us. He informed me the opening was very narrow, and could extend but a little way before it joined that which we had quitted this morning. Whilst he was on shore for the purpose of taking the necessary angles, a deer came down to the beach, which Mr. Le Mesurier,[2] the gentleman who had attended him in the boat, fired at, and fortunately killed. It proved to be a very fine buck, and afforded our people a good fresh meal, which was some compensation for the disappointment we experienced in not finding a passage home by the route we had lately pursued.

About day-break, as usual, on Tuesday morning the 29th, we again resumed our voyage towards the ships, which were now distant about 45 miles. Towards noon we landed on the north point of entrance into the second opening we had passed on Saturday evening; the latitude of which is 47° 15½′.[3] The strength of the ebb tide facilitated our progress, and our conjectures were soon proved to have been well founded in this being the same inlet, which I had directed the other party to examine. We were carried with great rapidity for some time up the branch leading to the northward,[4] and through this channel we arrived in the evening on board, without seeing any other opening leading to the westward. The land composing the eastern shore of this channel, and the western shore of that we had pursued on Saturday morning, was now ascertained to be the most extensive island we had yet met with in our several examinations of this coast; which after my friend Captain Vashon of the navy, I have distinguished by the name of VASHON'S ISLAND.[5]

Late on the preceding Saturday night, or rather on Sunday morning, our other party had returned. It was them we had seen the first evening of our excursion from the island, and they very distinctly saw our fire; but as they did not hear the report of the muskets, concluded it a fire of the natives, not having the least idea of any of our boats being in that neighbourhood. They

---

[1] The entrance to Pickering Passage.

[2] William LeMesurier, master's mate of the *Chatham*.

[3] The entrance to Carr Inlet, between Fox and McNeil islands. If the S point of Fox Island was meant, the lat. would be 47° 13′ N.

[4] Colvos Passage.

[5] James Vachon, later Admiral Vachon, who was captain of the *Europa* when Vancouver served in her as first lieutenant in 1787–89.

had explored all those parts of the inlet we had passed by, and found the three openings we left unexamined, the first afternoon, leading to the westward, to be channels dividing that shore into three islands;[1] and those we had not attended to on Monday morning formed two small branches leading to the S.W.; the westernmost of which extends to the latitude 47° 6′,[2] about two leagues to the westward of our researches in that direction; that in which the deer was shot communicated with the S.W. branch of the inlet by a very narrow channel.[3] They had also passed the opening we had pursued leading towards mount Rainier;[4] but agreeably to my directions had not prosecuted its examination; the termination of every other opening in the land they had ascertained. Thus by our joint efforts, we had completely explored every turning of this extensive inlet; and to commemorate Mr. Puget's exertions, the south extremity of it I named PUGET'S SOUND.[5]

The Chatham had sailed on Monday, and Mr. Whidbey had departed in the Discovery's launch for the purpose of carrying into effect the orders I had left with Mr. Broughton.

Mr. Puget had little more to communicate respecting his late expedition than what had fallen under my own observation, excepting the disorderly behaviour of an Indian tribe, he had met with at some distance up the first arm leading to the westward within the narrows,[6] whose conduct had materially differed from that of the natives in general; and in particular from that of a party consisting of about twenty natives whom they had before seen in that route, and who had behaved with their usual friendship and civility. In this arm they found the shores in general low and well wooded. About eight in the evening, attended by some of the natives in two canoes, they landed for the night. These people could not be invited nearer our party than about an hundred yards, where they remained attentive to all the operations until the tents were pitched, when it became necessary to discharge some loaded muskets, the noise of which they heard without any apparent surprize, and exclaimed *poo!* after every report. They soon afterwards paddled away to the westward. The next morning Mr. Puget proceeded up the arm, which took a N.E. direction about a mile wide, narrowing as they advanced to one-fourth of that width; the soundings were found regular from eight to thirteen fathoms. In this situation they saw a canoe making towards them, on which they rested on their oars to wait its approach. The canoe suddenly stopped, and no offers of presents, nor signs of friendly inclinations, could induce the

[1] Fox, McNeil and Anderson islands.
[2] Totten Inlet. The lat. given is that of the W end of Oyster Bay, at the extremity of the inlet.
[3] Pickering Passage.
[4] Commencement Bay.
[5] As already noted, this name is now generally applied to the whole of the waterways S of the Strait of Juan de Fuca, but Vancouver's chart indicates that he intended it to apply only to the southern waters, which Puget had explored.
[6] Carr Inlet is meant.

Indians to venture near the boat. In order to remove their apprehensions, Mr. Puget fastened some medals, copper, and trinkets, to a piece of wood which he left floating on the water; and when the boat was at a sufficient distance, the Indians picked it up. After repeating this twice or thrice they ventured, though not without some trepidation, alongside the boats. In their persons they seemed more robust than the generality of the inhabitants; most of them had lost their right eye, and were much pitted with the small pox. They now attended the boats for a short time, and having received some additional presents, returned to the shore. The whole of their conduct exhibited much suspicion and distrust. When any question was endeavoured to be put to them, they replied by *poo! poo!* pointing at the same time to a small island on which the party had breakfasted, and where some birds had been shot.[1] They seemed well acquainted with the value of iron and copper, but would not dispose of their weapons, or any other article in exchange for either. About noon the party landed to dine;[2] and whilst they were preparing to haul the seine before a fresh water brook, six canoes were seen paddling hastily round the point of the cove they were in, and directing their course towards the boats. The suspicious behaviour of those whom they had parted with in the morning, rendered it highly expedient that they should be upon their guard against any hostile design of these people; on whose approach, a line on the beach was drawn, to separate the two parties from each other; which was readily understood, and obeyed. They now divided their numbers into two sets, one remaining on shore with their bows and quivers, and other retiring to their canoes, where they quietly seated themselves.

Thus, with every appearance of good order being established, the officers went to dinner, on an elevated spot a few yards from the water-side, where the crews were dining in their respective boats, and in readiness to act in case of any alarm. On a seventh canoe joining the Indian party, those on the beach immediately embarked; and the whole number, amounting to twenty four persons, evidently entered into a consultation, during which they frequently pointed to those in the boats, as well as to the officers on the hill. This conduct tended to increase the suspicions that their inclinations were otherwise than friendly, however imprudent they might deem it, on the present moment, to carry their intentions into execution. But as our party could not be surprized, and as they were ready to act immediately on the defensive, Mr. Puget and the other gentlemen did not consider their situation alarming, and preferred quietly finishing their repast, to that of indicating any signs of distrust or apprehension, by a precipitate retreat. Towards the conclusion of their conference, three of their canoes were stealing near to the boats; but, on finding they were discovered by the officers, instantly returned. At this time, an eighth

---

[1] Raft Island. Referred to by Puget as Crow Island, because of the great number of crows there, some of which were shot for food.

[2] The landing was probably in Von Geldern Cove. After the brush with the Indians Puget referred to it as Alarm Cove.

canoe joined the party; on which all of them paddled to the beach, jumped on shore and strung their bows. This was manifestly preparing for an attack, as they had not ever been seen, on any former occasion, with their bows strung. The very man who appeared the principal in the canoe, they had met in the morning, and with whom so much trouble was taken to obtain his good opinion, now seemed the leader of this party; and, with an arrow across his bow in readiness for immediate use, advanced towards the station of the officers, whilst others of the party were moving that way. Such measures however were prudently resorted to, without proceeding to extremities, as obliged them all to retreat to the line of separation, where they again held a close and long consultation; and our gentlemen having now no object to detain them on shore, they re-embarked, leaving the Indians at the line of separation, sharpening their arrows and spears on stones, apparently much inclined, though irresolute, to attempt hostilities. In this undecided state of their minds, Mr. Puget thought it might answer a good purpose to fire a swivel, shotted; the effect of which, might teach them to respect, hereafter, our powers of defence, and induce them, on the present occasion, to prefer a pacific deportment, and preserve the lives of many, that must have been lost, had they been so injudicious as to have commenced an attack. Although, on the report of the gun, or the distant effect of the shot, which was fired over the water, not the least visible astonishment or apprehension was expressed, yet, the measure was almost instantly attended with every expected good consequence. Their bows were soon unstrung; and instead of their menacing a combat, their weapons became articles of traffic, in common with other trifles they had to dispose of, for copper, buttons, knives, beads, and other ornaments; in which friendly intercourse, they accompanied the boats until towards the evening, when they peaceably took their leave, and returned to their home.[1]

From Mr. Puget I likewise understood, that, in the course of his excursion, himself and party had visited, and had received the visits of several other tribes of Indians, whose behaviour had been uniformly civil, courteous, and friendly. Why this party, whose unfriendly intentions were too evident to be mistaken, should have been induced to assume, without the least provocation, a character so diametrically opposite to that which, in every other instance, seemed to govern their general conduct, is certainly very mysterious, and renders the foregoing an extraordinary circumstance, for which it is difficult to account.

The country we had mutually explored,[2] did not appear, to either party,

[1] Vancouver's account of this near-clash with the Indians was derived from the first-hand descriptions given by Puget and Menzies in their journals and differs from them only in a few minor details.

[2] Vancouver does not do justice to Puget's survey, which included Colvos Passage, The Narrows, Hale Passage, Carr Inlet, Nisqually Reach, Case Inlet, Pickering Passage, and Totten, Eld and Budd inlets. Many details are given in a narrative appended to Puget's log. He bestowed names on seven features, but Vancouver did not adopt any of them: Dinner Point (now Fosdick Point), Indian Cove (Wollochet Bay), Crow Island (Raft

from our transient view of it, materially to differ from that which has already been described, either in its several productions from the soil, or in its general appearance of fertility. It did not, however, possess that beautiful variety of landscape; being an almost impenetrable wilderness of lofty trees, rendered nearly impassable by the underwood, which uniformly incumbers the surface.

By the termination of the western range of snowy mountains in their southern direction, taking place considerably to the north-westward, and the more elevated land intercepting the view of such mountains as may extend from the eastern range, southward of mount Rainier, we were presented with more than the whole southern horizon of land moderately high, extending as far as the eye could reach, diversified by eminences and vallies, affording a probability of an easy intercourse by land with the sea coast; where some places of shelter for small vessels may possibly still be found, which, in the event of an establishment being formed, would prove highly advantageous.

The scarcity of water has before been mentioned as the only disadvantage that the interior country seemed to labour under; but in Mr. Puget's survey, a greater supply of water was found than in the inlets and bays that underwent my own particular examination. The country had also been considered by us as nearly destitute of inhabitants; but this opinion we found to be erroneous, from the other party having, by accident, fallen in with near 150 Indians, and having seen several deserted villages.

The point near our present station, forming the north point of the bay, hitherto called the Village point, I have distinguished by the name of RESTORATION POINT, having celebrated that memorable event, whilst at anchor under it;[1] and from the result of my observations made on the spot, it is situated in latitude 47° 30', longitude 237° 46'.[2] During our stay the tides were observed to be materially affected, by the direction or force of the winds, not only in respect to their rise and fall, but as to the time of high water. The former seldom exceeded seven or eight feet: and the latter generally took place about 4^h 10' after the moon passed the meridian. The variation of the compass, by six sets of azimuths taken on board, differing from 18° to 22°, gave the mean result of 19° 36' east variation.

Nothing occurring to detain us, on Wednesday morning, the 30th, with a pleasant southerly breeze, we directed our course to the opening under the examination of Mr. Broughton;[3] the entrance of which lies from Restoration point, N. 20 E. five leagues distant. The breeze, as was usual, dying away, we advanced very slowly; towards noon, it was succeeded by a N.W. wind, accompanied with the flood-tide, so that, by the time we had worked up the

Island), Alarm Cove (probably Von Geldern Cove), Long Island (Ketron Island), Wednesday Island (probably Herron Island) and Friendly Inlet (Eld Inlet, in which Puget visited a village of friendly Indians).

[1] 'Fired 17 Guns it being the Anniversary of King Charles's happy Restoration [in 1660].' – Puget, May 29.

[2] Its position is approximately lat. 47° 35' N, long. 122° 29' W (237° 31' E).

[3] Possession Sound.

opening, the ebb tide was returning not only with great strength, but attended by a sort of counter-tide, or under tow, that so affected the ship, as to render her almost unmanageable, notwithstanding we had a fresh breeze, and were assisted in working in by our boats. Having advanced about three miles within the entrance, which we found about half a league across, and, in the evening, seeing no appearance of the Chatham, a gun was fired, which was immediately answered from behind a point of land, on the starboard, or eastern shore,[1] where, soon afterwards, we saw the Chatham bearing a light at her mast-head for our guidance; and, though within the distance of two miles, it was near midnight before we anchored in 32 fathoms water, about a cable's length from her; not having been able to gain soundings with 110 fathoms of line, until we reached this station.

The next morning, Thursday 31st, we found ourselves about a cable's length from the shore, in a capacious sound; whose entrance bore by compass from S. 2 W. to S. 30 W., about six miles from us, from whence it extended in a true N.N.E. direction. To the north was a high round island,[2] bearing from N. 18 W. to N. 33 W.; on each side of which an opening was seen stretching to the northward.[3] These openings were separated by a high narrow slip of land,[4] which also appeared to be insular.[5] The eastern side of the sound formed a deep bay, apparently bounded by solid compact land of a moderate height.

Mr. Broughton informed me, he had navigated the east side of the round island in the brig, and had examined the eastern shore of the sound, which was, as it appeared to be, a compact shore. Mr. Whidbey, in our launch, accompanied by Lieutenant Hanson in the Chatham's, had, on the 29th, been dispatched to the two openings to the northward, with directions to examine the right hand, or easternmost, first; and, on finding its termination, to return with such information to the Chatham, before they proceeded to visit the other; that, in the event of the Discovery's arrival previous to their return, the vessels might follow them in such pursuit, observing to keep on the eastern shore until they should find it divided into two branches. This being the third day of their absence, it was concluded they had found the easternmost opening to be of considerable extent; in consequence of which I determined to follow them, but the weather being calm and gloomy, with some rain, we were prevented moving. On a low point of land near the ship, I observed the latitude to be 47° 57½', longitude 237° 58'. A light favourable breeze sprang up shortly after noon; but before the anchor was at the ship's bows it again fell calm,

---

[1] Now Elliot Point. 'Mr. Broughton named the Point from the vast abundance of wild roses that grew upon it *Rose Point*.' – Menzies, May 31.

[2] Gedney Island, known locally as Hat Island.

[3] Port Susan to the E and Saratoga Passage to the W.

[4] The narrow peninsula at the S end of Camano Island. (When Henry Kellet, R. N., named the island in 1846 or 1847 he misspelled Caamaño's name.)

[5] 'insulated' in the first edition.

with much rain, which obliged us to remain quiet. The Chatham however weighed, and being soon off the bank, which does not reach a quarter of a mile from the shore, was instantly out of soundings, and was driven by the ebb-tide until nine in the evening to the entrance of the sound. At this time a fresh southerly breeze springing up we weighed, and directed our course northward, to pass on the western side of the round island.

We had now been stationary upwards of 20 hours, and during that time the tide or current had constantly sat out; the like was observed by Mr. Broughton during his continuance in the same place. The southerly wind, attended by a heavy fall of rain, soon became so faint, that by eleven at night we had proceeded only five miles. Here we were obliged to anchor in twenty fathoms water, hard sandy bottom, near half way between the island and the point that divides the two openings,[1] which are about a league asunder.

About six in the morning of Friday, June the first, assisted by the flood tide, and a light southeasterly wind, we proceeded up the eastern arm; the entrance of which is about a mile wide,[2] with soundings from 75 to 80 fathoms, dark sandy bottom. The weather being rainy, calm, or attended with light variable winds, most of the forenoon we made little progress. During this interval the Chatham gained some advantage of us, and about noon proceeded with a favourable breeze from the southward up the opening. The haze which had obscured the land all the fore part of the day, gave the inlet an extensive appearance, without any visible terminatiom: but on the fog's dispersing, it seemed to be closed in every direction, excepting that by which we had entered; but as soundings could not be gained with fifty fathoms of line, we continued our course up the inlet until about two o'clock, at which time we had advanced six miles from the entrance; and being perfectly satisfied that the inlet finished in the manner common to all we had hitherto examined, the signal was made for the Chatham to bring up, and we shortened sail accordingly. In a few minutes she was discovered to be a-ground, and had made the signal for assistance. On this we stood towards her, and anchored about a mile from her in 20 fathoms water, sandy bottom, and about half that distance from the eastern shore,[3] which was the nearest land. Our boats were immediately sent to her relief; but as the tide subsided very fast, they could only lay out anchors for heaving her off on the returning flood. Although the upper part of the inlet had appeared to be perfectly closed, yet it was not impossible a channel might exist on the western or opposite shore, which by interlocking points might have been invisible to us on board, and through which our absent party might have found a passage. To ascertain this fact, I went in the yawl; and found the depth of water suddenly to decrease on leaving the ship to ten, seven, and two fathoms. We continued our

[1] Between Gedney Island and Camano Head, the S end of Camano Island.
[2] Its width is about two miles.
[3] This anchorage was about a mile N of Kayak Point, on the E shore of Port Susan.

researches in one and two fathoms water to the opposite side,[1] where we landed nearly a-breast of the ship, and found the shores of the inlet to be straight, compact, and about two miles apart. In several places we attempted to land near the upper end, but found ourselves as often repulsed by a flat sandy shoal, which extended directly across. The land there seemed of a swampy nature, was thinly wooded, and through it was the appearance of a shallow rivulet falling into the sea; further back it was more elevated, and the surrounding country being covered with a similar growth of timber to that before noticed, made us conclude the land to be equally fertile.

This examination perplexed me extremely to account for an error that had certainly taken place. For under the conviction that this inlet had been found navigable by the boats, I should not have hesitated to have prosecuted my way hither in the ship at midnight, in consequence of the party not having made any report to the contrary. This could only be attributed to a misunderstanding of the orders given, or to some unfortunate accident having befallen them. The latter we had no reason to apprehend, unless from an attack of the Indians, which was not very likely to have happened, as we saw not the least indication of either permanent or temporary habitations. I called on board the Chatham on my return, and was happy to understand that there was little probability of her receiving any injury, having grounded on a muddy bank; and that there was every prospect of her floating off the next tide.[2] In sounding to lay out their anchors, it became evident that in the very direction in which they had sailed to their then station, they had run upwards of half a mile on this bank in two fathoms water, in consequence of the unpardonable negligence of the man at the lead, who had announced false soundings, and for which he was deservedly punished.[3] She was hove off about midnight, and anchored near us without having received the least damage.

The Chatham being in readiness by ten the next morning, Saturday the 2d, with a light northerly breeze, attended with gloomy weather and some rain, we directed our route back by the way we had come, and it was not until three o'clock that we reached the sound, where we again anchored in fifty fathoms, a quarter of a mile from the eastern shore, and about six times that distance to the eastward of the arm we had quitted, which forms an excellent harbour, well sheltered from all winds; but during our short stay there we saw no appearance of any fresh water. Here our position was before

[1] The whole of the N part of Port Susan is very shallow. Davis Slough provides a narrow communication between its NE corner and Skagit Bay to the N, but shoals made it impossible for Vancouver to become aware of this. As it is Davis Slough that cuts Camano Island off from the mainland, he was also unaware that it was in fact an island.

[2] The grounding was turned to some account: [we] 'took this opportunity of repairing part of the Copper on the Starbd. Bow which had rubb'd off by the Bill of the Anchor.' – Heddington, June 2.

[3] Presumably the culprit was David Dorman, seaman, who was punished with three dozen lashes on June 2 for neglect of duty.

a small bay,[1] into which flowed two excellent streams, but these were so nearly on a level with the sea, that it became necessary either to procure the water at low tide, or at some distance up the brook; which latter was easily effected, as our boats were admitted to where the fresh water fell from the elevated land. In this situation the observed latitude was 48° 2½′, longitude 237° 57½′, being six miles S.S.E. from our last anchorage.

As there was little doubt now remaining that the party had proceeded to the examination of the other inlet, and as the weather was thick and hazy with some rain, a gun was now and then fired to direct them to the ships in case they should be on their return.

In the course of the afternoon we were tolerably successful with the seine, as we had also been in the above harbour, in taking a quantity of fish similar to those we procured in port Discovery. About eight in the evening we had the satisfaction of hearing our gun answered; and at nine the boats safely returned to the vessels.

Mr. Whidbey informed me, that on his return from the survey of the port we had quitted in the morning, he saw the Chatham working off the east end of the round island at so little distance, that he concluded the boats could not have escaped the observation of those on board; and under that impression, and his anxiety to forward this tedious service, he had availed himself of a favorable southerly wind, and flood tide, to prosecute his examination of the other branch,[2] whose entrance he had found something wider than the harbour we had left, having sixty fathoms depth of water, with a soft muddy bottom. Its general direction led N.N.W. Having advanced about four miles, they found, on a low projecting point of the western shore,[3] a village containing a numerous tribe of the natives. But as my orders, as well as the general inclination of the officers, were to prevent by all possible means the chance of any misunderstanding, it was the uniform practice to avoid landing in the presence of considerable numbers; and as it was now the dinner time of our party, Mr. Whidbey very prudently made choice of the opposite shore, in the hope of making a quiet meal without the company of the Indians. Having reached the place where they intended to land, they were met by upwards of two hundred, some in their canoes with their families, and others walking along the shore, attended by about forty dogs in a drove, shorn close to the skin like sheep. Notwithstanding their numbers, it was important to land for the purpose of taking angles; and they had the satisfaction of being received on shore with every mark of cordial friendship. Mr. Whidbey however, thought it prudent to remain no longer in their society than was absolutely necessary; and having finished the business for which he had landed, he instantly embarked, and continued his route up the inlet until the evening, when he landed for the night about nine miles within its entrance. In the morning they again pursued their inquiry, and soon after they had landed to

[1] Tulalip Bay.
[2] Saratoga Passage.   [3] Probably East Point.

breakfast, they were visited by a large canoe full of Indians, who were immediately followed by an hundred more of the natives, bringing with them the mats for covering their temporary houses, and seemingly, every other article of value belonging to them.[1]

On landing, which they did without the least hesitation, their behaviour was courteous and friendly in the highest degree. A middle-aged man, to all appearance the chief or principal person of the party, was foremost in shewing marks of the greatest hospitality; and perceiving our party were at breakfast, presented them with water, roasted roots, dried fish, and other articles of food. This person, in return, received some presents, and others were distributed amongst the ladies and some of the party. The chief, for so we must distinguish him, had two hangers, one of Spanish, the other of English manufacture, on which he seemed to set a very high value. The situation of the spot where they had landed was delightful; the shores on each side the inlet being composed of a low country, pleasingly diversified by hills, dales, extensive verdant lawns, and clear spaces in the midst of the forest, which, together with the cordial reception they had met from the natives, induced Mr. Whidbey to continue his examination on shore; on this occasion he was accompanied by the chief and several of the party, who conducted themselves with the greatest propriety; though with no small degree of civil curiosity in examining his clothes, and expressing a great desire to be satisfied as to the colour of the skin they covered; making signs, that his hands and face were painted white, instead of being black or red like their own; but when convinced of their mistake by opening his waistcoat, their astonishment was inexpressible. From these circumstances, and the general tenor of their behaviour, Mr. Whidbey concluded they had not before seen any Europeans, though, from the different articles they possessed, it was evident a communication had taken place; probably by the means of distinct trading tribes. The people, who had been met in that inlet removing with their families, and all their moveable property, were not unlikely to be of this commercial description; particularly, as their voyage was towards the sea-coast, where, in some convenient situation near to the general resort of Europeans, they might fix their abode until an opportunity was afforded them to barter their commodities for the more valuable productions of Europe, which are afterwards disposed of to the inhabitants of the interior country at a very exorbitant price. This circumstance tends, in some degree, to corroborate an opinion hazarded on a former occasion to this effect.

On the boats being ordered on shore to receive Mr. Whidbey and the gentlemen who had attended him in his walk, the launch grounded, which was no sooner perceived by the Indian chief, than he was foremost in using every exertion to shove her off. This being effected, and the gentlemen embarked, most of these good people took their leave, and seemed to part

[1] These would be Skagit Indians, who lived in Skagit Bay, around the mouth of the Skagit River, and on the central parts of Whidbey Island, which forms the W. shore of Saratoga Passage.

with their newly-acquired friends with great reluctance. The chief, and a few others, accompanied our party, until they had advanced about fourteen miles from the entrance, when they, very civilly, took their departure; here the arm branched off from its former direction of about N.N.W., to the westward, and N.E.[1] The latter being the object of their pursuit, they soon arrived off another extensive and populous village, whence several canoes came off with not less than seventy of the natives in them; and several others were seen coming from the different parts of the shore. Those who approached the boats conducted themselves with the utmost propriety, shewing, by repeated invitations to their dwellings, the greatest hospitality, and making signs that they had plenty of food to bestow. In these entreaties the ladies were particularly earnest, and expressed much chagrin and mortification that their offers of civility were declined. As the boats sailed past the village those in the canoes returned to the shore.

The direction which the land took to the N.E. conducted them to a considerable branch[2] whose outer points lie from each other N. 20 W., about a league asunder. From its eastern shore a shallow flat of sand, on which are some rocky islets and rocks, runs out, until within half a mile of the western shore, forming a narrow channel, navigated by them in nearly a N.N.W. direction, for about three leagues. The depth, at its entrance, was twenty fathoms; but gradually decreased to four, as they advanced up the channel which is formed by the western shore,[3] and the sand-bank, continuing, with great regularity, about half a mile wide, to the latitude of 48° 24′, longitude 237° 45′, where it then ceased to be navigable for vessels of any burthen, in consequence of the rocks and overfalls from three to twenty fathoms deep, and a very irregular and disagreeable tide. On meeting these impediments, the party returned,[4] with intention of exploring the opening leading to the westward. As they repassed the village, they were again visited by their friendly chief, attended by two or three canoes only, who presented them with a most welcome supply of very fine small fish which, in many respects, resembled, and most probably were, a species of the smelt. He accepted, with apparent pleasure, an invitation into the launch, where he remained with Mr. Whidbey until the evening, ate and drank of such things were offered with the greatest confidence, and on being made acquainted that the party was going to rest, bad them farewell with every mark of respect and friendship.

In the morning, the examination of the western branch[5] was pursued, and found to terminate in a very excellent and commodious cove or harbour, with regular soundings from 10 to 20 fathoms, good holding ground. Its western extent situated in latitude 48° 17′, longitude 237° 38′, is not more than a league

[1] Penn Cove, to the W and Skagit Bay to the NE.
[2] Skagit Bay.
[3] Most of Skagit Bay is filled with flats, bare at low water, but a narrow channel of sorts, to which Vancouver refers, runs along its W shore. Even this channel is only a few fathoms deep.
[4] If Whidbey's lat. is correct, the party turned back in the vicinity of Hope Island.
[5] Penn Cove.

from the eastern shore of the main inlet, within the straits.[1] On each point of the harbour, which in honor of a particular friend I call PENN'S COVE,[2] was a deserted village; in one of which were found several sepulchres formed exactly like a sentry box. Some of them were open, and contained the skeletons of many young children tied up in baskets; the smaller bones of adults were likewise noticed, but no one of the limb bones could here be found, which gave rise to an opinion that these, by the living inhabitants of the neighbourhood, were appropriated to useful purposes, such as pointing their arrows, spears, or other weapons. The surrounding country, for several miles in most points of view, presented a delightful prospect, consisting chiefly of spacious meadows, elegantly adorned with clumps of trees; amongst which the oak bore a very considerable proportion, in size from four to six feet in circumference. In these beautiful pastures, bordering on an expansive sheet of water, the deer were seen playing about in great numbers. Nature had here provided the well-stocked park, and wanted only the assistance of art to constitute that desirable assemblage of surface, which is so much sought in other countries, and only to be acquired by an immoderate expence in manual labour. The soil principally consisted of a rich, black vegetable mould, lying on a sandy or clayey substratum; the grass, of an excellent quality, grew to the height of three feet, and the ferns, which, in the sandy soils, occupied the clear spots, were nearly twice as high. The country in the vicinity of this branch of the sea is, according to Mr. Whidbey's representation, the finest we had yet met with, notwithstanding the very pleasing appearance of many others; its natural productions were luxuriant in the highest degree, and it was, by no means, ill supplied with streams of fresh water. The number of its inhabitants he estimated at about six hundred, which I should suppose would exceed the total of all the natives we had before seen; the other parts of the sound did not appear, by any means, so populous, as we had been visited by one small canoe only, in which were five of the natives,[3] who civilly furnished us with some small fish. The character and appearance of their several tribes here seen did not seem to differ in any material respect from each other, or from those we have already had occasion to mention.

A fortnight had now been dedicated to the examination of this inlet; which I have distinguished by the name of ADMIRALTY INLET: we had still to return about forty miles through this tedious inland navigation, before we could arrive on a new field of enquiry. The broken appearance of the region before us, and the difficulties we had already encountered in tracing its various shores,

[1] The most westerly part of the cove is in lat. 48° 14′ N, long. 122° 44′ W (237° 16′ E). The head of the cove is less than a mile from the E shore of the entrance to Admiralty Inlet.
[2] The 'particular friend' has been identified by Sir James Watt as Granville Penn (1761–1844), a grandson of William Penn, the founder of Pennsylvania, who lived in Richmond and who witnessed Vancouver's will.
[3] These would be Snohomish Indians. It is surprising that Vancouver did not meet more of them, as they had four villages in the S part of Possession Sound.

incontestibly proved, that the object of our voyage could alone be accomplished by very slow degrees. Perfectly satisfied with the arduousness of the task in which we were engaged, and the progress we were likely to make, I became anxiously solicitous to move the instant an opportunity should serve. The two following days were however unfavorable to that purpose, and after the great fatigue our people had lately undergone, were well appropriated to holidays. Sunday, the 3d, all hands were employed in fishing with tolerably good success, or in taking a little recreation on shore; and on Monday, the 4th, they were served as good a dinner as we were able to provide them, with double allowance of grog to drink the King's health, it being the anniversary of His Majesty's birth; on which auspicious day, I had long since designed to take formal possession of all the countries we had lately been employed in exploring, in the name of, and for His Britannic Majesty, his heirs and successors.[1]

To execute this purpose, accompanied by Mr. Broughton and some of the officers, I went on shore about one o'clock, pursuing the usual formalities which are generally observed on such occasions, and under the discharge of a royal salute from the vessels, took possession accordingly of the coast, from that part of New Albion, in the latitude of 39° 20′ north, and longitude 236° 26′ east, to the entrance of this inlet of the sea, said to be the supposed straits of Juan de Fuca; as likewise all the coast islands, &c. within the said straits, as well on the northern as on the southern shores; together with those situated in the interior sea we had discovered, extending from the said straits, in various directions, between the north-west, north, east, and southern quarters; which interior sea I have honored with the name of THE GULF OF GEORGIA,[2] and the continent binding the said gulf, and extending southward to the 45th degree of north latitude, with that of NEW GEORGIA, in honor of His present Majesty.[3] This branch of Admiralty inlet obtained the name of POSSESSION SOUND; its western arm, after Vice Admiral Sir Alan Gardner, I distinguish by the name of PORT GARDNER,[4] and its smaller eastern one by that of PORT SUSAN.[5]

[1] Vancouver took this action either on his own reponsibility or in response to verbal instructions, as no mention of taking formal possession is made in the written instructions he received from the Admiralty. As all concerned were well aware that Spain claimed the area, the omission (if such it was) is not surprising.

[2] The S part of Vancouver's 'interior sea' is now the Strait of Juan de Fuca, a name Vancouver intended to limit to the entrance of the strait. The large part N of the San Juan Islands is now the Strait of Georgia. Here and elsewhere in the first edition the word 'gulf' is spelled 'gulph'.

[3] The name never came into general use.

[4] Vancouver's chart shows that he intended this name to apply to the whole of what is now Saratoga Passage. It is now confined to a small area comprising the outer harbour of the city of Everett. It was named after Vancouver's friend and patron, Captain Sir Alan Gardner, who had recommended him for the command of the expedition. Gardner attained the rank of Admiral in 1799 and was raised to the peerage in 1800.

[5] Named for Lady Gardner (née Susanna Gale). Vancouver's chart shows that he named the tip of Camano Island Alan Point, after Sir Alan Gardner. The name was later corrupted to Point Allen, and has now been changed to Camano Head.

CHAPTER VII.

Quit Admiralty Inlet and proceed to the Northward—Anchor in Birch Bay—
Prosecute the Survey in the Boats—Meet two Spanish Vessels—Astronomical
and nautical Observations.

A LIGHT breeze springing up from the N.W. about seven in the morning of
Tuesday the 5th June, we sailed down Possession sound. This wind brought
with it, as usual, serene and pleasant weather. Whilst we were passing gently
on, the chief, who had shewn so much friendly attention to Mr. Whidbey and
his party, with several of his friends came on board, and presented us with
some fruit and dried fish. He entered the ship with some reluctance, but was
no sooner on deck than he seemed perfectly reconciled; and with much
inquisitive earnestness regarded the surrounding objects, the novelty of which
seemed to fill his mind with surprise and admiration. The unaffected hospitable
attention he had shewn our people, was not likely upon this occasion to be
forgotten. After he had visited the different parts of the ship, at which he
expressed the greatest astonishment, I presented him and his friends with an
assortment of such things as they esteemed to be most valuable; and then they
took their leave, seemingly highly pleased with their reception.

The N.W. wind was unfavorable after we were clear of Possession sound,
and obliged us to work to windward, which discovered to us a shoal lying
in a bay, just to be westward of the north point of entrance into the sound,[1]
a little distance from the shore. It shews itself above water, and is discoverable
by the soundings gradually decreasing to ten, seven, and five fathoms, and
cannot be considered as any material impediment to the navigation of the bay.
As the ebb-tide was greatly in our favour, I did not wait to examine it further,
but continued plying to windward until midnight, when being unable to gain
any ground against the strength of the flood, we anchored in 22 fathoms water
about half a mile from the western shore of Admiralty inlet, and about half
way between Oak cove and Marrowstone point; the Chatham having
anchored before us some distance astern.

The ebb again returned at the rate of about three miles per hour; but as
it was calm we did not move until the N.W. wind set in about seven in the
morning of Wednesday the 6th, when we worked out of the inlet.

Having reached its entrance, we were met by several canoes from the

---

[1] Cultus Bay, much of which is bare at low water.

westward. Some of the headmost, when they had advanced near to the ship made signs of peace, and came alongside, giving us to understand that their friends behind wished to do the same, and requested we would shorten sail for that purpose. They seemed very solicitous to dissuade us from proceeding to the northward by very vociferous and vehement arguments; but as their language was completely unintelligible, and their wishes not appertaining to the object of our pursuit, so far as we were enabled to comprehend their meaning, we treated their advice with perfect indifference, on which they departed, joined the rest of their countrymen, and proceeded up Admiralty inlet, whose north point, called by me POINT PARTRIDGE, is situated in latitude 48° 16', longitude 237° 31',[1] and is formed by a high white sandy cliff, having one of the verdant lawns on either side of it. Passing at the distance of about a mile from this point we very suddenly came on a small space of ten fathom water, but immediately again increased our depth to 20 and 30 fathoms.[2] After advancing a few miles along the eastern shore of the gulf, we found no effect either from the ebb or flood tide, and the wind being light and variable from the northward, at three in the afternoon we were obliged to anchor in 20 fathoms water, sandy bottom.[3]

In this situation New Dungeness bore by compass S. 54 W.; the east point of Protecton island S. 15 W.; the west point of Admiralty inlet, which after my much esteemed friend Captain George Wilson of the navy, I distinguished by the name of POINT WILSON, S. 35 E. situated in latitude 48° 10', longitude 237° 31';[4] the nearest shore east, two leagues distant; a low sandy island,[5] forming at its west end a low cliff, above which some dwarf trees are produced from N. 26 W. to N. 40 W.; and the proposed station for the vessels during the examination of the continental shore by the boats, which, from Mr. Broughton who had visited it, obtained the name of STRAWBERRY BAY,[6] N. 11 W. at the distance of about six leagues, situated in a region apparently much broken and divided by water. Here we remained until seven in the evening; we then weighed, but with so little wind, that after having drifted to the southward of our former station, we were obliged again to anchor until six the next morning, Thursday the 7th, when we made an attempt to proceed, but were soon again compelled to become stationary near our last situation.

On reflecting that the summer was now fast advancing, and that the slow progress of the vessels occasioned too much delay, I determined, rather than

---

[1] Vancouver's brother John married a Martha Partridge; Wagner suggests that this may explain the name. It had been named Punta de Melendez, probably by Quimper in 1790. The correct position is lat. 48° 13' 30" N, long. 122° 46' W (237° 14' E).

[2] Partridge Bank, parts of which are as shallow as 2¼ fathoms.

[3] Whitebrook believes that Vancouver crossed the E end of Partridge Bank and anchored not far beyond it. The bearings given confirm this.

[4] Its position is lat. 48° 08' N, long. 122° 45' W (237° 15' E).

[5] Smith Island, which, with its small neighbour, Minor Island, had been named Islas de Bonilla by the Spaniards in 1791.

[6] On the W side of Cypress Island.

lose the advantages which the prevailing favorable weather now afforded for boat expeditions, to dispatch Mr. Puget in the launch, and Mr. Whidbey in the cutter, with a week's provisions, in order that the shores should be immediately explored to the next intended station of the vessels, whither they would proceed as soon as circumstances would allow. In this arrangement I was well aware, it could not be considered judicious to part with our launch, whilst the ship remained in a transitory unfixed state in this unknown and dangerous navigation; yet she was so essentially necessary to the protection of our detached parties, that I resolved to encounter some difficulties on board, rather than suffer the delay, or lose so valuable an opportunity for the prosecution of the survey. In directing this, orders were given not to examine any openings to the northward, [1] beyond Strawberry bay, but to determine the boundaries of the continental shore leading to the north and eastward, as far as might be practicable to its parallel, whither they were to resort after performing the task assigned. On this service they departed, and directed their course for the first opening on the eastern shore about 3 or 4 leagues distant, [2] bearing by compass from the ship N. by E.

Having repaired to the low sandy island already noticed, for the purpose of taking some angles, I found some rocks lying on its western side nearly three quarters of a mile from its shores; and that the eastern part of it was formed by a very narrow low spit of land, over which the tide nearly flowed. Its situation is in latitude 48° 24′, longitude 237° 26½′. [3] Amongst the various bearings that it became necessary to take here, were those of the two remarkably high snowy mountains so frequently mentioned. Mount Baker bore N. 63 E.; mount Rainier S. 27 E.; and from a variety of observations purposely made for fixing their respective situations, it appeared that mount Baker was in latitude 48° 39′, longitude 238° 20′, and mount Rainier in latitude 47° 3′, longitude 238° 21′. [4] To the southward of these were now seen two other very lofty, round, snowy mountains, [5] lying apparently in the same north and south direction, or nearly so; but we were unable to ascertain their positive situation. The summits of these were visible only at two or three stations in the southern parts of Admiralty inlet; they appeared to be covered with perpetual snow as low down as we were enabled to see, and seemed as if they rose from an extensive plain of low country.

When due attention is paid to the range of snowy mountains that stretch to the southward from the base of mount Rainier, a probability arises of the same chain being continued, so as to connect the whole in one barrier along

[1] 'north-westward' in the first edition.

[2] Deception Pass.

[3] The spit runs NE about a mile to Minor Island. The position of Smith Island is lat. 48° 19′ N, long. 122° 50′ 30″ W (237° 09′ 30″ E).

[4] Mount Baker is in lat. 48° 48′ N, long. 121° 50′ W (238° 10′ E); the position of Mount Rainier is lat. 46° 52′ N, long. 121° 45′ W (238° 15′ E).

[5] Mount St. Helens (9,671 ft.) and Mount Adams (12,307 ft.).

the coast, at uncertain distances from its shores;[1] although intervals may exist in the ridge where the mountains may not be sufficiently elevated to have been discernible from our several stations. The like effect is produced by the two former mountains, whose immense height permitted their appearing very conspicuously, long before we approached sufficiently near to distinguish the intermediate range of rugged mountains that connect them, and from whose summits their bases originate.

About six in the evening, with a light breeze from the S.W. we weighed and stood to the northward; but after having advanced about 11 miles, the wind became light and obliged us to anchor about nine that evening, in 37 fathoms water, hard bottom, in some places rocky;[2] in this situation we were detained by calms until the afternoon of the following day, Friday the 8th. Our observed latitude here, was 48° 29′, longitude 237° 29′: the country, occupying the northern horizon in all directions, appeared to be excessively broken, and insulated. Strawberry bay bore, by compass, N. 10 W. about three leagues distant; the opening on the continental shore, the first object for the examination of the detached party,[3] with some small rocky islets before its entrance that appeared very narrow, bore, at the distance of about five miles, S. 87 E.; point Partridge S. 21 E.; the low sandy island south; the south part of the westernmost shore, which is composed of islands and rocks, S. 37 W. about two miles distant; the nearest shore was within about a mile; a very dangerous sunken rock, visible only at low tide, lies off from a low rocky point on this shore, bearing N. 79 W.;[4] and a very unsafe cluster of small rocks, some constantly, and others visible only near low water, bore N. 15 W. about two miles and a half distant.

This country presented a very different aspect from that which we had been accustomed to behold further south. The shores now before us were composed of steep rugged rocks, whose surface varied exceedingly in respect to height, and exhibited little more than the barren rock, which in some places produced a little herbage of a dull colour, with a few dwarf trees.

With a tolerably good breeze from the north, we weighed about three in the afternoon, and with a flood tide, turned up into Strawberry bay, where, in about three hours, we anchored in 16 fathoms, fine sandy bottom. This bay is situated on the west side of an island, which, producing an abundance of upright cypress, obtained the name of CYPRESS ISLAND.[5] The bay is of small extent, and not very deep; its south point bore by compass S. 40 E.; a small

---

[1] This 'probability' was borne out as Vancouver's survey progressed northward. The Cascade Range in Washington, whose higher peaks are visible from Puget Sound, the Coast Mountains and St. Elias Range in British Columbia, and the Chugach Mountains in Alaska form a virtually continuous barrier all the way from the sound to Cook Inlet.

[2] This anchorage was off the SE corner of Lopez Island.

[3] Deception Pass. Quimper had named it Boca de Flon in 1790.

[4] Kellett Ledge, off Cape St. Mary, Lopez Island.

[5] Named Isla de San Vicente by the Spaniards in 1791.

islet, forming nearly the north point of the bay,[1] round which is a clear good passage west; and the bottom of the bay east, at the distance of about three quarters of a mile. This situation, though very commodious, in respect to the shore, is greatly exposed to the winds, and sea in a S.S.E. direction.

In consequence of the wind ceasing, the Chatham, whilst endeavouring to gain this anchorage, was, by a strong flood tide, driven to the eastward of the island,[2] where she was compelled to anchor. The next morning, Saturday 9th, I received from Mr. Broughton a letter acquainting me, that, having been obliged to anchor on a rocky bottom, on account of the strength and irregularity of the tide, their stream cable had been cut through by the rocks; and that, after several attempts to recover the anchor, the rapidity of the tide had rendered all their efforts ineffectual; and he was very apprehensive that, remaining longer in that situation, for the purpose of repeating his endeavours, might endanger the loss also of the bower anchor by which they were then riding. In reply, I desired, if the anchor could not be regained by the next slack tide, that they would desist, rather than run a risk of still greater importance.

A fine sandy beach, forming the shores of the bay, gave us the hope of procuring a good supply of fish, as the Chatham, on her former visit, had been very successful, we were however, unfortunately mistaken; the seine was repeatedly hauled, but to no effect.

The Chatham arrived in the bay on Sunday morning, the 10th, with the loss of her stream anchor,[3] and in the afternoon the boats returned from their survey.

From the officers, I became acquainted, that the first inlet communicated with port Gardner, by a very narrow and intricate channel, which, for a considerable distance, was not forty yards in width, and abounded with rocks above and beneath the surface of the water. These impediments, in addition to the great rapidity and irregularity of the tide, rendered the passage navigable only for boats or vessels of very small burthen. This determined all the eastern shore of the gulf, from S.W. point of this passage, in latitude 48° 27′, longitude 237° 37′, to the north point of entrance into Possession sound, in latitude 47° 53′, longitude 237° 47′, to be an island, which, in its broadest part, is about ten miles across; and in consequence of Mr. Whidbey's circumnavigation, I

[1] Strawberry Island.
[2] Menzies explains that she 'was impelled by a strong flood Tide into an opening a little more to the Eastward, in which situation as neither helm nor canvass had any power over her, all were alarmd for her safety & anxious to hear her fate.' – June 8.
[3] 'the loss of it was more severely felt as it was the only one of the kind they had been supplied with.' – Menzies, June 9. Vancouver's displeasure at the loss of the anchor (which he twice refers to) may have been reflected in an incident recorded by Heddington: 'We began painting the Vessel but as Capt. Vancouver refus'd to assist us with a little oil which we wanted; we were oblig'd to leave the Sides one Yellow, and the other we painted black, as we had black paint mix'd'. – June 10.

distinguished it by the name of WHIDBEY'S ISLAND: and this northern pass, leading into port Gardner, DECEPTION PASSAGE.[1]

Hence they proceeded to the examination of the continental coast leading to the northward, and entered[2] what appeared to be a spacious sound, or opening, extending widely in three directions to the eastward of our present station. One, leading to the southward,[3] and another, to the eastward,[4] they examined, and found them to terminate alike in deep bays, affording good anchorage, though inconvenient communication with the shores; particularly towards the head of each bay, on account of a shallow flat of sand or mud, which met them at a considerable distance from the land. Having fixed the boundaries of the continent as far to the north as the latitude of this island, agreeably to their directions, they returned, leaving unexplored a large opening which took a northern direction, as also the space that appeared to be the main arm of the gulf, to the north-westward, where the horizon was unbounded, and its width seemed very considerable.[5] The country they had seen to the north-east of Deception passage, is much divided by water, and bore nearly the same steril appearance with that of our present situation; excepting near the heads of the two large bays, which they had examined on the continental shore. There the land was of a moderate height, unoccupied by rocky precipices, and was well wooded with timber. In the course of this expedition, several deserted villages had been seen, and some of the natives met with, who differed not, in any material particular, as to their persons, nor in their civil and hospitable deportment, from those we had been so happy, on former occasions, to call our friends.

As our present anchorage was much exposed, and supplied us with no sort of refreshment, excepting a few small wild onions or leeks, I determined, on this information, to proceed with the vessels up the gulf, to the N.W. in quest of a more commodious situation, from whence Mr. Whidbey might be dispatched, to complete the examination of the arm which had been left unfinished, and another party, to prosecute their inquiries to the N.W. or in such other direction as the gulf might take.

With a light breeze from the S.E. about four o'clock in the morning of Monday the 11th, we quitted this station, and passed between the small island and the north point of the bay to the north-westward, through a cluster of numerous islands, rocks, and rocky islets. On Mr. Broughton's first visit hither, he found a great quanity of very excellent strawberries, which gave it the name of Strawberry bay; but, on our arrival, the fruit season was passed.[6] The bay

---

[1] Both names still apply. Whidbey Island is the modern spelling.
[2] Through Guemes Channel.
[3] Fidalgo Bay.   [4] Padilla Bay.
[5] From the N end of Padilla Bay Puget and Whidbey would have a clear view into Bellingham Bay, and to the NW they would see the main portion of the Strait of Georgia.
[6] This is surprising in view of Puget's experience at Flounder Bay, at the NW corner of Fidalgo Island, where he had encamped on the spit: 'Here we passed a most

affords good and secure anchorage, though somewhat exposed; yet, in fair weather, wood and water may be easily procured. The island of Cypress is principally composed of high rocky mountains, and steep perpendicular cliffs, which, in the centre of Strawberry bay, fall a little back, and the space between the foot of the mountains and the sea-side is occupied by low marshy land, through which are several small runs of most excellent water, that find their way into the bay by oozing through the beach. It is situated in latitude 48° 36½', longitude 237° 34'.[1] The variation of the compass, by eighteen sets of azimuths differing from 18° to 21° taken on board, and on shore, since our departure from Admiralty inlet, gave the mean result of 19° 5' eastwardly. The rise and fall of the tide was inconsiderable, though the stream was rapid: the ebb came from the east, and it was high water 2^h 37' after the moon had passed the meridian.

We proceeded first to the north-eastward, passing the branch of the gulf that had been partly examined, and then directed our course to the N.W. along that which appeared a continuation of the continental shore,[2] formed by low sandy cliffs, rising from a beach of sand and stones. The country moderately elevated, stretched a considerable distance from the N.W. round to the south-eastward, before it ascended to join the range of rugged, snowy mountains. This connected barrier, from the base of mount Baker, still continued very lofty, and appeared to extend in a direction leading to the westward of north. The soundings along the shore were regular, from 12 to 25 and 30 fathoms, as we approached, or increased our distance from, the land, which seldom exceeded two miles: the opposite side of the gulf to the south-westward, composed of numerous islands, was at the distance of about two leagues. As the day advanced, the S.E. wind gradually died away, and, for some hours, we remained nearly stationary.

In the evening, a light breeze favoring the plan I had in contemplation, we steered for a bay that presented itself,[3] where, about six o'clock, we anchored in six fathoms water, sandy bottom, half a mile from the shore. The points of the bay bore by compass S. 32 W. and N. 72 W.; the westernmost part of that which we considered to be the main land west, about three leagues distant;[4] to the south of this point appeared the principal direction of the gulf, though a very considerable arm seemed to branch from it to the north-eastward. As soon as the ship was secured, I went in a boat to inspect the shores of the bay, and found, with little trouble, a very convenient situation for our several necessary duties on shore; of which the business of the obervatory was my chief object, as I much wished for a further trial of the rate of the chronometers,

uncomfortable Night tormented by Musquito's & Sand Flies, which however was in some Measure forgot in the Morning by a large supply of Strawberries and Wild Onions, which we found growing Spontaneously close to the Tents.' – June 11. Botanist Menzies makes no comment in his journal.

[1] The position of the bay is lat. 48° 33' 30" N, long. 122° 43' W (237° 17' E).
[2] Lummi Island and the mainland N of it.
[3] Birch Bay.   [4] Point Roberts.

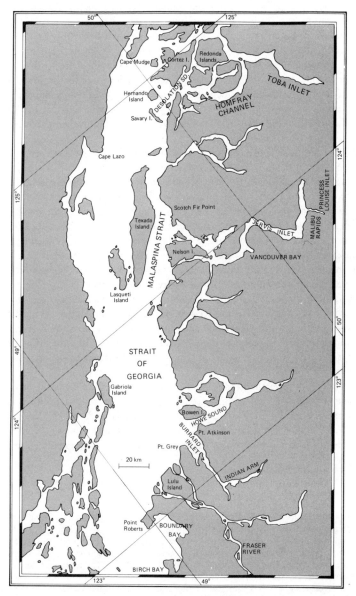

Figure 2. Birch Bay to Cape Mudge. *Base map by Michael E. Leek.*

now that it was probable we should remain at rest a sufficient time to make the requisite observations for that purpose. Mr. Broughton received my directions to this effect, as also, that the vessels should be removed, the next morning, about a mile further up the bay to the N.E. where they would be more conveniently stationed for our several operations on shore; and as soon as the business of the observatory should acquire a degree of forwardness, Mr. Whidbey, in the Discovery's cutter, attended by the Chatham's launch, was to proceed to the examination of that part of the coast unexplored to the S.E.; whilst myself, in the yawl, accompanied by Mr. Puget in the launch, directed our researches up the main inlet of the gulf.

Matters thus arranged, with a week's provision in each boat, I departed at five o'clock in the morning of Tuesday the 12th. The most northerly branch, though attracting our first attention, caused little delay; it soon terminated in two open bays; the southernmost,[1] which is the smallest, has two small rocks lying off its south point; it extends in a circular form to the eastward, with a shoal of land projecting some distance from its shores. This bay affords good anchorage from seven to ten fathoms water: the other is much larger, and extends to the northward;[2] these, by noon, we had passed round, but the shoals attached to the shores of each, and particularly to those of the latter, prevented our reaching within four or five miles of their heads. The point constituting the west extremity of these bays, is that which was seen from the ship, and considered as the western part of the main land, of which it is a small portion, much elevated at the south extremity of a very low narrow peninsula; its highest part is to the S.E. formed by high white sand cliffs falling perpendicularly into the sea; from whence a shoal extends to the distance of half a mile round it, joining those of the larger bay; whilst its southwest extremity, not more than a mile in an east and west direction from the former, is one of those low projecting sandy points, with ten to seven fathoms water, within a few yards of it. From this point, situated in latitude 48° 57′, longitude 237° 20′, (which I distinguished by the name of POINT ROBERTS, after my esteemed friend and predecessor in the Discovery)[3] the coast takes a direction

[1] Semiahmoo Bay.

[2] Boundary Bay. The 49th parallel, the boundary between Canada and the United States, runs through Semiahmoo and Boundary bays. The tip of Point Roberts, just south of the parallel, is American territory.

[3] Named Cape Roberts on Baker's MS chart (and in Menzies' journal) but Point Roberts on the engraved chart. Its position is lat. 48° 58′ N, long. 123° 05′ W (236° 55′ E). Point Roberts was named Isla de Zepeda by Narváez in 1791, under the impression that it was an island; Galiano changed this to Punta de Zepeda in 1792. Vancouver makes no mention of a deserted village on the point that Puget found interesting: 'This must by its Size have formerly been the habitation of Near four hundred People, but was now in perfect Ruins and overrun with Nettles & some Bushes, but as this Village differs materially from what we have already seen I shall notice what their construction appeared to be. The Body of the Village, consists of three Rows of Houses each Row divided by a Narrow Lane & partitioned off into four or Six Square houses & every one large and capacious. This Frame the only Remnant of the Village must have [caused] the Native Inhabitants an Infinite

N. 28 W. and presented a task of examination to which we conceived our equipment very unequal. That which, from hence, appeared the northern extreme of the continental shore, was a low bluff point, that seemed to form the southern entrance into an extensive sound,[1] bearing N. 25 W. with broken land stretching about 5° farther to the westward. Between this direction and N. 79 W. the horizon seemed uninterrupted, excepting by the appearance of a small though very high round island, lying N. 52 W. apparently at the distance of many leagues.[2] Having thus early examined and fixed the continental shore to the furthest point seen from the ship, I determined to prosecute our inquiries to the utmost limits that care and frugality could extend our supplies; and, having taken the necessary angles, we proceeded, but soon found our progress along the eastern or continental shore materially impeded by a shoal that extends from point Roberts N. 80 W. seven or eight miles, then stretches N. 35 W. about five or six miles further, where it takes a northerly direction towards the above low bluff point.[3] Along the edge of this bank we had soundings from ten to one fathom, as we increased or decreased our distance from the eastern shore; to approach which all our endeavours were exerted to no purpose, until nine in the evening, when the shoal having forced us nearly into the middle of the gulf, we stood over to its western side, in order to land for the night, and to cook our provisions for the ensuing day, which being always performed by those on watch during the night, prevented any delay on that account, in the day time. As we stood to the westward, our depth soon increased to 15 fathoms, after which we gained no bottom until we reached the western shore of the gulf, where, on our arrival about one o'clock in the morning, it was with much difficulty we were enabled to land on the steep rugged rocks that compose the coast, for the

trouble in the Construction, & it still remains a Mystery, to me, by what powers of Machinism they have been able to lift up the heavy and long Logs of Timber which are placed on the top of the Standards. These last are 2½ feet in circumference & erected perpendicular about fourteen feet from the Ground. On the Top of these Standards or Posts is a Notch cut to receive the Rafter, which from its length will serve for two houses or perhaps more, each Side and End of the house having three Standards to support it; Besides the Rafters going length ways, they are likewise laid across & with their Standards Partition off the Different Habitations. I have no Doubt that when occupied, the Sides and Tops are boarded in as large planks smoaked dried were found contiguous to the Village.' – June 12. This would be a village of the Semiahmoo Indians, a Coast Salish tribe that lived around the bay of that name and straddled the present international boundary to the N.

[1] Point Grey, the S point of entrance of Burrard Inlet. Here again the Spaniards tentatively gave the name of Isla de Langara in 1791 and revised this to Punta de Langara in 1792.

[2] Mount Shepherd, on Texada Island. Although it is nearly 30 miles long, the island is narrow, and Vancouver was viewing it end on.

[3] Roberts Bank and Sturgeon Bank, two extensive alluvial deposits from the Fraser River. They extend all the way from Point Roberts to Point Grey, a distance of about 22 miles. The Fraser empties into the Strait of Georgia through several channels between these two points.

purpose of cooking only, and were compelled, by this unfavorable circumstance, to remain and sleep in the boats.[1]

At five in the morning of Wednesday the 13th, we again directed our course to the eastern shore, and landed about noon, on the above-mentioned low bluff point. This, as was suspected, formed the south point of a very extensive sound, with a small arm leading to the eastward: the space, which seemed to be its main direction, and appeared very extensive, took a northerly course.[2] The observed latitude here was 49° 19', longitude 237° 6', making this point (which, in compliment to my friend Captain George Grey of the navy, was called POINT GREY)[3] seven leagues from point Roberts. The intermediate space is occupied by very low land, apparently a swampy flat, that retires several miles, before the country rises to meet the rugged snowy mountains, which we found still continuing in a direction nearly along the coast. This low flat being very much inundated, and extending behind point Roberts, to join the low land in the bay to the eastward of that point; gives its high land, when seen at a distance, the appearance of an island: this, however, is not the case, notwithstanding there are two openings between this point and point Grey. These can only be navigable for canoes, as the shoal continues along the coast to the distance of seven or eight miles from the shore, on which were lodged, and especially before these openings, logs of wood, and stumps of trees innumerable.[4]

From point Grey we proceeded first up the eastern branch of the sound,[5] where, about a league within its entrance, we passed to the northward of an

[1] The night was probably spent off Gabriola Island. The failure to find a camping place ashore was exasperating: 'This Disappointment we much regretted as the People had been incessantly on the Oars Ten Hours and an Half'. – Puget, June 12.

[2] The 'extensive sound' evidently included both Burrard Inlet ('the arm leading to the eastward') and Howe Sound, which 'took a northerly course'.

[3] George, third son of the 1st Earl Grey, was born in 1767 and entered the Navy in 1781. As the party had landed at noon to dine, Puget dubbed the point 'Noon Breakfast Point'. Its location is lat. 49° 16' N, long. 123° 16' W (236° 44' E).

[4] This large 'swampy flat' was the broad estuary of the Fraser River. It was probably in flood, with the spring freshet, and in 1792 large areas that have since been reclaimed would be under water at high tide. The 'two openings' were the river channels N and S of Lulu Island, which occupies much of the midde of the mouth of the river. Vancouver makes no specific reference to a river, but Puget suspected its existence: 'Two Places in that Direction [eastward] had much the Appearance of large Rivers, but the Shoals hitherto have prevented our having any Communication with them.' – 12 June. The Spaniards had come to the same conclusion in 1791. Describing the explorations of Narváez and Pantoja, Eliza reported: 'they thought there must be a very copious river, because the schooner being anchored 2 miles out they collected and drank sweet water. They could not look for it on account of bad weather.' – H. R. Wagner, Spanish Explorations in the Strait of Juan de Fuca (Santa Ana, Calif., 1933), pp. 151–2. Eliza mistakenly placed the river between Howe Sound and Point Atkinson instead of between Point Grey and Point Roberts, but he had not visited the area himself.

[5] Burrard Inlet, the W limit of which is a line from Point Grey directly N to Point Atkinson, a distance of 4 miles.

island which nearly terminated its extent, forming a passage from ten to seven fathoms deep, not more than a cable's length in width.[1] This island lying exactly across the channel, appeared to form a similar passage to the south of it, with a smaller island lying before it.[2] From these islands, the channel, in width about half a mile, continued its direction about east. Here we were met by about fifty Indians, in their canoes, who conducted themselves with the greatest decorum and civility, presenting us with several fish cooked, and undressed, of the sort already mentioned as resembling the smelt. These good people, finding we were inclined to make some return for their hospitality, shewed much understanding in preferring iron to copper.

For the sake of the company of our new friends, we stood on under an easy sail, which encouraged them to attend us some little distance up the arm.[3] The major part of the canoes twice paddled forward, assembled before us, and each time a conference was held. Our visit and appearance were most likely the object of their consultation, as our motions on these occasions seemed to engage the whole of their attention. The subject matter, which remained a profound secret to us, did not appear of an unfriendly nature to us, as they soon returned, and, if possible, expressed additional cordiality and respect. This sort of conduct always created a degree of suspicion, and should ever be regarded with a watchful eye. In our short intercourse with the people of this country, we have generally found these consultations take place, whether their numbers were great or small; and though I have ever considered it prudent to be cautiously attentive on such occasions, they ought by no means to be considered as indicating at all times a positive intention of concerting hostile measures; having witnessed many of these conferences, without our experiencing afterwards any alteration in their friendly disposition. This was now the case with our numerous attendants, who gradually dispersed as we advanced from the station where we had first met them, and three or four canoes only accompanied us up a navigation which, in some places, does not exceed an hundred and fifty yards in width.

We landed for the night about half a league from the head of the inlet,[4] and about three leagues from its entrance. Our Indian visitors remained with us until by signs we gave them to understand we were going to rest, and after receiving some acceptable articles, they retired, and by means of the same

[1] The First Narrows, the entrance to Vancouver's inner harbour. Stanley Park, on the S side, with the high bluff of Prospect Point, could easily have been mistaken for an island, but it is connected with the mainland by low lying ground. The 'passage' is somewhat wider than Vancouver estimated.

[2] The 'similar passage' would be False Creek. The land Vancouver thought formed 'a smaller island' has not been identified.

[3] The 'arm' is now Vancouver's inner harbour, with the city on its S shore.

[4] Baker's chart indicates that Vanvouver went up the inlet sufficiently far to see its end at Port Moody. He spent the night on the S shore, opposite the entrance to Indian Arm, which would be about 4 miles from the end, not 'about half a league' as Vancouver suggests.

language promised an abundant supply of fish the next day; our seine having been tried in their presence with very little success. A great desire was manifested by these people to imitate our actions, especially in the firing of a musket, which one of them performed, though with much fear and trembling. They minutely attended to all our transactions, and examined the color of our skins with infinite curiosity. In other respects they differed little from the generality of the natives we had seen: they possessed no European commodities, or trinkets, excepting some rude ornaments apparently made from sheet copper; this circumstance, and the general tenor of their behaviour, gave us reason to conclude that we were the first people from a civilized country they had yet seen. Nor did it appear that they were nearly connected, or had much intercourse with other Indians, who traded with the European or American adventurers.

The shores in this situation were formed by steep rocky cliffs, that afforded no convenient space for pitching our tent, which compelled us to sleep in the boats. Some of the young gentlemen, however, preferring the stony beach for their couch, without duly considering the line of high water mark, found themselves incommoded by the flood tide, of which they were not apprized until they were nearly afloat; and one of them slept so sound, that I believe he might have been conveyed to some distance, had he not been awakened by his companions.

Perfectly satisfied with our researches in this branch of the sound, at four in the morning of Thursday the 14th, we retraced our passage in; leaving on the northern shore, a small opening extending to the northward,[1] with two little islets before it of little importance, whilst we had a grander object in contemplation; and more particularly so, as this arm or channel[2] could not be deemed navigable for shipping. The tide caused no stream; the colour of its water, after we had passed the island the day before, was green and perfectly clear, whereas that in the main branch of the sound, extending nearly half over the gulf, and accompanied by a rapid tide, was nearly colourless, which gave us some reason to suppose that the northern branch of the sound might possibly be discovered to terminate in a river of considerable extent.[3]

As we passed the situation from whence the Indians had first visited us the preceding day, which is a small border of low marshy land on the northern

[1] Indian Arm. It extends N for about 10 miles but only the first reach would be visible from the spot where Vancouver spent the night: 'Opposite to our Sleeping place is a Small Branch, which I suppose terminates in our view, but its Narrowness would not be any prevention of its being examined, had we not been certain that it possibly could not run far.' – Puget, June 13. Ten days later Indian Arm was explored by two Spanish officers from the Galiano-Valdéz expedition, whose presence was still unknown to Vancouver.

[2] Here as elsewhere 'channel' has been substituted for 'canal' in the first edition.

[3] It is surprising that Vancouver makes no comment about the colour of the water off the mouth of the Fraser. Normally at freshet time the silt-laden river water spreads out into the Strait and into parts of Burrard Inlet, and there is a very distinct line of demarcation between the water of the river and the sea.

shore, intersected by several creeks of fresh water,[1] we were in expectation of their company, but were disappointed, owing to our travelling so soon in the morning. Most of their canoes were hauled up into the creeks, and two or three only of the natives were seen straggling about on the beach. None of their habitations could be discovered, whence we concluded that their village was within the forest. Two canoes came off as we passed the island, but our boats being under sail, with a fresh favorable breeze, I was not inclined to halt, and they almost immediately returned.

The shores of this channel, which, after Sir Harry Burrard of the navy, I have distinguished by the name of BURRARD'S CHANNEL,[2] may be considered, on the southern side, of a moderate height, and though rocky, well covered with trees of large growth, principally of the pine tribe. On the northern side, the rugged snowy barrier, whose base we had now nearly approached, rose very abruptly, and was only protected from the wash of the sea by a very narrow border of low land. By seven o'clock we had reached the N.W. point of the channel, which forms also the south point of the main branch of the sound:[3] this also, after another particular friend, I called POINT ATKINSON,[4] situated north from point Grey, about a league distant. Here the opposite point of the entrance into the sound bore by compass west, at the distance of about three miles;[5] and nearly in the centre between these two points, is a low rocky island producing some trees, to which the name of PASSAGE ISLAND was given. We passed in an uninterrupted channel to the east of it, with the appearance of an equally good one on the other side.

Quitting point Atkinson, and proceeding up the sound, we passed on the western shore some detached rocks, with some sunken ones amongst them, that extend about two miles, but are not so far from the shore as to impede the navigation of the sound; up which we made a rapid progress, by the assistance of a fresh southerly gale, attended with dark gloomy weather, that greatly added to the dreary prospect of the surrounding country. The low fertile shores we had been accustomed to see, though lately with some interruption, here no longer existed; their place was now occupied by the base

---

[1] These were Squamish Indians, a Coast Salish tribe, who had a village, Homulchesun, on the N shore at the First Narrows, beyond the several mouths of Capilano Creek. Puget, presumabliy in error, refers to the narrow entrance and adds. 'On its South Side is a Village from which we were visited by about 30 Indians.' — June 13. A second village, Whoi-Whoi, did exist on the S shore in what is now Stanley Park.

[2] Burrard's Canal in the first edition; now Burrard Inlet. Vancouver and its satellite cities have been built on its shores. There is some difference of opinion as to whether Vancouver was honoring the first baronet, who died 12 days after the *Discovery* sailed from England, or his nephew, Sir Harry Burrard, later Sir Harry Burrard-Neale. The weight of the evidence seems to favour the latter, who had been a shipmate of Vancouver in the *Europa*. See Sir Gerald Burrard, 'The Naming of Burrard Inlet', BCHQ x (1946), 143–50, and W. Kaye Lamb, 'Burrard of Burrard's Canal', BCHQ x (1946), 276–80. Narváez suspected the existence of the inlet and named it Canal de Floridablanca in 1791.

[3] Howe Sound.

[4] The friend has not been identified.   [5] Point Cowan, on Bowen Island.

of the stupendous snowy barrier, thinly wooded, and rising from the sea abruptly to the clouds; from whose frigid summit, the dissolving snow in foaming torrents rushed down the sides and chasms of its rugged surface, exhibiting altogether a sublime, though gloomy spectacle, which animated nature seemed to have deserted. Not a bird, nor living creature was to be seen, and the roaring of the falling cataracts in every direction precluded their being heard, had any been in our neighbourhood.

Towards noon I considered that we had advanced some miles within the western boundary of the snowy barrier, as some of its rugged lofty mountains were now behind, and to the southward of us. This filled my mind with the pleasing hopes of finding our way to its eastern side. The sun shining at this time for a few minutes afforded an opportunity of ascertaining the latitude of the east point of an island which, from the shape of the mountain that composes it, obtained the name of ANVIL ISLAND, to be 49° 30', its longitude 237° 3'.[1] We passed an island the forenoon of Friday the 15th, lying on the eastern shore, opposite to an opening on the western, which evidently led into the gulf nearly in a S.W. direction,[2] through a numerous assemblage of rocky islands and rocks, as also another opening to the westward of this island, that seemed to take a similar direction.[3] Between Anvil island and the north point of the first opening, which lies from hence S. by W. five miles distance, are three white rocky islets, lying about a mile from the western shore.[4] The width of this branch of the sound is about a league; but northward from Anvil island it soon narrows to half that breadth, taking a direction to the N.N.E. as far as latitude 49° 39', longitude 237° 9', where all our expectations vanished, in finding it to terminate in a round bason,[5] encompassed on every side by the dreary country already described. At its head, and on the upper part of the eastern shore, a narrow margin of low land runs from the foot of the barrier mountains to the water-side, which produced a few dwarf pine trees, with some little variety of underwood. The water of the sound was here nearly fresh, and in color a few shades darker than milk; this I attributed to the melting of the snow, and its water passing rapidly over a chalky surface, which appeared probable by the white aspect of some of the chasms that seemed formerly to have been the course of water-falls but were now become dry.

The gap we had entered in the snowy barrier seemed of little importance, as through the vallies, caused by the irregularity of the mountain's tops, other mountains more distant, and apparently more elevated, were seen rearing their lofty heads in various directions. In this dreary and comfortless region, it was

[1] The S point of Anvil Island is in lat. 49° 30' N, long. 123° 18' W (236° 42' E).

[2] The island was Bowyer Island; the 'opening to the westward' was the channel across the N end of Bowen Island, leading to Collingwood Channel, which runs down the W side of the Island to the Strait of Georgia.

[3] The entrance to Thornbrough Channel: 'this island' was Anvil Island, not Bowyer Island, as the wording suggests.

[4] Only two are noticed in the official sailing directions: Christie Islet and Pam Rock.

[5] Squamish, the town now at the head of the sound, is in lat. 49° 41' N, long. 123° 09' W (236° 51' E).

no inconsiderable piece of good fortune to find a little cove in which we could take shelter, and a small spot of level land on which we could erect our tent; as we had scarcely finished our examination when the wind became excessively boisterous from the southward, attended with heavy squalls and torrents of rain, which continuing until noon the following day, Friday the 15th, occasioned a very unpleasant detention. But for this circumstance we might too hastily have concluded that this part of the gulf was uninhabited. In the morning we were visited by near forty of the natives, on whose approach, from the very material alteration that had now taken place in the face of the country, we expected to find some difference in their general character. This conjecture was however premature, as they varied in no respect whatever,[1] but in possessing a more ardent desire for commercial transactions; into the spirit of which they entered with infinitely more avidity than any of our former acquaintances, not only in bartering amongst themselves the different valuables they had obtained from us, but when that trade became slack, in exchanging those articles again with our people; in which traffic they always took care to gain some advantage, and would frequently exult on the occasion. Some fish, their garments, spears, bows and arrows, to which these people wisely added their copper ornaments, comprized their general stock in trade. Iron, in all its forms, they judiciously preferred to any other article we had to offer.

The weather permitting us to proceed, we directed our route along the continental or western shore of the sound, passing within two small islands and the main land,[2] into the opening before mentioned, stretching to the westward from Anvil island.[3] At the distance of an hundred yards from the shore, the bottom could not be reached with 60 fathoms of line, nor had we been able to gain soundings in many places since we had quitted point Atkinson with 80 and 100 fathoms, though it was frequently attempted; excepting in the bason at the head of the sound, where the depth suddenly decreased from sixty fathoms to two. We had advanced a short distance only in this branch, before the colour of the water changed from being nearly milk white, and almost fresh, to that of oceanic and perfectly salt. By sun-set we had passed the channel which had been observed to lead into the gulf, to the southward of Anvil island; and about nine o'clock landed for the night, near the west point of entrance into the sound, which I distinguished by the name of HOWE'S SOUND, in honor of Admiral Earl Howe;[4] and this point, situated in latitude 49° 23′, longitude 236° 51′, POINT GOWER;[5] between which and point Atkinson, up to Anvil island, is an extensive group of islands of various

[1] These again would be Squamish Indians.

[2] Defence Island and the smaller island near it.   [3] Thornbrough Channel.

[4] Now Howe Sound. The name appears as Lord Howe's Sound on Baker's MS chart but as Howe's Sound on the engraved chart. The Spaniards had named the sound Bocas del Carmelo in 1791.

[5] The name is Gore Point on both Baker's MS chart and the engraved chart, but the spelling is Gower (the present name) in both editions of the *Voyage*. Meany and Walbran both conclude that the person honored was Captain (later Admiral) Sir Erasmus Gower. The position of the point is lat. 49° 23′ N, long. 123° 32′ W (236° 28′ E).

sizes.[1] The shores of these, like the adjacent coast, are composed principally
of rocks rising perpendicularly from an unfathomable sea; they are tolerably
well covered with trees, chiefly of the pine tribe, though few are of a luxuriant
growth.

At four o'clock on Saturday morning the 16th, we resumed our course
to the northwestward, along the starboard or continental shore of the gulf of
Georgia, which from point Gower takes a direction about W.N.W. and affords
a more pleasing appearance than the shores of Howe's sound. This part of the
coast is of a moderate height for some distance inland, and it frequently jets
out into low sandy projecting points. The country in general produces forest trees in great abundance, of some variety and magnitude; the pine is the
most common, and the woods are little encumbered with bushes or trees of
inferior growth. We continued in this line about five leagues along the coast,
passing some rocks and rocky islets, until we arrived at the north point of
an island about two leagues in circuit, with another about half that size to
the westward of it, and a smaller island between them.[2] From the north point
of this island, which forms a channel with the main about half a mile wide,
and is situated in latitude 49° 28½', longitude 236° 31',[3] the coast of the
continent takes a direction for about eight miles N. 30 W. and is composed
of a rugged rocky shore, with many detached rocks lying at a little distance.
The track we thus pursued had not the appearance of the main branch of the
gulf, but of a channel between the continent and that land, which, from point
Roberts, seemed like a small though very high round island.[4] This now
appeared of considerable extent, its N.E. side formed a channel to the N.W.
as far as the eye could reach, above five miles in width. The main branch of
the gulf, apparently of infinitely greater extent, took a direction to the
south-westward of this land, which now looked more like a peninsula than
an island. Along this rocky shore of the main land we passed in quest of a
resting place for the night, to no effect, until after dark; when we found shelter

[1] Vancouver, primarily interested in the continental shore, neither notices nor names
the two islands of considerable size in Howe Sound – Bowen Island and Gambier
Island – but on Baker's chart the two are named Jarvis's Isles. Probably he had in mind
Admiral Sir John Jervis (later Earl St. Vincent). In 1791 the Spaniards had named Bowen
and nearby islands the Islas de Apodaca.

[2] North Thormanby Island and South Thormanby Island. The third 'smaller island'
is Merry Island, which is SE of them, not between them as Vancouver states. South
Thormanby Island had been named Isla de San Ignacio by the Spaniards in 1791.

[3] Welcome Pass. The names of the pass and the islands adjacent are an interesting
example of the way in which fortuitous circumstances can influence nomenclature.
Welcome Pass was so named in 1860 by Captain Richards of the survey ship *Plumper*
because he had received the welcome news that the horse named Thormanby had won
the Derby; J. C. Merry was the horse's owner. North Thormanby Island is in lat. 49° 30′ N,
long. 123° 58′ W (236° 02′ E).

[4] Texada Island, originally named Isla de San Felix by the Spaniards in 1791 but renamed
Isla de Texada later the same year. The name Texada had been first applied to nearby
Lasqueti Island.

in a very dreary uncomfortable cove near the south point of an island, about
a mile long, and about two miles to the S.S.E. of a narrow opening leading
to the northward.[1] This on the return of day-light on Sunday the 17th, we
proceeded to examine; and passed through a very narrow, though navigable
channel, amongst a cluster of rocks and rocky islets, lying just in the front
of its entrance, which is situated in latitude 49° 35½', longitude 236° 26'. It
is about half a mile wide, winding towards the N.N.E. for about three leagues,
where it divides into two branches, one stretching to the eastward, the other
to the westward of north, with an island before the entrance of the latter.[2]
Agreeably to our general mode of proceeding, the north-easterly branch
became the first object of our attention, and was found from hence to continue
in an irregular course to the latitude of 49° 49', longitude 236° 35½'; where,
finding a tolerably comfortable situation, we rested for the night.[3]

We had seen about seventeen Indians in our travels this day, who were much
more painted than any we had hitherto met with. Some of their arrows were
pointed with slate, the first I had seen so armed on my present visit to this
coast; these they appeared to esteem very highly, and like the inhabitants of
Nootka, took much pains to guard them from injury. They however spoke
not the Nootka language, nor the dialect of any Indians we had conversed
with; at least, the few words we had acquired were repeated to them without
effect; in their persons they differed in no other respect, and were equally civil
and inoffensive in their behaviour.[4] The shores we passed this day are of a
moderate height within a few miles of this station, and are principally
composed of craggy rocks, in the chasms of which a soil of decayed vegetables
has been formed by the hand of time; from which pine trees of an inferior
dwarf growth are produced, with a considerable quantity of bushes and

[1] Beaver Island, S of the mouth of Agamemnon Channel. Fearney Point, the NW point
of entrance to the channel, is in lat. 49° 39' N, 124° 05' W (235° 55' E).

[2] Vancouver had come to the point where Agamemnon Channel joins Jervis Inlet, a
major waterway whose main entrance is about 7 miles up the coast from Fearney Point.
The island at the junction is now Captain Island. Vancouver seems not to have noticed
Skookumchuck Narrows, to the SE, which lead to Sechelt Inlet, some 16 miles in length,
off which branch Narrows Inlet and Salmon Inlet. The omission is surprising, but was of
no consequence from the point of view of the prime purpose of the survey.

[3] Puget might have questioned the description 'tolerably comfortable': 'we brought
up for the Night in a Rocky Cove, driven there perfectly by Necessity...it was not till
11 at Night that we landed, after a most disagreeable & laborious Row, the Boats and their
Furniture were all wet nor was there a Spot to shelter us from the Inclemency of the
Weather, & as it was equally uncomfortable either remaining in the Water afloat or on
Shore most of us preferred the Ground & Fire for the Remainder of the Night; from which
however we experienced little or no Inconvenience except the being under the Necessity
of laying down in wet Cloaths.' – June 17. In 1862 Capt. G. H. Richards of the survey
ship *Hecate* concluded that the party had spent the night in the cove on the E side of Jervis
Inlet that he named Vancouver Bay. The small Vancouver River empties into it.

[4] Vancouver was still in the area inhabited by the Coast Salish Indians and would meet
other Salish bands during the next fortnight. The Salishan language was split into many
tribal dialects, not all of which were mutually intelligible.

underwood. We passed a few rocky islets near the division of the inlet. These seemed steep, as soundings with the hand line could not be gained; nor had we any where in mid-channel been able to reach the bottom with 100 fathoms of line, although the shores are not a mile asunder.

The next morning, Monday the 18th, as usual, at four o'clock, we proceeded up the inlet about three miles in a N.N.W. direction, whence its width increases about half a league in a direction nearly N.E. to a point which towards noon we reached, and ascertained its latitude to be 50° 1', longitude 236° 46'.[1] The width of this channel still continuing, again flattered us with discovering a breach in the eastern range of snowy mountains, notwithstanding the disappointment we had met with in Howe's sound; and although since our arrival in the gulf of Georgia, it had proved an impenetrable barrier to that inland navigation, of which we had heard so much, and had sought with sanguine hopes and ardent exertions hitherto in vain, to discover.

By the progress we had this morning made, which comprehended about six leagues, we seemed to have penetrated considerably into this formidable obstacle; and as the more lofty mountains were now behind us, and no very distant ones were seen beyond the vallies caused by the depressed parts of the snowy barrier in the northern quarters, we had great reason to believe we had passed the centre of this impediment to our wishes, and I was induced to hope we should yet find this inlet winding beyond the mountains, by the channel through which we had thus advanced upwards of 11 leagues, though for the most part it was not more than half a mile wide. Under these circumstances, our reduced stock of provisions was a matter of serious concern, fearing we might be obliged to abandon this pursuit without determining the source of this branch of the sea, having now been absent six days with subsistence for a week only, which would consequently very materially retard our survey, by rendering a second visit to this inlet indispensably necessary. The surrounding country presented an equally dreary aspect with that in the vicinage of Howe's sound; and the serenity of the weather not adding at present to the natural gloominess of the prospect, was counterbalanced by the rugged surface of the mountains being infinitely less productive. A few detached dwarf pine trees, with some berry, and other small bushes, were the only signs of vegetation. The cataracts here rushed from the rugged snowy mountains in greater number, and with more impetuosity than in Howe's sound; yet the colour of the water was not changed, though in some of the gullies there was the same chalky aspect. Hence it is probable, that the white appearance of the water in Howe's sound, may arise from a cause more remote, and which we had no opportunity of discovering.

Having dined, we pursued our examination. The inlet now took a N.W. by W. direction, without any contraction in its width, until about five o'clock in the evening, when all our hopes vanished, by finding it terminate, as others had done, in swampy low land producing a few maples and pines, in latitude

[1] Patrick Point, in lat. 50° 05' 30″ N, long. 123° 48' 30″ W (236° 11' 30″ E).

50° 6′, longitude 236° 33′.[1] Through a small space of low land, which extended from the head of the inlet to the base of the mountains that surrounded us, flowed three small streams of fresh water, apparently originating from one source in the N.W. or left hand corner of the bay, formed by the head of this inlet; in which point of view was seen an extensive valley, that took nearly a northerly uninterrupted direction as far as we could perceive, and was by far the deepest chasm we had beheld in the descending ridge of the snowy barrier, without the appearance of any elevated land rising behind. This valley much excited my curiosity to ascertain what was beyond it. But as the streams of fresh water were not navigable, though the tide had risen up to the habitations of six or seven Indians, any further examination of it in our boats was impracticable, and we had no leisure for excursions on shore. From the civil natives who differed not in any respect from those we had before occasionally seen, we procured a few most excellent fish, for which they were compensated principally in iron, being the commodity they most esteemed and sought after. In all these arms of the sea we had constantly observed, even to their utmost extremity, a visible, and sometimes a material rise and fall of the tide, without experiencing any other current than a constant drain down to seaward, excepting just in the neighbourhood of the gulf.

On our approach to the low land, we gained soundings at 70 fathoms, which soon decreased as we advanced, to 30, 14, and 3 fathoms, on a bank that stretches across the head of the inlet, similar to all the others we had before examined. So far as these soundings extended, which did not exceed half a league, the colour of the water was a little affected, probably by the discharge of the fresh water rivulets, that generally assumed a very light colour. Beyond these soundings the water again acquired its oceanic colour, and its depth was unfathomable.

Not a little mortified that our progress should be so soon stopped, it became highly expedient to direct our way towards the ships, to whose station, by the nearest route we could take, it was at least 114 miles. This was now to be performed, after the time was nearly expired for which our supply of provisions had been calculated. Necessity directed that no time should be lost; especially as I was determined to seek a passage into the gulf by the branch of the inlet that we had passed the preceding day, leading to the N.W. conceiving there was a great probability that this branch might lead into the gulf at some distance beyond where we had entered this inlet; in which course we should have an opportunity of fixing the boundaries of the continent to the utmost extent that our present equipment would afford. For as our people had become wise by experience, I entertained little doubt of their having so husbanded their provisions as to enable our effecting this service; by which means any other excursion this way would be rendered unnecessary.[2]

[1] The head of the inlet is in lat. 50° 13′ N, long. 123° 59′ W (236° 01′ E).
[2] Every effort was made to live off the country: 'some birds the Gentlemen Shot, afforded us an Excellent Repast, these were principally Curlews. But neither Eagles or

About two leagues from the head of the inlet we had observed, as we passed upwards on the northern shore, a small creek with some rocky islets before it, where I intended to take up our abode for the night. On our return, it was found to be a fall of salt water,[1] just deep enough to admit our boats against a very rapid stream, where at low tide they would have grounded some feet above the level of the water in the inlet. From the rapidity of the stream, and the quantity of water it discharged, it was reasonable to suppose, by its taking a winding direction up a valley to the N.E. that its source was at some distance. This not answering our purpose as a resting place, obliged us to continue our search along the shore for one less incommodious, which the perpendicular precipices precluded our finding until near eleven at night, when we disembarked on the only low projecting point the inlet afforded.

At four, on the morning of Tuesday the 19th, we again started, but having a strong southerly gale against us, it was past nine at night before we reached a small bay, about a mile to the north of the north point of the arm leading to the north-westward,[2] where we rested for the night; and, at day-light, proceeded, as usual, along the continental shore.

This first stretched a little way to the north-westward, and then to the S.W. into the gulf, as I had imagined it would; forming, irregularly, a much more spacious channel than that by which we had entered, having an island lying between the two channels about three leagues in length, with several small islets about it.[3] This island, and its adjacent shores, like those in the other channel, are of a moderate height, and wear a similar appearance. It was nearly noon before we reached the north point of the inlet; which, producing the first Scotch firs we had yet seen, obtained the name of SCOTCH-FIR POINT, and is situated in latitude 49° 42′, longitude 236° 17′.[4] To this arm of the sea, I gave the name of JERVIS's CHANNEL, in honour of Admiral Sir John Jervis.[5]

The boundary of the continental shore I now considered as determined to this point, from a full conviction that the inlet under the examination of Mr. Whidbey, would terminate like those we had visited. Presuming our time to have been not ill spent, we directed our course to the station where we had left the ships now at the distance of 84 miles, steering for the opposite shore, being the land before adverted to, as appearing to form an extensive island,

Crows would then have been rejected, which though Coarse food were sometimes eat by us & frequently By the Boats Crews & it was by these Additions that the Provisions were made to last far beyond their proportioned time.' – Puget, 17 June.

[1] Malibu Rapids, at the narrow entrance to Princess Louisa Inlet, a branch of Jervis Inlet 4 miles in length.

[2] Probably Goliath Bay.　　　　　　　　　[3] Nelson Island.

[4] The name has been retained. The position of the point is lat. 49° 45′ N, long. 124° 16′ W (235° 44′ E).

[5] Jervis's Canal in the first edition; now Jervis Inlet. Spelled Jarvis's Canal on both the manuscript and engraved charts. Vancouver gave no name to Agamemnon Channel (so named in 1860); it had been named Boca de Moniño in 1791 by the Spaniards, who had seen its entrance but did not explore it.

or peninsula; the nearest part of which was about five miles across from Scotch-fir point; and with the continental shore still formed a passage, to all appearance, of the same width, in a direction N. 62 W., with an uninterrupted horizon in that point of view; so that, whether it was an island or peninsula, remained still to be determined.

The shores of this land, nearly straight and compact, are principally formed of rocky substances of different sorts; amongst which, slate was in abundance; and the trees it produced were of infinitely more luxuriant growth than those on the opposite shore. In the forenoon of Thursday the 21st, we passed the south point of this land, and in remembrance of an early friendship, I called it POINT UPWOOD, situated in latitude 49° 28½′, longitude 236° 24′.[1] This land, though chiefly composed of one lofty mountain,[2] visible at the distance of 20 leagues and upwards, is very narrow, appearing to form, with the western shore of the gulf, a channel nearly parallel to that which we had last quitted; though considerably more extensive, and containing some small islands. Its horizon was bounded by the summits of high distant detached mountains.

As we were rowing, on the morning of Friday the 22d, for point Grey, purposing there to land and breakfast, we discovered two vessels at anchor under the land.[3] The idea which first occurred was, that, in consequence of our protracted absence, though I had left no orders to this effect, the vessels had so far advanced in order to meet us; but on a nearer approach, it was discovered, that they were a brig and a schooner, wearing the colours of Spanish vessels of war, which I conceived were most probably employed in pursuits similar to our own; and this on my arrival on board, was confirmed. These vessels proved to be a detachment from the commission of Sen[r] Malaspina, who was himself employed in the Phillippine islands; Sen[r] Malaspina had, the preceding year, visited the coast; and these vessels, his Catholic Majesty's brig the Sutil, under the command of Sen[r] Don D. Galiano, with the schooner Mexicana, commanded by Sen[r] Don C. Valdes, both captains of frigates in the Spanish navy, had sailed from Acapulco on the 8th of March, in order to prosecute discoveries on this coast.[4] Sen[r] Galiano, who

[1] Its position is lat. 49° 29′ N, long. 124° 07′ W (235° 53′ E).

[2] Texada Island. A curious remark, as Mount Shepherd is near the S end of an island over 30 miles in length.

[3] The ships were not anchored off Spanish Bank, to the N of Point Grey and E of it, as is often assumed. The narrative of the voyage states that they 'let the anchor fall in 10 [fathoms] with the most northern end of Punta de Langara [Point Grey] bearing E 05° N from us.' – Wagner, *Spanish Explorations of the Strait of Juan de Fuca*, p. 262; a translation of the *Viage de las goletas Sutil y Mexicana* (Madrid, 1802). This places the ships W of the point, a little to the S of it, and sufficiently offshore to be clear of the shallows on the W side of the point. To Vancouver, rowing down the Strait of Georgia, they would appear to be 'under the land'.

[4] The survey had been planned in accordance with Malaspina's recommendations and it was commanded by two of his officers – Dionisio Alcalá Galiano and Cayetano Valdés – who had been made available for the purpose, but it was not otherwise connected

spoke a little English,[1] informed me, that they had arrived at Nootka on the 11th of April, from whence they had sailed on the 5th of this month, in order to complete the examination of this inlet, which had, in the preceding year, been partly surveyed by some Spanish officers whose chart they produced.[2]

I cannot avoid acknowledging that, on this occasion, I experienced no small degree of mortification in finding the external shores of the gulf had been visited, and already examined a few miles beyond where my researches during the excursion, had extended; making the land, I had been in doubt about, an island;[3] continuing nearly in the same direction, about four leagues further than had been seen by us; and, by the Spaniards, named Favida.[4] The channel, between it and the main, they had called Canal del Neustra Signora del Rosario,[5] whose western point had terminated their examination; which seemed to have been entirely confined to the exterior shores, as the extensive arms, and inlets, which had occupied so much of our time, had not claimed the least of their attention.

The Spanish vessels, that had been thus employed last year, had refitted in the identical part of port Discovery, which afforded us similar accommodation. From these gentlemen, I likewise understood, that Senr Quadra, the commander in chief of the Spanish marine at St Blas and at California, was, with three frigates and a brig, waiting my arrival at Nootka, in order to negotiate the restoration of those territories to the crown of Great Britain. Their conduct was replete with that politeness and friendship which characterizes the Spanish nation; every kind of useful information they cheerfully communicated, and obligingly expressed much desire, that circumstances might so concur as to admit our respective labours being carried on together;[6] for which purpose,

with his own expedition. Both Galiano and Valdés were experienced navigators with considerable knowledge of surveying. In 1805 both served at Trafalgar and Galiano was killed in the battle.

[1] 'we conceived ourselves particularly fortunate that this Gentleman spoke English with great Ease and Fluency.' – Puget, 22 June.

[2] Presumably the chart of Eliza's discoveries drawn by Juan Carrasco. At some stage Vancouver was evidently given a copy or permitted to make one.

[3] Texada Island.

[4] Feveda on both Baker's MS chart and the engraved chart. This was a misreading of Texada, which is clearly marked on Carrasco's chart.

[5] Adopting what he thought was the Spanish name, Vancouver named the present Malaspina Strait, between Texada Island and the mainland, Canal de Nuestra Señora del Rosario, but he was mistaken. The Spaniards had applied the name to the whole Strait (Vancouver's Gulf) of Georgia. Vancouver retained his own name for the main waterway, and the name Rosario is now confined to a strait through the San Juan Islands.

[6] The diary or journal kept by Galiano and Valdes suggests that they were less enthusiastic about collaboration than this implies. They state that Vancouver put forward 'his argument that our vessels should join his so as to be able to work together. He did this in such terms that not only were we obliged to agree but we comprehended that if we did not it would be discreditable, not only as far as we were concerned, but even for the public credit of the nation.' They evidently regarded Vancouver with some suspicion: by cooperating 'we might discern their views relative to these countries and the true object

or, if from our long absence and fatigue in an open boat, I would wish to remain with my party as their guest, they would immediately dispatch a boat with such directions as I might deem necessary for the conduct of the ships, or, in the event of a favorable breeze springing up, they would weigh and sail directly to their station; but being intent on losing no time, I declined their obliging offers, and having partaken with them, a very hearty breakfast, bad them farewell, not less pleased with their hospitality and attention, than astonished at the vessels in which they were employed to execute a service of such a nature. They were each about forty-five tons burthen, mounted two brass guns, and were navigated by twenty-four men, bearing one lieutenant, without a single inferior officer. Their apartments just allowed room for sleeping places on each side, with a table in the intermediate space, at which four persons, with some difficulty, could sit, and were, in all other respects, the most ill calculated and unfit vessels that could possibly be imagined for such an expedition;[1] notwithstanding this, it was pleasant to observe, in point of living, they possessed many more comforts than could reasonably have been expected. I shewed them the sketch I had made of our excursion, and pointed out the only spot which I conceived we had left unexamined, nearly at the head of Burrard's channel:[2] they seemed much surprized that we had not found a river said to exist in the region we had been exploring, and named by one of their officers Rio Blancho,[3] in compliment to the then prime minister of Spain; which river these gentlemen had sought for thus far to no purpose. They took such notes as they chose from my sketch, and promised to examine the small opening in Burrard's channel, which, with every other information they could procure, should be at my service on our next meeting.

From these new and unexpected friends we directed our course along the shoal already noticed, which I now called STURGEON BANK, in consequence of our having purchased of the natives some excellent fish of that kind, weighing from fourteen to two hundred pounds each. To avoid this bank, which stretches from point Roberts to point Grey,[4] a most excellent leading

of their explorations in them, gaining at the same time an idea of their methods of service and mode of working.' – Wagner, *Spanish Explorations*, p. 215.

[1] Though they differed in rig, the two Spanish vessels were otherwise identical; both were originally schooners. They were built at San Blas, had an overall length of 50 feet 3 inches, and a width of 13 feet 10 inches. Tonnage was 46. The Spaniards 'held that these vessels combined the advantage of light draught [about 6 feet],...[and] of handiness under sail or when rowed.' But they were lightly built and had had to be overhauled and strengthend at Acapulco before sailing northward.

[2] Indian Arm.

[3] The Spaniards suspected the existence of the Fraser River, but at this time confused its mouth with Burrard Inlet. The narrative of the expedition notes that as they sailed N from Point Roberts they 'were already in water almost fresh, and saw great logs floating, these signs confirming us in the idea that the inlet we called Floridablanca [Burrard Inlet] was the mouth of some large river.' – Wagner, *Spanish Explorations*, p. 262.

[4] The name is still used, but the S part of the bank, between Point Roberts and the main (southern) channel of the Fraser River is now called Roberts Bank.

mark was observed along its western extremity, being Passage and Anvil islands in one, which lead by its edge in six fathoms water, deepening suddenly to the westward, and in many places to the eastward, shoaling as suddenly to three, two, and one fathom. The circle which this bank occasioned us to make, made the distance to point Roberts upwards of 30 miles. We were likewise unfortunate in having two flood tides against us. These, together with a light southerly breeze that prevailed the whole time, obliged us to be constantly rowing from nine in the forenoon until after midnight, before we could reach the point, which was at length effected; though not before we were nearly exhausted by fatigue. Here we slept, and in the morning of Saturday the 23rd, against a strong easterly breeze, about ten in the forenoon we reached the ships, after having traversed in our boats upwards of 330 miles. [1]

The broken part of the coast that Mr. Whidbey had been employed in examining, was found to extend but a few miles to the northward of the spot where his former researches had ended; forming altogether an extensive bay, which I have distinguished as BELLINGHAM'S BAY. [2] It is situated behind a cluster of islands, from which a number of channels lead into it: its greatest extent in a north and south direction, is from the latitude 48° 36', to 48° 48'; the longitude of its eastern extremity 237° 50'. [3] It every where affords good and

[1] 'In this Expedition By the Geometrical Mensuration the Boats have run 315 Miles, in 11 Days, on an Average at the Rate of 28' a Day. This certainly is an Immense Distance, considering the very lumbered and heavy Situation of the Boats on their first Outset & the Quantity of Articles which must to the End of the Cruise be in them & consequently retard their Progress.' – Puget, 23 June. Vancouver does not mention an incident that resulted in an estrangement between him and Manby. On the evening of 19 June, returning down Jervis Inlet, the boats reached the point where Agamemnon Channel joins the main channel of the inlet, which runs W to Malaspina Strait. Vancouver and Puget were ahead in the pinnace; Manby was far behind in the launch. As usual, Vancouver wished to trace the continental shore and therefore followed the main channel; unaware of this, Manby turned S into Agamemnon Channel. His account reads: 'in the dark we parted company and did not again meet untill we joined the Ship. In a deplorable state I remained three days without a thing to eat, but what my Gun afforded, and destitute of a Compass, to regain my way to the Discovery....On the 24th The Captain arrived on board, his salutation I can never forget, and his language I will never forgive, unless he withdraws his words by a satisfactory apology.' Two years later, in June 1793, John Carter, a seaman in the *Discovery*, would die of mussel poisoning in a cove farther up the coast. It seems not to have been noticed that on his way back to the ship, Manby's crew suffered from the same malady: 'My Boats Crew suffered every hardship fatigue and hunger could inflict, in a small cove I passed a Night that abounded with Muscles. A fire soon cooked us sufficient to make a voracious Meal of. In the course of an hour, the whole of us were taken violently ill, and experienced every agony a poisoned set of beings could feel, I gorged them all, with hot water, which had the desired effect, by clearing the Stomach from this dangerous food, it threw one Man into a Fever, the rest fortunately recovered.' – Manby, Letters, June.

[2] Named for Sir William Bellingham, controller of storekeeper's accounts of the Navy. Vancouver also named Point William and Frances Point, which he evidently considered the N and S points of entry to the bay; the names appear on his chart. Frances Point (wrongly spelled Francis on the chart) was named for Bellingham's wife, Lady Frances.

[3] The correct long. would be about 122° 30' W (237° 30' E).

secure anchorage; opposite to its north point of entrance the shores are high and rocky, with some detached rocks lying off it. Here was found a brook of most excellent water. To the north and south of these rocky cliffs the shores are less elevated, especially to the northward, where some of those beautiful verdant lawns were again presented to our view. Near the north entrance into this bay, the two Spanish vessels had been descried by Mr. Whidbey, who returned, and communicated the intelligence to the ships; in consequence of which the Chatham weighed and spoke them off point Roberts; they having passed our ships during the night undiscovered.[1]

Having now fixed the continental shore so far as from this station was within our reach, and having obtained sufficient observations for correcting the rate of our chronometers, every thing was immediately re-embarked, and we were in readiness to proceed in the morning.

During my absence, the boats of the Discovery and Chatham had been employed in attempting to gain some further knowledge of the numerous islands we passed on our arrival in this bay; but they were found so abundantly dispersed as to preclude any correct examination, without having sufficient leisure for the purpose.

Nothing further occurred at this station worthy of notice, if we except an observation which had been repeatedly made, that in proportion as we advanced to the northward, the forests were composed of an infinitely less variety of trees, and their growth was less luxuriant. Those most commonly seen were pines of different sorts, the arbor vitæ, the oriental arbutus, and I believe, some species of cypress. On the islands some few small oaks were seen, with the Virginian juniper; and at this place the Weymouth pine, Canadian elder, and black birch; which latter grew in such abundance, that it obtained the name of BIRCH BAY.[2] The S.E. part of this bay is formed by nearly perpendicular rocky cliffs, from whence the higher woodland country retires a considerable distance to the north eastward, leaving an extensive space of low land between it and the sea, separated from the high ground by a rivulet of fresh water that discharges itself at the bottom, or northern extremity of

[1] When sailing northward the Spaniards had seen Whidbey's boats in Lummi Bay. Their appearance caused no surprise: 'We did not doubt that they belonged to the two English ships which according to the information from our friend Tetacus [an Indian chief at Neah Bay] were in the strait.' After darkness fell the Spanish ships sailed past Birch Bay 'and saw lights within it, which told us that the ships to which the smaller vessels belonged were lying at that anchorage.' – Wagner, Spanish Explorations, p. 249; translation of the Viage de las goletas Sutil y Mexicana.

[2] There is some confusion about the name given to the bay by the Spaniards, but it appears to have been the Ensenada or Puerto de Garzon. Vancouver's officers and men alike found it attractive: 'by far the most pleasing Place we have been at on the Coast of America.' – Heddington, 12 June. 'We found it an excellent Station for all our purposes, the water was good & easy & expeditious in the filling. the plain on which the Observatory was fixed, was of considerable extent & clear of Wood, affording a pleasant place of exercise for our people & likewise an abundance of wild fruit & vegetables of different kinds.' – Baker, 24 June.

the bay. On the low land very luxuriant grass was produced, with wild rose, gooseberry, and other bushes in abundance.

I shall conclude this chapter by stating that, by the mean result of eleven meridional altitudes of the sun, we found Birch bay situated in latitude 48° 53½′; the longitude 237° 33′,[1] was deduced from the observations made use of for settling port Discovery, including twenty-eight sets of lunar distances taken at this station, whence on the 22d, at noon, Kendall's chronometer was found to be 54′ 11″ 29‴ fast of mean time at Greenwich, and by six days corresponding altitudes, to be gaining on mean time at the rate of 12″ 45‴ per day. Mr. Arnold's on board the Chatham, from the same authority was, on the same day at noon, fast of mean time at Greenwich, 3ʰ 14′ 46″, and gaining at the rate of 25″ 15‴ per day. The variation of the compass, by nineteen sets of azimuths, differing from 17½ to 21 degrees, gave a mean result of 19° 30′ eastwardly variation.

The vertical inclination of the marine dipping needle,

Marked end,	North face	East	72° 18′
Ditto,	Ditto	West	73
Ditto,	South face	East	73 28
Ditto,	Ditto	West	74 20

The mean vertical inclination of the magnetic needle 73 13

The tides were found to be very inconsiderable, but were not particularly noticed.

[1] The position of the centre of the bay is about lat. 48° 55′ N, long. 122° 46′ W (237° 14′ E).

Plate 25. Dionisio Alcalá Galiano.

Plate 26. Cayetano Valdés.

CHAPTER VIII.

The Vessels continue their Route to the Northward—Anchor in Desolation Sound—
The Boats dispatched on surveying Parties—Discover a Passage to Sea—Quit
Desolation Sound—Pass through Johnstone's Straits.

WITH a fine breeze, and very pleasant weather, we sailed out of Birch bay, on Midsummer morning;[1] and, with the wind from the eastward, we directed our course up the gulf, to the north-westward. About two in the afternoon of Sunday the 24th, we were joined by the Spanish vessels, who saluted by cheering. This was returned; after which their respective commanders favored me with their company on board the Discovery; and we pursued our way up the gulf together.

Senr Galiano informed me, that they had examined the small branch I had passed by in Burrard's channel,[2] which was found very narrow, leading in a north direction nearly three leagues, where it terminated in a small rivulet. They favored me with a copy of their sketch of it, as also with their good company until sun-set, when they returned to their vessels; point Roberts then bearing by compass S. 68 E. point Grey, N. 64 E.; which, being the nearest part of the continental or eastern shore, was at the distance of about three leagues; and the nearest part of the opposite shore of the gulf, bearing S.W. was distant about two leagues.

During the night, and until noon the next day, Monday the 25th, the winds were light and baffling. In the course of the forenoon a great number of whales were playing about in every direction; and though we had been frequently visited by these animals in this inland navigation, there seemed more about us now, than the whole of those we had before seen, if collected together.

This circumstance, in some measure, favored the assertion in Mr. Meares's publication, that a passage to the ocean would be found by persevering in our present course; though this was again rendered very doubtful, as we had understood, from our Spanish friends, that, notwithstanding the Spaniards had lived upon terms of great intimacy with Mr. Gray and other American traders at Nootka, they had no knowledge of any person having ever performed such a voyage, but from the history of it published in England; and so far were these gentlemen from being better acquainted with the discoveries of De Fuca or De Fonte than ourselves, that, from us, they expected much information

---

[1] June 24, an English quarter day.　　　　　　　[2] Indian Arm.

as to the truth of such reports. Senr Valdes, who had been on the coast the preceding year, and spoke the Indian language very fluently, understood, from the natives, that this inlet *did* communicate with the ocean to the northward, where they had seen ships. He was, however, too well acquainted with their characters as reporters, to place much dependance on their information, which was incompetent to the forming of any idea how far remote such ocean might be.[1]

A gentle gale springing up from the eastward, soon after mid-day, we brought to for the Spanish vessels, who were at some distance astern. When they came up, we were honored with the company of the commanders to dinner; and then made sail, directing our course through the channel del Neustra Signora del Rosario,[2] whose whole extent nearly in a direction N. 53 W. is about 10 leagues from point Upwood, the S.W. point, to POINT MARSHALL, the N.W. point of the island of Feveda,[3] which point is situated in latitude 49° 48', longitude 235° 47½'.[4] From Scotch-Fir point, the shores of the channel approximated, until they became within two miles of each other, at its western end; and are, as well on the island as on the continental side, nearly straight, perfectly compact, and rise gradually, particularly on the continental shore, from a beach of sand and small stones, to a height that might be considered rather elevated land, well clothed with wood, but without any

[1] Puget implies that Spanish expectations were somewhat more definite: 'It Appears that some of their Pilots had previously been employed in this Service & by the Plans there seemed a great Probability of our finding a Passage through, though materially Different from what Mr. Mears represents to be the Route of the Sloop Washington.' – June 22. At this time both the fabled straits of Juan de Fuca and Bartholomew de Fonte threatened to become realities that could jeopardize Spain's claim to the ownership of Northwest Coast unless the Spaniards explored them promptly. In July 1787 Captain C. W. Barkley, in the ship *Imperial Eagle*, had sighted an opening which, in his wife's words, he 'immediately recognized as the long lost strait of Juan de Fuca'. Brief visits by trading ships followed, notably that by Robert Gray in the *Lady Washington*, who, according to Meares, had circumnavigated what is now Vancouver Island. Spain reacted by an effort to protect her sovereignty by exploring whatever waterways actually existed inside and beyond the strait. The Quimper, Eliza and Galiano expeditions were successive parts of this effort. By the time Vancouver reached the coast the Spaniards were also following up a clue that suggested that de Fonte's strait, which he claimed to have explored in 1640, actually existed. In 1791, when Colnett was about to sail from Nootka in the repossessed *Argonaut*, he had given Eliza a copy of a map in which he had charted his movements during his earlier visit to the Northwest Coast in 1787–88. De Fonte was supposed to have found his strait or river at lat. 53° N. Colnett had seen the outlets of several inlets thereabouts, and seems to have assumed that one of them, probably Douglas Channel, was de Fonte's strait. Eliza sent Colnett's map to the Viceroy in Mexico, who took steps immediately to have the area explored. The result was the Caamaño expedition of 1792, which was already far up the coast by the time Vancouver met Galiano.

[2] Malaspina Strait.

[3] Texada Island.

[4] The NW point of Texada Island is Kiddie Point, and it seems likely that it was this point that Vancouver named Point Marshall. If so, the name has migrated a mile to the S to the present Marshall Point. The derivation of the name is not known. Kiddie Point is in lat. 49° 48' N, long. 124° 38' W (235° 22' E).

signs of being inhabited. From hence the continental shore took a N.W. direction. From point Marshall, N. 35 W. about a league distant, lies an island of a moderate height, four miles in circuit, with a smaller one about a mile to the S.W. of it: between this, which I named HARWOOD'S ISLAND,[1] and point Marshall, are some rocky islands and sunken rocks.

On the coast of the main land opposite this island is a small brook,[2] probably of fresh water; from whence, as we advanced, the shores put on a very dreary aspect, chiefly composed of rugged rocks, thinly wooded with small dwarf pine trees. The islands, however, which appeared before us, were of a moderate height, and presented a scene more pleasing and fertile. About five in the evening we passed between the main and an island lying in an east and west direction, which I named SAVARY'S ISLAND,[3] about two leagues long, and about half a league broad: its N.E. point, situated in latitude 49° 57½′, longitude 235° 54½′,[4] forms a passage with the continental shore, along which, in a N.W. direction, we continued at a distance from half a mile to half a league. On the south side of Savary's island were numberless sunken rocks, nearly half a league from its shores, visible I believe only at low water.

We seemed now to have forsaken the main direction of the gulf, being on every side encompassed by islands and small rocky islets; some lying along the continental shore, others confusedly scattered, of different forms and dimensions. South-westward of these islands, the main arm of the gulf extended in a north west direction, apparently three or four leagues wide, bounded by high though distant land. Through this very unpleasant navigation we sailed, still keeping close to the continental shore, which was compact. About dark we entered a spacious sound stretching to the eastward.[5] Here I was very desirous of remaining until day-light; but soundings could not be gained though close to the shore.

The night was dark and rainy, and the winds so light and variable, that by the influence of the tides we were driven about as it were blindfolded in this labyrinth, until towards midnight, when we were happily conducted to the north side of an island in this supposed sound,[6] where we anchored in company with the Chatham and the Spanish vessels, in 32 fathoms water, rocky bottom. At break of day on Tuesday the 26th, we found ourselves about half a mile from the shores of a high rocky island, surrounded by a detached and broken country, whose general appearance was very inhospitable.

[1] Harwood Island. Walbran states that it was named after Edward Harwood, who served for many years as a surgeon in the Royal Navy.

[2] The Powell River, which is much larger than Vancouver suggests. It now provides hydro-electric power for large pulp and paper mills.

[3] Savary's Isle on the engraved chart. The derivation of the name is not known.

[4] Mace Point, in lat. 49° 57′ N, long. 124° 45′ W (235° 15′ E). The discrepancy in long., which is unusually large (almost 40′), may be due to a misprint in the *Voyage*.

[5] Desolation Sound.

[6] Kinghorn Island, lying just within the entrance to the sound. The Spaniards named it Isla de la Quema because a fire was seen on it. Baker's MS chart shows that Vancouver's ships anchored on the N side of the island.

Stupendous rocky mountains rising almost perpendicularly from the sea, principally composed the north west, north and eastern quarters; on these, pine trees, though not of luxuriant growth, nor of much variety, were produced in great numbers. The pleasing prospects which the shores on the eastern side of the gulf afforded by their contrast with the mountains of the snowy barrier, giving a grand and interesting character to the landscape, here no longer existed; nor had we been enabled to trace that range of mountains far to the north-westward of Scotch-Fir point, where the line of coast forms a very considerable angle with that of the barrier mountains. It is however probable, that at some distance from our present anchorage, where the perpendicular precipices we were now under would no longer have obstructed our view of the inland country, their lofty summits would have been still visible. The tops of the rugged mountains that compose these shores were not sufficiently elevated to retain the snow in summer, which, in all probability, clothes them during the winter season.

The infinitely divided appearance of the region into which we had now arrived, promised to furnish ample employment for our boats.

To Lieutenant Puget and Mr. Whidbey, in the Discovery's launch and cutter, I consigned the examination of the continental shore, from the place where we had lost sight of it the preceding evening. Mr. Johnstone, in the Chatham's cutter, accompanied by Mr. Swaine in her launch, were directed to investigate a branch of this sound leading to the north-westward; and Senr Valdes undertook the survey of the intermediate coast;[1] by which arrangement the whole, or if not a very considerable extent, would soon be determined. Whilst the boats were equipping, Mr. Broughton went in quest of a more commodious situation for the ships up the sound to the north west.[2]

The weather, which was serene and extremely pleasant, afforded me an opportunity, in company with Senr Galiano and some of our officers, to visit the shore of the island, near which we were at anchor, and to determine the situation of its west point to be in latitude 50° 6′, longitude 235° 26′. With the former Senr Galiano's observations agreed, but by his chronometer the longitude was made more westerly. My observations being deduced from the

---

[1] Menzies' journal throws some light on the arrangements made for the survey parties: 'On the morning of the 26th Don Alcala Galeano...came on board the Discovery to make overtures to Capt Vancouver of a juncture of the two parties to facilitate the examination of this intricate Country, saying, that his Boats & Crews were ready to aid in the execution of any plan of operation that might be devised for that purpose, & as his Vessels were of a small draught of Water they might be commodiously employd on difficult & distant excursions, offering at the same time the chief direction of the parties to Capt Vancouver, which was declined – & Capt Galeano then proposd to send one of his Boats to examine a large opening leading to the Northward & on his returning on board, he dispatched Don Valdes Commander of the Schooner in one of their Launches upon that service.' – 26 June. It will be noted that Vancouver took care to ensure that he himself or his officers should continue to trace the continental shore; he was not prepared to delegate this essential task to anyone else.

[2] Lewis Channel.

watch, according to its rate as settled in Birch bay, which was not very likely to have yet acquired any material error, inclined me to believe we were probably the most correct.[1]

Early in the afternoon Mr. Broughton returned, having found a more eligible anchorage, though in a situation equally dreary and unpleasant. The several gentlemen in the boats being made acquainted with the station to which the ships were about to resort, departed agreeably to their respective instructions.

The wind, that since noon had blown fresh from the S.E. attended with heavy squalls and much rain, drove us, by its increased violence, from our anchorage, and almost instantly into 70 and 80 fathoms water. The anchor was immediately hove up, and we steered for the rendezvous Mr. Broughton had pointed out, where, about six in the evening, we arrived in company with our little squadron. Our situation here was on the northern side of an arm of the sound leading to the north-westward,[2] a little more than half a mile wide, presenting as gloomy and dismal an aspect as nature could well be supposed to exhibit, had she not been a little aided by vegetation; which though dull and uninteresting, screened from our sight the dreary rocks and precipices that compose these desolate shores, especially on the northern side; as the opposite shore, though extremely rude and mountainous, possessed a small space of nearly level land, stetching from the water side, on which some different sorts of the pine tribe, arbor vitæ, maple, and the oriental arbutus, seemed to grow with some vigour, and in a better soil.

The very circumscribed view that we had of the country here, rendered it impossible to form the most distant idea of any circumstances relative to the situation in which we had become stationary; whether composed of islands, or of such arms of the sea as we had lately been employed in examining, or how long there was a probability of our remaining in anxious expectation for the return of our friends. Our residence here was truly forlorn; an awful silence pervaded the gloomy forests, whilst animated nature seemed to have deserted the neighbouring country, whose soil afforded only a few small onions, some samphire, and here and there bushes bearing a scanty crop of indifferent berries. Nor was the sea more favorable to our wants, the steep rocky shores prevented the use of the seine, and not a fish at the bottom could be tempted to take the hook.

I had absented myself from the present surveying excursions, in order to procure some observations for the longitude here, and to arrange the charts of the different surveys in the order they had been made. These, when so methodized, my third lieutenant Mr. Baker had undertaken to copy and embellish, and who, in point of accuracy, neatness, and such dispatch as

[1] Vancouver placed the point some distance E of its true position, which is lat. 50° 05′ N, long. 124° 51′ 30″ W (235° 08′ 30″ E).
[2] Baker's chart shows that the anchorage was off the N shore of Teakerne Arm, a little E of the entrance.

circumstances admitted, certainly excelled in a very high degree. To conclude our operations up to the present period some further angles were required. Beside these I was desirous of acquiring some knowledge of the main channel of the gulf we had quitted on Monday afternoon, and to which no one of our boats had been directed.

Early in the morning of Saturday the 30th, I set out in the yawl on that pursuit, with a favorable breeze from the N.W. which shortly shifted to the opposite quarter, and blew a fresh gale, attended with a very heavy rain. Having reached by ten in the forenoon no further than the island under which we had anchored at midnight on the 25th, a prospect of a certain continuance of the unsettled weather obliged me to abandon my design, and return to the ship; where I had the pleasure of hearing the launch and cutter had arrived soon after my departure, after having completed the examination of the continental coast from the place where we had left it, the night we had entered the sound, to about three leagues north-westward of our present station, making the land near which we were then at anchor on our northern side, an island, or a cluster of islands of considerable extent. These gentlemen were likewise of opinion, that all the land before us to the westward and N.W. from its insular appearance, formed an immense archipelago; but knowing Mr. Johnstone was directed to examine that quarter, and coming within sight of the ships, they had returned on board for further instructions.

On the commencement of their survey, they found the continental shore continue nearly in its N.W. direction to the eastern point of entrance into this sound, which I called POINT SARAH, and is situated in latitude 50° 4½′; longitude 235° 25½′; its opposite point, which I named POINT MARY,[1] lying N. 72 W. about half a league distant; from point Sarah they proceeded along the continental shore up a very narrow channel,[2] rendered almost inaccessible by the number of sunken rocks and rocky islets which it contained. It was found to lead in a south-easterly direction, almost parallel with, and two or three miles from, the northern shore of the gulf at the distance of about three leagues, with a smaller branch near the middle,[3] extending about a league from its northern shore to the N.N.E. From this channel they continued along the continental shore in an easterly and N.E. direction,[4] which led to that part of the coast under the inspection of Senr Valdes. The eastern shore, for the space of two leagues, was found much indented; and several small islands and rocks were seen lying near it to the latitude of 50° 10′, longitude 235° 35′.

[1] Named after Vancouver's sisters. No agreement had been reached with the Spaniards regarding place names, and each expedition named geographical features independently. In general, those given by Vancouver have prevailed. The Spanish names for Sarah and Mary points were Punta de Sarmiento and Punta de Magellanes. The position of Sarah Point is lat. 50° 04′ N, long. 124° 40′ W (235° 10′ E).

[2] Malaspina Inlet, which continues as Okeover Inlet.

[3] Lancelot Inlet. Puget's account shows that they also examined Theodosia Inlet, which branches off Lancelot Inlet.

[4] That is, up Homfray Channel, between the Redondo Islands and the mainland.

Here these rocky islets disappeared, and the coast took a winding course N.W. and westward, to a point bearing from the above station N. 35 W. distant about two leagues, and forming the east point of an arm of the sound, whose entrance, about half a league wide, has two islets lying in it.[1] About a mile up this arm they met Senr Valdes, who informed them he had thoroughly explored that place,[2] and that in the channel leading to the north-westward[3] he had spoken with Mr. Johnstone, so that there could be no doubt of a passage to the ships by that route. Senr Valdes intimated that he considered any further investigation of that place totally unnecessary; but the officers not having on this occasion any directions of a discretionary nature, acted according to the directions they had formerly received for the execution of such service, and prosecuted its examination.[4] They found it extend in an irregular north-easterly direction to the latitude of 50° 22', longitude 235° 46', where it terminated in shallow water and a little low land; through which flowed two small rivulets.[5] In these rivulets, and on the shoal parts, several wears were erected. Along the shores of the upper part of this arm, which are mostly composed of high steep barren rocks, were several fences formed by thin laths, stuck either in the ground, or in the chinks of the rocks, with others placed along them; some in horizontal, others in oblique, and different directions. Ranges of these were fixed along the rocky cliffs in the line of the shore, others varied from that direction, and from their appearance were supposed to be intended for the purpose of drying fish; but as similar works, though perhaps not quite so extensive, had been often observed without being appropriate to that use, and always at a considerable distance from any known habitation; the object they were designed for, remained as uncertain to us,[6] as the application of the high beacons we found so frequently erected on the more southern part of New Georgia.

The surrounding country up this arm nearly corresponded with that in the neighbourhood of Howe's sound; and, like it, was nearly destitute of inhabitants. Two canoes were seen, which the owners had very recently

[1] Channel Island and Double Island.

[2] Toba Inlet. Valdés seems not to have mentioned that on 27 June, while exploring the inlet, he had happened upon a board or tablet that the Indians had covered with hieroglyphics. A sketch was made of it which was reproduced in the atlas accompanying the account of the Galiano-Valdés expedition. In view of this discovery the Spaniards named the inlet Brazo de la Tabla, but on the Galiano-Valdés map of 1795 the name appears as Brazo de Toba. Wagner suggests that the change was made to honor Antonio Toba (or Tova) Arredondo, an officer of the Malaspina expedition, from which Galiano and Valdés had been seconded.

[3] Pryce Channel.

[4] Further evidence that Vancouver was unwilling to accept any survey of the continental shore except his own.

[5] The head of the inlet is in about lat. 50° 30' N, long. 124° 22' W (235° 38' E).

[6] In spite of Vancouver's doubts (which were shared by Puget), these were undoubtedly for drying fish. Menzies noted that they were 'erected from the ground in a slanting manner, for the purpose of exposing the fish fastened to them to the most advantageous aspect for drying.' – 27 June.

quitted, as their garments and many of their utensils were remaining in them, to which the officers added some articles of iron, copper, beads, and other trinkets. From hence they directed their course towards the ship, and arrived as before stated. The country they had visited differed little, excepting in one or two small spots, from the region in which we were then stationed: the whole presented one desolate, rude, and inhospitable aspect. It has already been considered as not entirely destitute of the human race; and that it had been more populous than at present, was manifested by the party having discovered an extensive deserted village,[1] computed to have been the residence of nearly three hundred persons. It was built on a rock, whose perpendicular cliffs were nearly inaccessible on every side; and connected with the main, by a low narrow neck of land, about the centre of which grew a tree, from whose branches planks were laid to the rock, forming by this means a communication that could easily be removed, to prevent their being molested by their internal unfriendly neighbours; and protected in front, which was presented to the sea, from their external enemies, by a platform, which, with much labour and ingenuity had been constructed on a level with their houses, and overhung and guarded the rock. This, with great stability, was formed by large timbers judiciously placed for supporting each other in every direction; their lower ends were well secured in the chasms of the rocks about half way to the water's edge, admitting the platform to be so projected as to command the foot of the rock against any attempt to storm the village. The whole seemed so skilfully contrived, and so firmly and well executed, as rendered it difficult to be considered the work of the untutored tribes we had been accustomed to meet; had not their broken arms and implements, with parts of their manufactured garments, plainly evinced its inhabitants to be of the same race.

Whilst examining these abandoned dwellings, and admiring the rude citadel projected for their defence, our gentlemen were suddenly assailed by an unexpected numerous enemy, whose legions made so furious an attack upon each of their persons, that unable to vanquish their foes, or to sustain the conflict, they rushed up to their necks in water. This expedient, however, proved ineffectual; nor was it till after all their clothes were boiled, that they were disengaged from an immense hord of fleas, which they had disturbed by examining too minutely the filthy garments and apparel of the late inhabitants.[2]

The weather continued very rainy and unpleasant until the forenoon of Saturday the 1st of July, when, on its clearing up, Mr. Puget and Mr. Whidbey were again dispatched, to execute the task I had the preceding day attempted;

[1] Newcombe, who knew the locality well, places this village in Prideaux Haven, Homfray Channel. *Menzies' Journal*, p. 66.

[2] Puget states that they found in the village 'an astonishing Quantity of Filth and Dirt, with a very offensive Smell.' – 28 June. Menzies was convinced that the filth and fleas had forced the natives to leave. The village was named Flea Village and 'a high conspicuous Mountain to the Westward [actually N] of it on the opposite side of the Arm [now Mount Addenbroke] was named from its figure *Anvil Mountain*.' – June 27.

as likewise to gain some information of the southern side of the gulf, and the broken country, which existed between it and our present anchorage.

The securities about the head of the Discovery being constantly out of repair, our carpenters were now employed on that service; and, here also, we brewed some spruce-beer, which was excellent.

The next day, Monday the 2d, in the afternoon, Mr. Johnstone returned, who, after having met Sen[r] Valdes, as before stated, abandoned his pursuit of that which appeared to him to be the main shore leading to the eastward,[1] and prosecuted his researches in the opposite direction, leading to the west, N.W. and to the north, in a channel of an irregular width, where, after examining a small opening, in a northerly direction,[2] he shortly discovered another, about two miles wide, in latitude 50° 21', longitude 235° 9';[3] along which, he kept the starboard or eastern shore on board, which was compact; but the western side, for some miles on which some fires were observed, seemed somewhat divided by water.[4] This inlet, in general, from one to two miles wide, led them in an irregular northern direction to the latitude of 50° 52', longitude 235° 19',[5] where, in the usual manner, it terminated by a small tract of low land, from whence a shallow bank stretched into the arm, which soon increased, from 2 to 50, 70, and 100 fathoms in depth, and then became unfathomable. Behind this low small spot of land, the mountains rose very abruptly, divided by two deep vallies, whence issued streams of fresh water,[6] though not sufficiently capacious to admit the boats. In these vallies, and on the low plains, pine-trees grew to a tolerable size; the few seen on the mountains were of very stunted growth. High steep barren rocks, capped with snow, formed the sides of this channel, the water of which at its head, was nearly fresh, and of a pale colour, as was that in the arm where Mr. Puget met Sen[r] Valdes. It was noon on the 30th before we[7] reached that part of the western shore, which had appeared broken, and on which the fires of the natives had been observed on entering this channel, which I distinguished by the name of BUTE'S CHANNEL.[8] Here was found an Indian village, situated

---

[1] The N shore of Pryce Channel.

[2] Ramsay Arm.

[3] The entrance to Bute Inlet, which is in lat. 50° 21' N, long. 125° 05' W (234° 55' E). The lat. 50° 21' is misprinted 52° 21' in the second edition.

[4] Presumably referring to the channels on either side of Stuart Island, on the W side of the entrance to the inlet.

[5] Waddington Harbour, at the head of the inlet, is in lat. 50° 55' N, long. 124° 50' W (235° 10' E).

[6] The Homathko River and its canyon to the N, and the Southgate River, in the Pigeon Valley, to the E.

[7] Vancouver was not a member of the survey party; he was quoting or paraphrasing Johnstone's journal, and twice in this sentence inadvertently retained the first person pronoun.

[8] Bute's Canal in the first edition and on the engraved chart; now Bute Inlet. Named in honour of John Stuart, 3rd Earl of Bute, whose son, the Hon. Charles Stuart, was a midshipman in the Discovery. (Hence Stuart Island, at the entrance to the inlet.)

on the face of a steep rock, containing about one hundred and fifty of the natives, some few of whom had visited our party in their way up the channel, and now many came off in the most civil and friendly manner, with a plentiful supply of fresh herrings and other fish, which they bartered in a fair and honest way for nails. These were of greater value amongst them, than any other articles our people had to offer. From the point on which this village is erected, in latitude 50° 24', longitude 235° 8', a very narrow opening was seen stretching to the westward, and through it flowed so strong a current, that the boats, unable to row against it, were hauled by a rope along the rocky shores forming the passage.[1] In this fatiguing service the Indians voluntarily lent their aid to the utmost of their power, and were rewarded for their cordial disinterested assistance, much to their satisfaction. Having passed these narrows, the channel widened, and the rapidity of the tide decreased. Mr. Johnstone, in the cutter, had alone been able to pass; to whom it was evident that this narrow passage had communication with some very extensive inlet of the sea; but, as the weather was now very boisterous, with heavy rain, and a thick haze, and as the launch had not yet made her appearance, he returned in search of her, and found the party using their utmost endeavours to get through the narrows by the same friendly assistance of the natives he had before experienced; which being now no longer required these good people returned to their habitations, apparently well satisfied with the kind offices they had rendered, and the acknowledgments they had received. The boats now sought shelter from the inclemency of the weather in a small cove on the south side of the arm they had quitted, where the same cause operated to detain them until the morning of the 2d of July, when the time for which they were supplied with provisions being nearly expired, it was deemed most expedient to return to the ships.

By these two expeditions the boundary of the continental shore was completely ascertained to the above narrow passage; and the strongest presumption induced that the whole of the coast on our western side, southward of that passage was composed of innumerable islands.

The weather being tolerably fair, Mr. Johnstone and Mr. Swaine were the next day, Wednesday the 5th, again dispatched with a week's provisions, to examine the continental shore through the narrow passage from whence they had returned; by the means of which, and the survey then prosecuting under Lieutenant Puget and Mr. Whidbey, who were to commence their inquiries in an opposite point, the whole extent of the gulf would be finally determined; or, in the event of the Indian's information being correct, its further navigable communication to the northward would be discovered.

By what I had seen of the gulf on the evening we entered this sound, though

---

[1] The village was at the entrance to the Arran Rapids, which are between the N end of Stuart Island and the mainland. Tidal streams attain speeds of 7 to 9 knots. The entrance is in lat. 50° 25' N, long. 125° 08' W (234° 52' E). The rapids were named in 1863 after the island of Arran, in the Firth of Clyde, in the County of Bute, Scotland.

Figure 3. Seymour Narrows to Queen Charlotte Strait. *Base map by Michael E. Leek.*

its western extremity was certainly bounded, yet the appearance of the land in that direction favored the opinion of its being composed of islands, though the whole might be united by low land not perceptible at so great a distance.

On Friday the 5th in the afternoon, the officers in the launch and cutter returned,[1] from whom I understood, that they had found the western side of the gulf of Georgia, from that part opposite to point Marshall,[2] to be compact, rising in a gentle ascent from the sea shore to the inland mountains, (some of which were covered with snow) wearing a pleasant and fertile appearance; along this shore they continued their route and entered an inlet,[3] whose eastern side is formed by a long narrow peninsula, the south extreme of which is situated in latitude 50°, longitude 235° 9′. This promontory, after my first lieutenant, who had also discovered the inlet from the top of a mountain he had ascended in this neighbourhood, obtained the name of POINT MUDGE.[4] It forms a channel with the main land of the western side of the gulf of about a mile in width, nearly in a N.N.W. direction; this was pursued about three or four leagues without any apparent termination; the further they advanced the more extensive it was found. The tide, which was regular, was also rapid, and the flood evidently came from the north-westward; all these circumstances indicating the channel to be of considerable extent, they returned to communicate this intelligence.

On point Mudge was a very large village of the natives,[5] many of whom visited the party on their passing and repassing by it, who uniformly conducted themselves with the greatest civility and respect. On the western shore, immediately without the entrance of the inlet, they found a rivulet of excellent fresh water.[6] The passage up the inlet is perfectly free from danger, and affords good anchorage.[7] Round point Mudge, at the distance of about half a mile, is a ledge of sunken rocks; these are, however, easily avoided by the weeds

[1] Puget and Whidbey.

[2] Puget describes the expedition in considerable detail. Late on the first night they reached the N shore of Savary Island – 'our Night Quarters & snug ones they were, for we found a Most delightful Plain to pitch the Tents on & a fine Smooth Beach for the Boats.' The next morning they continued on S to Harwood Island, where they encountered some Indians whom Puget found interesting but unattractive. When opportunity offered his party 'set off & stopped for Breakfast on the SE point of the Island to be clear of the Inhabitants whose Company on these Occasions is particularly offensive from the Intolerable Stench of the Whale Oil in general use among all the tribes we have seen.' Some of their habits were equally unlovely, but Puget was fair minded: 'it would be doing them Injustice not to mention that in all our Dealings, since we began the Examination of the Continental Shores of America we have found the Inhabitants conducting themselves with strictest Honesty & Friendship towards us (except in Alarm Cove.)' – July 2 and 3. From Harwood Island the boats crossed the Strait of Georgia to the E coast of Vancouver Island.

[3] Discovery Passage.

[4] Now Cape Mudge, and so named on Baker's MS chart, but Point Mudge on the engraved chart. The lat. given is correct but the long. is 125° 11′ W (234° 49′ E).

[5] Yaculta, the first Kwakiutl village known to have been visited by Europeans.

[6] The Campbell River.

[7] Johnstone's discoveries, soon to be mentioned, overshadowed those of Puget, the great significance of which Vancouver does not even mention. Referring to Discovery Passage,

which they produce. From hence their way was directed to the northward, in order to join the ship through the broken land that exists between our present station and point Mudge. This was effected through a very intricate channel full of sunken rocks and rocky islets, leading them to the north point of the island[1] which formed our S.W. shore, and bearing from hence N. 53 W. distant about four miles.

After receiving this information, I waited with no little impatience the return of the other boat party; in the hope that, if no intelligence should be derived to facilitate the progress of the ships, there was yet a great probability of finding a more comfortable resting place than that we then occupied. This afforded not a single prospect that was pleasing to the eye, the smallest recreation on shore, nor animal or vegetable food, excepting a very scanty proportion of those eatables already described, and of which the adjacent country was soon exhausted, after our arrival. Nor did our exploring parties meet with a more abundant supply, whence the place obtained the name of DESOLATION SOUND;[2] where our time would have passed infinitely more heavily, had it not been relieved by the agreeable society of our Spanish friends.

The week, for which Mr. Johnstone and his party were furnished with supplies, having been expired some time, I began to be anxiously solicitous for their welfare; when, about two in the morning of Thursday the 12th, I had the satisfaction of having their arrival announced, all well, and that a passage leading into the Pacific Ocean to the north-westward had been discovered.

Mr. Johnstone had succeeded in finding his way into the arm leading to the westward through the narrows,[3] where they were assisted by the friendly natives, about a league to the south of the passage by which he had before entered it; making the intermediate land, lying before the entrance into Bute's channel, nearly a round island three or four leagues in circuit, which obtained the name of STUART'S ISLAND. This channel was not less intricate than the other, neither of which he considered a safe navigation for shipping, owing to their being so narrow, to the irregular direction and rapidity of the tides, and to the great depth of water; which even close to the shore, was no where less

Puget wrote: 'For the first time since our Entrance into the Streights [of Juan de Fuca] we perceived the Water flowing by the Shore & the Stream running at the Rate of five Knots from the Northward. This certainly was the most favorable prospect, we had had of finding a passage to the Northward for the Ships & most gladly did we pursue this Inlet which trended in a N^d 11 W^d Direction & was little better than a Mile in Breadth...We were however willing to flatter ourselves that by this Branch we should find a Communication with a Passage leading to the Sea; with this Intelligence I thought it necessary to join the Discovery as soon as possible...' He was hopeful that Johnstone's expedition would 'pitch on a better Channel, as the present one by the Rapidity of the Tides could not be altogether reckoned safe without being further sounded.' – 5 July.

[1] Cortes Island. Puget makes no mention of any 'intricate channel'. Sutil Channel would seem to be the obvious route back to the ships.

[2] On his chart Vancouver applied this name to the waterways extending all the way from Sarah Point to Bute Inlet. It is now confined to the sound immediately N of Sarah Point, round about Kinghorn Island.   [3] The Yaculta Rapids.

than sixty fathoms. From this passage the northern shore was pursued, and two small arms leading to the N.W. each about a league in extent, were examined.[1] Here was met a canoe in which were three Indians, who fled to the woods with the utmost precipitation, leaving their canoe on the shore. In it Mr. Johnstone deposited some trifling articles, in the hope of dissipating by this means, their ill-grounded apprehension of danger. As he proceeded, he passed a spacious opening leading to the S.W.[2] which he supposed communicated with the gulf some distance to the westward of our present station. The principal channel of the western arm still preserving a west direction, was about a mile wide; and as they advanced in it, they arrived at another branch nearly about the same width, in latitude 50° 26′ longitude 234° 35′, with an islet and some rocks lying off its east point of entrance.[3] Conformably to our mode of tracing the continental shore, they were led up this opening; and in the night found themselves incommoded by the flood tide,[4] although they had conceived from their former observations on the tides, that, at the time of their being disturbed at their resting place on shore, it would be nearly low water, as the moon was then passing the meridian. But, as the tide here varied upwards of four hours earlier than in the gulf of Georgia, and as the night had been still and pleasant, no accidental cause could be referred to, which was likely to have produced so material an alteration: the period of flowing, however, nearly corresponded with that of the tides at Nootka, and on the sea-coast to the north of that place; which left little doubt, in the mind of Mr. Johnstone, that this unexpected circumstance had been occasioned by the channel they were in communicating with the ocean to the north-westward. The examination of the arm was continued, the next morning, to the latitude of 50° 46′, longitude 234° 41′, where it was thought to end. But this appearance proved to be a contraction only of the channel, by two interlocking points, from whence the Spaniards, who afterwards pursued its course, found its final termination in a N.E. by N. direction about three leagues further.[5] They again reached the entrance in the evening, where the party rested for the night. This channel, which I

[1] Frederick Arm and Phillips Arm. Johnstone was following Cordero Channel, now taken as extending from Stuart Island to Loughborough Inlet. Its W section was named Canal de Cordero by the Galiano-Valdés expedition. José Cordero (or Cardero) was an artist with the expedition and author of the narrative that describes it.

[2] Nodales Channel; another Spanish name (Canal de los Nodales) which has survived.

[3] Loughborough Inlet. Named Brazo de Salamanca by the Spaniards when they passed this way the following month. Its entrance is in lat. 50° 27′ N, long. 125° 35′ W (234° 25′ E).

[4] 'in the middle of the night they were hastily roused from their repose by the flowing of the Tide, which had risen so much higher than they expected & rushd upon them so suddenly, that every person got completely drenched before they could remove to the higher ground.' – Menzies, 12 July.

[5] The inlet narrows at Towry Head, in lat. 50° 40′ N, and beyond it swings to the E and NE. Unless a boat goes beyond Towry Head it could appear to end there. It extends only about 5 miles farther, not three leagues, and its head is in lat. 50° 43′ N.

distinguished by the name of LOUGHBOROUGH's CHANNEL,[1] was about a mile wide, between steep and nearly perpendicular mountains, from whose lofty summits the dissolving snow descended down their rugged sides in many beautiful cascades.

In the morning of the 6th, their researches were continued along the western channel,[2] in which they found the tide favoring their former conjectures, by the flood evidently approaching them from the westward. About two leagues to the west of the arm they had quitted, the channel again branched off in two directions, one stretching a little to the northward,[3] the other a little to the southward of west.[4] The former demanded their attention first, and was found to be an intricate channel, containing many sunken rocks and rocky islets, occasioning great irregularity in the tides, which were here extremely violent; this continued about two leagues, where the channel widened,[5] and the water became less agitated. Their course along the continental shore led them into a continuation of the western channel,[6] which they had forsaken for the purpose of pursuing this more northerly one along the shore of the main land, by which means the southern side of the channel they had passed through was proved to be an island, about four leagues in extent.[7] From hence they continued along the northern shore of the great western channel for the most part upwards of half a league wide, in the firm reliance of finding it lead to the ocean. Under this impression, Mr. Johnstone thought it of importance to ascertain that fact as speedily as possible; for which purpose, he steered over to the southern shore, leaving some openings, with some islands and rocks, on the northern side, for future examination. The southern shore was found nearly straight, and intire, rising abruptly from the sea to mountains of great height. Here they passed some small habitations of the natives, but the northern shore presented not the least sign of its being inhabited to the westward of the narrows. A slow progress was now made to the westward, in consequence of a fresh gale from that quarter, most part of the day; and the nights and mornings, often obscured in a thick fog, were generally calm.

On the morning of the 8th they were much surprized by the report of a gun at no very great distance. This was immediately answered by a swivel;

[1] Loughborough's Canal in the first edition and on Vancouver's chart; now Loughborough Inlet. Named after Alexander Wedderburn, appointed chief justice and created first Baron Loughborough in 1780; later the first Earl of Rosslyn. He was an intimate friend of the Earl of Bute, which probably suggested the name to Vancouver, who had recently named Bute Inlet.

[2] Chancellor Channel, the continuation of Cordero Channel W of the entrance to Loughborough Inlet.

[3] Wellbore Channel.

[4] The continuation of Chancellor Channel, which joins Johnstone Strait about three miles to the W.

[5] The channel both widened and turned to the SW. Johnstone was entering Sunderland Channel. He was travelling around Hardwicke Island, which is bounded by Wellbore Channel, Sunderland Channel, Johnstone Strait and the W end of Chancellor Channel.

[6] Johnstone Strait.   [7] Hardwicke Island.

but no return was heard. On the fog clearing away, a small canoe appeared, which attended them until they reached a village of greater consequence, in point of size, than any they had before seen, situated on the front of a hill near the sea-side.[1] The two Indians in the canoe, finding they were seen by those on shore, ventured alongside our boats; and, in the canoe was a musket with its appendages, and an eagle recently shot, which easily accounted for the discharge heard in the fog. As they approached the village several canoes visited the party; each of which was armed with a musket, and provided with ammunition; in one canoe there were three;[2] these were considered as belonging to a chief, who informed them, that the village was under the authority of *Maquinna*,[*] the chief of Nootka,[3] who, they gave our party reason

[1] The village of Cheslakees, a Kwakiutl chief, at the mouth of the Nimpkish River. Vancouver visited it later and both he and Menzies describe it and its inhabitants in some detail.

[2] Bell describes the transition from copper to muskets: 'a Sheet of Copper that at one time wou'd purchase four Skins, at last wou'd not purchase at some places one. Muskets were early given them in Barter which they could not use without Powder and Ball, these they then demanded for their Skins, and got them, and for a length of time no Skins could be purchased without ammunition and Fire Arms, some of the first Muskets that were sold procured 6 and Seven Skins, now, two Skins, but more commonly one, is the price. At the district of Wickananish, that Chief can turn out four hundred men, arm'd with Muskets and well Stored with ammunition, a considerable part of which have been given him in barter by a Mr. Kendrick Master of an American Vessel call'd the Washington. Their former Weapons, Bows and Arrows, Spears and Clubs are now thrown aside & forgotten. at Nootka it was the same way, every one had his Musket. Thus they are supplied with weapons which they no sooner possess than they turn them against the donors. – Every Season produces instances of their daring treacherous conduct, few Ships have been on the Coast, that have not been attacked or attempted to be attacked, and in general many lives have been lost on both sides.' – October 1792 (at Nootka). Although trading vessels found it necessary to take measures to guard against Indian attacks, Bell's last sentence exaggerates. Robin Fisher has pointed out that F. W. Howay, who gathered evidence of such attacks over the 20-year period 1785–1805 'lists only fifteen instances that could possibly be described as attacks on vessels, and at least five of these are highly doubtful cases'. – *Contact and Conflict* (Vancouver, 1977), p. 17n. But Mozino supports Bell's charge that Kendrick played an important part in initiating the trading of firearms to the natives. Kendrick 'for ten guns and a little powder, bought a piece of land in Maquinnas [territory] on which to spend the winter....I cannot say whether it was self-interest or rivalry with the English that suggested to the Americans the perverse idea of teaching the savages the handling of firearms – a lesson that could be harmful to all humanity. He [Kendrick] gave Maquinna a swivel gun; he furnished Wickananish with more than two hundred guns, two barrels of powder, and a considerable portion of shot'. – *Noticias de Nutka*, Wilson translation (Seattle, 1970), pp. 70–71.

[*] So called by the Spaniards, but known by the name of *Maquilla* by the English. [Meares spelled the name *Maquilla*, probably its first appearance in print in English. *Maquinna* has long been the usual spelling, but in *Flood Tide of Empire* Warren Cook has preferred the variant *Ma-kwee-na*.]

[3] The village was not 'under the authority' of Maquinna, as Vancouver thought at this time, but Indians in the village and area had become heavily dependent upon trading relations with him. When describing Johnstone's expedition Menzies noted that some of the Indians 'could blab several English words, from which it evidently appeard that they had some late intercourse with the English or American Traders. They also talked much

to believe, was then on shore. The village had the appearance of being constructed with much regularity; its inhabitants numerous, and all seemingly well armed: under these circumstances it was passed by, without further inquiry, agreeably to our established maxim, never to court a danger on shore when necessity did not compel our landing.

A small sandy island, lying to the eastward of the village, affords between it and the land on which the town is situated, a small, but very commodious, anchorage.[1] This is not, however, to be approached by the passage to the south of the island, that being navigable only for very small craft. To the south of the village a valley extended, apparently to a considerable distance, in a south-westerly direction. Through it a very fine stream of fresh water emptied itself into the sea,[2] and, from the many wears that were seen in it, it was unquestionably well stocked with fish, though not any was offered for sale, notwithstanding the solicitations of our party, in the Nootka language, with which the natives seemed well acquainted.[3]

After the chief had received some presents, amongst which copper seemed to him the most valuable, he, with most of his companions, returned to the shore; and, on landing, fired several muskets, to shew, in all probability, with what dexterity they could use these weapons, to which they seemed as familiarized as if they had been accustomed to fire-arms from their earliest infancy.

The shores on each side of the channel had materially decreased in height. That to the northward appeared very much broken, and mostly composed of islands; whilst that to the southward, which was pursued, remained compact and entire. The islands to the north were generally formed by low land near the shore, rising to a moderate height, well wooded, and on them the smoke of several fires was observed. This circumstance, together with the number of inhabitants on the southern shore, and the many canoes that were seen passing and repassing, evidently bespoke this country to be infinitely more populous than the shores of the gulf of Georgia.

of Maquinna the Chief of Nootka Sound with whom they seemed to have kept up a considerable commercial intercourse as they spoke of having received from him almost every article of Traffic in their possession such as Cloths Muskets &c.' and Menzies concluded that it appeared 'extremely probable that *Maquinna* has been the grand agent through which the Bartering Commerce of this interior Country has been carried on by some inland communication'. – July 12.

[1] Flagstaff Islet seems to be the most likely identification.

[2] The Nimpkish River.

[3] Vancouver's remark indicates that some member or members of his expedition could make themselves understood in the Nootkan language. Presumably this competence would be confined to those who had made a previous visit to the Northwest Coast, and only Vancouver, Menzies and Johnstone are known to have done so. Of the three, Menzies seems to have taken the most interest in the various languages and dialects that were encountered. The Nootkan vocabulary in Cook's journal, consisting of several hundred words, which Beaglehole thinks was compiled by Anderson, may have been of assistance to them. – Cook, *Journals*, III, 323–30.

The evening brought our party to the termination of the compact southern shore in its west direction, by a narrow channel leading to the south;[1] and the main arm, which from that station took a north direction, spread very considerably; but the view to the westward was greatly interrupted by small islands. In the hope of reaching the westernmost island in sight, and by that means of determining the great object of their pursuit, they proceeded with a fresh gale from the east, attended by a great fall of rain, until midnight; when, supposing themselves at the limits they had seen before it was dark, they came to a grapnell under the lee of a small island, which in some degree sheltered them from the inclemency of the night. This extremely unpleasant weather continued without intermission, the whole of the next day, and until the morning of the 10th. They had now been absent six days out of the seven for which they had been provided, and the small remains of their stock were becoming hourly more insufficient for the distant voyage they had yet to perform in returning to the ships, which greatly increased the mortification they experienced by this very unlooked for detention; but a westerly wind and pleasant weather returning with the morning of the 10th, they rowed to an island conspicuously situated, from whence their expectations were gratified by a clear though distant view of the expansive ocean. The land constituting the different shores of the passage appeared of moderate height, much broken, and seemed to form various other channels to sea. This was however the most capacious; the westernmost land of which, on the northern side, bore by compass N. 62 W. about five leagues; and the westernmost land on the southern side N. 80 W. about four leagues distant. This island obtained the name of ALLEVIATION ISLAND,[2] from whence they directed their course homeward, being upwards of 120 miles from the ships.

Impelled by reasons of the most pressing nature, no time was lost in taking advantage of the prevailing favorable gale, with which they kept on their return until midnight, when as usual, they landed for the night on the southern shore, nearly opposite the west end of the island that forms the south side of the intricate passage they had passed through on the 6th.[3] As the survey from the ship had been carried on by that route, and confined to the examination of the northern or continental shore to that station, through passages rendered by various impediments ineligible as a navigation for the ships, Mr. Johnstone was desirous of pursuing another which led more southerly, and appeared less liable to such objections. Though he much regretted the lost opportunity of returning by the favorable gale that continued all night, he waited the approach of day, and departing with the dawn, had his wishes gratified by sailing through a clear and spacious channel, in width about half a league,[4]

[1] Presumably Hardy Bay is meant.

[2] The island is shown on Baker's MS chart but not on the engraved chart. The name has not survived and positive identification is not possible. It was probably the present Pine Island, which is about 16 miles NW of Hardy Bay and would provide the clear view of the ocean to which Vancouver refers.

[3] Hardwicke Island.   [4] Johnstone Strait.

without the smallest interruption, or the least irregularity in the tides. The southern shore, which from the large village was nearly straight, afforded some few small bays, the land mostly rising in an abrupt manner from the sea to mountains of considerable height, divided by valleys that appeared to extend a great way back into the country; the shores were tolerably well inhabited by the natives who lived in small villages near the water side. The northern shore was neither so high nor so compact; several detached rocks were seen lying near it, and it was, generally speaking, composed of rugged rocks, in the fissures of which an abundance of pine trees were produced, constituting, as on the southern shore, one intire forest. As they advanced in this channel, leading nearly in an east and west direction, they observed another which led to the south, south eastward,[1] bearing every appearance of being clear, navigable, and communicating with the gulf; and one also stretching to the north-eastward,[2] which they had little doubt was the same they had seen after passing the narrows on the 4th, leading to the S.W. The former of these they much wished to explore, but their provisions being totally exhausted, it became expedient they should join the ships without further delay, and therefore pursued that leading to the north-eastward, by which they arrived as already related.[3]

This information left me scarcely a doubt that the channel Mr. Johnstone had declined pursuing south eastwardly towards the gulf, was the same our boats had entered leading to the northward from point Mudge, and which, on comparing the sketches of the several surveys, was as nearly as possible reduced to a certainty. I derived no small degree of satisfaction in finding my expectations so far advanced, for had our efforts proved ineffectual in discovering a communication with the ocean, it would have occupied the remaining part of the season to have examined the numerous openings on the opposite shores of the gulf, which were now proved to form the north-eastern side of an extensive island or archipelago, on whose south-western coast Nootka is situated;[4] hence this task now became unnecessary, and I was flattered with the hope of yet extending our researches during the summer months a considerable distance to the northward.

Sen[r] Galiano and Valdes I made acquainted with our discoveries; and with my intention of departing, in consequence of the information we had gained, the first favourable moment.

When the village was pointed out where *Maquinna* was supposed to have been, Sen[r] Valdes was of opinion, that circumstance was highly probable,

---

[1] Discovery Passage, the S part of which Puget and Whidbey had explored.

[2] Nodales Channel.

[3] Menzies describes the plight of Johnstone and his crew when they returned. They had 'hastend night & day to join the Ships...harassed with hunger & fatigue being for the last two days upon a single scanty meal & without any rest or out of the Boats for the last 24 hours.' – July 12.

[4] This was the first determination by Europeans of the insularity of Vancouver Island.

knowing he had authority over an extensive country to the north-westward of Nootka.[1]

These gentlemen received such information of all our discoveries up to this period as they required, and now begged leave to decline accompanying us further, as the powers they possessed in their miserable vessels, were unequal to a cooperation with us, and being apprehensive their attendance would retard our progress. Senr Galiano favoured me with a copy of his survey, and other particulars relative to this inlet of the sea, which contained also that part of the neighbouring coast extending north-westward from the straits of De Fuca, beyond Nootka to the latitude of 50° 3′, longitude 232° 48′.[2] He likewise gave me a letter to be forwarded to Senr Quadra at Nootka, by *Maquinna*, or any of his people with whom we might chance to meet, together with an introductory one to Senr Quadra, when I should have the pleasure of meeting him at Nootka. After an exchange of good wishes, we bad each other farewell, having experienced much satisfaction, and mutually received every kindness and attention that our peculiar situation could afford to our little society. From these gentlemen we were assured, that on our arrival at Nootka we should meet a most cordial reception, and be more pleasantly situated than we could imagine, as the houses had lately undergone a thorough repair, and all the gardens had been put and kept in the highest order, for the purpose of being so delivered into our possession.

With a light breeze from the northward, in the morning of Friday the 13th, we weighed and left our Spanish friends at anchor, who intended to pursue their researches to the westward through the channel Mr. Johnstone had discovered; and in commemoration of whose exertions was by me named JOHNSTONE'S STRAITS;[3] and the island described by him on the 6th, was in compliment to Mr. Swaine, who commanded the other boat, distinguished by the name of HARDWICKE'S ISLAND, after the noble earl of that title;[4] towards which straits our course was now bent to the southward, trusting we should find a passage into them to the westward of point Mudge.

Little remains further to add respecting the station we had just quitted, but to state the general satisfaction that prevailed on leaving a region so truly desolate and inhospitable. During our stay at that gloomy place, I was enabled

[1] Valdés (or Vancouver) was mistaken; this was a Kwakiutl village over which Maquinna had no authority except through trading relations.
[2] The chart showing the W coast of Vancouver Island was probably a copy of the map drawn at Nootka after the return of the Eliza expedition in 1791. This extends to Cape Cook (shown as Punta de Boyse), which is in lat. 50° 08′ N. It was probably drawn by Juan Carrasco.
[3] Now Johnstone Strait.
[4] Walbran explains: 'Swaine was a protégé of the Hardwicke family, his father being a gentleman of influence and position in the county of Cambridge, for which county Philip Yorke, a member of the Hardwicke family, was M.P., 1780–1790, when he succeeded to the earldom [as third Earl of Hardwicke] on the death of his uncle.' – *British Columbia Coast Names* (Ottawa, 1909), p. 480.

to take only ten sets of lunar distances; which, with six sets taken at our anchorage near the entrance of the sound, gave a mean result for the longitude 235° 5′ 30″. Kendal's chronometer, by ten sets of altitudes taken on different days, shewed the mean result, allowing the Birch bay rate to be 235° 21′. This I considered to be nearer the truth than that deduced from the few lunar observations above mentioned, and have accordingly adopted it as the longitude of Desolation sound, whose latitude by six meridional altitudes of the sun was found to be 50° 11′.[1] The mean result of eighteen sets of azimuths taken on board, differing from 17° 45′ to 23°, gave 19° 16′ easterly variation; seventeen sets taken on shore differed from 14° 26′ to 19° 30′, gave a mean result of 16° variation in the same direction. The irregularity of the tides was such that no correct inferences could well be drawn. They appeared to be principally influenced by local or incidental causes; possibly by the operation of both. They were greatly affected by the direction or force of the winds, which seemed as equally to act on the rise and the fall, as on the current when there was any. This, however, was not always the case; as in the course of some days there would not be the least perceptible stream; and in others a very rapid one, that generally continued in the same direction twenty four hours, and sometimes longer. The time of high water was equally vague and undefinable; that I attributed to its insular situation, nearly at the extremity of the influence of two tides flowing from directly opposite points, causing their divided streams to act, according to the incidental circumstances that might operate upon them.

In this route we passed through the assemblage of islands and rocks lying at some distance before the entrance into Desolation sound; some of which presented an appearance infinitely more grateful than that of the interior country. These were mostly of a moderate height from the sea, tolerably well wooded, and the shores not wholly composed of rugged rocks, afforded some small bays bounded by sandy beaches. The wind continued light from the northern quarter, and the weather being serene and pleasant, made a most agreeable change. Numberless whales enjoying the season, were playing about the ship in every direction; as were also several seals; the latter had been seen in great abundance during our residence in Desolation sound, and in all the remote excursions of our boats, but they were so extremely watchful and shy, that not one could be taken. These animals seemed to have had the exclusive possession of the gloomy region we had just quitted; but the scene now before us was more congenial to our minds, not only from the different aspect of the shores, but from the attention of the friendly Indians, who, as we were crossing the gulf, visited us in several canoes, with young birds, mostly sea fowl, fish, and some berries, to barter for our trinkets and other commodities. Soon after mid-day we anchored about half a mile to the northward of point

[1] The precise location where Vancouver made his observations is not clear. Joyce Point, on the S side of Teakerne Arm and close to the anchorage as shown on Baker's MS chart, is in lat. 50° 10′ N, long. 124° 54′ W (235° 06′ E).

Mudge, in 37 fathoms water, on a bottom of black sand and mud. A very strong *flood tide* came from the northward,[1] and although nearly convinced that our conjectures were right, the launch and cutter with lieutenant Puget and Mr. Whidbey, were immediately dispatched to examine the channel as to its communication with Johnstone's straights; that in the event of there being any obstructions where such rapid tides were running, we might have sufficient notice, and be prepared to avoid them.

From the village situated on point Mudge, we were visited by several of the natives, who brought fish and the wild fruits of their country, which they exchanged for our European articles, in a very fair and honest manner.

After dinner, accompanied by Mr. Menzies and some of the officers, I went on shore to return the visit of our friends, and to indulge our curiosity. On landing at the village, which is situated a little to the N.W. within the promontory, and nearly at the summit of a steep sandy cliff, we were received by a man who appeared to be the chief of the party. He approached us alone, seemingly with a degree of formality, though with the utmost confidence of his own security, whilst the rest of the society, apparently numerous, were arranged and seated in the most peaceable manner before their houses. I made him such presents as seemed not only to please him excessively, but to confirm him in the good opinion with which he was prepossessed; and he immediately conducted us up to the village by a very narrow path winding diagonally up the cliff, estimated by us to be about an hundred feet in height, and within a few degrees of being perpendicular. Close to the edge of this precipice stood the village, the houses of which were built after the fashion of Nootka, though smaller, not exceeding ten or twelve feet in height, nearly close together in rows, separated by a narrow passage sufficiently wide only for one person. On the beach, at the foot of the cliff, were about seventy canoes of small dimensions, though amongst them were some that would carry at least fifteen persons with great convenience. On a computation, therefore, deduced from these and other circumstances, we were led to consider that this village, though occupying a very small space, could not contain less than three hundred persons.[2] The spot where it was erected appeared to be well chosen to insure its protection; the steep loose sandy precipice secured it in front, and its rear was defended by a deep chasm in the rocks; beyond these was a thick and nearly impenetrable forest: so that the only means of access was by the narrow path we had ascended, which could easily be maintained against very superior numbers. Having gratified our curiosity, and, in return for the cordial attention

[1] 'In the vicinity of Cape Mudge, the tidal streams attain velocities of from 5 to 7 knots, the flood flowing south and the ebb north.' – *Sailing Directions – British Columbia Coast (South Portion)* (9th ed., Victoria, B.C., 1974), p. 237.

[2] According to Menzies the village consisted 'of about 12 houses or Huts plankd over with large boards some of which were ornamented with rude paintings particularly those on the fronts of the houses. They were flat roofed & of a quadrangular figure and each house contained several families to the number of about 350 inhabitants in all on the most moderate calculation...' – 13 July.

of these friendly people, made our acknowledgments by presents of such trivial articles as we had about us, we took our leave of the village for the purpose of indulging ourselves before dark, with a refreshing walk, on a low margin of land extending from the more elevated woodland country, some distance along the water-side to the northward; a luxury we had not for some time experienced. In this excursion, which was extremely grateful and pleasant, we saw two sepulchres built with plank about five feet in height, seven in length, and four in breadth. These boards were curiously perforated at the ends and sides, and the tops covered with loose pieces of plank, as if for the purpose of admitting as great a circulation of air as possible to the human bones they enclosed, which were evidently the relics of many different bodies. A few of the Indians attended us in our walk, picking the berries from the trees as we passed, and with much civility presenting them to us on green leaves. The evening approaching obliged us to return on board, against a very strong ebb tide.

The Chatham having been detained some hours in Desolation sound after we had sailed, had now arrived and anchored near us. She had been stopped by her anchor when nearly half up, hooking a rock; every means that could be devised had been resorted to without effect, until the moment when they were about to cut it away, it cleared itself, which fortunately saved the anchor and cable.

With a fresh breeze from the N.W. and a continuation of pleasant weather, at high water about three o'clock on the morning of Saturday the 14th, we were under sail, and with the assistance of the ebb tide, turned about four leagues up the inlet towards a commodious anchoring place, that had been discovered by our boats, and was the appointed rendezvous on the return of the launch and cutter. About six o'clock we arrived and anchored in 24 fathoms water, sandy bottom. In this situation each side of the arm formed a bay affording commodious anchorage; and that on the western side being the most extensive was preferred.[1] Nearly in the centre is a shallow bank of sand, with a navigable passage all around it.[2] The ships were stationed between this bank and the north side of the bay, near a small Indian village, whose inhabitants had little to dispose of, though they were very civil and friendly. Whilst turning up in the ship, many of the natives came off; but the swiftness of our motion prevented their coming on board.

The clearness of the sky and atmosphere enabled me to procure some observations, by which our latitude was ascertained to be 50° 7′ 30″.[3] Ten sets of lunar distances, with those made in Desolation sound, amounting in all to twenty-six sets taken on different sides of the moon, brought forward by Kendal's chronometer and the protraction, agreeing extremely well together; gave the mean result of the longitude by the lunar distances 15′ 15″ to the westward of the watch. On such authority, however, I could not

[1] Menzies Bay.   [2] Defender Shoal.
[3] The lat. of Menzies Bay is 50° 07′ N.

possibly determine that the chronometer erred so materially; yet had reason to believe, that it was not gaining at the rate we had allowed since our departure from Birch bay. The *true longitude*, therefore, of the respective places hereafter mentioned, from Desolation sound to Nootka, will be deduced from such observations as I was enabled to make at the latter place for correcting the error of the chronometer; by which, according to the Birch bay rate, the longitude of our present rendezvous was 234° 57'; its true longitude, by subsequent observations, 234° 52½';[1] the variation of the compass by three set of azimuths, 18° 30' eastwardly.

From point Mudge to this bay the channel is nearly straight; the western shore is compact, the eastern one has some rocky islets and rocks lying near it; it is about half a league wide; in turning up we found not the smallest obstruction; and the shores are sufficiently bold for vessels to stand as close to them as inclination may direct. Immediately above this station the channel contracts to a short half mile, by the projecting land that forms the north sides of these two bays, and by an island on the eastern shore[2] (navigable round for boats only) which projects so far as to reduce the channel to nearly one half its width. The tide, setting to the southward through this confined passage, rushes with such immense impetuosity as to produce the appearance of falls considerably high; though not the least obstruction of either rocks or sands, so far as we had an opportunity of examining it, appeared to exist. The returning tide to the north, though very rapid, does not run with such violence; this was estimated to move at the rate of about four or five miles; the other, at seven or eight miles per hour.[3] They seemed regular in their quarterly change, but the visible rise and fall by the shore in this situation was so inconsiderable as to allow us merely to distinguish the ebb from the flood tide.

In the evening of the 14th our boats returned, having found the channel from these narrow parts gradually increasing its width to a mile, and half a

---

[1] This was still too far to the E; the correct long is 125° 22' W (234° 38' E).
[2] Maud Island.
[3] The 'confined passage' was Seymour Narrows. Here 'the tidal streams attain velocities up to 15 knots, the flood setting south, and the ebb in the opposite direction. When either stream is running at full strength, the eddies and swirls are extremely heavy, and when these are opposed by a strong wind, the races become very dangerous to small vessels.' – *Sailing Directions – B.C. Coast*, p. 244. Vancouver did not detect the notorious Ripple Rock, for many years a major hazard to navigation for vessels of any size. It lay almost in mid-channel, at the S entrance to the Narrows. The Government of Canada decided finally that it must be removed; this required the excavation of a tunnel 2400 feet long under the Narrows, and a 300-foot shaft up into the base of the rock. The upper end of the shaft was packed with explosives which were set off in April 1958. The result was the greatest non-nuclear blast in history and the destruction of the rock as a navigational hazard. The Indians are said to have punished men by marooning them on the rock at low water, leaving them to drown when the tide rose. Considering the hazards, Vancouver's ships passed through the Narrows with astonishing ease. Baker remarks that they were 'soon drifted through these Narrows by the strength of the tide.' – 16 July.

league, and to communicate with Johnstone's straits in nearly the same
N.N.W. direction, about four leagues further, without any visible obstruction
or impediment to the navigation. The eastern shore, like that to the northward,
was much broken; the western shore continued firm, and afforded some small
bays in which there was good anchorage. As they proceeded, not any
inhabitants were seen, but, on returning, they met twenty canoes filled with
Indians, who, at first, were a little distant, but at length approached our party
with confidence, and with every appearance of civility and friendship.

These were observed to be more variously painted than any of the natives
our gentlemen had before seen. The faces of some were made intirely white,
some red, black, or lead colour; whilst others were adorned with several
colours; and the generality had their hair decorated with the down of young
sea-fowl. In these respects they evidently approached nearer to the character
of the people of Nootka, than of any other we had yet seen, either in the
entrance of the straits of De Fuca, or in the gulf of Georgia.

The winds being too light and variable to command the ship against the
influence of such rapid tides, we were under the necessity of waiting for the
ebb in the afternoon of the following day, Sunday the 15th, when, with
pleasant weather and a fresh breeze at N.W. we weighed about three o'clock,
turned through the narrows, and, having gained about three leagues by the
time it was nearly dark, we anchored on the western shore in a small bay,[1]
on a bottom of sand and mud, in 30 fathoms water, to wait the favorable return
of tide. On Monday morning the 16th, with the assistance of a fresh N.W.
wind, and the stream of ebb, we shortly reached Johnstone's straits; passing
a point which, after our little consort, I named POINT CHATHAM, situated in
latitude 50° 19½′, longitude 235° 45′.[2] This point is rendered conspicuous by
the confluence of three channels, two of which take their respective directions
to the westward and south-eastward towards the ocean,[3] as also by a small
bay on each side; by three rocky islets close to the south, and by some rocks,
over which the sea breaks to the north.

Immediately on our entering these straits, we were affected by more swell
than we had experienced in this inland navigation, indicating that the ocean,
in a westerly direction was not quite so remote as, by Mr. Johnstone, it had
been estimated.

In the bay, to the north-westward of point Chatham, was situated an Indian
village, from whence some of the natives attempted to give us their company;
but the wind, blowing heavily in squalls, prevented their venturing alongside.
After we had proceeded about ten miles from point Chatham, the tide made
so powerfully against us as obliged us, about breakfast time, to become again

[1] Elk Bay.
[2] Chatham Point, in lat. 50° 20′ N, long. 125° 26′ W (234° 34′ E). Vancouver's lat. is
misprinted 53° 19½′ in the second edition.
[3] Johnstone Strait to the W and Discovery Passage to the SE. The third channel is
Nodales Channel, leading NE to Cordero Channel.

stationary in a bay on the northern shore[1] in 32 fathoms water. The land, under which we anchored, was a narrow island, which I distinguished by the name of THURLOW'S ISLAND,[2] it is about eight leagues long, and was passed to the northward by Mr. Johnstone in going, and to the S.E. on his return. The bay was observed to be in latitude 50° 23', longitude 234° 32';[3] three sets of azimuths gave the variation 19° eastwardly; it affords good anchorage; and wood and water may be easily procured. Our efforts with the seine, though unremitted, were ineffectual, not having afforded us the least supply since our departure from Birch bay; nor, with the hooks and lines, had we been more successful. About four in the afternoon, we again proceeded, but made little progress against a fresh westerly gale. In the evening we passed another village, when the inhabitants, more knowing than their neighbours, embracing the opportunity of the ship being at stays, of selling a few small fresh salmon. They had some with them ready cooked, and they seemed to have great pleasure in throwing them on board as we passed their canoes. We anchored again about nine in the evening, on the southern shore, nearly abreast of the west end of Thurlow's island, in 22 fathoms, sandy bottom; having gained, this tide, little more than three leagues.[4]

The wind blew strong from the westward, with squalls, during the night; and when we weighed, at three in the morning of Tuesday the 17th, we were obliged to ply, under double-reefed topsails, to windward, with little prospect of making much progress, until we had passed Thurlow's and Hardwick's islands.

The meeting of the channels added great velocity to the tides; and, as the day advanced, the weather became fair and pleasant, which enabled us to spread all our canvass; yet we were very apprehensive of losing, by the adverse tide, all we had gained by the favorable stream; not having been able to reach the bottom with 100 fathoms of line, although repeated trials had been made, on traversing within a ship's length of each shore. At last, about eleven, in a small bay on the southern side,[5] soundings were gained at the depth of fifty fathoms, where we instantly anchored, about half a cable's length from the rocks, to wait the return of the favorable current, not knowing by what name to call it. That which came from the eastward we had stiled the ebb; but, on going on shore to observe the latitude, the stream that came rapidly from the westward, appeared to be the reflux, as the water on the shore, during the afternoon, had evidently retired, though to no very great distance.

Our station here was nearly opposite the first opening on the northern shore,

[1] Knox Bay must be meant, although it is only about 7 miles from Chatham Point.
[2] There are two islands, not one, as Vancouver thought: West Thurlow Island, relatively narrow, and East Thurlow Island, much broader, divided by Mayne Passage. Their combined length is about 18 miles. They were named in honour of Edward, first Baron Thurlow, Lord Chancellor from 1778 to 1792.
[3] Vancouver's lat. is correct, but the long. is 125° 36' 30" W (234° 23' 30" E).
[4] They had advanced only about two leagues, not three.
[5] St. Vincent Bight.

passed by unexamined by Mr. Johnstone;[1] who had also declined visiting two others, apparently on the continent, further to the westward. Lieutenant Puget and Mr. Whidbey, were dispatched in the launch and cutter, in order to explore the former, lying from us N. 50 E.; about a league distant, with instructions to join me, in the ship, either in the third unexplored opening on the north side of the straits, or at the village where *Maquinna* was stated to be; it being my intention, that the Chatham should pursue the second opening, whilst I proceeded in order to procure an interview with *Maquinna*, through whom I might be able to inform Sen[r] Quadra of the time he might expect to see us, and forward Sen[r] Galiano's letter.

In the afternoon we were visited by two canoes, having a musket, with all the necessary appurtenances in each. These were the first fire-arms we had seen from the ships, but, from the number Mr. Johnstone had seen in his late excursion, it would appear, that the inhabitants of this particular part are amply provided with these formidable weapons.

Having the tide in our favor, at four o'clock we quitted this station, the latitude of which was found to be in 50° 27′, longitude 235° 53′.[2] At this time, it appeared to be low tide, the water having fallen, since my landing in the forenoon, nearly five feet; the stream was in our favor, though running at a very gentle rate, and the wind from the N.W. being very light, we advanced so slowly, that, by ten at night, we had only gained three leagues, where another small bay, or cove, was seen on the southern shore, with low land extending some distance from the mountains. Here I was in hopes of finding a commodious resting place, but was obliged to stand very near to the shore before soundings could be gained; at length, with forty fathoms of line, the bottom was reached, and on wearing, which the ship did very briskly, in order to anchor in a less depth of water, our next cast was ten fathoms, when the anchor was instantly let go; yet, before we had veered a third of the cable, the ship grounded abaft; but, on heaving in a few fathoms of the cable, she very easily swung off the bank. The Chatham grounded also, and was likewise got off with little difficulty.

At this station, it was again low water about four on Wednesday morning, or nearly so, as the inner part of the bank on which we had grounded, and at that time was covered with water, was dry at no great distance from us.[3] We again proceeded, with the current in our favor, to the westward; and on passing two small villages of the natives, a few of the inhabitants, from each, paid us their respects. At this time we were nearly abreast of the second opening,[4] passed by unexamined by Mr. Johnstone. It appeared infinitely more capacious than the other, which, agreeably to my former intentions,

[1] Port Neville.
[2] Again, the lat. is correct but the long. is 126° 10′ W (233° 50′ E). Vancouver's figure is obviously a misprint for 233° 53′ E.
[3] The ships were in the shallow bight at the mouth of the Adam River.
[4] Havannah Channel, leading to Call Inlet.

Mr. Broughton was directed to pursue, appointing the same rendezvous with him, that had been fixed for the boats.

We remained under sail the whole day, but made so little way, that by nine at night, we had advanced about five leagues only. Then, in a small bay, close to the rocks on the southern shore, we again anchored, in forty-five fathoms water, sandy bottom.[1]

Light variable winds prevented our sailing until eight in the morning of Thursday the 19th, when, with a gentle breeze from the eastward, we weighed; and, what was not a little extraordinary, without heaving the least strain on the cable, on fishing the anchor, its lower arm was discovered to be broken off close to the crown, and to have been left at the bottom. On further examination, it proved to have been just welded round the surface, so as barely to hold the parts together, within which the bars, composing the internal mass, preserved their original unaltered shape, distinctly separate from each other; and, in the spaces remained the blacksmith's coal, without any appearance of their having undergone the action of fire.

Whilst we remained inactive the fore part of the morning, our time was not unprofitably employed, in receiving the welcome visits of some hospitable friends from the shore; who brought us such an abundant supply of fresh salmon, that we purchased a sufficient number to serve the crew as long as they would keep good; which was a great relief from our salted provisions, being a luxury we had not lately experienced.

We had not long been under sail, when the officers, who had been dispatched in the boats on the 17th, arrived on board. From these gentlemen I became acquainted, that they had examined the inlet to which they had been directed.[2] Off its western point lies a small island;[3] its entrance is about half a mile wide, but with no more than four fathoms water in mid-channel; from whence it extends about eight miles, in a direction N. 75 E.; this depth however increased as they advanced, to five, six, and seven fathoms, affording good anchorage about two thirds of the way up: beyond which limits, like all the channels of this kind that we had explored, it terminated in shallow water. The country bore a more pleasing aspect than that seen from Johnstone's straits; and the soil, where they landed, at the upper part, was composed of black mould and sand, producing pine-trees of large dimensions. They saw one run of water at the head; but the shoal stretching from thence prevented their ascertaining its qualities; yet as a deserted village was observed half way up on the northern shore, in all probability this place is not destitute of wholesome water, the only undiscovered requisite to constitute it a very snug and commodious port; to which I gave the name of PORT NEVILLE.[4]

---

[1] Probably Robson Bight.
[2] Port Neville.   [3] Milly Island.
[4] Walbran suggests (without giving any evidence) that the inlet was named after Lieut. John Neville, Royal Marines, later killed on board Lord Howe's flagship in the battle of the 'Glorious First of June' in 1794.

The weather was serene and pleasant, but the wind so light and variable, that, although we were not more than four leagues from the village where we expected to meet *Maquinna*; it was not until past ten at night that we reached that station, when we anchored just without the sandy island, in seven fathoms water.

The next morning shewed the village in our neighbourhood to be large; and, from the number of our visitors, it appeared to be very populous. These brought us the skins of the sea-otter, of an excellent quality, in great abundance, which were barted for sheet-copper, and blue cloth; those articles being in the highest estimation amongst them. Most of these people understood the language of Nootka, though it did not appear to be generally spoken.[1]

The *Ty-eie*, or chief of the village, paid us an early visit, and received from me some presents which highly delighted him. I understood his name to be *Cheslakees*.[2] He ackowledged *Maquinna* to be a greater chief; as he also did *Wicananish*; but, so far as I could learn, he did not consider himself to be under the authority of either.

On inquiring if *Maquinna* was at the village, he answered in the negative, saying they seldom visited; and that it was a journey of four days across the land to Nootka sound, which from hence towards the S.S.W. is about twenty leagues distant.

Accompanied by some of the officers, Mr. Menzies, and our new guest *Cheslakees*, I repaired to the village, and found it pleasantly situated on a sloping hill, above the banks of a fine freshwater rivulet, discharging itself into a small creek or cove. It was exposed to a southern aspect, whilst higher hills behind, covered with lofy pines, sheltered it completely from the northern winds. The houses, in number thirty-four, were arranged in regular streets; the larger ones were the habitations of the principal people, who had them decorated with paintings and other ornaments, forming various figures, apparently the rude designs of fancy; though it is by no means improbable, they might annex some meaning to the figures they described, too remote, or hieroglyphical, for our comprehension. The house of our leader *Cheslakees* was distinguished by three rafters of stout timber raised above the roof,

[1] Neither Vancouver nor Menzies seems yet to have grasped the fact that they had met Indians belonging to another tribe – the Kwakiutl – who had their own language and were not subject to Maquinna's authority. Menzies goes so far as to state that 'they spoke the Nootka language' and that 'it was evident to us at first sight that they were of the same Tribe by their crying *Wakash Wakash*...which is their expression for friendship...' – 18 July. But in fact their knowledge of the Nootkan language was due simply to social and commercial contacts.

[2] Menzies spells the chief's name Cathlagees and gives the name of the village as Whannoc. Bell's version of the two names are Cathlaginess and Whulk. The village was later abandoned and the Indians established a new settlement at Alert Bay, on nearby Cormorant Island. The terraces upon which the houses stood are still visible. Galiano and Valdés visited the village three weeks after Vancouver, at the invitation of a chief named Sisiaquis. They named it the Rancheria de Sisiaquis.

according to the architecture of Nootka, though much inferior to those I had there seen in point of size; the whole, from the opposite side of the creek, presented a very picturesque appearance.

On our landing, three or four of the inhabitants, only, came down to receive us at the beach; the rest quietly remained near their houses. These, *Cheslakees* informed me, were his near relations, who consequently received, in the shape of presents, compliments from me, with which they seemed greatly pleased.

The houses were constructed after the manner at Nootka, but appeared rather less filthy, and the inhabitants were undoubtedly of the same nation, differing little in their dress, or general deportment. Several families lived under the same roof; but their sleeping apartments were separated, and more decency seemed to be observed in their domestic economy, than I recollected to be the practice at Nootka. The women, who in proportion appeared numerous, were variously employed; some in their different household affairs, others in the manufacture of their garments from bark and other materials; though no one was engaged in making their woollen apparel, which I much regretted. The fabrication of mats for a variety of purposes, and a kind of basket, wrought so curiously close, as to contain water like an earthern vessel without the least leakage or drip, comprehended the general employment of the women, who were not less industrious than ingenious.

As inquiries into the laudable ingenuity of others are not to be satisfied in the civilized world without some expence, so investigations of the like nature amongst the uncultivated regions were not to be had in this society without due acknowledgments, which were solicited by these female artizans in every house we entered; and so abundant were their demands, that although I considered myself amply provided for the occasion with beads, hawk's bells, and other trinkets, my box, as well as my pockets, and those of the gentlemen who were of the party, were soon nearly emptied. At the conclusion of this visit we were entertained at the house of an elderly chief, to whom *Cheslakees*, and every other person paid much respect, with a song by no means unmelodious, though the performance of it was rendered excessively savage, by the uncouth gestures, and rude actions accompanying it, similar to the representations I had before seen at Nootka. The song being finished, we were each presented with a strip of sea-otter skin; the distribution of which occupied some time. After this ceremony a song from the ladies was expected; and during this interval, I observed in the hands of the numerous tribe that now surrounded us, many spears pointed with iron, clubs, large knives, and other weapons with which they were not furnished on our first approach to the village. I was not altogether satisfied with this change in their appearance, though I had every reason to believe their intentions were of the most inoffensive nature, and that it was most probable they had thus produced their arms to shew their wealth, and impress us with an idea of their consequence: I deemed it, however, most advisable to withdraw; and having distributed the few remaining articles we had reserved, *Cheslakees* was informed I was about to return; on which he, with his relations who had attended us through the village, accompanied us to the sandy island, whither I went to observe its latitude.

Some few others of the Indians attended us on this occasion, whose behaviour being orderly and civil, they were permitted to assemble round me whilst observing. They were excessively amused with the effect of the sun's rays through the reading glass; and the extraordinary quality of the quicksilver used for the purpose of an artificial horizon, afforded them the greatest entertainment, until our business was ended, when they in a very friendly manner took leave, and confirmed me in the opinion, that the martial appearance they had assumed, was purely the effect of ostentation.

In most of the houses were two or three muskets, which, by their locks and mounting, appeared to be Spanish. *Cheslakees* had no less than eight in his house, all kept in excellent order: these, together with a great variety of other European commodities, I presumed, were procured immediately from Nootka, as, on pointing to many of them, they gave us to understand they had come from thence, and in their commercial concerns with us, frequently explained, that their skins would fetch more at Nootka than we chose to offer. Their total number we estimated at about five hundred. They were well versed in the principles of trade, and carried it on in a very fair and honorable manner. Sea-otter skins were the chief objects of our people's traffic, who purchased nearly two hundred in the course of the day.[1] Mr. Menzies informed me, that these had been procured at least an hundred per cent. dearer than when he visited the coast on a former occasion,[2] which manifestly proved, that either a surplus quantity of European commodities had been since imported into this country, or more probably, that the avidity shewn by the rival adventurers in this commerce, and the eagerness of an unrestrained throng of purchasers from different nations, had brought European commodities into low estimation. Iron was become a mere drug; and when we refused them fire arms and ammunition, which humanity, prudence, and policy directed to be with-held, nothing but large sheets of copper, and blue woollen cloth engaged their attention in a commercial way; beads and other trinkets they accepted as presents, but they returned nothing in exchange.

[1] Menzies estimated that 'upwards of 200' were procured, and Baker states that 'between 3 & 4 hundred were purchased on board the Discovery'. – July 21.

[2] Menzies states that 'consequently many of our Articles of Commerce begin now to lose their intrinsic Value amongst them [the Indians]. Iron though valuable to most other Indian Natives was here scarcely sought after. The articles they most esteemed were Sheet Copper & coarse broad blue Cloth; Of the former they took from half a sheet to two thirds for a Skin, & of the latter a piece about a yard square of the Cloth, but they sometimes preferrd Woollen Cloth made up in the form of short Jackets or Trowsers. They likewise eagerly asked for fire arms powder & shot, but both policy & prudence should ever prevent them from being distributed amongst them'. – July 20.

These were the principal circumstances that occurred to me on our short visit to this station. The further and more general observations, that fell under my notice respecting the very extraordinary region we had lately passed through, and which were not noticed in the narratives of the several parties who were employed in exploring it, I shall now briefly state, with such reflections as were consequent thereon.

The length of coast from point Mudge to this station, about thirty-two leagues, forms a channel which, though narrow, is fair and navigable; manifested by the adverse winds obliging us to beat to windward every foot of the channel, and to perform a complete traverse from shore to shore through its whole extent, without meeting the least obstruction from rocks or shoals. The great depth of water not only here, but that which is generally found washing the shores of this very broken and divided country, must ever be considered as a very peculiar circumstance, and a great inconvenience to its navigation. We however found a sufficient number of stopping places to answer all our purposes, and, in general, without going far out of our way. In coming from the westward, through Johnstone's straits, the best channel into the gulf of Georgia in thick weather might, though not easily, be mistaken. Such error however may be avoided, by keeping the southern shore close on board, which is compact, and so steep, that it may be passed within a few yards in the greatest safety; indeed I have every reason to believe the whole of the passage to be equally void of dangers that do not evidently shew themselves. The height of the land that composes these shores and the interior country, has been already stated to decrease as we proceeded westward. The land on the southern side, which is an extensive island, appeared to be the most elevated, composed of very lofty mountains, whose summits, not very irregular, were still in some places covered with snow. The northern side, for a considerable distance, seemed less elevated, and the intire forest that covered its surface, might have favored the belief of great fertility, had we not known that pine trees innumerable are produced from the fissures and chasms of the most barren rocks, of which, we had great reason to suppose, the whole of the country before us was composed. Its low appearance may possibly be occasioned by its being much divided by water, as we evidently saw, through an opening, about four miles only to the westward of that appointed for our rendezvous, a much greater space so occupied, than that which comprehended these straits. Our general view to the northward, was, however, bounded by a mountainous country, irregular in the height of its eminences, and some of them capped with snow. The retired hills of the most eastern part of the straits, were, as we passed, so obscured by the high steep rocky cliffs of the shores, that we were unable to describe them with any precision. As the elevation of the northern shore decreased, I was in expectation of seeing a continuation of that lofty and connected range of snowy mountains, which I have repeatedly had reason to consider, as the insurmountable barrier to any

Plate 27. 'Village of the Friendly Indians at the entrance of Bute's Canal.'

CHESLAKEE'S VILLAGE in JOHNSTONE'S STRAITS.

Plate 28. 'Cheslakee's Village in Johnstone's Straits.'

extensive inland navigation. Herein I was disappointed, as this lofty structure either decreases in its vast degree of elevation, or it extends in a more inland direction.

The residence of all the natives we had seen, since our departure from point Mudge, was uniformly on the shores of this extensive island, forming the southern side of Johnstone's straits, which seems not only to be as well inhabited as could be expected in this uncultivated country, but infinitely more so, than, we had reason to believe, the southern parts of New Georgia were. This fact established, it must be considered as singularly remarkable, that, on the coast of the opposite or continental shore, we did not discover even a vestige of human existence, excepting the deserted villages! This circumstance, though it countenances the idea of the original inhabitants of the interior country having migrated, fallen by conquest, or been destroyed by disease; still leaves us unable to adduce any particular reason as the cause of this evident depopulation.[1] The width of the passage scarcely any where exceeding two miles, can hardly have induced the inhabitants of the northern side, to quit their dwellings for a residence on the opposite shore, merely for the purpose of being that small distance nearer to the commerce of the sea-coast. On regarding the aspect of the two situations, and on reflecting that the winter season under this parallel must be severe and inclement, it appears reasonable to suppose, that any human beings, not restrained in fixing their abode, would not hesitate to choose the very opposite side to that which is here preferred, where, in general, their habitations front a bleak northern aspect, with mountains rising so perpendicularly behind them, that, if they do not totally, they must in a great measure, exclude the cheering rays of the sun for some months of the year. The northern side labours not under this disadvantage, and enjoying the genial warmth denied to the other, at certain seasons, most probably, possesses the requisites necessary to their present mode of life, at least in an equal degree; especially, as this country has, in no instance, received the advantages of cultivation. This would appear to be the situation of choice, the other of necessity; for the same source of subsistence, which is evidently the sea, affords equal supplies to the inhabitants of either shore. And that there was a time, when they resided on both, is clearly proved, by their deserted habitations, yet in existence, on the northern shore.

As neither *Maquinna*, nor any of his people, were at this village, I intrusted to the brother of a man named *Kaowitee*, who seemed next of importance

---

[1] Robin Fisher comments: 'Voyagers would attribute the supposed depopulation to disease, whereas villages were clearly abandoned for a variety of reasons. Seasonal migrations, the exhaustion of resource areas, and moves to be closer to the centres of the fur trade were all reasons for an Indian band to relocate its village. Furthermore, most voyagers came to the coast in the summer months when the Indians were more mobile, and there was a greater number of "deserted" villages.' – *Contact and Conflict* (Vancouver, 1977), p. 22. To these reasons Menzies would have added the filth and stench in the villages, which he was convinced would force their abandonment from time to time.

to *Cheslakees*, the letter I received from Senr Galiano, as also one from myself, to be forwarded to Senr Quadra at Nootka, which this man undertook to deliver, on the promise of being handsomely rewarded for his service.[1]

The sandy island, by my observations, is situated in latitude 50° 35½', longitude 232° 57';[2] the variation of the compass here being 20° 45' eastwardly.

[1] 'Capt. Vancouver with great difficulty endeavoured to make the Chief dispatch one of the Natives over Land to Nootks, he appeared to comprehend the Meaning & seemed unwilling to engage in a Promise for its Delivery, he however took charge of a Letter for the purpose.' Puget, July 20. The letter never reached Nootka.

[2] If the 'sandy island' was Flagstaff Islet, the correct position would be lat. 50° 34' N, long. 126° 58' W (233° 02' E).

CHAPTER IX.

Pass through Broughton's Archipelago, to pursue the continental Shore—The Vessels get aground—Enter Fitzhugh's Sound—Reasons for quitting the Coast and proceeding to Nootka.

HAVING replaced our broken anchor with a new one from out of the hold, which had employed the whole of the preceding day, about ten in the forenoon of Saturday the 21st we proceeded with a favourable breeze from the westward, to the appointed rendezvous, that lies from the sandy island N. 89 E. at the distance of about fourteen miles, where, at three in the afternoon, we anchored in twenty fathoms water, sandy bottom, about a cable's length from the shore, of a similar nature to those already described.

Wishing to acquire some idea of the probable extent of this opening, I left the ship after dinner, and was not a little surprized to find it communicate with the extensive space of water, to the north of the channel or straits already mentioned, making the land under which we were at anchor, an island[1] about a league and a half long, nearly in a direction N. 70 W. with many rocky islets and rocks lying about its western extremity, some along its north side, and others off the east end. Northward of this island, and a chain of others which lie to the westward of it, an arm of the sea, not less than four or five leagues across, stretched westward towards the ocean,[2] where the horizon, in that direction, appeared to be intercepted only by a few small islands; the eastern and northern shores seemed wholly composed of rocky islands and rocks, and presented in their examination a very laborious task, to ascertain the continental boundary. But as this important line had been already determined to the entrance of an opening, not more than three leagues to the eastward of our present station, now under the survey of Mr. Broughton in the Chatham, and as a branch of this opening to the eastward of us took a direction that way through a multitude of islands, any investigation of this broken country was rendered unnecessary, until I should understand how far the Chatham had been able to succeed in fixing the continuation of the continental shore.

Our very inactive, unpleasant situation, whilst we anxiously waited the arrival of our consort, was somewhat relieved by the visits of a few Indians from the southern shore of the straits, who brought us a small supply of fish,

---

[1] Hanson Island.   [2] Queen Charlotte Strait.

very acceptable, being unable to obtain any by our own efforts. Among the number of our visitors we were honored with the company of *Cheslakees*, with whose importunities for various articles I had with pleasure complied. He remained on board most part of the day; and as he sat at my elbow whilst writing, saw me frequently advert to a small memorandum book, which he managed to take away in the most dexterous manner, unperceived. Having occasion for its use, and knowing no other person had been near me, the purloiner could not be mistaken. A Sandwich island mat which I had given him, he had contrived to fold up in a very small compass, and in the centre of it was the missing book. He appeared somewhat ashamed at the detection, but more mortified at my taking away the presents he had received; these were however, about two hours afterwards restored, on his contrition, and penitential application. Stealing a book, incapable of being in the least degree serviceable to him, or useful to any other person than the owner, strongly marked that natural inordinate propensity to thieving, which, with few exceptions, influences the whole of the uncivilized world, as if impelled by mere instinct and destitute of reason, they were unable to restrain such inclinations.[1]

Without any occurrence of an interesting nature,[2] we remained uncomfortably idle until the arrival of Mr. Broughton in the afternoon of Friday the 27th, who came on board in his cutter, the Chatham having been obliged, by adverse winds, to anchor the preceding evening three leagues to the westward of our rendezvous.

Mr. Broughton informed me, that after he had entered the opening he had been sent to examine, the eastern point of which is situated in latitude 50° 32′, longitude 233° 32′,[3] he found it take an irregular course towards the N.E. passing a narrow branch leading to the westward.[4] This opening, about a mile in width,[5] occupied their attention until sun-set, when they anchored at its

[1] In the second edition changes in wording were made in the latter part of this sentence and in the first sentence of the next paragraph, but the sense was not changed.

[2] Vancouver does not mention that Puget left on a short expedition on 22 July, the day after the *Discovery* anchored near the E end of Hanson Island: 'The Cutter was sent to examine an Arm to the Eastward....I found the Arm [Baronet Passage] very narrow trending in that Direction which carried me into a more Spacious Inlet [Clio Channel]. This after a Day's Examination I concluded by its NE turn would in all Probability lead into the Branches the Chatham was exploring I therefore according to Capt. Vancouvers Orders returned.' Indians caused him some annoyance: 'As I had only the Cutter, it was a greater Inducement to the Natives to follow us. One Large Canoe full of People kept hovering round the Boat the whole afternoon but finding us on our Guard prudently went away. These People would paddle towards the Cutter with great force; look on for a few Minutes & then as hastily withdraw to the Shore.' – July 22. Menzies states that the cutter was sent 'to look for the Chatham, with orders not to go far', but Puget makes no mention of this. Menzies, 21 July.

[3] Broughton was entering Havannah Channel, leading to Call Inlet. The position of the Broken Islands, on the E side of the entrance, is lat. 50° 31′ N, long. 126° 18′ W (233° 42′ E).

[4] Chatham Channel.   [5] Call Inlet is meant, not the 'narrow branch'.

head in 35 fathoms water, and found it to terminate like the many others already described, in latitude 50° 42½', longitude 234° 3½': which, after Sir John Call, was named CALL'S CHANNEL.[1] On the evening of the next day they reached the narrow branch leading to the westward, which lies from their last place of anchorage S. 68 W. about four leagues distant. Here the Chatham stopped for the night in 17 fathoms water, near a small village of the natives, who brought them an abundance of fresh salmon. Mr. Broughton examined this narrow branch, and found it communicating with an arm of the sea in latitude 50° 43', longitude 233° 33', just navigable for the Chatham;[2] and with the assistance of a strong flood tide, and their boats, they passed it the next morning, through a channel that continued for about half a league, not a hundred yards wide. The shallowest water, from three fathoms, gradually increased to seven fathoms, as they approached the arm of the sea,[3] which is about two miles wide, and extends in an east and west direction. Here the Chatham anchored, and Mr. Broughton pursued its eastern course in his boat along the continental shore, leaving a branch leading to the northward,[4] near the entrance of which are two islands and some rocks. This arm of the sea continued a little to the northward of east, six leagues, to the latitude of 50° 45', where its width increased to near a league, taking an irregular northerly direction to its final termination in latitude 51° 1', longitude 234° 13'. To this, after Captain Knight of the navy, Mr. Broughton gave the name of KNIGHT'S CHANNEL.[5] The shores of it, like most of those lately surveyed, are formed by high stupendous mountains rising almost perpendicularly from the water's edge. The dissolving snow on their summits produced many cataracts that fell with great impetuosity down their barren rugged sides. The fresh water that thus descended gave a pale white hue to the channel, rendering its contents intirely fresh at the head, and drinkable for twenty miles below it. This dreary region was not, however, destitute of inhabitants, as a village was discovered a few miles from its upper extremity, which seemed constructed like that described in Desolation sound, for defence; the inhabitants were civil and friendly. Near this place Mr. Broughton joined the Chatham on the morning of the 23d, and proceeded in her towards the branch above mentioned, leading to the northward.[6] This in the evening he reached, and anchored for the night in 75 fathoms water. The next morning its course was pursued about three leagues towards the N.E. where this direction terminated in latitude 50° 51½',

---

[1] Call's Canal in the first edition; now Call Inlet. It ends in about lat. 50° 38' N, long. 125° 56' W (234° 04' E). Sir John, a military engineer, had a short but distinguished career in India, where he rose to be chief engineer of the East India Company.
[2] Littleton Point, where Chatham Channel meets Knight Inlet is in lat. 50° 38' N, long. 126° 18' W (233° 42' E).
[3] Knight Inlet.   [4] Tribune Channel.
[5] Knight's Canal in the first edition and on the charts; now Knight Inlet. Knight and Broughton had served together in the American Revolutionary War. The inlet terminates in lat. 51° 06' N, long. 125° 36' W (234° 24' E).
[6] Tribune Channel.

longitude 233° 49',[1] from whence it irregularly stretched to the N.W. and westward. Inhabitants were still found on these inhospitable shores, who brought fish and skins of the sea-otter to sell, demanding in return blue great coats. A passage through this channel was accomplished on the 25th, notwithstanding the wind was very fickle and blew hard in squalls, attended with much lightning, thunder, and rain: the night was nearly calm, gloomy, and dark; and not being able to gain soundings, although within thirty yards of the rocky shores, they were driven about as the current of the tides directed, and happily escaped, though surrounded on all sides by innumerable rocks and rocky islets. On the 26th, the boundary of the continent was determined to a point, which, from its appearance and situation, obtained the name of DEEP SEA BLUFF, in latitude 50° 52', longitude 232° 29'.[2] This station Mr. Broughton judged to be as far to the westward as the appointed rendezvous; and for the purpose of repairing thither, directed his course to the south-westward, through a channel that bore every appearance of leading to the sea,[3] as had been understood from the natives. With the assistance of a fresh gale from the N.E. he shortly arrived at its southern entrance, which presented the opening I had seen on the day we arrived at this station. Across it his course was directed to the southward, leaving between his present track and the route he had pursued to the northward, an extensive cluster of islands, rocky islets, and rocks. These, in commemoration of his discovery, I distinguished by the name of BROUGHTON'S ARCHIPELAGO.[4]

Whilst at this station, I had an opportunity of observing the latitude by five meridional altitudes of the sun to be 50° 35', its longitude 233° 19'.[5] The variation of the compass, differing in eight sets of azimuths from 18° 30' to 23° 53', shewed a mean result of 20° 5', eastwardly variation. The tides were irregular, on some days being very rapid, on others scarcely perceptible; the rise and fall, the time of high water, and other fluctuations and irregularities, I attributed, as already stated, to the influence of the winds, and the operation of other local causes on this insulated region.

With a fresh breeze from the E.N.E. we directed our course to the westward, on the morning of Saturday the 28th, in order to proceed to the northward round the west end of this island. The channel through which we passed, though very unpleasant on account of the many rocks in it, is infinitely less dangerous than that to the eastward of the island, which is by no means advisable for ships to attempt.

We had not been long under weigh before we were joined by the Chatham,

---

[1] Thompson Sound here branches off to the ENE. London Point, at its entrance, is in lat. 50° 46' N, long. 126° 07' W (233° 53' E).

[2] The N point of entrance to Tribune Channel, in lat. 50° 49' N, 126° 30' W (233° 30' E). Named Deep Water Bluff on Baker's MS chart.

[3] Fife Sound, leading to Queen Charlotte Strait.

[4] The name is no longer used.

[5] This was close to the correct position, which would be about lat. 50° 33' N, long. 126° 42' W (233° 18' E).

and steered to the northward for the channel leading to Deep Sea bluff, which I called FIFE'S PASSAGE.[1] As we crossed the main arm the squally hazy weather permitted our seeing, but very imperfectly, the several islands and rocks that it contains. About two o'clock in the afternoon, we entered Fife's passage, and found its eastern point (named by me, after Captain Duff of the royal navy, POINT DUFF) situated in latitude 50° 48′, longitude 233° 10′.[2] A small rocky island lies off point Duff, covered with shrubs; and off the west point of this passage, named POINT GORDON,[3] bearing N. 83 W. from point Duff, are several white flat barren rocks lying at a little distance from the shore. Although the tide appeared to be in our favor, we made so little progress in this inlet, that we were compelled to anchor at five in the afternoon not more than two miles within the entrance, in 20 fathoms water, on the northern shore, near some small rocky islets. The shores that now surrounded us were not very high, composed of rugged rocks steep to the sea, in the chasms and chinks of which a great number of stunted or dwarf pine trees were produced. Some few of the natives favored us with their company, but brought little to dispose of; these were not quite so much painted as the Indians of *Cheslakee*'s village, nor did they seem in the least acquainted with the Nootka language.

On Sunday morning the 29th, about nine, we were under sail, with a light favorable breeze, sufficient to have carried us at the rate of near a league per hour; yet the ship remained stationary and ungovernable, not answering to her helm in any direction. In this very unpleasant and disagreeable situation, attributed by us to a kind of under tow, or counter tide, we continued until near dark, when a most powerful breeze springing up, we reached Deep Sea bluff, and anchored about eleven at night in a small opening on its western side in 70 fathoms water; having passed a more extensive one to the south of this, which took its direction to the N.W.[4] On the next day, Monday the 30th, this appeared a very small branch of the sea; and as it was now manifest there was no certainty in confiding in appearances, directions were given that both vessels should be removed higher up near to a convenient spot for recruiting our wood and water; whilst, in the yawl, I proceeded to examine whither this arm was likely to lead. It continued about four miles from Deep Sea bluff to the north-eastward, then stretched to the westward, and terminated behind the hill under which the vessels were at anchor, about two

---

[1] Now Fife Sound.

[2] Its position is lat. 50° 45′ N, long. 126° 43′ W (233° 17′ E).

[3] The place names Fife, Duff and Gordon have a common origin. Captain George Duff was an officer in the *Europa* when Vancouver served in her. He was a grand nephew of Vice Admiral Robert Duff, who was a cousin of William Duff, first Earl of Fife. Presumably Vancouver had James Duff, second Earl of Fife (1729–1809) in mind when he named the sound. Alexander Gordon, 4th Duke of Gordon, was the friend and patron of Captain George Duff and did much to further his career in the Navy.

[4] The ships first anchored a little to the N of Deep Sea Bluff, on the E side of the entrance to Simoon Sound; later they moved some distance up the sound and anchored on the W side.

miles to the westward of them, forming a narrow isthmus, over which we walked, and had a distinct view of the opening before mentioned, extending to the westward.[1] Being perfectly satisfied on this head, I returned, and found the vessels at the appointed station, riding in 30 fathoms water near the western shore, conveniently situated for procuring the only supplies this dreary region seemed likely to afford. But, as tolerably secure anchorage was not on all occasions to be found, I determined the vessels should remain stationary here, whilst the boats explored the broken country before us; which promised to furnish other passages, into the great western channel we had quitted, and bore every appearance of leading to the Pacific Ocean.

The Discovery's yawl, launch and cutter, were ordered to be equipped, and in readiness to depart at day-light the next morning. Mr. Broughton accompanied me, attended by lieutenant Puget in the launch, and Mr. Whidbey in the cutter. On Tuesday the 31st, at sun-rise, our little squadron put off with intention of following up the continental shore, until we might find a more western passage leading to the sea; there to appoint a rendezvous for the launch and cutter, which were to continue the examination of the continental boundary, whilst we returned to conduct the vessels to the appointed station.

From Deep Sea bluff, the shore of the main, across this small opening, took a direction N. 50 W. for about four miles; then extended N.N.E. about a league to a point, where the arm took a more easterly course,[2] passing an island,[3] and several rocky islets, forming passages for boats only; whilst, to the westward of the island, the main channel was a mile in width,[4] and no doubt was entertained of our there finding a greater depth of water than we required for the vessels. We were however obliged to quit the direction of that which appeared, and afterwards proved to be the main channel, to pursue the continental line along this, which apparently led to the N.E. and eastward. In this route, a poor unfortunate deer, that seemed to have eluded the pursuers, had found an asylum in a small recess on the rocky precipice forming the shore, about twenty yards in a direction almost perpendicular to the water, from whence he could only escape by the way he had come. In this very exposed situation, the two headmost boats passed him unnoticed; but, on the third making the discovery, a platoon of muskets was discharged at the defenceless animal by the whole party without effect. On this a seaman landed, and, with a boat-hook, dragged him from the rocks by the neck, and secured to us this valuable acquisition. Upwards of twenty muskets on this occasion were fired, seven of which hit him, but no one mortally; or wounded him in such a manner as to have prevented his escaping, had not the over-hanging precipices

---

[1] Simoon Sound ends in O'Brien Bay; beyond it is the narrow isthmus that separates it from Shawl Bay. From the isthmus Vancouver would see the entrance to Sutlej Channel, leading NW.

[2] Kingcome Inlet. [3] Gregory Island.

[4] Sutlej Channel is meant.

of the rocks rendered it impossible. Venison had long with us been a scarce commodity; our buck proved excellent, and afforded us all one or two excellent fresh meals.

We pursued the examination of this arm to its head in latitude 51°, longitude 233° 46';[1] where it terminated in a similar way to the many before described. Its shores, about a mile apart, were composed of high steep craggy mountains, whose summits were capped with snow; the lower cliffs, though apparently destitute of soil, produced many pine trees, that seemed to draw all their nourishment out of the solid rock. The water, near four leagues from its upper end, was of a very light chalky colour, and nearly fresh. From its shores two small branches extended, one winding about four miles to the S.E. and S.W.[2] the other about a league to the N.N.W.[3] The examination of this branch employed us until noon the next day, Wednesday the 1st of August, when we pursued that which appeared to be the main channel leading to the westward,[4] having several rocky islets and rocks off its north point of entrance. This I called POINT PHILIP,[5] lying N. 56 W. from Deep Sea bluff, at the distance of not more than eight miles. So tardy was our progress in fixing the boundary of this broken continental shore, which we traced from point Philip, about two leagues in the direction of N. 78 W. when it again became divided into various channels. The most spacious one, leading to the south-westward, presented an appearance of communicating with the sea.[6] The shores, on all sides, were high, steep and rocky; though they seemed tolerably well clothed with pines of different sorts.

We kept the continental shore on board through a very intricate narrow branch that took a direction E. by N. for near two leagues,[7] and then terminated as usual at the base of a remarkable mountain, conspicuous for its irregular form, and its elevation above the rest of the hills in its neighbourhood. This I have distinguished in my chart by the name of MOUNT STEPHENS, in honor of Sir Philip Stephens of the Admiralty. It is situated in latitude 51° 1', longitude 233° 20',[8] and may serve as an excellent guide to the entrance of the various channels with which this country abounds.

As we prosecuted our researches, we visited a small Indian village situated on a rocky islet. The whole of it was nearly occupied, well constructed for its protection, and rendered almost inaccessible by platforms similar to that before described though not so strong, nor so ingeniously designed. The inhabitants did not exceed thirty or forty persons, who exactly corresponded with those seen to the southward of Deep Sea bluff, and from whom we met

---

[1] Close to the true position, which is about lat. 50° 57' N. long. 126° 12' W (233° 48' E).
[2] Belleisle Sound.
[3] Wakeman Sound, about 6 miles in length.   [4] Sutlej Channel.
[5] Wrongly spelled Point Phillip on the engraved chart. Named in association with Mount Stephens.   [6] Wells Passage.
[7] Mackenzie Sound.
[8] The mountain (5665 ft.) is about 7 miles N of Philip Point, in approximately lat. 50° 58' N, long. 126° 40' W (233° 20' E).

with, as usual, a very cordial reception.[1] A few indifferent sea-otter skins, for which they demanded more iron than we were inclined to give, comprehended all their stock in trade; they had a distant knowledge of a few words of the Nootka language, but did not always seem properly to apply them. The narrow passage by which we had entered, is a channel admissible for boats only;[2] and thence, to the foot of mount Stephens, was merely a chasm in the mountains, caused, probably, by some violent efforts of nature. This idea originated in its differing materially in one particular from all the channels we had hitherto examined; namely, in its having regular soundings, not exceeding the depth of 13 fathoms, although its shores, like all those of the channels which had no bottom within the reach of line, were formed by perpendicular cliffs, from their snowy summits to the water's edge.

The stupendous mountains on each side of this narrow chasm, prevented a due circulation of air below, by excluding the rays of the sun; whilst the exhalations from the surface of the water and the humid shores wanting rarefaction, were, in a great measure, detained, like steam in a condensed state; the evaporation thus produced a degree of cold and chillness which rendered our night's lodging very unpleasant.

We quitted this unwholesome situation, at the dawning of the next day, Thursday the 2d, and directed our course through another passage, which, from the northern shore, led about a league to the westward, and then turned to the south.[3] This channel is excessively dangerous, owing to the number of rocky islets, sunken rocks, and, by the tides setting through it with great rapidity and irregularity. By breakfast time we reached the opening leading to the southwestward, about half a league from the village we had visited the preceding day. Here I intended to conclude my excursion as soon as a place of rendezvous for the vessels and boats should be found; in quest of which we proceeded down the opening leading to the south-westward; which I called WELLS'S PASSAGE;[4] this now seemed, on a certainty, to communicate with the great channel, which we supposed to lead to sea. But another branch soon appearing, that stretched a little to the south-westward of west,[5] I was in hopes my object would have been further attained, by finding some more

[1] Puget gives a quite different account of the village, which he describes as large, 'situated on an Elevated Rock', and consisting of three rows of buildings. 'Small as the Rock appeared to be, still it contained about Two Hundred People of all Ages and Descriptions...Captain Vancouver having distributed some trifling Presents among the Populace & given the Chief some Copper &c for his Civility and Trouble, we took our leave & glad I was once more to get to the Boats, for the intolerable Stench that came from all parts owing to Stinking Fish & every thing that was bad absolutely made me Sick; we however procured from them some excellent salmon.' – 3 August.

[2] Hopetown Passage.

[3] Kenneth Passage, which leads to the NW from Mackenzie Sound and meets Grappler Sound, which extends southward to the N entrance of Wells Passage.

[4] Now Wells Passage. Walbran states that it was named in honour of Captain John (later Admiral Sir John) Wells.

[5] Stuart Narrows, leading to Drury Inlet.

westerly station for our rendezvous than the end of Wells's passage. In this hope we continued our examination about two leagues, leaving some part of the shore to the north of us, not fully explored. On landing to dine about the time of high water, we soon perceived a rapid ebb tide coming from the westward. This rendered a communication with the ocean in that direction, if not impossible, at least very improbable; and as the time its examination was likely to engage from its apparent extent, might render my design ineffectual, I determined to return, leaving the launch and cutter to carry on the survey. Our future meeting I appointed near the west point of Wells's passage; this, after Captain Boyles of the navy, I named POINT BOYLES; it is situated in latitude 50° 51′, and in longitude 232° 52′.[1]

About one o'clock the next day, Friday the 3d, we arrived on board, and immediately proceeded with the vessels towards the rendezvous, but so slowly that it was not till the evening of Saturday the 4th, that we arrived within two leagues of the S.E. of it. There the boats joined us, and the want of wind obliged us to anchor in 60 fathoms water, on the S.W. side of a low island, about half a league from its shores, bearing by compass from N. 42 E. to N. 38 W.; point Duff N. 87 E.; the land of the southern shore from S. 50 E. to S. 22 W.; a high island appearing to lie nearly in mid-channel, from S. 55 W. to S. 64 W.; and point Boyles N. 84 W.; having many rocky islets and rocks in view, too numerous to be here noticed.[2]

I now became acquainted, that the officers had returned, as directed, to the examination of the continental shore from the place where I had quitted it, and on pursuing it to the southward, they had found it indented with small bays, that afforded, like the narrow arm before mentioned, snug and convenient anchorage; but the passages into them were intricate and dangerous, owing to the strong currents, and the many rocky islets, and sunken rocks, in their neighbourhood. The arm, leading to the westward, that I had been in, was traced to the latitude of 50° 59′, longitude 232° 36′.[3] In it were many rocky islands and sunken rocks; which, with the velocity of the tide, rendered it dangerous, even for the navigation of boats. Near its termination, they pursued a very narrow opening on its northern shore, winding towards the E.N.E. replete with overfalls and sunken rocks, and ending by a cascade similar to several that had before been observed.[4] These are perfectly salt, and seem to owe their origin to the tidal waters, which, in general, rise seventeen feet, and, at high water, render these falls imperceptible, as the bar or obstruction, at that time, lies from four to six feet beneath the surface of the

---

[1] Now Boyles Point. Named for Captain (afterwards Vice Admiral) Charles Boyles. The point is in lat. 50° 49′ N, long. 127° 01′ W (232° 59′ E).

[2] The bearings given and Baker's MS chart show that the ships anchored near the largest of the Polkinghorne Islands.

[3] Drury Inlet does not extend as far W as the long. given; it ends at about 232° 49′ E (127° 11′ W). The lat. (and Baker's chart) show that Puget explored Actaeon Sound and Tsibass Lagoon, N of the W end of the inlet.

[4] The tidal rapids in the narrow entrance to Tsibass Lagoon.

sea, and consequently at low water causes a fall of ten or twelve feet; some of which are twenty yards in width. One of these Mr. Whidbey ascended nearly at low water, and found the internal reservoir to be a small lake, or rather a large pond, seemingly of deep water, divided into several branches, winding some distance through a low, swampy, woodland country. These salt-water cascades may probably be occasioned by the great rapidity of the tides, after they have risen above these obstructions, (acting with considerable pressure) and rushing forward in those inland narrow channels, where they soon overflow the plain, and finding an extensive field for their expansion, a sufficient quantity of water, with the addition of the drains and springs of the country, is thus collected, to replenish these reservoirs every twelve hours, and to cause a constant fall during the reflux of the tide. Within a few yards of one of these cascades was discovered a considerable stream of *warm* fresh water.

By this expedition, the continental shore was traced to the westernmost land in sight. We had now only to proceed along it, as soon as the wind and weather would permit our moving. This, however, a thick fog and a calm prevented, until the afternoon of Sunday the 5th, when a light breeze between S.W. and west enabled us, by sun-set, to advance about two leagues to the westward of point Boyles, which, by compass, bore from us S. 85 W.; an island, previously considered to lie in mid-channel, but now discovered to be divided into four or more islets, S. 38 E.; the most distant part of the opposite shore south, four or five leagues off; and the nearest taken by us to be an island,[1] W.S.W. about a league. These positions are not, however, to be received as correct, because the fog, still continuing, alternately obscured place after place, in the southern quarters, so as to render it impracticable either to acquire the true position, or even gain a distinct view of those shores. The northern, or continental side, was not in the like manner obscured; its nearest part bore by compass north about half a league from us; and its western extremity, N. 78 W. Between this point and a cluster of islands, bearing west, a channel appeared to lead along the coast of the main land,[2] in which were some small islets and rocks; south of the cluster, the haze and fog rendered it impossible to determine of what the region principally consisted, though the imperfect view we obtained, gave it the appearance of being much broken. In this situation, we had 60 and 70 fathoms, muddy bottom; but as we had sufficient space to pass the night in under sail, I preferred so doing, that we might be ready to pursue the above-mentioned channel in the morning.

The wind continuing light in the S.W. quarter, we plied until day-break on Monday 6th, when the breeze was succeeded by a calm, and a very thick fog that obscured every surrounding object until noon, without our being able to gain soundings; so that we were left to the mercy of the currents, in a situation that could not fail to occasion the most anxious solicitude. The fog had no sooner dispersed, than we found ourselves in the channel for which

[1] The largest of the Numas Islands.

[2] Richards Channel, between the Millar Group of islands and the N shore of Queen Charlotte Sound.

I had intended to steer, interspersed with numerous rocky islets and rocks, extending from the above cluster of islands towards the shore of the continent. The region to the S.W. still remained obscured by the fog and haze; at intervals, however, something of it might be discerned, serving only to shew there was no great probability of our finding a less intricate passage to navigate, than that immediately before us along the continental shore; which must either be now traced by the ship, or by the boats on a future occasion. This made me determine on the former mode, although there was reason to apprehend it would engage our utmost attention, even in fair weather to preserve us from latent dangers. The dispersion of the fog was attended by a light breeze from the N.N.W., and as we stood to windward, we suddenly grounded on a bed of sunken rocks about four in the afternoon.[1] A signal indicating our situation was immediately made to the Chatham, she instantly anchored in fifty fathoms water, about a cable and a half distant from us, and we immediately received all her boats to our assistance. The stream anchor was carried out, and an attempt made to heave the ship off, but to no effect. The tide fell very rapidly; and the force with which the ship had grounded, had occasioned her sewing[2] considerably forward. On heaving, the anchor came home, so that we had no resource left but that of getting down our topmasts, yards, &c. &c. shoaring up the vessel with spars and spare topmasts, and lightening her as much as possible, by starting the water, throwing overboard our fuel and part of the ballast we had taken on board in the spring. Soon after the ship was aground, the tide took her on the starboard quarter; and as she was afloat abaft it caused her to take a sudden swing, and made her heel so very considerably on the starboard side, which was from the rocks, that her situation, for a few seconds, was alarming in the highest degree.[3] The shoars were got over with all possible dispatch, but notwithstanding this, by the time it was low water, the starboard

[1] The ships were following the N (continental) shore westward, passing through Richards Channel, and Menzies states that they were 'standing in towards the North Shore of the Sound' when the *Discovery* grounded. Next morning, once more afloat, she anchored about a quarter of a mile from the reef. 'About noon,' Menzies records, 'it cleard up a little so as to enable us to ascertain our Latitude which was 50° 55′ North...' – 6–7 August. It is not possible to identify the precise reef or pinnacle on which the ship grounded, but Richards Channel narrows to a width of four cables between Jeanette Island and Ghost Island and the reef was probably not far from the latter. Jeanette Island is in lat. 50° 55′ N.

[2] Being left high and dry.

[3] Menzies, Puget and Manby all give graphic accounts of the mishap: 'the yards and Top Masts were struck and got over in hopes of preventing her tumbling over, our fears were too well founded, after laying upright half an hour, a terrible crash ensued, that brought the Ship on her broadside...Seven long and tedious hours we sat on the Ships side without the ability of giving her any assistance, but that of carrying out an anchor and three Cables ready to heave upon the high Water...' – Manby, letters, 7 August. 'About an hour before Low Water the Ship suddenly swung with her head off it was then thought all was over; & that she would immediately upset but providentially the Shores of a projecting Rock as we supposed under her Starboard Bilge brought her timely up.' – Puget, 7 August. As usual in accounts of moments of great stress, details differ. Mudge states that 7 tons of water were thrown overboard; Swaine increases this to 8 tons, and Menzies increases it further to 17 tons.

main chains were within three inches of the surface of the sea. Happily, at
this time, there was not the smallest swell or agitation, although we were in
the immediate vicinity of the ocean. This must ever be regarded as a very
providential circumstance, and was highly favorable to our very irksome and
perilous situation,[1] in which, under the persuasion of the tide falling as low
as had been lately observed in our several boat expeditions, nothing short of
immediate and inevitable destruction presented itself, until towards the latter
part of the ebb tide, when more than one half of the ship was supported by
such a sufficient body of water, as, in a great measure, to relieve us from the
painful anxiety that so distressing a circumstance necessarily occasioned. When
the tide was at the lowest, about nine at night, the ship's fore foot was only
in about three and a half feet water, whilst her stern was in four fathoms.

In this melancholy situation, we remained, expecting relief from the
returning flood, which to our inexpressible joy was at length announced by
the floating of the shoars, a happy indication of the ship righting. Our exertions
to lighten her were, however, unabated, until about two in the morning of
Tuesday the 7th; when the ship becoming nearly upright, we hove on the
stern cable, and, without any particular efforts, or much strain, had the
inexpressible satisfaction of feeling her again float, without having received
the least apparent injury. We brought up in 35 fathoms water, about a quarter
of a mile from the bed of rocks from whence we had so providentially escaped.
After about three hours rest, all hands were employed in the re-equipment
of the ship. The main top-gallant top-rope unluckily broke, and by this
accident, John Turner, a seaman, had his arm fractured.[2] By noon, the hold
was restowed, and the ship, in every respect, ready again to proceed.

A light breeze springing up from the S.W. about one o'clock, we were
again under sail, and knowing of no safer channel, we directed our course
through that before us, along the continental shore. This was a narrow passage,
and as we advanced, became more intricate by an increased number of rocky
islets and rocks, as well beneath, as above the surface of the water; the former
being ascertained by the surf breaking with some violence upon them. This
dangerous navigation seemed to continue as far as was discernible towards the
ocean, between the shore of the continent and the land forming the opposite
side of the channel, which appeared to be an extensive range of islands.

Having so recently been preserved from the dangers of a most perilous
situation, the scene before us, in presenting a prospect of many such snares,
was extremely discouraging. We had, however, not the least hope of finding
a less difficult way for the execution of the adventurous service in which we

---

[1] 'irksome and unpleasant situation' in the first edition.
[2] Hewett adds a note, as usual critical of Vancouver: 'This Man's Arm continued many
Months weak when he was ordered to do what little Duty he could but it proved too
heavy for him and [he] fell Overboard for which Capn. Vancouver ordered him to be
flogged.' Brown's log records that on 19 March 1793 Turner was given 24 lashes for
'neglect of duty'.

were engaged; nor any alternative but to proceed with all the circumspection and caution that the nature of our situation would permit, through a channel not more than half a mile wide, bounded on one side by islands, rocks, and breakers, which in some places appeared almost to meet the continental shore on the other. However intricate, this was apparently the only navigable channel in the neighbourhood.[1] About five in the afternoon we had fortunately escaped through its narrowest part; the wind now became light and baffling; the ebb tide sat us towards the ocean, where we had a view of the distant horizon, although intercepted by the same rocky region that surrounded us in every direction. About six o'clock some of its hidden dangers arrested the progress of the Chatham. We instantly anchored in seventy fathoms water, and sent our boats to her assistance. Thus, before we had recovered from the fatiguing exertions and anxious solicitude of one distressing night, the endurance of a similar calamity was our portion for the next.

I had less reason at first to hope for the preservation of the Chatham under the circumstances of her disaster, than I had the preceding night for that of the Discovery; as the oceanic swell was here very perceptible, and caused a considerable surf on the shore. On the return of our small boat, I became acquainted that, in consequence of its having fallen calm, she had been driven by the tide on a ledge of sunken rocks, but had the consolation of hearing, that although she had frequently struck when lifted by the surge, it had not been violently; that no damage had yet been sustained; and that her present very uncomfortable situation could not be of long duration, as it was nearly half ebb when she grounded.

Our present anchorage bore by compass from the rocks, on which the Discovery had struck, though intercepted by various others, S. 42 E. five miles, and from the ledge of rocks on which the Chatham was then lying. S. 61 E. three miles distant. Our estimated latitude was 51° 2', longitude 232° 25'.[2] Since the commencement of the month of August, the foggy weather had totally precluded our making any celestial observations; the situation therefore of the islands, coasts, rocks, &c. westward from Deep Sea bluff, could only be ascertained by an estimated protraction,[3] which may be liable to errors we had no means to detect; hence this portion of intricate navigation is not to be implicitly depended upon in this particular, as exhibited by the chart; but the continued direction of the continental shore, (the nearest part now bearing by compass N.E. at the distance of about half a league) was positively ascertained to this station; and I trust, its latitude and longitude will not be found to deviate many miles from the truth.

The rocks between our present anchorage and the ocean having the

[1] The navigation channels now used by large vessels are on the S side of Queen Charlotte Strait.

[2] This position is too far N; it would be about 10 miles, not five, from the position (based on observation) given by Menzies for the grounding of the Discovery.

[3] Estimated courses and distances based on observations made previously.

appearance of being almost impenetrable, Mr. Whidbey was dispatched to discover the most safe channel for us to pursue. The day-light just served him to execute his commission; and on his return at night he informed me, that there were three passages; one nearly through the centre of the rocks; another about midway between the continental shore, and a very broken country to the southward of us; and a third between the nearest cluster of rocks and the continent.[1] This for a small distance seemed to be clear; but further to the north-westward a labyrinth of rocks appeared to stretch from the continent towards land, forming like two islands. These rocks nearly joined to the north-easternmost about nine miles from us, bearing by compass N. 50 W. the westernmost at about the same distance, N. 64 W.

The nearest cluster of rocks, whose southern part was almost in a line with the easternmost island, not quite a league from us, we were to pass to the south of; between them and other rocks and rocky islets, to the westward and S.W. forming a channel about two miles wide, in which no visible obstruction had been discovered by Mr. Whidbey. These rocks and rocky islets presented an appearance of being as nearly connected with the southern broken shore, as those further north did with the continent, giving us little to expect but a very intricate and hazardous navigation.

An extremely thick fog ushering in the morning of the 8th, precluded our seeing or knowing any thing of the Chatham's situation; and obliged us to remain in the most painful state of suspense until about nine in the forenoon, when the fog in some measure dispersing, we had the satisfaction of seeing our consort approaching us under sail; and having a light southerly breeze, with the ebb tide in our favor, we immediately weighed in order to proceed together through the channel before mentioned between the rocks.[2]

On the return of the boats, Lieutenant Baker, who had been with our people assisting the Chatham during the night, informed me that latterly she had struck so hard, as intirely to disable both the spare topmasts, which had been used for shoars;[3] but that about half past one they succeeded in heaving her off, without the appearance of her having sustained any very material damage.[4] Our sails were scarcely set when the wind became variable; and soon after mid-day partial fogs and a clear atmosphere succeeded each other in every direction. These by one o'clock obliged us again to anchor in fifty-five fathoms water, as did the Chatham about two miles to the northward of our

[1] The three passages were respectively Europa Passage, the W end of Gordon Channel and a channel along the N shore of Queen Charlotte Strait, beyond the W end of Richards Channel.

[2] Europa Passage, between the Storm Islands and Pine Island.

[3] Menzies adds an interesting detail: 'They were obligd to shore her up on both sides, but not having a sufficient number of Spars on board for the purpose, the Tide happened to drift a very good one along side at the moment they wanted it & which was made use of...' – 8 August.

[4] The damage was minor, as Vancouver states, but the Chatham was hauled ashore at Nootka for repairs, of which details are given later.

Plate 29. 'The *Discovery* on the Rocks in Queen Charlotte's Sound.'

Plate 30. Sketch, believed to represent the *Daedalus*, in a rough
journal by William Gooch.

FRIENDLY COVE, NOOTKA SOUND.

Plate 31. 'Friendly Cove, Nootka Sound.'

The letters A–B, close to shore at right, indicate 'the Territories, which in Sept. 1792 were offer'd by
Spain to be ceded to Great Britain'.

MACUINA,
Xefe de Nutka.

Plate 32. Chief Maquinna.

former station, and within a quarter of a mile of the continental shore. Here we were detained until nine the following morning of Thursday the 9th, when with a light eastwardly breeze, and clear weather, we directed our course as before stated. On passing near the rocks on the eastern side of the channel, we had soundings at the depth of twenty-eight fathoms, rocky bottom; but immediately afterwards gained no ground with sixty and seventy fathoms of line. As it was my intention to seek a channel between the two islands,[1] the Chatham's signal was made to lead. The wind being light we advanced slowly, passing some very dangerous rocks, whose situation was only to be known by the breakers upon them at low tide, lying about two miles to the S.E. of the north-easternmost island.

Though clear immediately overhead, the horizon was encumbered with partial fogs in every direction. This rendered the view of surrounding objects not less limited than undefined, and prevented such observations being made, as were necessary for ascertaining our positive situation. About noon we were becalmed between these islands, whose shores are about two miles and a half asunder; soundings were obtained at the depth of seventy fathoms, rocky bottom. They lie from each other about north and south; the southernmost is about a league in circuit, with a small island lying off its eastern extremity.[2] The northernmost, instead of being one island, as had been supposed, was now found to comprehend eight or nine small islets, lying in a direction about N. 50 W. and occupying in that line an extent of four miles; their breadth about half, or perhaps three quarters of a mile.[3] With the assistance of the boats a-head, we passed through this channel about one o'clock. At this time a light breeze springing up from the north-westward, we stood towards the southern shore; it was not however, as was usual with the north-westerly winds, attended with clear and pleasant weather, but with a remarkably thick fog; and having no soundings we were obliged to ply to windward under an easy sail until about five o'clock, when we gained bottom, and anchored in fifty-five fathoms water. The fog soon cleared away, and discovered our situation to be near the southern shore, before a small opening at the distance of about a mile.[4] This by compass bore S. 7 W.; a channel that appeared to stretch to the S.E. through the range of islands to the southward of that we had navigated, bore S. 80 E. and seemed tolerably clear of those dangers and impediments with which we had lately contended.[5] The southernmost of the

[1] Europa Passage.
[2] Pine Island and the Tree Islets.   [3] The Storm Islands.
[4] The ships were off the entrance to Shadwell Passage, at the E end of Hope Island. Nigei Island lies to the E. On his chart Vancouver named these islands Galiano and Valdes (Isles of Galiano and Valdes on Baker's MS chart). He may have applied these names after he heard that Galiano and Valdes had sailed through Goletas Channel, betweeen the islands and the coast of Vancouver Island. In 1900 the Geographic Board of Canada renamed the islands to prevent confusion with other islands with the same names in the Strait of Georgia. Valdes Island became Hope Island and Galiano Island was named Nigei Island.
[5] Gordon Channel, now the principal navigation channel through the strait.

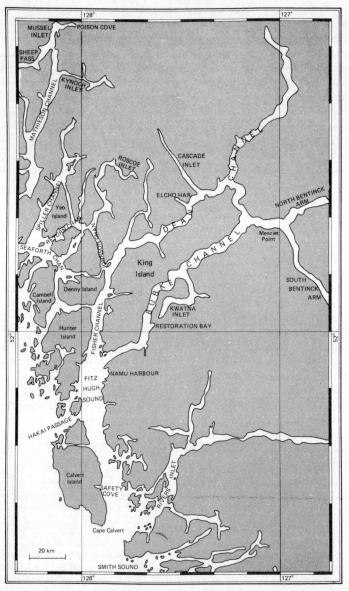

Figure 4. Calvert Island to Poison Cove, including Fitz Hugh Sound, Burke Channel and Dean Channel. *Base map by Michael E. Leek.*

islands we had passed at noon bore by compass N. 7 E. at the distance of about a league; and the north-westernmost of the islets, N. 8 W. distant about two leagues; a low point of land forming the south point of an opening on the continental shore N. 14 W. a high distant mountain being the northernmost land in sight N. 30 W. and the westernmost land on the southern shore S. 55 W. Between these latter directions the oceanic horizon seemed perfectly clear and uninterrupted.

We now appeared to have reached the part of the coast that had been visited and named by several of the traders from Europe and India. The Experiment, commanded by Mr. S. Wedgborough, in August, 1786, honoured the inlet through which we had lately passed, with the name of 'QUEEN CHARLOTTE'S SOUND;'[1] the opening on the continental shore was discovered, and called 'SMITH'S INLET,' by Mr. James Hanna,[2] the same year; the high distant mountain that appeared to be separated from the main land, formed part of a cluster named by Mr. Duncan 'CALVERT'S ISLANDS;'[3] and the channel between them and the main land, was by Mr. Hanna called 'FITZHUGH'S SOUND.'[4] These being the names given, as far as I could learn, by the first discoverers of this part of the coast, will be continued by me, and adopted in my charts and journal.

Destitute of any other authority, our estimated latitude in this situation was 51° 4' longitude 232° 8'. In the evening I visited the shores, and found the opening take a winding southerly direction, dividing the land most probably into two or more islands.[5] Westward of the opening a sandy beach stretched along the coast, and afforded tolerably good shelter, with anchorage from six to twenty fathoms depth of water. Some detached rocks were observed to lie at a little distance from these shores.

Having a fine breeze from the eastward on the morning of Friday the 10th, we weighed at seven, and stood across Queen Charlotte's sound for the entrance of Smith's inlet. The Chatham being ordered to lead, at half past ten made the signal for soundings, at the depth of ten to eighteen fathoms. In this situation the island, near which the Chatham had grounded, bore S. 43 E. distant about six or seven leagues; and the labyrinth of rocks that before

---

[1] Captain Guise was in command of the *Experiment*, not Wedgborough, but Walbran hazards the guess that Wedgborough may have been an officer of the ship and possibly in temporary command. Meares published a sketch of Friendly Cove by Wedgborough in his *Voyages*.

[2] The broad entrance is now Smith Sound. The name Smith Inlet is confined to one of the two branches into which the sound divides, the other being Boswell Inlet. Hanna was captain of the *Sea Otter*.

[3] Charles Duncan, commander of the *Princess Royal*, companion vessel to the *Prince of Wales*, Captain James Colnett. Duncan bestowed the name 'Calvert's Island' (not Islands) in 1788.

[4] Named by Hanna in 1786. Now spelled Fitz Hugh Sound.

[5] Vansittart Island divides Bate Passage and Shadwell Passage, which separate Hope and Nigei islands. The position of the island is lat. 50° 55' N, long. 127° 48' W (232° 12' E). Vancouver cannot have been very far from this position.

had appeared to extend along the continental shore, now seemed to exist no further than a low sandy point bearing by compass E.S.E. at the distance of about two leagues. The shores of the main from this point seemed free from rocks, and possessed some small sandy bays to the south point of entrance into Smith's inlet, which bore by compass N. 18 W. about a league distant; where detached rocks were again seen to incumber the shore.

The weather, less unfavorable to our pursuits than for some time past, permitted our having a tolerably distinct view of the surrounding country. The opening before us, Fitzhugh's sound, appeared to be extensive in a northerly direction. At noon we found our observed latitude to be 51° 21', longitude 232° 4'. In this situation, the south point of Calvert's island bore by compass N. 29 W. its westernmost part in sight N. 60 W. two clusters of rocks S. 73 W. and N. 70 W. these were discovered by Mr. Hanna, who named the former 'VIRGIN,' the latter 'PEARL ROCKS,'[1] both which being low, and at some distance from the shore, are dangerously situated. The south point of Smith's inlet terminating the continental shore in a north-westwardly direction, bore by compass S. 40 E. from which the Virgin rocks, about thirteen miles distance, lie N. 75 W. and the Pearl rocks N. 38 W. distant about eight miles.

Intending to continue the investigation of the continental shore up Smith's inlet, the Chatham was directed that way; but as we advanced, the great number of rocky islets and rocks, as well beneath as above the surface of the sea, and the irregularity of the soundings, induced me to abandon this design, and to steer along the eastern side of Calvert's island, forming a steep and bold shore, in quest of 'Port Safety,' laid down in Mr. Duncan's chart,[2] or of any other convenient anchorage we might find; and from thence to dispatch two parties in the boats, one to prosecute the examination of the broken shores to the south-eastward of us, the other to explore the main branch of Fitzhugh's sound leading to the northward. In consequence of this determination, the necessary signal was made to the Chatham for quitting her pursuit; and we made all sail to the northward.

On passing that which we had considered as the south point of Calvert's island, it proved to be two small islets lying near it;[3] and from the southern-most of them, the Virgin and Pearl rocks in a line lie S. 68 W. the former eleven, and the latter four miles distant.

As we proceeded up this sound, the eastern shore still continued to be much divided by water; towards the sea it was of moderate height, though the interior country was considerably elevated; the whole was apparently one

[1] Both names still apply, but Menzies states correctly that Hanna named the Pearl Rocks the Peril Rocks. – August 10. How Pearl Rocks came to be substituted in Vancouver's text and on his chart does not appear. The rocks are unnamed on Baker's MS chart.

[2] Named by Duncan in 1788; as will appear, Vancouver changed the name to Safety Cove, which is still used. Duncan's chart of the cove was engraved and published by Dalrymple in 1789. Vancouver had a copy.

[3] The Sorrow Islands.

intire forest of pine trees produced from the chasms in the rugged rocks of which the country is formed. The western, or shore of Calvert's islands is firm, and rose abruptly from the sea to a very great height, seemingly composed of the same rocky materials, and like the eastern shore, intirely covered with pine trees. About four in the afternoon of Saturday the eleventh, a small cove was discovered on the western shore, bearing some resemblance to Mr. Duncan's port Safety, but differing in its latitude according to our run since noon.[1] Appearing however likely to answer all our purposes, we hauled in for it; the shores we found to be bold, steep on either side, and soundings at the entrance were from twenty-three to thirty fathoms, soft bottom. We anchored about six in the evening in seventeen fathoms on the south side of the cove, as did the Chatham on the opposite shore, steadying the vessels with hawsers to the trees. My first object after the ship was secured, was to examine the cove. It terminated in a small beach, near which was a stream of excellent water and an abundance of wood: of these necessaries we now required a considerable supply; and as the field of employment for our boats would be extensive, there was little doubt of our remaining here a sufficient time to replenish these stores. Being tolerably well sheltered in this cove, I was willing to hope the Chatham might with security, and without much difficulty, be laid on shore to examine if she had sustained any damage whilst striking on the rocks.

After giving directions for the execution of these services, I ordered the yawl, launch, and two cutters belonging to the Discovery, and the Chatham's cutter to be equipped, supplied with a week's provisions, and to be in readiness to depart early the next morning. The boats being prepared and supplied, agreeably to my wishes, we departed about five o'clock; and having proceeded together nearly into the middle of the sound, I directed Lieutenant Puget and Mr. Whidbey, in the Discovery's launch and large cutter, to examine the coast we had left unexplored to the south-eastward, from the termination of the continent in its N.W. direction, to a certain point on the eastern shore, where Mr. Johnstone, in the Chatham's cutter, attended by Mr. Humphreys in the Discovery's small cutter, would commence his inquiry. Conceiving the northern survey would be infinitely more extensive than that to the south, I joined Mr. Johnstone's party,[2] in order to fix on a rendezvous where, agreeably to my proposed plan, he would on his return find the vessels, or they would be on their way from the cove to the place so appointed.

Our separation had scarcely taken place, when our southerly breeze freshened to a brisk gale, attended by a torrent of rain. The wind however having favored our pursuit, we reached the eastern shore about five miles to the northward of the cove where the ships rode. It was low but compact, with one

[1] Duncan gave the lat. as 51° 41' N. Menzies gives it as 51° 30' N. The correct figure is 51° 32' N.

[2] These details are somewhat confusing, as the fifth boat is not accounted for. This was the yawl (referred to by Puget and Menzies as the pinnace) in which Vancouver travelled.

small opening only, impassable for our boats by breakers extending across it. On the western side two conspicuous openings had been observed; the southernmost had the appearance of being a very fine harbour;[1] the other, about two leagues further north, formed a passage to sea, in which were several rocky islets.[2] About noon we arrived at the point where Mr. Johnstone's researches were to commence, nearly in the direction of north from the ships, and at the distance of about sixteen miles. From this point,[3] the north point of the passage leading to sea, lies S. 39 W. four miles distant; but the thick rainy weather prevented our seeing any objects that were to the northward. Increased torrents of rain, and thick stormy weather from the S.E. obliged us to take shelter in the first safe place we could discover, which presented itself in a small cove, about a mile from the point above-mentioned,[4] where we were very unpleasantly detained until near noon the following day, Sunday the 12th, when the wind having moderated, and the rain in some degree abated, we resumed our examination along the starboard or continental shore, extending from the above point about a league and a half in a north direction. Here the inlet divided into two capacious branches; that which appeared to be the principal one still continued its northerly course,[5] the other stretched E.N.E. and was in general about a mile wide.[6] In order to prosecute the survey of the continental shore, which I presumed this to be, the latter became the first object of our examination, for which we quitted the former, whose width we estimated at a league. The intermission of the rain was for a short time only; at three in the afternoon it again returned with such squally and unpleasant weather, that we were necessitated, at six, to take up our abode for the night on a long sandy beach, about eight miles within the entrance of this eastern branch. In the S.E. corner of this beach was the largest brook of fresh water we had yet seen on the coast.[7] It bore a very high colour, and emptied itself into the sea with considerable velocity. Here the mountains, which appeared to be a continuation of the snowy barrier from mount Stephens, retired a small distance from the beach, and the low land, occupying the intermediate space, produced pine trees of inferior growth, from a bed of moss and decayed vegetables in the state of turf, nearly as inflammable as the wood which it produced. A continuation of the unpleasant weather confined us to this uncomfortable spot until the afternoon of Monday the 13th; when, about four, we again proceeded up the branch, which, from the beach, took a direction N. by E.; the furthest point seen in that line was at the distance of about three leagues; this, after passing an extensive cove on the starboard side,[8] we reached about nine at night. Excepting this cove, and that we had

[1] Kwakshua Channel. Vancouver could not see that it swung to the N, cutting off what appeared to be the N end of Calvert Island and forming Hecate Island.
[2] Hakai Passage, N of Hecate Island.
[3] Uganda Point.
[4] Warrior Cove, or Kiwash Cove, just N of it.
[5] Fisher Channel.
[6] Burke Channel.
[7] The Nootum River.
[8] Restoration Bay.

just before left, no other was seen; the sides of this channel were composed of compact, stupendous mountains, and nearly perpendicular, rocky cliffs, producing pine trees to a considerable height above the shores, and then nearly barren to their lofty summits, which were mostly covered with snow.

During the night we had much rain; the next morning, Tuesday the 14th, the weather was cloudy, with some passing showers, which at intervals enabled us to obtain a tolerably distinct view of the region before us; and for the first time, since the commencement of this expedition, it shewed the branch we were navigating to be about two miles wide, extending in a N.E. by E. direction, several leagues ahead. I had been in continual expectation of finding that the larboard shore would prove to be an island,[1] in which case, on the return of the launch and cutter, the vessels should have been removed to its northern extremity, and by that means the return of the boats, that were still to proceed, would be materially shortened; but, seeing little reason to indulge this hope any longer, I appointed a rendezvous with Mr. Johnstone, a little to the south of the entrance into this arm; where, on his return, he would find the vessels, or they would be on their way thither; and, after bidding him farewell, returned on my way towards the ships.

By noon we had reached the entrance of this branch of the inlet, where, on a small islet near its south point, I observed the latitude to be 51° 52',[2] making the station at which I had parted with Mr. Johnstone, and which I had concluded to be the continental shore, in latitude 52° 3', longitude 232° 19'.[3] This rendezvous was about 37 miles from the station of the vessels, in as desolate inhospitable a country as the most melancholy creature could be desirous of inhabiting. The eagle, crow, and raven, that occasionally had borne us company in our lonely researches, visited not these dreary shores. The common shell-fish, such as muscles, clams, and cockles, and the nettle samphire, and other coarse vegetables, that had been so highly essential to our health and maintenance in all our former excursions, were scarcely found to exist here; and the ruins of one miserable hut, near where we had lodged the preceding night, was the only indication we saw that human beings ever resorted to the country before us, which appeared to be devoted intirely to the amphibious race; seals and sea-otters, particularly the latter, were seen in great numbers.

Having dined, and dedicated a short interval of sun-shine to the drying of our wet clothes, we made the best of our way towards the ships; where, about midnight, we arrived, most excessively fatigued; the inclemency of the weather having, on this occasion, been more severely felt than in any of our former expeditions.

The same very disagreeable weather had prevailed during our absence, attended with much more wind than we had experienced. From the S.W. the

---

[1] As further exploration was to prove, Vancouver's surmise was correct; the larboard shore was King Island.
[2] Probably Kiwash Island, in lat. 51° 52' N, long. 127° 54' W (232° 06' E).
[3] This position is about a mile and a half N of Restoration Bay.

gale had blown particularly hard, which caused the most grateful reflections for our having providentially reached so comfortable a place of shelter, from the dangers that must necessarily have awaited our navigating, in such tempestuous weather, the intricate and unexplored region we had so recently quitted.

During our absence, a sufficient quantity of salmon had been taken, for every person on board the vessel; the necessary supplies of wood and water were nearly completed; but the rise and fall of the tide had not been equal to our wishes for the purpose of grounding the Chatham, without landing the greater part of her stores and provisions; and, as the bottom at low tide was found to be soft mud, unfavourable to such an operation, that business was necessarily deferred.

The weather, though clear at intervals for a short time, continuing very boisterous, filled our minds with much solicitude for the welfare of our friends in the boats; particularly those detached to the S.E. who were greatly exposed not only to its inclemency, but to the violence of the sea, which, from an uninterrupted ocean, broke with great fury on the southern shores. One consolation, however, always attended my anxious concern on these perilous occasions, that, in the exposure of my people to such fatiguing and hazardous service, I could ever depend on their cheerful and ready obedience to the prudent and judicious directions of the officers who were intrusted with the command of these adventurous expeditions.

Friday, the 17th. Whilst we thus remained under much concern for the safety of our detached parties, we were suddenly surprized by the arrival of a brig off the entrance of the cove, under English colours. A sight so uncommon, created a variety of opinions as to the cause that would induce any vessel in a commercial pursuit, (for so she appeared to be employed) to visit a region so desolate and inhospitable. Our suspense, however, was at an end on the return of Lieutenant Baker, who informed me she was the Venus belonging to Bengal, of 110 tons burthen, commanded by Mr. Shepherd,[1] last from Nootka, and bound on a trading voyage along these shores; that having found the price of skins so exorbitant on the sea-coast, he had been induced to try this inland navigation, in the hope of procuring them at a less extravagant price. By him we received the pleasant tidings of the arrival of the Dædalus store-ship, laden with a supply of provisions and stores for our use; and he acquainted Mr. Baker that Sen.r Quadra was waiting with the greatest impatience to deliver up the settlement and territories at Nootka. But, as fortune too frequently combines disastrous circumstances with grateful intelligence, Mr. Shepherd had brought with him a letter from Mr. Thomas New, master of the Dædalus, informing me of a most distressing and melancholy event. Lieutenant Hergest the commander, Mr. William Gooch the astronomer, with one of the seamen belonging to the Dædalus, had been

[1] Captain Henry Shepherd. The *Venus* was the companion ship of the *Halcyon*, Captain Charles W. Barkley.

murdered by the inhabitants of Woahoo, whilst on shore procuring water at that island.[1] A circumstance so much to be deplored, and so little to be expected, was sincerely lamented by us all, and sincerely felt by myself, as Mr. Hergest had, for many years, been my most intimate friend; he was a most valuable character; and I had ever esteemed him as a man not less deserving my respect than intitled to my regard. The loss of Mr. Gooch, though I had not the pleasure of his acquaintance, would unavoidably be materially felt in the service we had to execute during the ensuing part of our voyage. For although Mr. Whidbey, with the assistance of some of our young gentlemen, relieved me of considerable labour, by attending to nautical astronomy; yet, for the purpose of expediting this arduous service on which we were employed, the absence both of Mr. Whidbey and myself frequently became necessary, whilst the ships remained stationary for some days, in situations where many opportunities might occur of making various astronomical observations on shore. Although we were compelled to appropriate such time to those pursuits as were indispensibly requisite to determine the position of different points, promontories and stations, yet we had little leisure for making such miscellaneous observations as would be very acceptable to the curious, or tend to the improvement of astronomy.

The weather was less disagreeable and boisterous the next morning, Saturday the 18th, when, to our great satisfaction, the launch and cutter returned, without having met with any accident, although infinitely fatigued by the severity of the weather, with which they had so long contended.

The entrance into Smith's inlet was nearly closed by rocky islets, some producing shrubs and small trees, others none; with innumerable rocks as well beneath as above the surface of the sea, rendering it a very intricate and dangerous navigation for shipping. Within the islets and rocks the northern shore appeared the clearest; but the opposite side could not be approached without some difficulty, not only from the numerous rocks, but from a great oceanic swell occasioned by the prevailing tempestuous weather. From the entrance into the inlet, whose north point lies from its south point N. 20 E. about a league distant, they found it extend, nearly in an east direction, about six leagues; here it took a turn to the north-eastward, and terminated in latitude 51° 24', longitude 232° 47½'.[2] About three leagues within the entrance, the rocks and islets ceased to exist, and the inlet contracted to a general width of about half a mile; though, in particular places, it was nearly twice that distance from shore to shore; both of which were formed by high rocky precipices covered with wood.

About half way up the channel a village of the natives was discovered, which

[1] Vancouver deals with the whole matter of the murders in detail in his account of his second visit to the Sandwich Islands.
[2] Puget and Whidbey explored the full length of the Smith Inlet, the continuation of Smith sound to the E. The head of the inlet is in the lat. Vancouver gives, but the long. is about 127° 06' W (232° 54' E).

our gentlemen supposed might contain two hundred or two hundred and fifty persons. It was built upon a detached rock, connected to the main land by a platform, and, like those before mentioned, constructed for defence. A great number of its inhabitants, in about thirty canoes, visited our party, and used every endeavour they thought likely to prevail on them to visit their habitations. They offered the skins of the sea-otter and other animals to barter; and beside promises of refreshment, made signs too unequivocal to be misunderstood, that the female part of their society would be very happy in the pleasure of their company. Having no leisure to comply with these repeated solicitations, the civil offers of the Indians were declined;[1] and the party continued their route back, keeping the northern or continental shore on board. On the 16th they entered another opening, about a league to the north of the north point of Smith's inlet.[2] The entrance into this seemed less dangerous than the former; it had, however, on its southern side, many rocky islets and rocks; but they discovered no one below the surface of the water, nor any danger that could not easily be avoided; and, by keeping on the north side of the entrance, which is about half a league across, a fair navigable passage was found about half a mile wide, between the north shore and the rocky islets that lie off its southern side. Along this the continent was traced about a league, in an east direction, where the opening took its course N. 15 E. about 16 miles, and terminated in latitude 51° 42', longitude 232° 22'.[3] About a league and a half south of this station, a small branch extends about four miles to the W.N.W.; and, half a league further south, another stretches about the same distance to the N.E.[4]

In this inlet, which I have distinguished by the name of RIVER'S CHANNEL,[5] the land continued of a more moderate height, further up, than had generally been found to be the case: but where it branched off in the above directions

---

[1] While exploring a small branch on the S shore, Puget had found the Indians less friendly than Vancouver implies: 'we had many new Visitors and many more were perceived coming in. I must own their Numbers at first was not altogether pleasant, as those already near the Boats behaved in a most daring and insolent manner. Mr. Whidbey and me immediately consulted & we were both of Opinion, the Intention of the Natives was not friendly. The Boats were directly put in a State to act on the Defensive, but we were determined not to begin Hostilities without their absolutely attempting to take the Boats; Seeing us prepared and preparing to resist such an attempt, for a Lighted Match was close to the Swivels they thought proper to conduct themselves more quietly, though Still armed with Daggers and other offensive Weapons, we continued pulling out into the Main Branch, they following & dropping off as we came from the Cove.' – 13 August. This encounter probably took place in Takush Harbour.

[2] Rivers Inlet.

[3] The inlet ends in approximately lat. 51° 40' N, long. 127° 15' W (232° 45' E).

[4] This is a surprisingly inaccurate reference to Kilbella Bay and Moses Inlet (which extends 14 miles to the N). But both bay and inlet are shown with reasonable accuracy on both Baker's MS chart and the engraved chart, and both include Hardy Inlet, which branches off to the W from Moses Inlet.

[5] River's Canal in the first edition; now Rivers Inlet. Named after George Pitt, first Baron Rivers.

towards its head, the shores were composed of high steep rocky mountains, and, like Smith's inlet, and many other channels of this kind that we had examined, afforded no soundings in the middle with 80 fathoms of line; though in the bays, found in most of them, anchorage may, in all probability, be procured. Having finally examined these branches, they returned, by a very narrow intricate passage on the northern shore,[1] leading through an immensity of rocky islets and rocks, until they reached POINT ADDENBROOKE,[2] and again arrived on the eastern shore of Fitzhugh's sound; making the land they had passed, in going up this last inlet, on their larboard side, an island about six or seven miles long.[3] The continental shore, abreast of this station, having been so far ascertained, their supply of provisions being exhausted, and being greatly fatigued by the inclement weather, they returned on board without proceeding agreeably to my original design to the northern extremity allotted to their examination. The further labour, however, of this party, I deemed unnecessary, having become perfectly satisfied as to the intermediate space. Every thing was therefore directed to be taken from the shore, that we might sail in the morning towards the rendezvous I had appointed with Mr. Johnstone.

Since my return from the last boat expedition, I had fortunately obtained, during the few short intervals of fair weather that had occurred, some tolerably good observations for the latitude and longitude of this station. The former, by three meridional altitudes of the sun, appeared to be 51° 32', the latter, 232° 3' 15":[4] the variation of the compass, 17° 7' eastwardly. This cove is at its entrance, the points of which lie from each other N. 30 W. and S. 30 E., about a quarter of a mile wide; and from thence, to its head, in a direction S. 68 W., about a mile. A small rock and two rocky islets lie off its north point of entrance. It undoubtedly bore some resemblance at first to Mr. Duncan's port Safety; but on reference to particulars, differed very materially. Mr. Duncan places port Safety in latitude 51° 41'; and in his sketch takes no notice of the above-mentioned islets and rocks. By him port Safety is recommended as a very proper place for cleaning and refitting vessels; and he says, that the opposite shore is not more than six or seven miles distant. We however found the opposite shore within a league of us; and at the entrance of the cove, instead of 100 fathoms, as stated by Mr. Duncan, we had only 30 fathoms water; decreasing gradually to its head, the whole a soft muddy bottom, and consequently very improper for the operations of cleaning or repairing vessels. Notwithstanding this manifest disagreement, there were those amongst us, who having heard Mr. Duncan's discourse on this subject, insisted upon the certainty of its being his port Safety. In this opinion however, I could not concur, for the obvious reasons above stated,

[1] Darby Channel.
[2] Now spelled Addenbroke Point. The origin of the name is not known.
[3] Ripon and Walbran islands, which would appear to be one island.
[4] The lat. is correct; the long. is 127° 55' W (232° 05' E).

and was more inclined to suppose, that the opening I had seen when in the boats on this shore, to the south of that which led to sea,[1] was Mr. Duncan's port Safety, as that corresponded nearer in point of latitude, and had more the appearance of a *port* than this small cove: it however is the first place that affords safe and convenient anchorage on the western shore, within the south entrance into Fitzhugh's sound, and proved a comfortable retreat to us from the dangerous situations to which we had so recently been exposed. Hence I have distinguished it by the name of SAFETY COVE; and have only further to add, that the rise and fall of the tide was about ten feet, and that it is high water at the time the moon passes the meridian. The same circumstances respecting the tides were observed by those employed in the boat excursions from this station.

In the morning of Sunday the 19th, we sailed out of Safety cove, having for the first time since the commencement of the present month, a pleasant breeze from the S.E. with serene and cheerful weather. About eleven o'clock we had the gratification of being joined by our other boat party; and from Mr. Johnstone I learned, that about four miles to the N.E. of the spot where I had quitted them, they pursued a narrow branch of the inlet winding to the south and south-westward, to the latitude of 51° 57′, due south of the place of our separation.[2] The inclemency of the weather detained them in this situation until the 16th, when they pursued the main branch of the inlet, which is from one to two miles broad, in a north-easterly direction, to a point which I called by the name of POINT MENZIES, after Mr. Menzies who had accompanied me, and afterwards Mr. Johnstone, in this excursion; here the inlet divides into three branches, each nearly as wide as that they had navigated. The first led to the N.W. the second to the northward, and the other to the south.[3] Several leagues to the S.W. of point Menzies, the water had assumed a pale white colour, and was not very salt, which had encouraged them to push forward in constant expectation of finding its termination; but on reaching the above station, all hopes intirely vanished of carrying their researches further into execution, having extended their excursion beyond the time I had prescribed, and the period for which they had been supplied with provisions. These on the morning of the 17th, being nearly expended, Mr. Johnstone considered it most prudent to decline any further investigation, and to return to the ships. These they reached two days afterwards, almost exhausted with hunger and fatigue.

The country they had visited differed in no one respect from the general appearance we had long been accustomed to, nor did any thing occur to vary

[1] Kwakshua Channel.
[2] Kwatna Inlet. Misprinted 50° 57′ in the second ed.; the correct position is about 52° 02′ N.
[3] The three branches were Labouchere Channel, which branches off to the N about four miles and a half W of Menzies Point; and North Bentinck Arm and South Bentinck Arm, leading to the NE and SE respectively, into which Burke Channel divides beyond Menzies Point.

the continual sameness, or chequer the dreary melancholy scene before them, if we except their finding near the conclusion of their examination, a canoe about forty feet long, hauled up by the side of a miserable hut, near which was the remains of a fire still burning; indicating the vicinity of some human beings, for whom they left in the canoe some copper, nails, and other trifles, these on their return were found in the same state, without any appearance of the canoe or hut having been visited in their absence; but concluding the natives could not be far removed, they added a few more articles to their former donation. The soil in this place was principally composed of roots, leaves, and other decayed vegetable matter, and the fire that had been kindled, had caught this substance, and made considerable progress on the surface.

Had Mr. Johnstone found a termination to the inlet under his examination, I should have proceeded up the main arm of this sound to the northward along the shore of the continent, in quest of a more northerly passage to sea; but as that had not been effected, I pursued that which I had seen from the boats leading to the westward through Calvert's islands; being now resolved, in consequence of the intelligence I had received from Nootka, to abandon the northern survey of the continental shore for the present season. This I had otherwise intended to have continued at least a month longer; but as the distressing event of Mr. Hergest's death necessarily demanded my presence in the execution of His Majesty's commands at Nootka, I determined to repair thither immediately. This determination favored also another design I much wished to execute, namely, that of extending the examination of the coast this autumn, southward from cape Mendocino, to the southernmost point of our intended investigations in this hemisphere. Having the greatest reason to be satisfied with the result of our summer's employment, as it had by the concurrence of the most fortunate circumstances enabled us finally to trace and determine the western continental shore of North America, with all its various turnings, windings, numerous arms, inlets, creeks, bays, &c. &c. from the latitude of 39° 5′, longitude 236° 36′, to point Menzies, in latitude 52° 18′, longitude 232° 55′;[1] we took our leave of these northern solitary regions, whose broken appearance presented a prospect of abundant employment for the ensuing season, and directed our route through the passage above-mentioned,[2] in order to make the best of our way towards Nootka.

[1] This was very close to the correct position, which is lat. 52° 18′ N, long. 127° 02′ W (232° 58′ E).

[2] Hakai Passage.

CHAPTER X.

Passage from Fitzhugh's Sound to Nootka—Arrival in Friendly Cove—Trans-
actions there, particularly those respecting the Cession of Nootka—Remarks on
the Commerce of North-west America—Astronomical Observations.

HAVING on Sunday the 19th directed our course towards a passage, which appeared to lead to the ocean as stated in the last chapter, its N.E. point of entrance was found to be situated in latitude 51° 45′, longitude 232° 1′;[1] south of this point lies a sunken rock, which though near the shore is dangerous, being visible at low tide only by the surf that breaks upon it. In turning into the channel we must have passed twice very near it, but did not discover it until we were some distance beyond it; and had not light baffling winds retarded out progress, it would have escaped our notice. From the point above-mentioned the passage extends S. 60 W. about seven miles; its northern shore is composed of rocky islets and rocks, with some scattered rocks lying off its southern shore: between these and the rocky islets is the passage, generally from one to two miles wide, without any apparent obstruction, yet it is rendered unpleasant by the want of soundings, as within 50 and 100 yards of the shore, on either side, no bottom could be obtained, with 150 fathoms of line. In this very disagreeable situation we were detained by faint unsteady winds until eleven at night, when, by the assistance of a light breeze from the S.E. we reached the ocean, and stood to the south-westward.

The next morning, Monday the 20th, was very unpleasant; fresh squalls from the S.E. attended with thick rainy weather, continued until noon the following day, Tuesday the 21st, when it cleared up, and we saw Scot's islands, bearing S. 22 E. about seven leagues distant.[2] The wind during the day was light and variable, though attended with fair weather; in the evening it seemed fixed at S.S.W. when, not being able to pass to windward of Scot's islands, our course was directed to the north of them, towards cape Scot,[3] having soundings and a soft muddy bottom at the depth of eighty and ninety fathoms, until about nine in the evening, when the water suddenly shoaled from sixty to seventeen fathoms, and the bottom became rocky. On this we instantly

---

[1] Bayly Point. This is again very close to the correct position.
[2] Scot's Islands on Baker's MS chart but Scott's Islands on the engraved chart. Now Scott Islands.
[3] Cape Scott, the present name, on the engraved chart.

stood back to the westward, lest we should approach some danger, but we did not perceive either breakers or shoals, although the night was still and clear. These soundings were from the westernmost of Scot's islands N. 18 E. about five leagues; from this circumstance, and from the distant rocks and shoals we saw extending from the shores of Calvert's islands, it is highly necessary that the space between Calvert's and Scot's islands should be navigated with great caution.

We were detained about Scot's islands by light variable winds until Friday the 24th, when we passed to the south of them, and continued to the eastward along their southern shores.

The westernmost of them is situated in latitude 50° 52′ longitude 231° 2′. The group consists of three small and almost barren islands, with many small rocks and breakers about them.[1] West from the westernmost of them, a ledge of rocks extends about two miles, and south of it is another about a league distant. The easternmost of Scot's islands being much larger than the rest, may probably be the same to which Mr. Hanna gave the name of 'Cox's island:'[2] by others of the traders it has been represented as a part of the main; this is certainly wrong, and as Mr. Hanna's chart is very erroneous, even in point of latitude, no certain conclusion can be drawn.

The wind, which was from the westward, was so light, that it was not until the forenoon of Saturday the 25th, that we passed the N.W. point of the large island, which forms the south and western shores of the gulf of Georgia and Queen Charlotte's sound.[3] This point (called by former visitors 'Cape Scott') is situated in latitude 50° 48′, longitude 231° 40′,[4] and with the easternmost of Scot's islands, forms a passage which appears to be about four miles wide. About cape Scot the land is composed of hills of moderate height, though to the south-eastward it soon becomes very mountainous, and at the distance of three or four leagues appeared to be much broken and to form many inlets, coves, and harbours, all the way to Woody point, which we passed in the afternoon within the distance of about two miles; it is situated in latitude 50° 6′, longitude 232° 17′.[5] West from it lies a small rocky islet about half

---

[1] There are five islands and some smaller islets in the group. Triangle Island, westernmost of them, is in lat. 50° 52′ N, long. 129° 05′ W (230° 55′ E) – very nearly the location given by Vancouver.

[2] Now Cox Island; named by Hanna in 1786. It is not much larger than nearby Lanz Island and it seems probable that Vancouver thought the two were one; Menzies remarked that 'The easternmost & largest seems to be divided into two Islands...' – 24 August. The group was named twice in 1786: Strange bestowed the name Scott Islands, after David Scott, patron of his expedition; Hanna named them the Lance Islands. Galiano spelled the name Lanz and called the eastern islands Islas de Lanz. The name now applies only to the one island.

[3] Vancouver Island, not yet named.

[4] Its position is lat. 50° 47′ N, long. 128° 26′ W (231° 34′ E).

[5] Vancouver had returned to an area he had visited with Cook, who sighted and named Woody Point on 29 March 1778. The name was changed to Cape Cook in 1860. Its position is lat. 50° 08′ N, long. 127° 55′ W (232° 05′ E).

a league distant, and another larger one lying N. 28 W. about a league from the north part of the point,[1] which is an extensive and projecting promontory.

From Woody point as we sailed along the shore to the eastward, we saw several openings in the land, which was about three or four miles from us, that appeared like coves and harbours. Innumerable rocky islets and rocks lined the shores, which as we advanced became low, but the country behind swelled into hills of considerable height divided by many valleys; beyond these it rose to mountains so elevated, that even at this season of the year many patches of snow were yet undissolved.

As I intended to ascertain the outline of the coast from hence down to Nootka; at dark we brought to, about six leagues to the eastward of Woody point, in expectation of accomplishing this design the following day, but in this I was disappointed; the N.W. wind was succeeded by light winds, which continued until the afternoon of Tuesday the 28th, and prevented in the present instance my acquiring such authority as I deemed necessary for delineating this part of the coast.

Foggy weather during the forenoon precluded us the advantage of steering for Nootka with the favorable winds that prevailed from the N.W. but on its clearing away about two we steered for that port. On reaching its entrance we were visited by a Spanish officer, who brought a pilot to conduct the vessel to anchorage in Friendly cove, where we found riding his Catholic Majesty's brig the Active,[2] bearing the broad pendant of Senr Don Juan Francisco de la Bodega y Quadra,[3] commandant of the marine establishment of St. Blas and California.

The Chatham, by the partial clearing of the fog, had found her way in some time before us: the Dædalus store ship, and a small merchant brig called the Three Brothers of London, commanded by Lieutenant Alder of the navy, were also there at anchor.[4]

As Senr Quadra resided on shore, I sent Mr. Puget to acquaint him with our arrival, and to say, that I would salute the Spanish flag, if he would return an equal number of guns. On receiving a very polite answer in the affirmative, we saluted with thirteen guns, which were returned, and on my going on shore accompanied by some of the officers, we had the honor of being received with the greatest cordiality and attention from the commandant, who informed me he would return our visit the next morning.

[1] Solander Island, about a mile and a quarter SW of Cape Cook; Hackett Island is to the NE.

[2] The *Activa*, a new brigantine of 213·5 tons, built at San Blas in 1791.

[3] Now usually referred to (correctly) as Bodega, but for many years referred to in most English language publications as Quadra. As Vancouver used the latter name in his numerous references, it has been adopted in the introduction and notes of this work. This usuage cannot have been entirely unacceptable to the Spaniards, as the name appears in this form in place names on several of the contemporary Spanish charts.

[4] Lieut. William Alder. The *Three Brothers* (also referred to as the *3Bs*) was the consort of the schooner *Prince William Henry*, commanded by Captain Ewen.

Agreeably to his engagement, Senr Quadra with several of his officers came on board the Discovery, on Wednesday the 29th, where they breakfasted, and were saluted with thirteen guns on their arrival and departure: the day was afterwards spent in ceremonious offices of civility, with much harmony and festivity. As many officers as could be spared from the vessels with myself dined with Senr Quadra, and were gratified with a repast we had lately been little accustomed to, or had the most distant idea of meeting with at this place. A dinner of five courses, consisting of a superfluity of the best provisions, was served with great elegance; a royal salute was fired on drinking health to the sovereigns of England and Spain, and a salute of seventeen guns to the success of the service in which the Discovery and Chatham were engaged.

Maquinna,[1] who was present on this occasion, had early in the morning,

[1] The most influential chief of the Moachat group of the Nootka Indians, who occupied a number of the 22 villages said to have existed in Nootka Sound. Maquinna's principal residence and summer village, Yuquot (also spelled Yucuat), had long been established in Friendly Cove, but the Spaniards had taken possession of its site and had built their settlement there. (When they withdrew from Nootka in 1795 the Indians promptly demolished the Spanish buildings and Yuquot was reborn in its traditional location.) Maquinna's winter village, which Vancouver would visit with Quadra, was at the head of Tahsis Inlet. As the maritime fur trade developed, Friendly Cove became the most frequented harbour on the Northwest Coast, and Maquinna's dealings with the Spaniards and his many contacts with traders and explorers enhanced his prestige amongst the native tribes and made him the best known Indian on the coast. He is often said to have been the leading chief that Cook met in 1778, but this is very doubtful. Robin Fisher comments: 'Probably the most tantalizing gap in the entire documentary record surviving from Cook's visit to Nootka Sound is his failure to name this Indian leader. Many have subsequently assumed that the man was Maquinna.... Perhaps the assumption is correct, although it must be said that there is no evidence to support it.' – Robin Fisher and Hugh Johnston (eds.) *Captain James Cook and His Times* (Vancouver, 1979), pp. 89–90. Certainly the evidence is scanty and inconclusive. Martínez claimed in 1789 that Maquinna remembered his visit to Nootka in 1774, when the *Santiago* paused briefly at the entrance to the sound (ibid., p. 111), and E. O. S. Scholefield states that according to 'the legendary lore of the Indians' Tsaxawasip ('one of Chief Maquinna's names') sighted Cook's ships as they were approaching and had dealings with him. – *British Columbia* (Vancouver, 1914), I, 81. But the name Maquinna was borne by a succession of chiefs, and José Mariano Moziño, who spent five months at Nootka in the spring and summer of 1792, believed that Maquinna's father, presumably chief at the time of Cook's visit, had 'died after the year 1778 in a war'. – *Noticias de Nutka*, Wilson translation (Seattle, 1970), p. 31. Meares, who met Maquinna in 1788, describes him as being 'about thirty years [of age], of a middle size, but extremely well made, and possessing a countenance that was formed to interest all who saw him.' – *Voyages* (London, 1790), p. 113. Most opinions of him were favourable, but he evidently displeased Colnett, who described him early in 1791 as 'a most miserable, cowardly wretch', – *Journal* (Toronto, 1940), p. 208. Maquinna detested Martínez, who had appropriated the site of Yuquot village, and whom he held responsible for the death of his brother, Callacum, but a warm friendship had developed with Quadra. After the unfortunate initial rebuff, Maquinna and Vancouver were on good terms. Charles Bishop's log of the *Ruby* records that in September 1795, when he arrived in Friendly Cove, Maquinna 'came on board to Welcome the Ship, altho' extremely ill of an ague' and early in October, when the *Ruby* was in Clayoquot Sound, Chief Wickananish sent him a message that 'His Friend Maquinna had died'. – Michael Roe (ed.), *The Journal and Letters of Captain Charles Bishop...1794–1799* (Cambridge, The Hakluyt Society, 1967), pp. 94,

from being unknown to us, been prevented coming on board the Discovery by the centinels and the officer on deck, as there was not in his appearance the smallest indication of his superior rank. Of this indignity he had complained in a most angry manner to Senr Quadra, who very obligingly found means to sooth him; and after receiving some presents of blue cloth, copper, &c. at breakfast time he appeared to be satisfied of our friendly intentions: but no sooner had he drank a few glasses of wine, than he renewed the subject, regretted the Spaniards were about to quit the place, and asserted that we should presently give it up to some other nation; by which means himself and his people would be constantly disturbed and harassed by new masters. Senr Quadra took much pains to explain that it was our ignorance of his person which had occasioned the mistake, and that himself and subjects would be as kindly treated by the English as they had been by the Spaniards. He seemed at length convinced by Senr Quadra's arguments, and became reconciled by his assurances that his fears were groundless. On this occasion I could not help observing with a mixture of surprize and pleasure, how much the Spaniards had succeeded in gaining the good opinion and confidence of these people; together with the very orderly behaviour, so conspicuously evident in their conduct towards the Spaniards on all occasions.

The tents, observatory, chronometers, instruments, &c. were sent on shore the following day,[1] Thursday the 30th, and all hands were busily employed on the several necessary duties of the ship, such as caulking,[2] overhauling the rigging and sails, cleaning the hold and bread-room for the reception of stores

107. But this report was evidently untrue. When Jewitt was a captive at Nootka Sound in 1803, the Chief Maquinna who held him prisoner recalled incidents dating back to the first days of the maritime fur trade; the details are inaccurate, but this may be due to lapses in Jewitt's memory rather than in Maquinna's. – See Derik G. Smith (ed.), *The Adventures and Sufferings of John R. Jewitt* (Carleton Library ed., Toronto, 1974), pp. 79–80. Much more convincing is the narrative of Camille de Roquefeuil, who visited Nootka in 1817 and again in 1818, and had numerous conversations with Maquinna. He refers to 'the very animated discourse of the old chief' and remarks that 'he got on deck with great activity for his age'. He confirms Moziño's belief that 'the dignity of Tahi' [Chief] 'devolved upon Macouina, in the year 1778, when his father was killed by the Tahumasses, a nation inhabiting the other side of the island'. He records that Maquinna 'expressed great regret' at the departure of the Spaniards and 'spoke in high terms of the commanders, Quadra, Alava, and Fidalgo, and gave all the Spaniards in general, except Martinez, praises.... Macouina spoke also in praise of Vancouver, Broughton, and the English captains who frequented Nootka at the same time. He mentioned, among others, Meares...' – *A Voyage Round the World, 1816–1819, in the ship "Bordelais"* (London, 1823), pp. 28, 97, 103. Maquinna would have been chief for 40 years at the time of Roquefeuil's second visit.

[1] 'the new observatory, with the Circular Instrument, Astronomical Clock, three Time keepers [chronometers] & the other Astronomical Instruments that were sent out by the Board of Longitude with the unfortunate Astronomer Mr. Gooch were also sent on shore here.' – Bell, August. Two of the chronometers were by Arnold; the third was a pocket watch by Earnshaw.

[2] Here and elsewhere Vancouver employed local labour: 'with the assistance of the Spanish Caulkers & some from the Merchants Ships in the Cove they began to give the Discovery a thorough Caulking.' – Menzies, 29 August.

and provisions. The boats, in consequence of the services they had performed during the summer, were in want of much repair, and were hauled on shore for that purpose.

From the unfortunate death of Lieutenant Richard Hergest, late agent to the Dædalus, I considered it expedient that an officer should be appointed to that store-ship, and I therefore nominated Lieutenant James Hanson of the Chatham to that office; Mr. James Johnstone, master of the Chatham, I appointed to the vacant lieutenancy; and Mr. Spelman Swaine, one of my mates, to be master in the Chatham.

In the forenoon I received an official letter from Senr Quadra respecting the restitution of this place, with several copies of a correspondence resulting from the inquiries he had made during his residence here, respecting the English establishments on the coast, at the time the British vessels were captured, and the Spaniards effected an establishment at Nootka.[1] On this occasion I considered myself very fortunate in finding a young gentleman (Mr. Dobson) on board the store-ship, who spoke and translated the Spanish language very accurately, and who politely offered me his services.[2]

The Chatham was hauled on shore the next day to examine her bottom, and to repair the damage she had sustained by getting a-ground. A part of the gripe, a piece of the fore-foot with part of the main, and false keels, were broken off, and some of the copper was torn away in different places.

Senr Galiano and Valdes arrived the following day, Saturday, September the 1st, from the gulf of Georgia; they had pursued a route through Queen Charlotte's sound to the southward of that which we had navigated, and obligingly favored me with a copy of their survey of it.[3]

Mr. Dobson having translated Senr Quadra's letter and the documents accompanying it, it appeared that Senr Quadra had, after his arrival at Nootka in April, 1792, commissioned all the vessels under his command to inspect the coast;[4] in order that the proper limits to be proposed in the restitution of these

[1] Quadra to Vancouver 29 August. The enclosures consisted of a letter from Quadra to Francicso José Viana, nominal commander of the *Iphigenia*, the latter's reply, and a request for information sent by Quadra to Gray and Ingraham and their reply. This and subsequent correspondence are included in Vancouver's 'Narrative of my proceedings...from the 28th August to the 26th of September' (P.R.O., C.O. 5/187, ff. 106–124v), for which see the appendix.

[2] Thomas I. Dobson, midshipman, who joined the *Discovery* on 8 September. He was born at Clapham and was 21 years of age. Bell remarks that he 'fortunately spoke and wrote tolerably good Spanish. I say fortunately, for there was not any other person in the Cove that understood both Spanish and English except a Servant of Mr. Quadra's, and he could only *speak* them.' – September.

[3] The *Sutil* and *Mexicana* had passed through Goletas Channel, which they had named Salida de las Goletas.

[4] Three expeditions were in progress. Fidalgo arrived at Neah Bay (Núñez Gaona) in the *Princesa* on 29 May to establish a base there; Galiano and Valdés sailed from Nootka Sound on 5 June to extend the survey of the inland waterways begun by Quimper in 1790 and by Eliza's expedition in 1791; on 12 June Caamaño left Nootka in the *Aranzaza* with instructions to survey the coast from Bucareli Bay southward.

territories might be ascertained, and that the several commanders might inform themselves of all the matters and circumstances that preceded the capture of the Argonaut and Princess Royal merchantmen in the year 1789.

Senr Quadra stated, that the court of Spain had expended large sums in sustaining the department of St. Blas, with the sole view of its being an auxiliary to other establishments which were then in contemplation of being formed. That Nootka was seen in the year 1774, and in 1775 possession was taken 2° to the south, and 6° to the north of it; and as in this space Don Estevan Joseph Martinez found no kind of establishment whatever, that therefore no one should take it ill that he (Martinez) should dispute his prior right to the port. Under the orders of the viceroy of New Spain, Martinez entered Nootka, and took possession the 5th of May, 1789, with visible demonstrations of joy in the Indians; and afterwards fortified the place, without any objection being made on the part of a Portuguese commander of a trading brig called the Ephigenia, then in the cove. [1] On the arrival of the Columbia and Washington American vessels, he examined their papers and passports, as he had before done those of the Portuguese; and disapproving some expressions contained in those of the Columbia, she was detained until an explanation took place, when she was released. [2] The English schooner North West America, and sloop Princess Royal arrived soon afterwards, and were permitted to depart, after receiving the most friendly attention. [3] Captain Colnett, commanding the English vessel Argonaut, fearing to enter, the Spaniards visited him, and his fears vanished; but as Captain Colnett did not confine his views to the commerce of the country, but wished to fortify himself, and to establish an English factory, Martinez arrested him and sent him to St. Blas. The like conduct was observed towards Thomas Hudson, who commanded the Princess Royal, on his return to Nootka. The vessels of both were detained.

This was the real situation of things, says Senr Quadra, who offers to demonstrate in the most unequivocal manner that the injuries, prejudices, and usurpations, as represented by Captain Meares, were chimerical: that Martinez

---

[1] The *Iphigenia Nubiana* (seldom referred to by her full name), a British snow of 200 tons, was owned by the Associated Merchants trading to the North West Coast of America, in which Meares and his associates had joined forces with Messrs. Etches and their associates. Although British owned, she was trading under the Portuguese flag and had a Portuguese captain nominally in command; the owners were represented by Capt. William Douglas, who had commanded the ship on her first visit to the Northwest Coast in 1788. The Associated Merchants had four ships on the coast in 1789, the *Iphigenia, North West America, Princess Royal* and *Argonaut*, the latter commanded by James Colnett. The *Iphigenia* was detained by Martinez but was later released; the other three ships were all seized. For a detailed narrative describing the events at Nootka Sound in the summer of 1789 see Warren Cook, *Flood Tide of Empire*, chap. 5.

[2] Vancouver here paraphrases Quadra's letter inaccurately; it was the papers of the *Iphigenia* that were found unsatisfactory. Viana and Douglas were arrested on 13 May, but they were released and the *Iphigenia* sailed on 31 May.

[3] The *Princess Royal* was released but the *North West America* was confiscated and on 20 June was christened *Santa Gertrudis la Magna*.

had no orders to make prize of any vessels, nor did he break the treaty of peace, or violate the laws of hospitality: that the natives will affirm, and that the documents accompanying his letter will prove, that Mr. Meares had no other habitation on the shores of Nootka than a small hut, which he abandoned when he left the place, and which did not exist on the arrival of Martinez: that he bought no land of the chiefs of the adjacent villages; that the Ephigenia did not belong to the English; that Martinez did not take or detain the least part of her cargo; and that Mr. Colnett was treated with the greatest distinction of St. Blas, and his officers and crew received the wages of the Spanish navy for the time of their detention: that the vessel and cargo were restored, and that Mr. Colnett obtained a great number of skins on his return to Nootka.

These circumstances duly considered, adds Senr Quadra, it is evident that Spain has nothing to deliver up, nor damage to make good; but that as he was desirous of removing every obstacle to the establishment of a solid and permanent peace he was ready, *without prejudice to the legitimate right of Spain*, to cede to England the houses, offices, and gardens, that had with so much labour been erected and cultivated, and that himself would retire to Fuca:★ observing at the same time, that Nootka[1] ought to be the last or most northwardly Spanish settlement, that there the dividing point should be fixed, and that from thence to the northward should be free for entrance, use and commerce to both parties, conformably with the fifth article of the convention; that establishments should not be formed without permission of the respective courts, and that the English should not pass to the south of Fuca.

After enumerating these particulars, Senr Quadra concludes his letter by expressing, That if I should find any difficulty in reconciling what he had proposed, or if I should have any other honourable medium to offer that might be the means of terminating this negociation, and secure the desired peace, he begged I would communicate it to him.

The documents accompanying this letter were copies of a correspondence between Senr Quadra and Don Francisco Joseph De Viana, the commander of the Ephigenia; Mr. Robert Gray and Mr. Joseph Ingraham, commanders of the Columbia and Washington; from all of whom Senr Quadra appears to have solicited every information respecting the transactions at Nootka, previously to his arrival, and the reason which induced Mr. Meares to represent things to the prejudice of Don Estevan Joseph Martinez.[2] The Portuguese

★ Meaning an establishment they had in the entrance of De Fuca's straits [at Neah Bay].

[1] The post at Neah Bay, not Nootka, was suggested as the 'dividing point'; Vancouver misunderstood the antecedents of the phrase 'the above mentioned place' in Dobson's translation of Quadra's letter.

[2] A surprising number of those who had first-hand knowledge of the events at Nootka in 1789 were again in the vicinity in 1792. Quadra had arrived expecting to hand over the Sound to the English, but after questioning a number of these witnesses he became convinced that Meares's charges and claims were for the most part false and in no way justified a Spanish withdrawal. Manby believed that Captain Gray of the *Columbia* was

captain briefly sets forth, that his vessel was seized, and that he was made prisoner by Don Martinez; during his captivity he was very well treated, and on his being liberated, his vessel and cargo were completely restored, and he was furnished with whatever provisions and supplies he required. He also states, that when Don Martinez entered Nootka, there was not the least remains of a house belonging to the English.[1]

Sen[r] Quadra had addressed Mr. Gray and Mr. Ingraham jointly, and consequently they both replied to him in the same way. These gentlemen state, that on the arrival of Don Estevan Joseph Martinez, in Friendly cove, the 5th of May, 1789, he found there the Ephigenia only; the Columbia being at that time six miles up the sound at Mahwinna;[2] the Washington and North West America being then on a cruize. Martinez demanded the papers of each vessel, and their reasons why they were at anchor in Nootka sound, alledging that it belonged to his Catholic Majesty. Captain Viana, of the Portuguese vessel, answered, that he had put in there in distress to wait the arrival of Captain Meares from Macao,[3] who was daily expected with supplies, and that on his receiving them he should depart; that Captain Meares had sailed from Nootka in 1788, under the colours of Portugal, had a Portuguese captain with him on board, and was expected to return with him in the same vessel, which, with the Ephigenia, belonged to a merchant at Macao. The Ephigenia wanting provisions and stores, the same were supplied by Martinez, who seeming satisfied with the answers which he had received from the several commanders, not the least misunderstanding was suspected. On the 10th of May arrived the Carlos Spanish ship, Captain Arro,[4] and on the following day Martinez captured the Ephigenia, and his reason assigned for so doing, *as these gentlemen understood*, was, that in the Portuguese instructions, they (the Portuguese) were ordered to capture any English, Spanish, or Russian vessel they might meet

in great part responsible for this change of opinion: 'The arrival of an American Brig stopped the intended plan [to turn Nootka over to the British], the Master of her having sufficient influence with the Spaniards, persuaded them that the treaty between the two nations only gave the English the spot of which they were dispossessed of, by Senr. Martinez. This Brig was in the sound when Martinez seized the Vessels and Factory, belonging to Mr. Mears, in the publication of the latter Gentleman, we are informed, these very Americans assisted in forging the Irons to secure the Prisoners. Don Quadra on this information. sent an official letter to Captain Vancouver, acquainting him, that altho' he quitted Nootka Sound, he should not withdraw the claim, his Catholic Majesty had to the Territory, but at the same time willingly relinquished all Title to the spot, where the English Factory had been Erected.' – Manby, letters, 30 August.

[1] In his reply to Quadra, Viana stated that the house 'was very small and made from a few boards got from the Indians, and when we sailed it was pulled to pieces...' His signature is here spelled Vianna; Menzies' version is Vicana.

[2] Marvinas Bay, on the W side of Cook Channel, which runs to the N from Friendly Cove. Kendrick and Gray used it extensively and it is sometimes referred to as Kendrick's Cove.

[3] Meares did not visit the Northwest Coast himself in 1789. Colnett was in charge of trading by the Associated Merchants that year.

[4] The *San Carlos*, of 196 tons, commanded by López de Haro.

on the N.W. coast of America, and could take. This was afterwards said to have been a mistake, originating in a want of due knowledge in reading the Portuguese language. The vessel and cargo were liberated, and Martinez supplied the Ephigenia's wants from the Princessa,[1] enabling her, by so doing, to prosecute her voyage, without waiting for the return of Mr. Meares. They then proceeded to state that, on the arrival of the Columbia in the year 1788, there was a house, or rather a hut, made by the Indians, consisting of rough posts covered with boards; this was pulled down the same year, the boards were taken on board the Ephigenia, and the roof was given to Captain Kendrick, so that on the arrival of Martinez in May, 1789, there was no vestige of any house remaining. That Mr. Meares had no house, and as to land, they had never heard, although they had remained nine months amongst the natives, that he had ever purchased any in Nootka sound. From *Maquinna* and other chiefs they had understood, that Mr. Kendrick was the only person to whom they had ever sold any land.[2]

These gentlemen stated, that the North West America arrived the 8th of June, and that on the following day the Spaniards took possession of her; ten days afterwards came the Princess Royal, commanded by Mr. Hudson[3] from Macao, who brought the news of the failure of the merchant at Macao, to whom the Ephigenia and other vessels belonged.[4] That Martinez assigned this as a reason for his capturing the North West America, (although she was seized before the arrival of the Princess Royal) that he had detained her as an indemnification for the bills of exchange, drawn on her owner in favour of his Catholic Majesty. That Captain Hudson, after having been treated with the kindest attention by the commodore and his officers, sailed with the Princess Royal from Nootka, the 2d of July; and that the same evening arrived the Argonaut, Captain Colnett.

Mr. Gray and Mr. Ingraham state also, that they heard Mr. Colnett inform Don Martinez that he had come to hoist the British flag, and to take formal possession of Nootka; and that, in conjunction with Mr. Meares and some other English gentlemen at Macao, he had concluded to erect a fort, and settle a colony. To this the Spanish commodore replied, That he had taken possession already in the name of his Catholic Majesty. Captain Colnett then asked, if he should be prevented from building a house in the port? The commodore replied, That he was at liberty to erect a tent, to wood and to water, after which he would be at liberty to depart when he pleased. Captain Colnett said that was not what he wanted, that his object was to build a block-house, erect a fort, and settle a colony for the crown of Great Britain. To this Don Martinez

[1] The *Princesa*, a frigate of 189 tons, in which Martínez had come from San Blas.

[2] In July 1791 Kendrick purchased Marvinas Bay from Maquinna, with 'all the land, rivers, creeks, harbours, islands, etc., with all the produce of sea and land appertaining thereto.' – F. W. Howay, 'John Kendrick and his Sons', *Oregon Historical Quarterly*, XXIII (1922), p. 288.

[3] Captain Thomas Hudson.

[4] Gray and Ingraham spell his name Cavallo; Warren Cook gives it as João Carvalho.

answered, No; that in his acceding to such a proposal he should violate the orders of his king, relinquish the Spaniards' claim to the coast, and risk the losing of his commission. Beside which the commodore stated, that Mr. Colnett's vessels did not belong to the King of Great Britain, nor was Mr. Colnett invested with powers to transact any such public business. Captain Colnett replied, That he was a king's officer; but Don Martinez observed, That his being on half-pay, and in the merchants' service, rendered his commission as a lieutenant in the British navy of no consequence in the present business. In conversation afterwards on this subject, as we were informed, (say these gentlemen) for we were not present during this transaction, some dispute arose in the Princessa's cabin; on which Don Martinez ordered the Argonaut to be seized. Soon after this the Princess Royal returned, and, as belonging to the same company, the commodore took possession of her also. With respect to their treatment whilst prisoners, these gentlemen say, That although they have not read Mr. Meares's publication, they think it impossible that the officers and crew of the Argonaut can be backward in confessing, that Senr Don Estevan Martinez always treated them kindly, and consistently with the character of gentlemen.* They further state, That the captain, officers and crew of the North West America were carried by them to China, with one hundred sea-otter skins, valued at four thousand eight hundred and seventy-five dollars, which were delivered to Mr. Meares as his property.

To Senr Quadra's letter of the 29th of August, I replied to the following effect:[1] That I did not consider myself authorized to enter into a retrospective discussion on the respective rights and pretensions of the court of Spain or England, touching the western coasts of America, and islands adjacent, to the northward of California. That subject having undergone a full investigation, and having been mutually agreed upon and settled by the ministers of the respective courts, as appeared by the convention of the 28th of October, 1790, and Count Florida Blanca's letter of the 12th of May, 1791, I considered any interference, on my part, to be incompatible with my commission, being invested with powers only to receive the territories which, according to the first article of the convention, Senr Quadra was authorized to restore and to put me in possession of, viz. ('the buildings and districts, or parcels of land which were occupied by the subjects of his Britannic Majesty in April, 1789, as well in the port of Nootka or of St. Lawrence, as in the other, said to be called Port Cox,[2] and to be situated about 16 leagues distant from the former to the southward.') That agreeably to the express words of the fifth article in the said convention, ('It is agreed, That, as well in the places that are to be restored to the British subjects by virtue of the first article, as in all other

* Some circumstances in contradiction to the whole of these evidences, which afterwards came to my knowledge, will appear in a future chapter.

[1] Vancouver to Quadra, 1 September. The reply is considerably longer than this summary suggests.

[2] In Clayoquot Sound. Meares states that he named it in 1788 'in honour of our friend John Henry Cox, Esq.' a China merchant.

parts of the northwestern coast of North America, or of the islands adjacent, situated to the north of the parts of the said coast already occupied by Spain, wherever the subjects of either of the two powers shall have made settlements since the month of April, 1789, or shall hereafter make, any of the subjects of the other shall have free access, and shall carry on their trade without any disturbance or molestation.') I considered the Spanish settlement in the entrance of the straits of De Fuca, which I had reason to believe was formed no longer ago than May, 1792, to come within the meaning of a 'port of free access,' as well as all other establishments that have been, or that may hereafter be, formed from thence southward to port St. Francisco, conceiving port St. Francisco to be the northernmost settlement occupied by the subjects of His Catholic Majesty, in April, 1789.

In my way to the observatory, on Sunday, I waited upon Senr Quadra, who informed me, that Mr. Dobson had translated my letter to him; and he was pleased to say, That he derived the greatest satisfaction from finding a person of my character, with whom he was to transact the business of delivering up Nootka; that he should accept the civil offers contained in my letter, and remain on shore until the carpenters had finished some additional accommodation to his apartments on board his little brig; which being completed, he would either wait my departure, to accompany us in our researches to the southward, and to conduct us to any of the Spanish ports I might wish to visit; or he would sail, and wait my arrival at any place I should think proper to appoint, recommending St. Francisco or Monterrey for that purpose.

Senr Quadra requested to know who I intended to leave in possession of these territories; and being informed that it would be Mr. Broughton in the Chatham, in whose charge the remaining cargo of the Dædalus would be deposited, he gave directions that the store-houses should be immediately cleared, and begged I would walk with him round the premises, that I might be the better able to judge how to appropriate the several buildings; which for the most part appeared sufficiently secure, and more extensive than our occasions required. A large new oven had been lately built expressly for our service, and had not hitherto been permitted to be used. The houses had been all repaired, and the gardeners were busily employed in putting the gardens in order. The poultry, consisting of fowls and turkies, was in excellent condition, and in abundance, as were the black cattle and swine: of these Senr Quadra said he should take only a sufficient quantity for his passage to the southward, leaving the rest, with a large assortment of garden seeds, for Mr. Broughton. Sen^{rs} Galiano and Valdes added all they had in their power to spare, amongst which were three excellent goats; I had likewise both hogs and goats to leave with him; so that there was a prospect of Mr. Broughton passing the winter, with the assistance of the natural productions of the country, not very uncomfortably.

The orders under which I was to receive these territories, on the part of

His Britannic Majesty, were intirely silent as to the measures I was to adopt for retaining them afterwards. Presuming, however, that the principal object which His Majesty had in view, by directing this expedition to be undertaken, was that of facilitating the commercial advantages of Great Britain in this part of the world; and for that purpose it might not be impossible, that a settlement was in contemplation to be made at this important station, which had become the general rendezvous for the traders of almost all nations; I had determined, on leaving this port, to commit it to the charge and direction of Mr. Broughton, who would retain the possession of it, and whose presence might restrain such improper conduct as had already been manifested on the part of the several traders; whilst I should proceed to execute the remaining part of His Majesty's commands, until I should be furnished with further instructions for my future government.

Having satisfactorily arranged these matters, I gave directions for clearing the store-ship, which was set about accordingly.

The politeness, hospitality, and friendship, shewn on all occasions by Senr Quadra, induced Mr. Broughton and myself, with several of the officers and gentlemen of both vessels, to dine at his table almost every day, which was not less pleasant than salubrious, as it was constantly furnished with a variety of refreshments to most of which we had long been intire strangers.

Senr Galiano informed me, that he intended to take advantage of the present serene weather, which without interruption had prevailed since our arrival, and sail for the Spanish ports to the southward, either in the course of the night, or early the next morning; and obligingly undertook to forward a short letter to the Lords of the Admiralty, containing a brief abstract of transactions since our departure from the Cape of Good Hope.[1]

I had the honor of Senr Quadra's company on the morning of Monday the 3d at breakfast. He omitted no opportunity of impressing on the minds of the natives the highest and most favorable opinion of our little squadron; and the more effectually to insure a good understanding in future, he proposed a visit of ceremony to *Maquinna*; to him it would be grateful, and on my part he recommended it as essentially requisite. It was agreed we should set out the next morning for his royal residence, which was about seven leagues up the sound, at a place called Tahsheis.[2]

In the evening I received from Senr Quadra a letter in reply to mine of the 1st of September.[3]

Agreeably to appointment, about eight in the morning of Tuesday the 4th, Senr Quadra accompanied me in the Discovery's yawl, which, with our own and a Spanish launch, and the Chatham's cutter, containing as many Spanish and English officers as could be taken, we departed for Tahsheis; a message having been sent the preceding day to announce our intended visit.

[1] This letter seems never to have reached London.
[2] Now spelled Tahsis.
[3] Quadra to Vancouver, 2 September.

The weather though cloudy was very pleasant, and having a favourable breeze, we reached Tahsheis about two in the afternoon: *Maquinna* received us with great pleasure and approbation, and it was evident that his pride was not a little indulged by our shewing him this attention. He conducted us through the village, where we appeared to be welcome guests, in consequence perhaps of the presents that were distributed amongst the inhabitants, who all conducted themselves in the most civil and orderly manner. After visiting most of the houses, we arrived at *Maquinna*'s residence, which was one of the largest, though it was not intirely covered in; here we found seated in some kind of form, *Maquinna*'s daughter, who not long before had been publicly and with great ceremony proclaimed sole heiress to all his property, power, and dominion. Near her were seated three of his wives, and a numerous tribe of relations. The young princess was of low stature, very plump, with a round face, and small features; her skin was clean, and being nearly white, her person altogether, though without any pretensions to beauty, could not be considered as disagreeable. To her and to her father I made presents suitable to the occasion, which were received with the greatest approbation by themselves and the throng which had assembled; as were also those I made to his wives, brothers, and other relations. These ceremonies being ended, a most excellent dinner was served, which Senr Quadra had provided,[1] at which we had the company of *Maquinna* and the princess, who was seated at the head of the table, and conducted herself with much propriety and decorum.

After dinner *Maquinna* entertained us with a representation of their warlike achievements. A dozen men first appeared, armed with muskets, and equipped with all their appendages, who took their post in a very orderly manner within the entrance of the house, where they remained stationary, and were followed by eighteen very stout men, each bearing a spear or lance sixteen or eighteen feet in length, proportionably strong, and pointed with a long flat piece of iron, which seemed to be sharp on both edges, and was highly polished; the whole however appeared to form but an aukward and unwieldy weapon. These men made several movements in imitation of attack and defence, singing at the same time several war songs, in which they were joined by those with the muskets. Their different evolutions being concluded, I was presented with two small sea-otter skins, and the warriors having laid by their arms, performed a mask dance, which was ridiculously laughable, particularly on the part of *Maquinna*, who took a considerable share in the representation.

---

[1] Menzies records that Quadra 'had brought along with him on this occasion not only his Steward Cooks & culinary Utensils but even his *Plate*, so that our dinner was served up in a manner that made us forget we were in such a remote corner, under the humble roof of a Nootka Chief. Maquinna his Wives & Daughter, together with other Chiefs sat at the head of the Table, partook of the Entertainment & joind us in drinking a convivial glass of wine after dinner, while the rest of the Natives entertaind themselves at a Mess not less gratefull to their palate. It consisted of a large *Tunny* & a Porpus cut up in small pieces entrails & all into a large Trough with a Mixture of Water blood & fish Oil, & the whole stewed by throwing heated Stones into it.' – Menzies, 4 September.

We were not backward in contributing to the amusements of the day, some songs were sung which the natives seemed much to admire, and being provided with drums and fifes, our sailors concluded the afternoon's diversion with reels and country dances.

In the evening we took leave of *Maquinna*, who was scarcely able to express the satisfaction he had experienced in the honour we had done him, saying, that neither *Wacananish*, nor any other chief, had ever received such a mark of respect and attention from any visitors, and that he would in a few days return us the compliment; on which he was given to understand, he should be entertained in the European fashion.

From Tahsheis we proceeded a few miles in our way home, when, arriving at a convenient little cove, we pitched our encampment for the night, and passed a very pleasant evening.

After breakfast the following morning, Wednesday the 5th, we embarked and directed our route towards Friendly cove; the weather was pleasant though the wind was unfavorable; this occasioned our dining by the way on the rocks, for which however Senr Quadra was amply provided. About five we reached the cove, where I landed Senr Quadra and returned to the ship.

In our conversation whilst on this little excursion, Senr Quadra had very earnestly requested that I would name some port or island after us both, to commemorate our meeting and the very friendly intercourse that had taken place and subsisted between us. Conceiving no spot so proper for this denomination as the place where we had first met, which was nearly in the centre of a tract of land that had first been circumnavigated by us, forming the south-western sides of the gulph of Georgia, and the southern sides of Johnstone's straits and Queen Charlotte's sound, I named that country the island of QUADRA and VANCOUVER;[1] with which compliment he seemed highly pleased.

During my absence the Chatham had hauled off from the shore, but in consequence of the inconsiderable rise of the tide her damages had not been repaired; it was therefore necessary that she should remain light until the next spring tides; this however, under our present arrangements, was a matter of little importance.

Thursday 6th, *Maquinna* with his two wives and some of his relations returned our visit. They had not been long on board when I had great reason to consider my royal party as the most consummate beggars I had ever seen; a disposition which seemed generally to prevail with the whole of this tribe of Indians, and which probably may have been fostered by the indulgences

---

[1] Now Vancouver Island. Quadra's name appeared on some early Admiralty charts and (as Isla de Quadra y Vancouver) on a few Spanish maps, but at least as early as 1825 Hudson's Bay Company officials had shortened the name to Vancouver's Island. By mid-century the apostrophe had disappeared; on Arrowsmith's well-known 1857 *Map of North America* the name is Vancouver Island.

shewn them by the Spaniards.[1] They demanded every thing which struck their fancy, as being either useful, curious, or ornamental, though an article with which it might be impossible for us to gratify them; and if not immediately presented they would affect to be greatly offended, and would remain sulky for two or three days.

I was however particularly fortunate in having at hand every thing requisite to satisfy the demands of *Maquinna* and his party. The liberality I had so recently shewn to himself and family when at Tahsheis, was perhaps not yet quite forgotton; they nevertheless made a profitable visit, as what their modesty precluded their asking of me, I was afterwards informed was amply made up by their begging from the officers and others on board.

The exhibition of fire-works which I had promised the party, was anxiously waited for; towards the evening their impatience was almost unrestrainable, as they could not, or would not, understand that darkness was necessary to their entertainment, and accused us of a breach of promise and telling falsities. Sen[r] Quadra however, after much persuasion, prevailed upon them to stay the night, by which they were convinced that our assurances were not to be discredited. The night being favorable to our operations, they succeeded extremely well. The rockets, balloons, and other fire-works, were in a high state of preservation, and were regarded by the Indian spectators with wonder and admiration, mixed with a considerable share of apprehension;[2] for it was not without great difficulty that I prevailed on *Maquinna* and his brother to fire a few sky rockets, a performance that produced the greatest exultation. The Europeans present were not less entertained with the exhibition, than surprized that the several fire works should have remained so long on board in such excellent condition.

Saturday 8th, the Aransasu,[3] a Spanish armed ship, commanded by Sen[r] Caamano, arrived from a surveying expedition on the exterior coast to the north of Nootka, towards Biccareli,[4] of the charts of which I was promised a copy, as soon as they should be properly arranged.

Mr. Cranstoun, the surgeon of the Discovery, having been rendered incapable of his duty by a general debilitated state of health since our departure from the cape of Good Hope, requested permission to proceed to port Jackson in the Dædalus, from whence he might soon procure a passage to England; he was consequently discharged, and Mr. Archibald Menzies, a surgeon in the navy, who had embarked in pursuit of botanical information, having

---

[1] 'here we may say Mr. Quadra was *too good* a man, he ever treated the Indians more like Companions than people that should be taught subjection, – his house was open to them all, and a considerable number of them were fed there every day.' – Bell, September.

[2] 'this astonished the Natives, though in a much less degree than I expected, for such is their frigid inanimate disposition, that nothing will alter the Muscles of their Countenances, and the greater part of those present at this sight shewed as much unconcern and were as little moved by it, as if nothing of the kind was going on.' – Bell, September.

[3] The *Aranzazu*, a frigate of 205 tons.

[4] Bucareli Bay, in Alaska (lat. 55° 13·5′ N).

cheerfully rendered his services during Mr. Cranstoun's indisposition, and finding that such attention had not interfered with the other objects of his pursuit, I considered him the most proper person to be appointed in the room of Mr. Cranstoun.[1] The boatswain of the Discovery, Mr. William House, a careful, sober, and attentive officer, having laboured under a violent rheumatic complaint, since our departure from New Zealand, which had precluded his attention to any part of his duty, was on his application in like manner discharged; Mr. John Noot, boatswain of the Chatham, was appointed in his room, and Mr. George Philliskirk was appointed boatswain of the Chatham.[2]

Monday the 10th, I deemed it expedient, that their Lordships directions, prohibiting charts, journals, drawings, or any other sort of intelligence respecting our proceedings being made known or communicated, should be publicly read to the officers and persons under my command, and to urge every injunction in my power to enforce a due obedience to those orders.[3]

The letter I received the 2d of this month from Senr Quadra, not having been translated till this day, in consequence of Mr. Dobson's indisposition, I was not a little surprized to find it differ so much from what I had reason to expect.

In this letter Senr Quadra informs me, that in conformity to the first article of the convention, and the royal order under which he is to act, he can only restore to His Britannic Majesty the edifices, districts, or portions of land which in April, 1789, were taken from his subjects; that he was in possession of full proof that the small hut the English had was not in existence on the arrival of Martinez, and that the then establishment of the Spaniards was not in the place where the British subjects had theirs. That if I did not think myself authorized to subscribe to the tenor of his commission and instructions, he would recommend that each should lay before his respective court all the

[1] Menzies' account of the appointment is interesting: 'as Capt. Vancouver did not conceive himself warrantable to make a new Surgeon to fill up the vacancy on board the Discovery while I was on the spot, he solicited me to take charge of the Surgeon's duty, as the success of our expedition so much depended on the health & welfare of the Ship's Company, which he could more confidently entrust to my care & this he urged with a degree of earnestness that I could not well refuse, especially as he requested at the same time that in case of my not accepting it, to state my having refused it in writing, & as I did not know how far this might operate against my interest at the Navy Office, I with considerable hesitation accepted of the appointment, on Capt. Vancouver's promising me that he would take care it should not interfere with my other pursuits, more than the real exigencies of the service required, & as I had done the Surgeon's duty in the most critical situation [the epidemic of the flux] since we left the Cape of Good Hope, & constantly prescribed for Capt. Vancouver himself since we left England on account of Mr. Cranstoun's ill state of health, I conceived the difference of now attending the duty wholly would be very little especially as there were two assistant Surgeons on board, & the Ship in general healthy.' – 9 September.

[2] Phillips, carpenter of the Discovery, was also sent to Port Jackson in the Daedalus, en route to England, where he was to face charges of insolence, neglect of duty, etc.

[3] This order, brought from London by the Daedalus, had been sent at Vancouver's own request.

circumstances of the pending negociation, and wait for further instructions; in the mean time Senr Quadra offered to *leave me* in possession of what Mr. Meares had occupied, and *at my command* the houses, gardens, and offices then occupied by the Spaniards, whilst he retired until the decision of the two courts should be known.

To this letter I immediately replied,[1] that as, like his former one, it contained a retrospective view of matters which I had no authority to take cognizance of, I should accede to his proposal, and make a just and fair representation of all our proceedings to the court of Great Britain, and wait for further instructions. This letter I concluded by again repeating, that I was still ready to receive from Senr Quadra the territories in question, agreeably to the first article of the convention, and the letter of Count Florida Blanca.

In the course of the night arrived here the brig Hope, belonging to Boston in America, commanded by Mr. Joseph Ingraham,[2] the person who jointly with Mr. Gray had given Senr Quadra a statement of the conduct of Don Martinez, and of the transactions at this port in the year 1789.

About noon the next day, Wednesday the 12th, I received from Senr Quadra a letter dated the 11th of September, in answer to my last, expressive of his confidence that I should make a faithful and true representation of the proceedings that had taken place respecting the points in question; and repeating the offer contained in his former letter, of relinquishing the territories on the terms and conditions therein expressed. To this letter I immediately replied,[3] that I was ready whenever it suited Senr Quadra's convenience, to be put into possession of the territories on the N.W. coast of America, or islands adjacent, agreeably to the first article of the convention, and the letter of the Count Florida Blanca.

Having this day dined with Senr Quadra, on rising from table he requested, as no final determination had yet taken place respecting the restitution of these territories, to have some personal conversation on the subject, in hopes by that means of drawing the business to a more speedy conclusion. Besides ourselves there were present Senr Mozino[4] and Mr. Broughton; so that with the assistance of Mr. Dobson, and these gentlemen who spoke French extremely well, we had a prospect of coming to so perfect an explanation as to render any further epistolary altercation totally unnecessary. Senr Quadra vindicated the conduct of Martinez, and laid considerable stress on the concession of *Maquinna*, who had put them into complete possession of the lands they then occupied; on this circumstance, and on the information he had obtained since

[1] Vancouver to Quadra, 10 September.
[2] A brigantine of 70 tons, owned by Thomas H. Perkins and James Magee. She had traded on the coast in 1791, sailed for China in the autumn, and returned to the Northwest Coast in June 1792. Ingraham's journal gives a full account of these voyages.
[3] Vancouver to Quadra, 12 September.
[4] José Mariano Mozino, naturalist, who wrote an interesting and perceptive account of the events at Nootka in 1792 in his *Noticias de Nutka* (translated and edited by Iris Higbie Wilson; Seattle and Toronto, 1970).

his arrival at Nootka, certain parts of which he had by letter communicated to me, he seemed principally to establish the claims of the Spanish crown. The small spot on which Mr. Meares's house had been built, which did not then appear to be occupied by the Spanairds, Senr Quadra said I was at liberty to take possession of for His Britannic Majesty, whenever I should think proper. This offer being totally foreign to my expectations, and a repetition only of that which had taken place in our correspondence, Senr Quadra was made acquainted, that under such circumstances I did not feel myself justified in entering into any further discussion. The propriety of this determination being admitted, it was mutually agreed that we should each represent our objections and proceedings to our respective courts, and wait their decision on the important questions which had arisen in the negociation. In the mean time Senr Quadra proposed to leave me in possession of these territories, the instant his vessel was fitted for his reception. On his departure the Spanish flag was to be struck, and the British flag hoisted in its place, which Senr Quadra consented to salute, on my agreeing to return an equal number of guns. Thus did matters appear to be perfectly arranged, agreeably to the wishes of all parties, and the business brought to an amicable and pleasant conclusion, when to my great surprize I received on the morning of Thursday the 13th a letter from Senr Quadra,[1] setting forth that he was ready to deliver up to me, conformably to the first article of the convention, the territory which was occupied by British subjects in April, 1789, and to leave the Spanish settlement at Nootka until the decision of the courts of England and Spain were obtained; which was proceeding, he said, as far as his powers extended. This very unexpected letter produced an immediate reply from me,[2] wherein I stated, that the territories of which the subjects of His Britannic Majesty were dispossessed in April, 1789, and which by the first article of the convention were now to be restored, I understood to be this place (meaning Nootka) *in toto*, and port Cox. These I was still ready to receive, but could not entertain an idea of hoisting the British flag on the spot of land pointed out by Senr Quadra, not extending more than an hundred yards in any direction. I concluded by observing, that the offer made in Senr Quadra's two last letters differed materially from that contained in his first letter to me on this subject.

On the morning of Saturday the 15th, a young lad, who for about two days had been missing from Senr Quadra's vessel, was found in a cove not far from the ships, most inhumanly murdered. The calves of his legs were cut out, his head nearly severed from his body, and he had received several barbarous wounds in other parts. Doubts arose whether this horrid act had been perpetrated by the natives, or by a black man of most infamous character, who had deserted from the Spanish vessel about the time the boy was first missed. The prevailing opinion seemed to criminate the former, and on Senr Quadra demanding of *Maquinna* that the murderer should be given up, the

---

[1] Quadra to Vancouver, 11 September.
[2] Vancouver to Quadra, 13 September.

immediate departure of all the inhabitants of the sound from our neighbour-hood became a strong presumptive proof of their delinquency.[1]

Sen[r] Quadra gave an immediate answer to my letter of the 13th,[2] but as he therein did not depart from the terms of his late offer of *leaving me in possession only, not formally restoring* the territory of Nootka to the King of Great Britain; it became necessary on my part to demand a categorical and definitive answer from Sen[r] Quadra, whether he would or would not restore to me for His Britannic Majesty the territories in question, of which the subjects of that realm had been dispossessed in April, 1789.[3] These were Nootka and Clayoquot, or port Cox; the former is the place which was then occupied by the British subjects, from thence their vessels were sent as prizes, and themselves as prisoners to New Spain; this is the place that was forcibly wrested from them, and fortified and occupied by the officers of the Spanish crown; this place therefore, with Clayoquot or port Cox, were comprehended under the first article of the convention, and were by that treaty to be restored without any reservation whatsoever: on these terms, and on these only, could I receive the restitution of them. Sen[r] Quadra having also laid some stress upon Mr. Meares's vessels being under Portuguese colours, I took this opportunity of signifying, that I considered that circumstance equally foreign and unimportant, it having been set forth in Mr. Meares's original petition to the Parliament of Great Britain, and of course must have come under the consideration of the Spanish and English ministers. Unless our negociation could be brought to a conclusion on the terms pointed out in this as well as in my former letters, I begged leave to acquaint Sen[r] Quadra that I must positively decline any further correspondence on this subject.

It was a matter of no small satisfaction, that although on this subject such manifest difference arose in our opinions, it had not the least effect on our personal intercourse with each other, or on the advantages we derived from our mutual good offices; we continued to visit as usual, and this day Sen[rs] Quadra and Caamano, with most of the Spanish officers, honored me with their company at dinner.

On Monday morning the 15th, a Portuguese brig arrived here called the

---

[1] In the privacy of his rough journal, Puget tells a very different story. He believed that the boy (Quadra's servant) had been enticed away from the settlement and into a canoe 'on the promise that he would enjoy one of the girls, two of whom with a Man were in her. The Temptation was not to be guarded against, especially in the unthinking age of fifteen or Sixteen, he unfortunately obeyed the Dictates of Nature, & fell a Sacrifice to Indian Ferocity in the very height of his happiness.' But Puget seems not to have been completely satisfied that the murder had been committed by an Indian, for he goes on to comment upon the ferocity and savage disposition of the Spaniards, especially those from New Spain, and to suggest that the boy's body may have been mutilated to fix the blame on the Indians. – These notes are inserted, under the date 15 May 1794, in B.L., Add. MS 17548, the rough journal for the period January 1794–September 1795. A note in pencil gives the date of the murder as September 1792.

[2] Quadra to Vancouver, September 13.

[3] Vancouver to Quadra, September 15.

Fenis and St. Joseph, commanded by John de Barros Andrede, on board of which was a Mr. Duffin as super-cargo. In the evening I had Sen[r] Quadra's final determination;[1] which resting on the same point where it had originated, I considered any further correspondence totally unnecessary; and, instead, of writing, I requested in conversation the next day to be informed, if he was positively resolved to adhere, in the restitution of this country, to the principles contained in his last letter? and on receiving from him an answer in the affirmative, I acquainted him that I should consider Nootka as *a Spanish port*, and requested *his permission* to carry on our necessary employments on shore, which he very politely gave, with the most friendly assurance of every service and kind office in his power to grant.

On Tuesday the 18th, our negociation being brought by these means to a conclusion, Sen[r] Quadra informed me, that Sen[r] Caamano would be left in charge of the port, until the arrival of the Princessa, commanded by Sen[r] Fidalgo; with whom the government of the port of Nootka would be left, and from whom the English might be certain of receiving every accommodation.

Sen[r] Quadra was now making arrangements on board the Active for his departure, which he intended should take place in the course of a day or two. Agreeably to a former promise I had made him, he requested a copy of my charts for the service of His Catholic Majesty; but as our longitude of the several parts of the coast differed in many instances from that laid down by Captain Cook, I wished to embrace every future opportunity of making further observations whilst we might remain in this port, before a copy should be disposed of; but Sen[r] Quadra wishing to make certain of such information as we had acquired, and conceiving the further corrections we might be enabled to make of little importance, solicited such a copy as I was then able to furnish; which, with a formal reply to his last letter, I transmitted to him on the evening of Tuesday the 20th.[2] In this letter I stated the impossibility of my receiving the cession of the territories in question on the conditions proposed by Sen[r] Quadra, and that in consequence of the existing differences in our opinions on this subject, I should immediately refer the whole of the negociation to the court of London, and wait the determination thereof, for the regulation of my future conduct. The next day, Friday the 21st, Sen[r] Quadra acknowledged the receipt of my last letter, with the charts of this coast, &c.[3] which concluded our correspondence.

As Sen[r] Quadra intended to sail the next day, accompanied by most of the Spanish officers, he did me the honor of partaking of a farewell dinner, and was on this occasion received with the customary marks of ceremony and respect due to his rank, and the situation he here filled. The day passed with the utmost cheerfulness and hilarity: Monterrey was appointed as the rendezvous where next we should meet.

[1] Quadra to Vancouver, September 15.
[2] Vancouver to Quadra, September 20.
[3] Quadra to Vancouver, September 20.

Having understood that Mr. Robert Duffin, the supercargo on board the Portuguese vessel that had arrived on the 17th, had accompanied Mr. Meares in the year 1788,[1] and was with him on his first arrival in Nootka sound, I requested he would furnish me with all the particulars he could recollect of the transactions which took place on that occasion. This he very obligingly did,[2] and at the same time voluntarily made oath to the truth of his assertions. The substance of which was, that towards the close of the year 1787, two vessels were equipped for the fur trade on the N.W. coast of America, by John Henry Cox and Co. merchants at Canton. That the command and conduct of the expedition was given to John Meares, Esq. who was a joint proprietor also; that for the purpose of avoiding certain heavy dues, the vessels sailed under Portuguese colours, and in the name and under the firm of John Cavallo, Esq. a Portuguese merchant at Macao, but who had not any property either in the vessels or their cargoes, which were intirely British property, and were wholly navigated by the subjects of His Britannic Majesty: That Mr. Duffin accompanied Mr. Meares in one of these vessels to Nootka, where they arrived in May, 1788, when Mr. Meares, attended by himself and Mr. Robert Funter,[3] on the 17th or 18th of the same month, went on shore, and bought of the two chiefs, *Maquilla*[4] and *Calicum*, the whole of the land that forms Friendly cove, Nootka sound, in His Britannic Majesty's name, for eight or ten sheets of copper, and some trifling articles: That the natives were perfectly satisfied, and, with the chiefs, did homage to Mr. Meares as their sovereign, according to the custom of their country: That the British flag, and not the Portuguese flag, was displayed on shore, whilst these formalities took place between the parties: That Mr. Meares caused a house to be erected on the spot which was then occupied by the Chatham's tent, as being the most convenient place: That the chiefs and the people offered to quit their residence and to retire to Tahsheis, that consequently the English were not confined to that particular spot, but could have erected houses, had they been so inclined, in any other part of the cove: That Mr. Meares appointed Mr. Robert Funter to reside in the house, which consisted of three bed-chambers, with a mess-room for the officers, and proper apartments for the men; these were elevated about five feet from the ground, the under part serving as warehouses: That, exclusive of this house, there were several out-houses and sheds, built for the convenience of the artificers to work in: That Mr. Meares left the houses in good repair, and enjoined *Maquilla* to take care of them, until he, or some of his associates, should return: That he, Robert Duffin, was not at Nootka when Don Martinez arrived there; that he understood no vestige of the house remained at that time, but that on his return thither in July, 1789, he found

---

[1] Duffin was First Officer of the *Felice*, commander by Meares.

[2] Duffin to Vancouver; sworn to on 26 September 1792. P.R.O., C.O. 187/5, ff. 45–46v; duplicate original in Adm. 1/2628, ff. 640–641v.

[3] Commander of the *North West America*, launched at Nootka on 20 September 1788. Funter was in command from the time she entered service until she was seized by the Spaniards at Nootka on 9 June 1789.

[4] Meares' spelling of Maquinna.

the cove occupied by the subjects of His Catholic Majesty: That he then saw
no remains of Mr. Meares's house; and that on the spot on which it had stood
were the tents and houses of some of the people belonging to the Columbia,
commanded by Mr. John Kendrick, under the flag and protection of the
United States of America: That His Catholic Majesty's ships, Princessa and
San Carlos, were at this time anchored in Friendly cove, with the Columbia
and Washington American traders: That the second day after their arrival they
were captured by Don Martinez, and that the Americans were suffered to carry
on their commerce with the natives unmolested.

Senʳ Quadra, at my request, very obligingly undertook to forward, by the
earliest and safest conveyance, a short narrative of our principal transactions
at this port, for the information of the Lords of the Admiralty.[1]

On Saturday morning the 22d, he sailed from Friendly cove,[2] and having
saluted us with thirteen guns, I returned the compliment with an equal number.

Our attention had been most particularly directed to the re-loading of the
store-ship, and the re-equipment of the Chatham, whose hold had been intirely
cleared for the purpose of repairing the damages she had sustained.[3] The
Discovery being in all respects ready for sea, all hands were employed in the
execution of these services, which were materially retarded by the very bad
condition of the provision casks on board the Dædalus, most of which required
a thorough repair, and to be recruited with pickle. A very material loss was
also sustained in the spirits and wine; large quantities of the slop-clothing were
intirely destroyed, and many others, with some of the sails, were materially
damaged. Circumstanced as we were, these deficiencies and damages were
objects of the most serious concern, and appeared to have been intirely
occasioned by the very improper way in which the cargo had been stowed.[4]

[1] Only one item in the docket entrusted to Quadra seems to have survived: a duplicate
of Duffin's statement, the truth of which was attested to under oath before Vancouver.
It is endorsed: 'In Capt. Vancouver's Letter of 20 Sept 1792', but the covering letter is
missing. P.R.O., Adm. 1/2628, ff. 640–641v.

[2] A note in Menzies' journal illustrates the surprising extent of the traffic in and out
of Friendly Cove at this time. The morning Quadra sailed there were 'ten Vessels riding
at Anchor in this small Cove, besides two small ones building on shore...' – 22 September.
The ten were: the Spanish ships Activa and Aranzazu; Vancouver's three vessels; the
Columbia and her tender, the Adventure, and another American trader, the Margaret; the
British trading ship Jackal and the Portuguese Fenis and St. Joseph.

[3] Bell and Heddington give some details of the repairs required: 'On the 19th
[September] at high water, we hove the Vessel on the Blocks and repair'd that part of the
false keel that was knock'd off, the following day we hove her Broad Side on the beach
to repair some Copper, that was knock'd off her keel farther aft, and on the 21st the repairs
were finish'd, we hove off, and began reloading with all dispatch.' – Bell, September.
Everything possible was taken on shore to lighten the ship: 'Started the Water out of the
Fore Hold. Some of this was Thames Water and was as good as if it had just been
filled.' – Heddington, 1 September. Heddington also notes that the rudder had to be
unhung and taken ashore for repairs.

[4] Vancouver described some of the damage and made a vigorous complaint to the
Admiralty about the improper storage in a letter to the Admiralty written in the Discovery
at sea, 15 October 1792. – P.R.O., Adm. 106/1434.

The circumstances already related, with the correspondence at large between Sen[r] Quadra and myself, though comprehending the substance of the negociation which took place respecting the cession of these territories, may yet require some further explanation; and when the very important commerce of this country shall be properly appreciated, I trust the circumspection with which I acted will not be found liable to censure.

Our transactions here have been related with the greatest fidelity, and precisely in the order in which they occurred. Being unprovided with any instructions but such as were contained in the *convention*, and the very general orders I had received, it appeared totally incompatible with the intention of the British court, with the spirit and words of the said convention, or with those of the letter of Count Florida Blanca, that the identical space only on which Mr. Meares's house and breast-work had been situated in the northern corner of this small cove, and forming nearly an equilateral triangle not extending an hundred yards on any one side, bounded in front by the sea, and on the other two sides by high craggy rocks, which continued some distance down the beach, and, excepting at low tide, completely separated this triangular space from that occupied by the Spaniards' houses and gardens, could possibly be considered as the object of a restitution expressed by the terms '*tracts of land,*' according to the first article of the convention; the '*districts or parcels of land,*' mentioned in the letter of Count Florida Blanca; or the '*tracts of land, or parcels or districts of land,*' pointed out to me, and repeated in their Lordships' instructions communicated to me on that subject.

On due consideration, therefore, I concluded, that the cession proposed by Sen[r] Quadra could never have been that intended: that, at least, the whole port of Nootka, of which His Majesty's subjects had been forcibly dispossessed, and at which themselves, their vessels and cargoes had been captured, must have been the proposed object of restitution.

Under these impressions, I felt that if I had acceded to the proposals of Sen[r] Quadra, I should have betrayed the trust with which I was honored, and should have acted in direct opposition to my duty and allegiance, by receiving, without any authority, a territory for His Britannic Majesty, under the dominion of a foreign state.[1]

These principles uniformly governed the whole of my conduct throughout this negociation, in which I acted to the best of my judgment; should I be so unfortunate, however, as to incur any censure,[2] I must rely on the candour of my country, to do me the justice of attributing whatever improprieties I

---

[1] Menzies summarized the problem well in a few lines. Referring to Quadra and Vancouver he wrote: 'The former declared himself empowered by the Court of Spain to enter into a general discussion on this subject, in order to ascertain our claims on this Coast, & settle the line of demarcation. But the latter having no power to act in this way, nor any other instructions than merely to receive the place when it was given to him, could not enter into discussion.' – September 15.

[2] 'any *just* censure' in the first edition. Vancouver would certainly have objected to the deletion of the word 'just', which he emphasized by printing it in italics.

may appear to have committed, to the true and only cause; to a want of sufficient diplomatic skill, which a life wholly devoted to my profession had denied me the opportunity of acquiring.

After having so uniformly persisted in my determination of strictly adhering to the line of my duty, by an implicit obedience to the instructions I had received, in opposition to the judgment and opinion of Senr Quadra, and the evidences which he had proposed; I could not but consider the unexpected arrival of a gentleman, who had personally attended Mr. Meares on his forming the establishment at Nootka, and who it seems had been present on most occasions when differences had arisen between Senr Martinez and Captain Colnett, as a very fortunate circumstance, since his report and affidavit cleared up every point of which, from other testimonies, I could entertain any doubt, and confirmed me in the opinion, that the conduct I had pursued had not been incompatible with the trust committed to my charge and execution. On comparing his representation with that which had been communicated to me on the same subject by Senr Quadra, a very material difference appeared, which most probably operated to direct Senr Quadra's conduct, in refusing me possession of the country agreeably to the terms of my instructions.

The vessels employed in commercial pursuits this season on the north-west coast of America, have I believe found their adventures to answer their expectations: many were contented with the cargo of furs they had collected in the course of the summer;[1] whilst others who had prolonged their voyage, either passed the winter at the Sandwich islands, or on the coast, where they completed small vessels which they brought out in frame. An English and an American shallop were at this time on the stocks in the cove, and when finished were to be employed in the inland navigation, in collecting the skins of the sea-otter and other furs;[2] beside these, a French ship[3] was then engaged in the same pursuit, and the following vessels in the service of His Catholic Majesty: the Gertrudes and Conception of thirty-six guns each, the Active brig of twelve guns, Princessa, Aransasu, and St. Carlos, armed ships, with the

---

[1] Warren Cook believes that there were 22 trading vessels on the Northwest Coast in 1792; Menzies listed 21 in his journal and Vancouver named 18 in the narrative he sent to the Admiralty. Bell noted that it was difficult to ascertain how many furs were traded as reports seldom agreed, 'often varying hundreds of Skins, however I believe I may be somewhat tolerably near the truth in the quantities I have mention'd throughout...' He estimated that the *Hope* had collected 450 skins, the *Jackal* 700, the *Margaret* 1100 or 1200, and the *Columbia* and *Adventure* between them 1700 or 1800. Bell, September.

[2] One was a tender for the the British brig *Three Brothers*; the other was for the American ship *Margaret*: 'as she was to come on the Coast the following Season, she landed here on the beach the frame of a small Schooner, with one of her Mates, and a party of Seamen & Artificers who were to be her crew, these people were to remain here the Winter and build this little Vessel, so as to be ready to Start on the Coast the first of the ensuing Season...' – Bell, September. Both tenders were trading in 1793, but their names do not seem to have been recorded.

[3] *La Flavie*, of about 600 tons, by far the largest merchantman on the coast in 1792.

vessels of Sen^{rs} Galiano and Valdes.[1] Both these gentlemen had been, and were still employed, not only in geographical researches, but in acquiring every possible information respecting the commerce of the country; this circumstance, together with the guarded conduct observed by Senr Quadra, in his endeavours to retain the whole, or at any event to preserve a right in Nootka, evidently manifested the degree of jealousy with which the court of Spain regards the commercial intercourse that is likely to be established on this side of the world.

Considering it an indispensable duty, that the Lords of the Admiralty should, from under my own hand, become acquainted with the whole of my negociation at this port by the safest and most expeditious conveyance, a passage was procured for my first lieutenant Mr. Mudge on board the Fenis and St. Joseph, bound to China, from whence he was to proceed with all dispatch to England. To this gentleman I intrusted extracts from the most important parts of my journal, with a copy of our survey of this coast;[2] and I had every reason to indulge the hopes of his speedy return, with further instructions for the government of my conduct in these regions.

On this occasion, I appointed Lieutenant Puget and Baker to be first and second lieutenants, as also Mr. Spelman Swaine to be third lieutenant of the Discovery; and Mr. Thomas Manby to be master of the Chatham.

Senr Quadra having used no rigorous measures to detect and bring to justice the murderer of the young Spaniard, the alarm of the natives soon subsided, and in a day or two they visited us as usual. *Maquinna* and the other chiefs were not, however, so cordially received at the Spanish habitations as they had been in Senr Quadra's time;[3] at which they expressed much dislike to all the Spaniards, excepting Senr Quadra, and particularly to Martinez; who, *Maquinna* asserted, went on shore with a number of armed people, and obliged him by threats to make cession of Nootka to the king of Spain. He lamented also the prospect of our speedy departure, saying, that his people would always be harassed and ill-treated by new-comers, and intreated that I would leave some persons behind for their protection. Very little dependance, however, is to be placed in the truth or sincerity of such declarations; since these people, unlettered as they are, possess no small share of policy and

---

[1] The correct Spanish names of the eight were respectively *Santa Gertrudis, Nuestra Senora de la Concepción, Activa, Princesa, Nuestra Senora del Aranzazú, San Carlos, Sutil* and *Mexicana.*

[2] Although sent to Philip Stephens, Secretary of the Admiralty, the papers Mudge carried to London are now in the records of the Colonial Office. They are endorsed as having been received on 10 June 1793 and as having consisted of 'Narrative Copies of Correspondence & 4 Charts', for which see P.R.O., C.O. 187/5, ff. 43, 88–125.

[3] Quadra left Salvador Fidalgo in command at Nootka. His suspicious and unfriendly attitude was due to the murder of Antonio Serantes, his first officer, by the Indians at Neah Bay. Tribal tradition contends that Serantes made advances to an Indian woman and was killed by her native suitor. Menzies states that Serantes 'was murdered in a most shocking manner by the Natives who were afterwards seen rejoicing in their Savage Cruelties by placing part of his remains on a Stick & dancing round it in a Ring.' – October 1.

address, and spare no pains to ingratiate themselves, by the help of a little flattery (a commodity with whose value they seem perfectly acquainted) with strangers, to whom they represent their actions as resulting from the most sincere friendship; by which means they frequently procure very valuable presents, without making any return.

From the time of Senr Quadra's departure until Wednesday the 26th, my time had been mostly employed in preparing my dispatches for England; they were now completed, and Mr. Mudge would have sailed this day, had not a hard gale of wind from the S.E. attended with a heavy rain, prevented his departure, and retarded our operations in the equipment of the Chatham and Dædalus. This boisterous unpleasant weather continued until the 30th in the afternoon, when the wind shifting to the N.W. brought fair weather, with which the Fenis and St. Joseph sailed for China.[1]

On Tuesday, October the 2d, the Hope brig, which had sailed on the 20th of last month, and the Spanish armed ship Princessa, arrived here from the establishment before mentioned, that the Spaniards had formed near the southern entrance of the straits of De Fuca; which was the same open bay we had passed in the afternoon of the 29th of April last;[2] but it having been found much exposed, and the anchorage very bad, owing to a rocky bottom, the Spaniards, I was given to understand, had been induced intirely to evacuate it; and it appeared also that Senr Fidalgo had brought with him to this place all the live stock that had been destined for its establishment.

Our new suit of sails, after soaking some hours in the sea, were bent on Saturday the 6th. The observatory, with the instruments and chronometers, were on that day also taken on board, as well those supplied me by the Navy Board, as those intrusted by the Board of Longitude to the care of the late Mr. William Gooch the astronomer, intended for this expedition.

The very unsettled state of the weather much retarded our re-equipment, and the appearance of winter having already commenced, indicated the whole year to be divided here into two seasons only. The month of September had been delightfully pleasant, and the same sort of weather, with little interruption, had prevailed ever since the arrival of Senr Quadra in the spring; during which period of settled weather, the day was always attended with a refreshing gale from the ocean, and a gentle breeze prevailed through the night from the land; which not only renders the climate of this country extremely pleasant, but the access and egress to and from its ports very easy and commodious.

As my attention, during our continuance in this port, had been principally engrossed by the negociation already adverted to, I had little leisure to

[1] Vancouver gave Mudge a letter to the Committee of the East India Company to China, asking them to do everything possible to expedite Mudge's journey to England. The Committee received the letter on December 30, and according to the *Chronicles* of the Company not only helped with travel arrangements but advanced Mudge $1000 for his expenses. Cited in Godwin, *Vancouver. A Life* (London, 1930), p. 76. Mudge reached London early in May 1793.

[2] Neah Bay.

prosecute other inquiries; I shall therefore conclude this chapter by the insertion of such observations as were made on shore at the observatory.

The observations commenced on the 30th of August, at which time Kendall's chronometer, according to the Birch-bay rate gave the longitude   233° 58' 15"
By the Portsmouth rate   231° 16' 30"
Arnold's watch, on board the Chatham, by the Birch-bay rate   232° 47' 45"

1792.   Longitude of the observatory.

Sept. 7,	Myself, two sets of distances, moon and sun,	233° 22' 30"
—	Mr. Whidbey, two do. do.	19'
8,	ditto, eight ditto ditto	44' 20"
—	Myself, eight ditto ditto	38' 41"
9,	ditto, eight ditto ditto	31' 30"
—	Mr. Whidbey, eight do. do.	37' 17"
12,	ditto, eight ditto ditto	32' 32"
—	Myself, six ditto ditto	27' 5"
23,	ditto, eight ditto ditto	26' 34"
—	Mr. Whidbey, eight do. do.	13' 9"
23,	ditto, eight ditto ditto	12' 34"
—	Myself, eight ditto ditto	12' 50"
Oct. 1,	Mr. Whidbey, six ditto moon and aquila,	35' 25"
Aug. 22,	Five sets per ☽ a ☉, taken by myself at sea, and reduced at this place by the chronometer, according to its rate of going found here	49' 9"
—	Five sets, taken by Mr. Whidbey, ditto	36' 5"
24,	Four sets by myself, ditto	36' 49"
—	Four sets by Mr. Whidbey, ditto	34' 45"

The mean of the whole, *collectively* taken; being forty-nine sets by myself; and fifty-seven by Mr. Whidbey; amounting in all to one hundred and six sets of lunar distances gave the longitude   233° 31' 30"[1]

By which our observations place Nootka sound about 20' 30" to the eastward of the longitude assigned to it by Captain Cook, and about 10' to the eastward of Senr Malaspina's observations; whence it should seem to appear, that our instruments for the longitude were erring on the eastern side.

Although I should have been very happy to subscribe to the longitude as

---

[1] The long. of Friendly Cove is 126° 37' W (233° 23' E).

settled by astronomers of superior abilities, yet, on the present occasion, such a concession would have been attended with a very material inconvenience, in deranging the position of the different parts of the coast that have already been surveyed, and laid down by our own observations. For this essential reason, I have been induced to retain the meridian of Nootka, as ascertained by our own observations, which shewed Kendall's chronometer, on our arrival, to be 26′ 45″ to the eastward of what I have considered as the true longitude; and as I had reason to believe this error commenced about the time of our departure from Desolation sound, and that it had been regularly increasing since that period, the longitude has been corrected both in my journals and charts from that station.

On this authority, the errors of the chronometers have been found, which, on the 5th of October at noon, were as follow: (viz.)

Kendall fast of mean time at Greenwich 1^h 13′ 43″ 41‴

And gaining per day, on mean time, deduced from thirty-six sets of corresponding altitudes, at the rate of 11″ 15‴

Arnold's No. 82, on board the Chatham, fast of mean time at Greenwich 4^h 3′ 35″ 41‴

And gaining, per day, on mean time, at the rate of 28″ 7‴

Arnold's No. 14, from the Dædalus, fast of mean time at Greenwich 42′ 4″ 41‴

And gaining, per day, on mean time, at the rate of 14″ 45‴

Arnold's No. 176, fast of mean time at Greenwich 2^h 16′ 38″ 41‴

And gaining, per day, on mean time, at the rate of 32″ 27‴

Earnshaw's pocket watch, fast of mean time at Greenwich 1^h 7′ 39″ 41‴

And gaining, per day, on mean time, at the rate of 5″ 30‴

The calculations by the Portmouth rate of Kendall's chronometer have hitherto been noticed, in order to shew the degree of accuracy with which it had gone, according to its then ascertained motion, in encountering the various climates it had passed through since our departure from that port; but as I have no similar documents, or the least information, respecting the three chronometers I received from the Dædalus, to compare with the going of Kendall's, those calculations from hence will cease to attract our attention.

The latitude of the observatory, by thirty
meridional altitudes of the sun   49° 34′ 20″[1]

The variation of the compass, by thirty sets of
azimuths, taken by three different compasses,
varying from 16° to 21°, gave the mean result   18° 22′ east

The vertical inclination of the magnetic needle.
Marked end, North face East,   74° 0′
    Ditto,   West,   73° 47′
Marked end, South face East,   73° 7′
    Ditto,   West,   74° 52′
                                                             ————————
Mean inclination of the marine dipping needle   73° 56′

[1] The lat. of the Cove is 49° 35′ N.

CHAPTER XI.

Depart from Nootka Sound—Proceed to the Southward along the Coast—The Dædalus enters Gray's Harbour—The Chatham enters Columbia River—Arrival of the Discovery at Port St. Francisco.

THE inclemency of the weather prevented our proceeding in our several occupations, and detained us here until the afternoon of Friday, October the 12th, when, in company with the Chatham and Dædalus, we hauled out of the cove, in order to take the advantage of the land wind, which about ten o'clock enabled us to sail out of the port of Nootka; but the Chatham and Dædalus not following, we brought to about midnight, to wait their coming up. This however did not take place during the night, which was serene and pleasant, though we had a very heavy and irregular swell, which drove us so far to the westward, that by day-light we were not more than two miles to the southward of the ledge of rocks which lie two leagues to the westward of the west point of entrance into Nootka; our soundings were from 25 to 30 fathoms.

About nine the next morning, Saturday the 13th, the Chatham and Dædalus joined company. The Chatham, by the weather falling calm just as she had weighed anchor, became under no command, and was swept by the tide on the rocky point of the cove, where the sea broke with great violence; but by proper exertions, and immediate assistance from the Dædalus, which was in a fortunate situation for that purpose, she got off without receiving any apparent damage, though she had struck very heavily.

It is necessary here to state, that on the day previous to our sailing, I received on board two young women for the purpose of returning them to their native country, the Sandwich islands;[1] which they had quitted in a vessel that arrived at Nootka on the 7th instant, called the Jenny, belonging to Bristol. But as that vessel was bound from hence straight to England, Mr. James Baker her

[1] 'one of them was about fourteen years of age named Teheeopea & the other was a few years older named Tahomeeraoo.' – Menzies, 12 October. '...the Ladies accordingly removed into the Discovery, there the poor girls found themselves happy & satisfied, not only with the pleasing idea of getting soon home to their friends & Country, but having a Companion on board the Discovery (one of their Countrymen that Captn. Vancouver brought with him from Owhyee...) to whom they could converse, and who from his knowledge of our Language could contribute much to their comfort by interpreting their wants and desires.' – Bell, October.

commander very earnestly requested, that I would permit these two unfortunate girls to take a passage in the Discovery to Onehow,[1] the island of their birth and residence; from whence it seems they had been brought, not only very contrary to their wishes and inclinations, but totally without the knowledge or consent of their friends or relations; and of which transaction some particulars will hereafter be noticed, where they will not interfere with the regular progress of our narrative; which I now resume by observing, that after so long a continuance of unsettled weather, the present apparent re-established serenity encouraged me to hope I might be enabled in our route to the southward to re-examine the coast of New Albion, and particularly a river and a harbour discovered by Mr. Gray in the Columbia between the 46th and 47th degrees of north latitude, of which Sen[r] Quadra had favoured me with a sketch.[2] For this purpose our course was directed along shore to the eastward, which would also afford an opportunity of examining the Spanish survey between Nootka and De Fuca's straits.

Some observations were made to ascertain if any error had taken place in the chronometers since they had been received from the shore, and I had the satisfaction to find them all answer very well. Kendall's in particular was very exact, and its excellency having already been proved, I was determined to depend principally upon it until a further opportunity should offer for ascertaining the going of the others.

At noon our observed latitude was 49° 23′, the longitude 233° 28′. The northernmost land in sight by compass bore N.W.; Nootka N. 8 W.; the easternmost land in sight N. 88 E.; and point Breakers, our nearest shore, N. 30 E. distant four miles; whence that point is situated according to our observations, which were very good, made by different persons, and agreeing to a great nicety, in latitude 49° 25′, longitude 233° 32′.[3] Captain Cook states the latitude of point Breakers to be 49° 15′. The difference of 10′ is decidedly an error of the press, as by my own observations during that voyage point Breakers is placed in latitude 49° 24′.[4]

The wind at N.W. blew a pleasant gale until the evening, when it was succeeded by calms and light variable airs off the land, which continued until near noon of Sunday the 14th. During the fore part of the night the depth of water was from 70 to 90 fathoms, but by the morning we were drifted too far from the land to gain soundings. The weather, though clear over head, was hazy towards the horizon, and rendered the land very indistinct; in the

[1] Niihau.
[2] A copy of Gray's sketch of the Columbia River was included in the papers Vancouver sent to the Admiralty. It is now in P.R.O., C.P. 5/187.
[3] Estevan Point in lat. 49° 23′ N, long. 126° 33′ W (233° 27′ E). 'The SE extreme of the land formed a low point off which are many breakers...on this account it was called *point Breakers*.' – Cook, 29 March 1778; *Journals*, III, p. 294. The point had already been named Punta San Estéban by Pérez, and the Spanish name superseded Cook's.
[4] It was not 'an error of the press'; Cook's MS journal gives the lat. as 49° 15′. *Journals*, III, 294.

afternoon we had a fine breeze from the westward, which enabled us to steer in for the land, and to gain a distant view of Clayoquot and Nittinat, which, according to the Spaniards, are the native names of port Cox and Berkley's sound.[1] The east point of the former at sun-set by compass bore N. 50 W. about four leagues distant; the west point of the latter, our nearest shore, N. 28 E. about five miles distant, and the coast in sight extended from east to N. 63 W. We shortened sail for the night, and inclined our course towards cape Classet. I had been given to understand, that this promontory was by the natives called Classet; but now finding that this name had originated only from that of an inferior chief's residing in its neighbourhood, I have therefore resumed Captain Cook's original appellation of cape Flattery.[2]

The westwardly wind died away as the night approached, when we were in soundings from 30 to 40 fathoms; but light airs and calms succeeding, we were soon driven to a considerable distance from the land, which in the morning of Monday the 15th was nearly obscured by a thick haze at the distance of five or six leagues. The observed latitude at noon was 48° 41', longitude 234° 30'; the coast then in sight bearing by compass from N.W. to E. by N.

A want of wind until Tuesday the 16th much increased our distance from the shore, by our being set to the southward; and the land being still obscured by a dense haze, prevented our discovery that we had passed cape Flattery until ten in the forenoon, when it was announced by the rocks to the south of it; the largest of which, independently of Destruction island, is the most extensive detached land existing on the sea coast between cape Flattery and cape Mendocino.[3] It is of an oblong shape, and nearly level on the top, where it produces a few trees, its sides are almost perpendicular; near it are some small white barren rocks, some sunken ones, and some rocky islets of curious and romantic shapes. At noon the observed latitude was 48° 8', and the longitude, deduced from four different sets of obervations for the chronometer taken in the afternoon, was 235° 26'. In this situation the southernmost land in sight bore by compass S. 78 E. and the mountain before considered as mount Olympus, east. Whether our having been latterly accustomed to see more lofty mountains, or whether the mountain being disrobed of its winter garment (the snow now being only in patches) produced the effect, is not easily determined, but it certainly seemed of less stupendous height than when we first beheld it in the spring. A light favorable breeze from the N.W. during the afternoon, afforded a good opportunity for determining the situation of this cape,[4] and I had the satisfaction to find it correspond exactly with the

---

[1] Port Cox was an anchorage in Clayoquot Sound, not the sound itself. The rough sketch in Meares's *Voyages* suggests that it was in Templar Channel, with the soundings shown extending N into Van Nevel Channel. Nitinat, as Vancouver states, was the Indian name for Barkley Sound.

[2] In spite of this statement the cape is named Cape Classet on both Baker's MS map and the engraved chart.

[3] Ozette Island, which is half a mile long.   [4] Cape Flattery is meant.

position I had assigned to it, on passing it in the spring. This evinced the propriety of adopting the meridian of Nootka for our charts, agreeably to the result of the observations we had made for ascertaining it.

In the point of view we this day saw the entrance of De Fuca's straits, it appeared in no respect remarkable, or likely to be an opening of any considerable extent. The night being again almost calm, our distance from the land was increased as before. We approached it slowly in the forenoon of Wednesday the 17th, and at mid-day the coast by compass extended from N.N.W. to E.S.E.; mount Olympus bore N. 40 E. and the nearest shore N.E. about four leagues distant. Our observed latitude 47° 27', longitude 235° 38', agreed exceedingly well with our former position of this part of the coast.

A light N.W. breeze prevailed in the afternoon, which by sun-set brought us within four miles of the shore, having soundings from 50 to 30 fathoms. At eight the wind died away, and as we were now approaching a part of the coast which we had formerly passed at a greater distance than I could have wished, we anchored for the night to prevent the same thing happening a second time. The depth of water was 24 fathoms, black sandy bottom. At five in the morning of Thursday the 18th, with a gentle breeze from the land, we turned up along shore, and had soundings from 17 to 40 fathoms. The land breeze was succeeded by one from the N.W.; at noon the observed latitude was 47° 14', longitude 235° 59', very nearly corresponding with the position of this coast as laid down by us in the spring. In this situation the northernmost land in sight by compass bore N. 28 W.; the perforated rock noticed off point Grenville in the morning of the 28th of April, N. 15 W.; mount Olympus N. 14 E.; the nearest shore, being a small detached rock, S. 80 E. three or four miles distant; two low points of land which we considered to form the points of Gray's harbour, S. 40 E.; and S. 36 E.; and the southernmost land in sight S. 32 E. In the course of the morning we had seen a remarkably high round mountain, which now bore by compass N. 79 E. and rose conspicuously from a plain of low, or rather moderately elevated land, and was covered with snow as far down as the intervening hills permitted us to see. We entertained little doubt of its being mount Rainier, which was soon afterwards confirmed; its distance from us being an hundred geographical miles.

The weather and every other circumstance concurring to promote the design I had formed of re-examining this coast, I directed that Mr. Whidbey, taking one of the Discovery's boats, should proceed in the Dædalus to examine Gray's harbour, said to be situated in latitude 46° 53',[1] whilst the Chatham and Discovery explored the river Mr. Gray had discovered in the latitude of 46° 10'.[2] In the event of our not meeting with the Dædalus before we reached Monterrey, that port was appointed as a rendezvous. We proceeded to the

[1] Grays Harbor Light, on the S entrance point, is in lat. 46° 53·3' N.
[2] The Columbia River lightship, anchored off the entrance, is in lat. 46° 11·1' N.

southward at the distance of three or four miles from the shore, having regular soundings at a depth from 13 to 19 fathoms.

Towards midnight the light N.W. wind, which had prevailed during most part of the day, was succeeded by a calm, on which we anchored in 16 fathoms water, and at day-light the next morning discovered our situation to be off the bay we had endeavoured to enter the 27th of last April,[1] and about two miles from the outermost of the breakers, which bore by compass N. 73 E.; the southernmost part of the coast in sight S.S.E.; mount Rainier N. 66 E.; the S.E. point of Gray's harbour, which is low projecting land, covered with trees, N. 2 W.; and mount Olympus, our northernmost land in view, north. This by various observations, I found to be situated in latitude 47° 50′, longitude 236° 4′.[2] Here the bay before us did not appear to fall so far back as I had been led to suppose, but the low land projected further into the ocean than it had appeared to do on our former view of it; and instead of the breakers being intirely connected, two small openings were discovered, which, however, from the colour of the water, and the rising of the swell across them, must be very shallow. Broken water was also seen in every direction between the outer reefs and the shore, the latter of which was not discernible until eleven o'clock on Friday the 19th, when a breeze set in from the N.W. which dispersed the haze, and shewed the boundary of the coast to be one uninterrupted beach, lined with breakers at irregular distances from it. With this breeze we weighed anchor. The latitude observed at noon was 46° 42′, but observations for the chronometers were not procured.

With a pleasant gale and fine weather we coasted along this delightful and apparently fertile part of New Georgia, at the distance of about a league from the shoals, having soundings from ten to sixteen fathoms, until four in the afternoon, when having nearly reached cape Disappointment, which forms the north point of entrance into Columbia river, so named by Mr. Gray, I directed the Chatham to lead into it, and on her arrival at the bar should no more than four fathoms water be found, the signal for danger was to be made; but if the channel appeared to be further navigable, then to proceed.

As we followed the Chatham the depth of water decreased to four fathoms, in which we sailed some little time without being able to distinguish the entrance into the river, the sea breaking in a greater or less degree from shore to shore; but as the Chatham continued to pursue her course, I concluded she was in a fair channel. We however soon arrived in three fathoms, and as the water was becoming less deep, and breaking in all directions around us, I hauled to the westward in order to escape the threatened danger. In doing this we were assisted by a very strong ebb tide that sat out of the river, and which opposing a very heavy swell that rolled from the westward directly on the shore, caused an irregular and dangerous sea. By seven, our depth of water had increased to ten fathoms, where, conceiving ourselves in safety, we

---

[1] Willapa Bay.
[2] The position of Mount Olympus is lat. 47° 49′ N, long. 123° 42′ W (236° 18′ E).

anchored for the night, which passed very uncomfortably, owing to the violent motion of the vessel, and anxiety for the safety of the Chatham, from which a signal was made at the moment we hauled out of the breakers, which we were fearful might have been for assistance, as the closing in of the day prevented our accurately distinguishing the colour of the flags; but as she appeared to be perfectly under command, and as the rapidity of the tide and the heavy sea rendered any assistance from us impracticable, I was willing to hope the signal might have been for the bar, which, at day-light the next morning, was proved to be the case by her being seen riding in perfect safety, about two miles within the station we had taken.

The morning of Saturday the 20th was calm and fair, yet the heavy cross swell continued, and within the Chatham the breakers seemed to extend without the least interruption from shore to shore. Anxious, however, to ascertain this fact, I sent Lieutenant Swaine, in the cutter, to sound between us and the Chatham, and to acquire such information from Mr. Broughton as he might be able to communicate; but a fresh easterly breeze prevented his reaching our consort, and obliged him to return: in consequence of which a signal was made for the lieutenant of the Chatham, and was answered by Mr. Johnstone, who sounded as he came out, but found no bar, as we had been given to understand. The bottom was a dead flat within a quarter of a mile of our anchorage. From Mr. Johnstone I received the unpleasant intelligence, that by the violence of the surf, which, during the preceding night, had broken over the decks of the Chatham, her small boat had been dashed to pieces. Mr. Johnstone was clearly of opinion, that had the Discovery anchored where the Chatham did, she must have struck with great violence. Under this circumstance we undoubtedly experienced a most providential escape in hauling from the breakers. My former opinion of this port being inaccessible to vessels of our burthen was now fully confirmed, with this exception, that in very fine weather, with moderate winds, and a smooth sea, vessels not exceeding four hundred tons might, so far as we were enabled to judge, gain admittance. The Dædalus, however, being directed to search for us here, I was induced to persevere; particularly as, towards noon, a thick haze, which before had in a great degree obscured the land, cleared away, and the heavy swell having much subsided, gave us a more perfect view of our situation, and shewed this opening in the coast to be much more extensive than I had formerly imagined. Mount Olympus, the northernmost land in sight, bore by compass N. 7 W.; cape Disappointment N. 61 E. two miles, the breakers extending from its shore S. 87 E., about half a league distant; those on the southern or opposite side of the entrance into the river S. 76 E.: between these is the channel into the river, where at this time the sea did not break. The coast was seen to the southward as far as S. 31 E. The observed latitude 46° 20′,[1] which placed cape Disappointment one mile further north than did our former

---

[1] Cape Disappointment Light, on the SE point of the cape, is in lat. 46° 16·5′ N.

observations. The flood at one o'clock making in our favour, we weighed, with a signal as before for the Chatham to lead. With boats a-head sounding, we made all sail to windward, in four to six fathoms water. The Chatham being further advanced in the channel, and having more wind and tide, made a greater progress than the Discovery. About three o'clock a gun was fired from behind a point that projected from the inner part of cape Disappointment, forming, to all appearance, a very snug cove; this was answered by the hoisting of the Chatham's colours, and firing a gun to leeward, by which we concluded some vessel was there at anchor.[1] Soon afterwards soundings were denoted by the Chatham to be six and seven fathoms, and at four she anchored apparently in a tolerably snug birth. Towards sun-set, the ebb making strongly against us, with scarcely sufficient wind to command the ship, we were driven out of the channel into 13 fathoms water, where we anchored for the night; the serenity of which flattered us with the hope of getting in the next day.

The clearness of the atmosphere enabled us to see the high round snowy mountain, noticed when in the southern parts of Admiralty inlet, to the southward of mount Rainier; from this station it bore by compass N. 77 E. and, like mount Rainier, seemed covered with perpetual snow, as low down as the intervening country permitted it to be seen. This I have distinguished by the name of MOUNT ST. HELENS, in honor of His Britannic Majesty's ambassador at the court of Madrid. It is situated in latitude 46° 9', and in longitude 238° 4', according to our observations.[2]

All hopes of getting into Columbia river vanished on Sunday morning the 21st, which brought with it a fresh gale from the S.E. and every appearance of approaching bad weather, which the falling of the mercury in the barometer also indicated. We therefore weighed and stood to sea; soon after this some observations for the chronometer were obtained, which gave the longitude 236° 4' 30",[3] by which cape Disappointment appeared to be 3' in longitude further east than I had formerly esteemed it to be; it is however too trifling to demand correction, as such a difference, and even a much greater one, is liable to arise, by any little alteration in the rate of the chronometer.

The forenoon was employed in making the necessary preparations for bad weather, which was soon found to be an essential precaution. An increase of the gale, with a very heavy sea, obliged us about two in the afternoon to close-reef the topsails, and to hand the mainsail and mizen topsail.

Under this sail we stood to the S.W. until two in the morning of Monday the 22d, when, the wind in some degree moderating, we again made for the land, the gale subsided, and in the forenoon the wind from the S.E. was light and variable. The weather, however, was very unsettled, several water spouts

---

[1] The British schooner *Jenny* was anchored in Baker Bay.

[2] The position of Mount St. Helens is lat. 46° 12' N, long. 122° 11' W (237° 49' E). Alleyne Fitzherbert, 1st Baron St. Helens was the British ambassador extraordinary to Madrid who negotiated the Nootka Convention of October 1790.

[3] The W point of Cape Disappointment is in long. 124° 05' W (235° 55' E).

were seen, and some passed at no great distance from the ship. By a very indifferent observation, at noon, the latitude was ascertained to be 46° 4', and the longitude by the reckoning 234° 49'. About two in the afternoon, a strong gale, attended with heavy dark gloomy weather, suddenly arose from the N.W. and soon increased with such violence as obliged us afterwards to strike the top-gallant masts, close-reef the topsails, and to take in the main and the fore and mizen topsails. This boisterous weather, in addition to the advanced state of the season, induced me to abandon every idea of regaining Columbia river; and, under the conviction that from Mr. Broughton and Mr. Whidbey I should receive every information I required, not only of Gray's harbour but of Columbia river, which Mr. Broughton had entered, and who I was assured would not quit it without being satisfied in its examination, I directed our course to the southward.

The gale moderated next morning, Tuesday 23, veered to the S. and bringing with it more settled weather, we made all sail. At noon the observed latitude was 44° 31', longitude by the chronometer 234° 12'. This favourable appearance of the weather was however of short duration. The wind in the afternoon again blew a strong gale, which obliged us to stand to the S.W. under storm stay-sails until near midnight, when it veered to the S.W. became more moderate, and we were enabled to stand to the S.S.E. The weather, however, continued very unsettled, the sea was very heavy and irregular, and the wind became variable between S.W. and S.S.E. On Wednesday morning the 24th, some water spouts again appeared; and towards noon came on a very violent storm of lightning, thunder, and rain; about which time, very unexpectedly, we saw the land. I considered it to be part of the coast about cape Perpetua; it bore east, and was not more than six leagues from us, though, by our reckoning, it should have been more than twice that distance. The wind, with squalls from the S.S.W. now blew very hard, with which, in order to regain an offing, we stood to the westward; but this was accomplished so slowly, that at five in the evening the land was still in sight to the eastward, distant about six or seven leagues; and though the ship was already under a severe press of sail, it became necessary to make considerable addition, which the ship being unable to carry, the topsails were again close-reefed, under which and the two courses, we stood to the north-westward during the night, which was very stormy. The weather continued unsettled, although the wind became light and variable between the S. and S.W. attended with heavy rain and unpleasant weather, until Thursday afternoon the 25th, when the wind shifted to the N.W. blew a gentle breeze, and brought with it a clear atmosphere. To this favorable breeze we spread all our canvas, and directed our course for cape Orford,[1] in order to re-examine its position.

At noon the next day, Friday the 26th, our observed latitude was 43° 39', longitude 243° 51'.[2] Towards sun-set a distant view of the coast was gained,

---

[1] Now Cape Blanco, in lat. 42° 50' N.
[2] A misprint (in both editions) for long. 234° 51'.

bearing E.S.E. and by ten at night the wind veered again to the S.E. which, by noon of Saturday the 27th, reduced us to our close-reefed topsails. The gale moderated towards midnight, and once more we spread all our canvas to a moderate breeze, between the south and S.E. which was still attended with a heavy disagreeable cross swell, rendering the ship, with her then heavy cargo, very uneasy. The weather in general was much more pleasant than that which we had lately experienced, and as the wind veered, we occasionally tacked to get to the S.E. By these means, on the evening of Monday the 29th, the coast was seen extending by compass from N.E. by N. to S.E. by E.; cape Orford bearing E. by N. about four miles distant. By the observations made in the course of the day, the latitude of this cape, as before stated, was found to be correct;[1] the longitude as at cape Disappointment deviated three miles to the eastward. The next day, Tuesday the 30th, in the afternoon, I made some further observations to this effect, (not having proceeded more than three or four leagues to the southward of the cape) which produced the like result.

The wind continued nearly in the same direction, blowing a moderate breeze, with pleasant weather; but the very uncomfortable state of the vessel, in consequence of a disagreeable swell, was soon again aggravated by the increase of the S.E. wind, which, at sun-set, on Friday the 2d of November, reduced us to a close-reefed topsail and foresail. This gale was accompanied by a very high sea, which, about two o'clock in the morning of Saturday the 3d, carried away our spritsail yard in the slings. After day-break the wind shifted to the N.W.; with this we steered to the S.S.E. against a very heavy head sea, which washed overboard John Davison, a seaman, whilst rigging a new spritsail yard. This poor fellow being a good swimmer, was enabled to support himself until our small boat from the stern happily picked him up, when nearly exhausted.

The wind continuing to blow a fresh breeze to the westward of south, we made a fine slant along the coast to the south-eastward. The weather was delightfully pleasant until near midnight, when the wind veered to the S.E. and by four in the morning of Sunday the 4th, its violence obliged us to strike the top-gallant masts, and bring the ship under the foresail and storm staysails; even this low sail was more than prudence could authorize, yet I was, and had been, throughout the whole of this stormy weather, necessitated to resort to this measure, lest we should lose, in these tempestuous returns, the distance which the short intervals of moderate weather permitted us to gain. This gale moderated in the evening; close-reefed topsails were set; towards midnight the wind veered to the westward, and the next morning, Monday the 5th, we again stood to the south. The wind between N.W. and W. attended still with the same heavy irregular swell, blew a moderate breeze with fair and pleasant weather, which gave us again, on the following day, Tuesday the 6th, sight of the land extending by compass from N.W. by N. to E. $\frac{1}{2}$ S. The

[1] Vancouver's reading was lat. 42° 52′ N, very near the correct position, which is 42° 50′ N.

southernmost promontory of cape Mendocino, N. 40 E. distant five or six leagues. At noon in this situation our latitude was 40° 10′, longitude 235° 33′. From the observations on this occasion, I found the latitude of cape Mendocino exactly to correspond, and the longitude to be within 3′ of the position I had before assigned to it.[1] This circumstance afforded me much satisfaction, as it proved the accuracy of our survey in the spring, and flattered me with the hope, that future visitors to this coast would find the several projecting points, as well to the north of cape Mendocino, as to the south of it, which we were now bound to visit, laid down with tolerable accuracy in our chart.

The wind, however, proved adverse to our southern progress; it again veered to the S.E. and as usual was attended with squalls and torrents of rain, which kept us under close-reefed topsails until Wednesday morning the 7th, when the gale gradually died away, and was succeeded by a calm; the same heavy irregular sea, thick weather, and a deluge of rain continued until the morning of Thursday the 8th, when a gentle breeze sprang up from the N.W. and the atmosphere once more assumed a clear and pleasant appearance.

We had now passed to the south of cape Mendocino, and with this favorable change in the weather lost not a moment in making all sail towards the land to the S.E. of the cape, which at noon was in sight, extending by compass from N. by E. to E. by N.; the nearest shore bearing N. 55 E. about eight leagues distant. The latitude observed was 39° 51′, longitude 235° 48′. We had approached about dark nearly within a league of the shore, and as we had now to commence the examination of the coast to the southward, we hauled our wind and plied under an easy sail until day-light in the morning of Friday the 9th, when we again resumed our course along shore with a light northerly breeze, which by noon brought us to that part of the coast we first made on the 17th of last April. It extended by compass from S. 43 E. to N. 33 W.; the nearest shore bearing E. by N. about two leagues distant. In this situation our latitude was 39° 25′, longitude 236° 32′, which places the coast under this parallel near a quarter of a degree more to the eastward than I had considered it on our former visit. The land to the southward, which had then appeared to have been much broken, was now proved to be compact, the deception having been occasioned by our distance from it, and the irregularity of its surface, which rises abruptly in low sandy cliffs from a connected beach which uniformly composes the sea shore. The interior country appeared to be nearly an uninterrupted forest, but towards the sea side was a pleasing variety of open spaces.

From the south promontory of cape Mendocino to the land we were abreast of the preceding night, the coast takes a direction about S. 40 E. for about 12 or 13 leagues, and there forms something of a projection, whence it falls back about two leagues to the eastward, and then stretches about S. 15 E. in

---

[1] By 'the southernmost promontory of Cape Mendocino' Vancouver meant what is now Punta Gorda. Its position is lat. 40° 16′ N, long. 124° 21′ 30″ W (235° 38′ 30″ E). Vancouver had placed it in lat. 40° 19′ N, long. 235° 53′ E (124° 07′ W).

which direction we sailed at the distance of four or five miles from the shore which still continued compact, with two or three small rocky islets lying near it. As we proceeded, a distant view was obtained of the inland country, which was composed of very lofty rugged mountains extending in a ridge nearly parallel to the direction of the coast. These were in general destitute of wood, and the more elevated parts were covered with perpetual snow.

In the evening we again hauled off from the shore to wait the return of day, Saturday the 10th, at which time a low projecting point, called by the Spaniards Punta Barro de Arena,[1] bore by compass S. 57 E. about two leagues from us. The wind blew a pleasant gale from the N.W. with fine weather, which made me much regret the delays our survey demanded, as these now prevented our embracing so favorable an opportunity of making the best of our way to those ports of refreshments now not far off, especially as some scorbutic symptoms had at length made their appearance. Six of the crew were affected, though not in such a degree as to cause confinement. The same attention had been unremittingly paid to the preservation of health as on all former occasions during the voyage, and I was unable to ascribe the appearance of this malady to any other cause than the laborious exertions which the nature of the service had demanded, and the scarcity of refreshments we had been enabled to procure in the course of the summer. The very unpleasant state of the ship during the late boisterous weather had undoubtedly operated in producing this calamity, by the crew being almost continually wet with the incessant rains, and from our having shipped a great quantity of water which had unavoidably kept the ship damp in spite of our utmost endeavors. The salubrious qualities of the sour krout, though served with the portable soup every day, and boiled not only in the peas for dinner, but every morning in the wheat for breakfast, ever since we had left Nootka, had not averted the evil. On the first symptoms of the disease, recourse was immediately had to the essence of malt, with the inpissated juice of orange and lemon, which from some removed the disorder, and checked its progress in others, though they still continued to labour under its influence.[2]

We pursued our line of direction slowly along the coast, owing to the late baffling winds that prevailed. At noon the observed latitude was 38° 48′, longitude 236° 42′; the southernmost land in sight bore by compass S. 67 E.; two small rocky islets lying near the coast N. 79 E.; the nearest shore about two leagues distant; and the point de Arena being nearly the northernmost land in sight N. 10 W. at the distance of about three leagues. According to

[1] Now Point Arena. Vancouver was mistaken in thinking that the Spaniards had so named it; this name made its first appearance on his own chart. The point had had at least four Spanish names, the first being Cabo de Fortunas, bestowed by Bartolomé Ferrer, who discovered it in 1543, and the last Punta Delgada, given by Quadra as recently as 1775.

[2] Scurvy is caused by a lack of vitamin C, which is not found in 'essence of malt' (a remedy in which Cook placed great faith); the chief source would be lemon juice, the curative properties of which had been demonstrated, but were not widely or officially acknowledged at this date.

our observations this point is situated in latitude 38° 56′, longitude 236° 44′;[1]
it forms a conspicuous mark on the coast; the shores to the north of it take
a direction N. 10 W.; its northern side is composed of black rugged rocks
on which the sea breaks with great violence; to the south of it the coast trends
S. 35 E.; its southern side is composed of low sandy or clayey cliffs, remarkably
white, though interspersed with streaks of a dull green colour; the country
above it rises with a gentle ascent, is chequered with copses of forest trees and
clear ground, which gave it the appearance of being in a high state of
cultivation. The land further south is high, steep to the sea, and presented a
rude and barren aspect. Our soundings were 75 and 70 fathoms. The calm
of the afternoon was succeeded by a S.E. wind and its usual attendant, a heavy
rain, which prevented our acquiring any further knowledge of the coast until
Monday the 12th, when, on the return of a favourable gale, we stood for the
land, which at noon extended by compass from N. 15 W. to S. 77 E.; the
nearest shore bore N.E. about five leagues distant, latitude 38° 17′, longitude
236° 59′. As we approached the shore, advancing to the southward, the
country became nearly destitute of wood and verdure, at least that part of it
in the vicinity of the sea shore, which was nearly straight and compact. The
more interior hills, rising behind those forming the coast, were tolerably well
wooded.

Being near the assigned situation of the bay in which Sir Francis Drake
anchored, and that of a port called by the Spaniards Bodega, our attention
was directed to the appearance of a port to the eastward, for which we
immediately steered. By sun-set we were close in with the shore, which
extended from N.W. by W. to S.S.E. ½ E., so that we were considerably
embayed. We were now off the northern point of an inner bay that seemed
divided into two or three arms, the soundings had been regular from 40 to
28 fathoms, the bottom a bed of coral rock, sand, and shells. Being anxious
not to leave any opening on the coast unexamined, and as the evening was
serene and pleasant, I was induced to anchor, though on a rocky bottom, off
this point for the night, which bore by compass from us N.E. by E. two miles
distant, that my design might early in the morning be carried into execution.
Our situation here was by no means pleasant; during the night two deep sea
lines were cut through by the rocks, and at four in the morning of Tuesday
the 13th the buoy was seen drifting past ship, and was proved to have been
severed in the same way. Lest the cable should share the same fate, no time
was lost in weighing the anchor; fortunately however the cable had not
received any injury. A light breeze from the land permitted us to stand across
the bay, which we soon discovered to be port Bodega;[2] its north point
according to our observations is situated in latitude 38° 21′, longitude
237° 21′.[3] This point is formed of low steep cliffs, and when seen from the

[1] Its position is lat. 38° 57·3′ N, long. 123° 44·4′ W (236° 15·6′ E).
[2] Now Bodega Bay.
[3] Bodega Head, in lat. 38° 18′ N, long. 123° 03·2′ W (236° 56·8′ E).

south has the appearance of an island, but is firmly connected with the main land. To the east the land retires and forms a small inlet, apparently favorable to anchorage; it has a flat rock on which the water broke in its entrance, and has not any other visible danger excepting that of being much exposed to the south and S.E. winds. Not being able to sail into the bay, we stood towards its south point,[1] which lies from the north point S. 30 E. at the distance of seven miles. Within these limits appeared three small openings in the coast, one already noticed to the eastward of the north point,[2] the other two immediately within the south point;[3] across these a connected chain of breakers seemed to extend, with three high white rocks, which nearly blockaded the passage. Although very solicitious of gaining more intelligence, this was all the information I was able to procure of this place, which required to be minutely surveyed by our boats before the vessel should enter; the state of the weather was ill calculated for such service: it was very dark and gloomy, and the depression of the mercury in the barometer indicated an approaching storm. Our soundings when under 35 fathoms were on a rocky bottom, and considering that any further examination at this time was not important, I steered along the coast to the southward for point de los Reys, so named by the Spaniards, which at noon bore by compass, S. 22 E. distant about two leagues: the latitude by an indifferent observation, 38° 7′. My apprehensions of bad weather were not ill-founded; after a few hours calm we were again visited by a S.S.E. gale, attended as before with heavy rain; this soon reduced us to close-reefed topsails, and brought with it a very heavy sea. Soon after midnight the wind suddenly shifted to the westward, the sky became clear, and we again steered for the land; about nine in the morning of Wednesday the 14th we passed point de los Reys, which I found to be situated in latitude 38° 0′, longitude 237° 24′.[4] This is one of the most conspicuous promontories southward of cape Flattery, and cannot easily be mistaken; when seen from the north, or south, at the distance of five or six leagues, it appears insular, owing to its projecting into the sea, and the land behind it being lower than usual near the coast; but the interior country preserved a more lofty appearance, although the mountains extended in a direction further from the coast than those we had lately noticed. From the south point of port Bodega, which is formed by steep rocky cliffs with some detached rocks lying near it, the coast makes a shallow open bay, which is bounded by a low sandy beach; towards the S.E. part of which the elevated land of point de los Reys again commences, and stretches like a peninsula to the southward into the ocean, where its highest part terminates in steep cliffs, moderately elevated, and nearly

[1] Tomales Point.

[2] Bodega Harbor.

[3] Vancouver evidently sighted part of Tomales Bay, which runs S from Tomales Point, parallel to the coast, for about 12 miles.

[4] Now Point Reyes. The Spanish name dated back to the Vizcaino expedition of 1603. Its position is lat. 37° 59·7′ N, long. 123° 1·3′ W (236° 58·7′ E).

perpendicular to the sea, which beats against them with great violence. Southward of this point the shore, composed of low white cliffs, takes, for about a league, nearly an eastern direction, and there forms the north point of a bay extending a little distance to the northward, which is intirely open, and much exposed to the south and S.E. winds.

The eastern side of the bay is also composed of white cliffs, though more elevated. According to the Spaniards, this is the bay in which Sir Francis Drake anchored;[1] however safe he might then have found it, yet at this season of the year it promised us little shelter or security. The wind blowing fresh out of the bay from the N.N.W., I did not think it proper to lose this opporunity of proceeding with all dispatch to St. Francisco; where there was little doubt of our obtaining a supply of those refreshments which were now much wanted by the whole crew.

Off point de los Reys are situated some rocks, called Farellones;[2] those we saw were tolerably high, and appeared to be in two distinct clusters of three or four rocks each, lying in a S.E. and N.W. direction from each other. The highest rock of the northernmost group lies from the extremity of point de los Reys, S. 13 W., distant 14 miles; the southernmost S. 5 E., at the distance of 17 miles. From unquestionable authority I learned, that a third cluster of rocks, scarcely above the surface of the sea, lies $12\frac{1}{2}$ miles distant from the above point S. 36 W.

With a favorable gale and pleasant weather we sailed, at the distance of two or three miles, along the coast; which, from point de los Reys to port Francisco, takes a direction S. 62 E. distant eight leagues. At noon the observed latitude was 37° 53′, longitude 237° 35′; in this situation point de los Reys bore by compass N. 72 W.; the supposed bay of Sir Francis Drake N. 45 W.; a low sandy projecting point, off which some breakers extended nearly two miles to the E.S.E., being our nearest shore, N. 34 W., about a league distant; the southernmost land in sight S.E.; and the south-easternmost of the Farellones S. 35 W.; to the eastward of the low sandy projecting point, the coast suddenly rises in abrupt cliffs, with very unequal surfaces, presenting a most dreary and barren aspect. A few scattered trees were growing on the more elevated land, with some patches of dwarf shrubs in the vallies; the rest of the country

---

[1] Although *United States Coast Pilot 7* (12th ed., 1976) accepts this opinion and states that Drakes Bay was 'named after English explorer Sir Francis Drake, who anchored here in 1579', the identity of the bay in which Drake refitted his ship is still a matter of controversy. Wagner, for example, considered that it was 'far more probable' that he visited Bodega Bay. – *Cartography of the Northwest Coast* (Berkeley, 1937), p. 385. Some still think his anchorage was in San Francisco Bay. Like many of the features on the coast, Drakes Bay had several Spanish names. Cermeño entered it in 1595 and named it La Bahia de San Francisco. Vizcaino passed it in 1603 and named it Don Gaspar. On the famous Briggs map of 1625 it was named Puerto de Sir Francisco Draco and this was copied on other maps. Adopting this name, the U.S. Coast Survey first named it Sir Francis Drake's Bay. This was later shortened to Drake's Bay, and the official spelling is now Drakes Bay. It appears on Vancouver's chart as Port Sir Francis Drake.

[2] The Farallon Islands.

presented either a surface of naked rocks, or a covering of very little verdure.

We had approached, by two in the afternoon, within a small distance of the entrance into port St. Francisco, and found a rapid tide setting against us; the depth of water regularly decreased from 18 to 4 fathoms, which appearing to be the continuation of a shoal that stretches from the northern shore, then distant from us not more than a league, I hauled to the S.W. in order to avoid it, but did not succeed in reaching deeper water, as the bank we were upon extended a long way in that direction, as was evident from the confused breaking sea upon it, and the smooth water on either side of it. We therefore made for the port, and soon increased the depth of water to eight and ten fathoms, until we arrived between the two outer points of entrance, which are about two miles and a half apart,[1] and bear from each other N. 10 W. and S. 10 E.; here we had 15 and 18 fathoms water, and soon afterwards we could gain no sounding with a handline.

Although favored with a pleasant breeze which impelled us at the rate of four or five knots an hour, it availed us no more than just to preserve our station against the ebb setting out of the port. We did not advance until four o'clock, and then but slowly, through the channel leading into this spacious port; lying in a direction N. 61 E. and S. 61 W.; it is nearly a league in length, with some rocks and breakers lying at a little distance from either shore. Those on the southern side were furthest, detached, and most conspicuous, especially one, about a mile within the S.W. point of entrance, which seemed to admit of a passage within it; but we had no opportunity of ascertaining that fact, nor is it of any importance to the navigation, as the main channel appeared to be free from any obstruction, and is of sufficient width for the largest vessels to turn in. Its northern shore, composed of high steep rocky cliffs, is the boldest; the southern side is much lower, though its south-eastern point[2] is formed of steep rocky cliffs, from the base of which a tract of sandy country commences, extending not only along the southern shore of the channel, and some distance along the exterior coast to the southward, but likewise to a considerable height on the more elevated land that borders thereon; and interspersed with huge massy rocks of different sizes, which, with the Farellones, render this point too conspicuous to be mistaken. Having passed the inner points of entrance, we found ourselves in a very spacious sound, which had the appearance of containing a variety of as excellent harbours as the known world affords. The Spanish establishment being on the southern side of the port, our course was directed along that shore, with regular soundings from nine to thirteen fathoms. Several persons were now seen on foot and on horseback coming to the S.E. point above mentioned; from

[1] Point Bonita and Point Lobos, the N. and S. entrance points of the Golden Gate. They are about two miles apart. They appear on Vancouver's chart as N.W. Point and S.W. Point.

[2] Fort Point, the 'S.E. Point' on Vancouver's chart.

whence two guns were fired, and answered by us, agreeably to the signal established between Senr Quadra and myself. As the night soon closed in, a fire was made on the beach, and other guns were fired; but as we did not understand their meaning, and as the soundings continued regular, we steered up the port, under an easy sail, in constant expectation of seeing the lights of the town, off which I purposed to anchor: but as these were not discoverable at eight at night, and being then in a snug cove,[1] intirely land-locked, with six fathoms water and a clear bottom, we anchored to wait the return of day.

[1] The ships anchored in Yerba Buena Cove, now covered by reclaimed land. The location is shown on Vancouver's chart of the 'Entrance of Port St. Francisco'. They had rounded the N end of the peninsula now occupied by the city of San Francisco and had turned S in San Francisco Bay.

BOOK THE THIRD.

TRANSACTIONS AT TWO SPANISH SETTLEMENTS IN NEW
ALBION; EXAMINATION OF COLUMBIA RIVER; OCCUR-
RENCES ON BOARD THE DÆDALUS; SECOND VISIT TO
THE SANDWICH ISLANDS.

CHAPTER I.

Visited by a Priest and a Spanish Sergeant—The Commandant visits the Ship—
Account of the Missions of St. Francisco and St. Clara—Arrival of the Chatham—
Departure from St. Francisco—Meet the Dædalus at Monterrey.

THURSDAY morning, Nov. 15th, we discovered our anchorage to be in a most
excellent small bay, within three fourths of a mile of the nearest shore, bearing
by a compass south; one point of the bay bearing N. 56 W., the other S.
73 E. the former at the distance of 2½, the latter about 3 miles. The herds of
cattle and flocks of sheep grazing on the surrounding hills were a sight we
had long been strangers to, and brought to our minds many pleasing
reflections. These indicated that the residence of their proprietors could not be
far remote, though we could perceive neither habitations nor inhabitants. On
hoisting the colours at sun-rise, a gun was fired, and in a little time afterwards
several people were seen on horseback coming from behind the hills down
to the beach, who waved their hats, and made other signals for a boat, which
was immediately sent to the shore, and on its return I was favored with the
good company of a priest of the order of San Francisco, and a sergeant in
the Spanish army to breakfast. The reverend father expressed, and seemingly
with great sincerity, the pleasure he felt at our arrival, and assured me that
every refreshment and service in the power of himself or mission to bestow,
I might unreservedly command since it would be conferring on them all a
peculiar obligation to allow them to be serviceable. The sergeant expressed
himself in the most friendly manner, and informed me, that in the absence
of the commandant, he was directed on our arrival to render us every
accommodation the settlement could afford.

We attended them on shore after breakfast, where they embraced the earliest opportunity of proving, that their friendly expressions were not empty professions, by presenting me with a very fine ox, a sheep, and some excellent vegetables. The good friar, after pointing out the most convenient spot for procuring wood and water, and repeating the hospitable offers he had before made in the name of the fathers of the Franciscan order,[1] returned to the mission of San Francisco, which we understood was at no great distance, and to which he gave us the most pressing invitation.

From these gentlemen we learned, that the station we had taken was far within the general anchoring place of the Spanish vessels, which they said was off that part of the shore where the light was shewn and guns fired the preceding night on the beach, near the entrance into the port. Our situation was however perfectly commodious and suitable to all our purposes, and with permission of the sergeant, I directed a tent to be pitched for the accommodation of the party employed in procuring wood and water; whilst the rest of the crew were engaged on board in repairing the damages sustained in our sails, rigging, &c. during the tempestuous weather with which we had lately contended.

We amused ourselves with shooting a few quails on the adjacent hills, and in the afternoon returned on board to partake of the excellent repast which had been supplied by our hospitable friends. Whilst we were thus pleasantly engaged, our boat brought off father Antonio Danti,[2] the principal of the mission of St. Francisco, and Sen[r] Don Heamegildo Sal,[3] an ensign in the Spanish army, and commandant of the port. This gentleman, like those who visited us in the morning, met us with such warm expressions of friendship and good-will, as were not less deserving our highest commendations, than our most grateful acknowledgments.

The happiness they seemed to anticipate did not appear to arise so much from any pleasure they might derive in our society, as from the comforts and assistance which it was in their power to administer; this was manifested by all their actions, and by their expressing that our arrival had empowered them to execute a task the most accordant to their own wishes, as well as to the directions of their sovereign, which had been communicated to them and to the neighbouring settlements and missions.

From Sen[r] Sal I was made acquainted, that although the situation we had taken might answer our purposes in a certain degree, yet there was one which we had passed by the preceding evening, that we should find infinitely more commodious, as we should then be more immediately in his neighbourhood,

[1] In 1772 the Order of St. Francis of Assisi was granted the exclusive right to establish missions in Alta California. The Mission San Francisco de Asís, later known as the Mission Dolores, was founded in 1776.

[2] Father Danti had come to the mission from Mexico in 1790 and remained there until 1796.

[3] Ensign Hermenegildo Sal, described by Menzies as 'an elderly man' had come to San Francisco in 1776, the year the Presidio was established. He was acting commandant from the spring of 1791 until the middle of 1794.

and more frequent opportunities would be afforded him of rendering us service. In addition to the motive of his politeness, I was induced to comply with his wishes by the falling tide discovering to us a very great obstacle to our communication with that part of the shore from whence the wood and water were to be procured. A large bank of soft mud was found at low water to extend nearly half way between the ship and the shore.

I understood from these gentlemen that Senr Quadra still waited our arrival at Monterrey; I therefore intrusted to them a letter informing him of our arrival in this port, to which Senr Sal said an answer would most likely be procured in the course of three or four days. Having joined with us in drinking the healths of our royal masters, they took their leave and returned to the shore.

In the afternoon a fresh breeze from the S.E. sprang up, attended with rainy disagreeable weather, which continued during the night; the next morning we had a strong gale from the S. and S.W. with heavy squalls and much rain. Having no time to spare, and the pilot sent by Senr Sal being arrived, we proceeded under double-reefed top-sails to the general place of anchorage, which we reached by noon, and took our station about a quarter of a mile from the shore in five fathoms water; the outer anchor was in 13 fathoms soft muddy bottom. In this situation the S.E. and N.W. points of the passage into this port in a line, bore by compass S. 80 W. distant about half a mile. [1] The flag staff at the Presidio bore S. 42 E.

The little we had seen of Port St. Francisco enabled us to decide that it was very extensive in two directions; one spacious branch took its course east and southward to a great distance from the station we had quitted in the morning, [2] the other apparently of equal magnitude led to the northward. [3] In this were several islands. Although I had been informed by Senr Quadra that the boundaries of this inlet had been defined, yet I was anxious to be more particularly acquainted with its extent, having since been given to understand that Senr Quadra's information was by no means correct.

Near the branch leading to the east and south-eastward above mentioned, is situated the mission of Santa Clara. [4] These gentlemen informed me, that this branch had been thoroughly examined, but that the branch leading to the north never had. I was, however, obliged to remain contented under the uncertainty of such contradictory information; for the port having been established by Spain, I did not consider it prudent to prosecute its examination without sufficient authority for so doing; [5] nor was the weather favorable for

[1] Vancouver means that the SE point (Fort Point) was about half a mile to the W.

[2] San Francisco Bay.

[3] San Pablo Bay, Angel Island, Goat Island and the notorious Alcatraz Island are all shown on Vancouver's chart, but without names.

[4] Santa Clara is S of the S end of San Francisco Bay. The mission there was founded in 1777.

[5] Vancouver expressed his wish to explore the shores of San Pablo Bay; Menzies records that when he did so 'the Commandant readily acquiesced, & offerd any assistance that might

such an undertaking, though it did not prevent the exercise of those friendly
dispositions in the Spanish commandant, which he had before professed. He
had been some time on the beach in the rain before we anchored, for the
purpose of instantly affording us any assistance in his power to supply. A
message to this effect was brought by three of the native Indians who spoke
Spanish, and who came on board in a canoe of the country; which with
another, (though perhaps the same) seen crossing the harbour the evening we
entered it, were the only Indian vessels we had met with, and were without
exception the most rude and sorry contrivances for embarkation I had ever
beheld. The length of them was about ten feet, the breadth about three or
four; they were constructed of rushes and dried grass of a long broad leaf,
made up into rolls the length of the canoe, the thickest in the middle, and
regularly tapering to a point at each end. These are so disposed, that on their
ends being secured and lashed together the vessel is formed, which being
broadest in the middle, and coming to a point at each extremity, goes with
either end foremost. These rolls are laid and fastened so close to each other,
that in calm weather and smooth water I believe them to be tolerably dry,
but they appeared to be very ill calculated to contend with wind and waves.
The wind now blew strong with heavy squalls from the S.W. and in the middle
of this spacious inlet the sea broke with much force; notwithstanding which,
as soon as these people had delivered their message, they crossed the inlet for
the purpose of catching fish, without seeming to entertain the least apprehension
for their safety. They conducted their canoe or vessel by long double-bladed
paddles, like those used by the Esquimaux. [1]

The S.W. wind attended by much rain, blew very hard until Saturday
morning the 17th, when the weather becoming more moderate I visited the
shore. I was greatly mortified to find that neither wood nor water could be
procured with such convenience, nor of so good a quality, as at the station

be necessary from the Settlement to accomplish it; but on mentioning this business to Sn.
Quadra after we arrived at Monterrey, that Gentleman said that he had no other objection
than the trouble it would give without any utility, as their extent had been already
ascertained in a journey by land, by a party who rode round the head of them a little above
where they terminate on Mr. Dalrymple's plan of the Harbour, which we found to be
a very exact representation as far as we had occasion to consult it.' – 24 November. The
plan referred to would be the *Plan of Port St. Francisco*, 'From a Spanish MS. Communicated
by John Henry Cox Esqr.', published by Dalrymple in 1789, not the less accurate map
printed in 1790. This gives a fair representation of the general shape and extent of San Pablo
Bay, but does not extend as far E as the mouth of the Sacramento River. By contrast, the
outline of San Francisco Bay is wildly inaccurate. A company of priests and soldiers from
the new establishments at San Francisco had visited the N and S arms of San Pablo Bay
in 1776, but no detailed survey had been made.

[1] This is a good description of the 'tule balsa, a shaped raft of rushes', the type of boat
used by the Costanoan Indians and many other tribes over a wide area of California. For
an illustration see R. F. Heizer and M. A. Whipple (comps. and eds.), *The California
Indians: A Source Book* (2nd ed., Berkeley and Los Angeles, 1971), p. 10. All the natives
encountered by members of the Vancouver expedition on this first visit to California were
Castanoan Indians.

we had quitted a league and a half within the entrance of the port on the southern shore; but as our Spanish friends had informed us that the water here was far superior in its quality to that of Monterrey, there was now no alternative but that of taking what the country afforded. A tent was immediately pitched on the shore, wells were dug for obtaining water,[1] and a party was employed in procuring fuel from small bushy holly-leaved oaks, the only trees fit for our purpose. A lagoon of seawater was between the beach and the spot on which these trees grew, which rendered the conveying the wood when cut a very laborious operation.

Whilst engaged in allotting to the people their different employments, some saddled horses arrived from the commandant with a very cordial invitation to his habitation; which was accepted by myself and some of the officers. We rode up to the Presidio, an appellation given to their military establishments in this country,[2] and signifying a *safe-guard*. The residence of the friars is called a Mission. We soon arrived at the Presidio, which was not more than a mile from our landing place. Its wall, which fronted the harbour, was visible from the ships; but instead of the city or town, whose lights we had so anxiously looked for on the night of our arrival, we were conducted into a spacious verdant plain, surrounded by hills on every side, excepting that which fronted the port. The only object of human industry which presented itself, was a square area, whose sides were about two hundred yards in length, enclosed by a mud wall, and resembling a pound for cattle.[3] Above this wall the thatched roofs of their low small houses just made their appearance. On entering the Presidio, we found one of its sides still uninclosed by the wall, and very indifferently fenced in by a few bushes here and there, fastened to stakes in the ground. The unfinished state of this part, afforded us an opportunity of seeing the strength of the wall, and the manner in which it was constructed. It is about fourteen feet high, and five feet in breadth, and was first formed by uprights and horizontal rafters of large timber, between which dried sods and moistened earth were pressed as close and as hard as possible; after which the whole was cased with the earth made into a sort of mud plaster, which gave it the appearance of durability, and of being sufficiently strong to protect them, with the assistance of their fire-arms, against all the force which the natives of the country might be able to collect.

---

[1] 'The watering party who landed before us could meet with no fresh water stream, they were therefore obliged to dig a Well in the Marsh to fill their Casks from, but the Water thus procur'd was afterwards found to be a little brackish, which might indeed be expected from the nature of the Soil which was loose & sandy, & the little distance it was from the sea on the one side & salt water ponds on the other.' – Menzies, 17 November.

[2] 'What was pompously called by this name had but a mean appearance at a distance & a near approach did not at all contribute to make its appearance more favorable.' – Menzies, 17 November.

[3] Menzies estimated that the Presidio 'occupied a square space of ground about four hundred yards on each side, walled in on three sides with Turf or Mortar Wall...' – 17 November.

Plate 33. 'The Mission of St. Carlos, near Monterrey.'

Plate 34. 'The Presidio of Monterrey.'

The Spanish soldiers composing the garrison amounted, I understood, to thirty-five;[1] who, with their wives, families, and few Indian servants, composed the whole of the inhabitants. Their houses were along the wall, within the square, and their fronts uniformly extended the same distance into the area, which is a clear open space, without buildings or other interruptions. The only entrance into it, is by a large gateway; facing which, and against the centre of the opposite wall or side, is the church; which, though small, was neat in comparison to the rest of the buildings. This projects further into the square than the houses, and is distinguishable from the other edifices, by being white-washed with lime made from sea-shells; lime-stone or calcareous earth not having yet been discovered in the neighbourhood. On the left of the church, is the commandant's house, consisting, I believe, of two rooms and a closet only, which are divided by massy walls, similar to that which encloses the square, and communicating with each other by very small doors. Between these apartments and the outward wall was an excellent poultry house and yard, which seemed pretty well stocked; and between the roof and ceilings of the rooms was a kind of lumber garret: those were all the conveniencies the habitation seemed calculated to afford. The rest of the houses, though smaller, were fashioned exactly after the same manner;[2] and in the winter, or rainy seasons, must at the best be very uncomfortable dwellings. For though the walls are a sufficient security against the inclemency of the weather, yet the windows, which are cut in the front wall, and look into the square, are destitute of glass, or any other defence that does not at the same time exclude the light.

The apartment in the commandant's house, into which we were ushered, was about thirty feet long, fourteen feet broad, and twelve feet high; and the other room, or chamber, I judged to be of the same dimensions, excepting in its length, which appeared to be somewhat less. The floor was of the native soil raised about three feet from its original level, without being boarded, paved, or even reduced to an even surface: the roof was covered in with flags and rushes, the walls on the inside had once been whitewashed; the furniture consisted of a very sparing assortment of the most indispensible articles, of the rudest fashion, and of the meanest kind; and ill accorded with the ideas we had conceived of the sumptuous manner in which the Spaniards live on this side of the globe.

It would, however, be the highest injustice, notwithstanding that elegancies were wanting, not to acknowledge the very cordial reception and hearty welcome we experienced from our worthy host; who had provided a

[1] Puget estimated that the total military strength of the garrison was 'a Company consisting of Sixty Effective Men and Officers, from it they Afford Protection to the Missions of St. Francisco and Sta Clara, to each a Corporals Guard is sent to protect the Padres from the violence of the Neighbouring Indians.' – November.

[2] One of the Spanish adobe buildings has survived and is now the Officers' Club at the Presidio.

refreshing repast, and such an one as he thought likely to be most acceptable at that time of the day; nor was his lady less assiduous, nor did she seem less happy than himself in entertaining her new guests.

On approaching the house we found this good lady, who, like her spouse, had passed the middle age of life, decently dressed, seated cross-legged on a mat, placed on a small square wooden platform raised three or four inches from the ground, nearly in front of the door, with two daughers and a son, clean and decently dressed, sitting by her; this being the mode observed by these ladies when they receive visitors. The decorous and pleasing behaviour of the children was really admirable, and exceeded any thing that could have been expected from them under the circumstances of their situation, without any other advantages than the education and example of their parents; which however seemed to have been studiously attended to, and did them great credit. This pleasing sight added to the friendly reception of our host and hostess, rendered their lowly residence no longer an object of our attention; and having partaken of the refreshments they had provided, we re-mounted our horses in order to take a view of the surrounding country before we returned on board to dinner, where Senr Sal and his family had promised to favor me with their good company, and who had requested my permission to increase their party by the addition of some other ladies in the garrison.

Our excursion did not extend far from the Presidio, which is situated as before described in a plain surrounded by hills. This plain is by no means a dead flat, but of unequal surface; the soil is of a sandy nature, and was wholly under pasture, on which were grazing several flocks of sheep and herds of cattle; the sides of the surrounding hills, though but moderately elevated, seemed barren, or nearly so; and their summits were composed of naked uneven rocks. Two small spaces in the plain, very insecurely inclosed, were appropriated to kitchen gardens; much labour did not appear to have been bestowed either in the improvement of the soil, in selecting the quality of the vegetables, or in augmenting their produce; the several seeds once placed in the ground, nature was left to do the rest without receiving any assistance from manual labour.

Senr Sal having been made acquainted with the difficulties we had to encounter in removing our wood to the sea side, politely offered us the carts he had for the use of the Presidio; but on their being produced, I was greatly disappointed, as they were by no means so well calculated as the miserable straw canoes for the service they were intended to perform.

Thus, at the expence of very little examination, though not without much disappointment, was our curiosity satisfied concerning the Spanish town and settlement of St. Francisco. Instead of finding a country tolerably well inhabited and far advanced in cultivation, if we except its natural pastures, the flocks of sheep, and herds of cattle, there is not an object to indicate the most remote connection with any European, or other civilized nation.

This sketch will be sufficient, without further comment, to convey some idea of the inactive spirit of the people, and the unprotected state of the establishment at this port, which I should conceive ought to be a principal object of the Spanish crown, as a key and barrier to their more southern and valuable settlements on the borders of the north Pacific. Should my idea of its importance be over-rated, certain it is, that considered solely as an establishment, which must have been formed at considerable expence, it possesses no other means for its protection than such as have been already described; with a brass three-pounder mounted on a rotten carriage before the Presidio, and a similar piece of ordnance which (I was told) was at the S.E. point of entrance lashed to a log instead of a carriage;[1] and was the gun whose report we heard the evening of our arrival. Before the Presidio there had formerly been two pieces of ordnance, but one of them had lately burst to pieces.

The examination of these few objects, and the consequent observations upon them, occupied our leisure until dinner time, when we returned on board, accompanyied by Senr Sal, his wife, and party, and one of the fathers of the mission of St. Francisco, Martin de Landaeta, who brought me a pressing and polite invitation from his brethren, and who proved to be a very pleasing and entertaining acquisition to our society.

The next day, Sunday the 18th, was appointed for my visiting the mission. Accompanied by Mr. Menzies and some of the officers, and our friendly Senr Sal, I rode thither to dinner. Its distance from the Presidio is about a league, in an easterly direction; our ride was rendered unpleasant by the soil being very loose and sandy, and by the road being much incommoded with low groveling bushes.[2]

Its situation and external appearance in a great measure resembled that of the Presidio; and, like its neighbourhood, the country was pleasingly diversified with hill and dale. The hills were at a greater distance from each other, and gave more extent to the plain, which is composed of a soil infinitely

[1] Menzies was his informant; he relates that he visited Fort Point '& to my great surprise found on this formidable eminence which perfectly commanded the entrance of the Harbour only a single piece of Artillery & that lash'd to a log of wood. It was a Brass Cannon of two or three pounders & I believe the only one which the whole Settlement could boast of.' – 20 November. The Spaniards were evidently concerned about the undefended state of San Francisco. Guns were sent up from San Blas in 1793, and in 1794 Castillo de San Juan was built on Fort Point.

[2] The two young Hawaiian women were included in the party 'as it was thought that the novelty of a short ride might be pleasing.... Hitherto these women had only been distant spectators of the Country & its produce, Black Cattle they had some idea of from having seen a few of them at Nootka, but Horses & the fleetness with which they saw them carry people about on their backs produced much admiration & afforded a fertile theme for conversation between them since they came into this Port; the proposal of a ride therefore much excited their curiosity & was readily accepted, & we no sooner landed than they mounted on Horse-back & kept their Seats throughout the journey without shewing the least sign of fear or timidity, in short with as much ease & apparent satisfaction as if they had been brought up or accustomd to such mode of conveyance from their infancy.' – Menzies, 18 November.

richer than that of the Presidio, being a mixture of sand and a black vegetable mould. The pastures bore a more luxuriant herbage, and fed a greater number of sheep and cattle.[1] The barren sandy country through which we had passed, seemed to make a natural division between the lands of the mission and those of the Presidio, and extends from the shores of the port to the foot of a ridge of mountains, which border on the exterior coast, and appear to stretch in a line parallel to it. The verdure of the plain continued to a considerable height up the sides of these hills; the summits of which, though still composed of rugged rocks, produced a few trees.

The buildings of the mission formed two sides of a square only, and did not appear as if intended, at any future time, to form a perfect quadrangle like the Presidio. The architecture and materials, however, seemed nearly to correspond.

On our arrival, we were received by the reverend fathers with every demonstration of cordiality, friendship, and the most genuine hospitality. We were instantly conducted to their mansion, which was situated near, and communicated with the church. The houses formed a small oblong-square, the side of the church composed one end, near which were the apartments allotted to the fathers. These were constructed neatly after the manner of those at the Presidio, but appeared to be more finished, better contrived, were larger, and much more cleanly. Along the walls of this interior square, were also many other apartments adapted to various purposes.

Whilst dinner was preparing, our attention was engaged in seeing the several houses within the square. Some were found appropriated to the reception of grain, of which, however, they had not a very abundant stock; nor was the place of its growth within sight of the mission; though the richness of the contiguous soil seemed equal to all the purposes of husbandry. One large room was occupied by manufacturers of a coarse sort of blanketting, made from the wool produced in the neighbourhood. The looms, though rudely wrought, were tolerably well contrived, and had been made by the Indians, under the immediate direction and superintendance of the fathers; who, by the same assiduity, had carried the manufacture thus far into effect. The produce resulting from their manufactory is wholly applied to the clothing of the converted Indians. I saw some of the cloth, which was by no means despicable; and, had it received the advantage of fulling, would have been a very decent sort of clothing. The preparation of the wool, as also the spinning and weaving of it, was, I understood, performed by unmarried women and female children, who were all resident within the square, and were in a state of conversion to the Roman Catholic persuasion. Besides manufacturing the wool, they are also instructed in a variety of necessary, useful, and beneficial employments

[1] Vancouver makes no mention of wild life, but Manby, the sportsman, found good hunting: 'About a Mile from the [Mission] House, I found most excellent shooting on a large Lagoon of fresh Water [the Laguna de los Dolores], in an hour I loaded my Horse with all kind of Wild fowl...' – Letters, 23 November.

until they marry, which is greatly encouraged; when they retire from the tuition of the fathers to the hut of their husband. By these means it is expected that their doctrines will be firmly established, and rapidly propagated; and the trouble they now have with their present untaught flock will be hereafter recompenced, by having fewer prejudices to combat in the rising generation. They likewise consider their plan as essentially necessary, in a political point of view, for insuring their own safety. The women and girls being the dearest objects of affection amongst these Indians, the Spaniards deem it expedient to retain constantly a certain number of females immediately within their power, as a pledge for the fidelity of the men, and as a check on any improper designs the natives might attempt to carry into execution, either against the missionaries, or the establishment in general.

By various encouragements and allurements to the children, or their parents, they can depend upon having as many to bring up in this way as they require: there they are well fed, better clothed than the Indians in the neighbourhood, are kept clean, instructed, and have every necessary care taken of them; and in return for these advantages they must submit to certain regulations; amongst which, they are not suffered to go out of the interior square in the day time without permission; are never to sleep out of it at night; and to prevent elopements, this square has no communication with the country but by one common door, which the fathers themselves take care of, and see that it is well secured every evening, and also the apartments of the women, who generally retire immediately after supper.

If I am correctly informed by the different Spanish gentlemen with whom I conversed on this subject, the uniform, mild, and kind-hearted disposition of this religious order, has never failed to attach to their interest the affections of the natives, wherever they sat down amongst them; this is a very happy circumstance, for their situation otherwise would be excessively precarious; as they are protected only by five soldiers who reside under the directions of a corporal, in the buildings of the mission at some distance on the other side of the church.

The establishment must certainly be considered as liable to some danger. Should these children of nature be ever induced to act an ungrateful and treacherous part, they might easily conceal sufficient weapons to effect any evil purpose.—There are only three fathers,[1] these live by themselves, and should any attempt be made upon them at night, the very means they have adopted for security might deprive them of any assistance from the guard until it might be too late; and individually, they could make but little resistance. Should a conspiracy for their destruction take place, the mission would soon

---

[1] Menzies states that there were 'two Fathers' and the list of priests given by Zephryin Englehardt in his *San Francisco or Mission Dolores* (Chicago, 1924) indicates that only Fathers Danti and Landaeta were at the mission at the time of Vancouver's visit. However, Father Diego Noboa visited the mission occasionally, and Vancouver may have been so informed and have included him.

fall, and there would be little doubt of the conspirators being joined by the Indians of the village, which is in the vicinity of the mission, and was said to contain six hundred persons, but on visiting it, I considered their number greatly over-rated. The major part of them, I understood, were converted to the Roman Catholic persuasion; but I was astonished to observe how few advantages had attended their conversion.

They seemed to have treated with the most perfect indifference the precepts, and laborious example, of their truly worthy and benevolent pastors; whose object has been to allure them from their life of indolence, and raise in them a spirit of emulous industry; which, by securing to them plenty of food and the common conveniences of life, would necessarily augment their comforts, and encourage them to seek and embrace the blessings of civilized society. Deaf to the important lessons, and insensible of the promised advantages, they still remained in the most abject state of uncivilization; and if we except the inhabitants of Tierra del Fuego, and those of Van Dieman's land, they are certainly a race of the most miserable beings, possessing the faculty of human reason, I ever saw. Their persons, generally speaking, were under the middle size, and very ill made; their faces ugly, presenting a dull, heavy, and stupid countenance, devoid of sensibility or the least expression. One of their greatest aversions is cleanliness, both in their persons and habitations; which, after the fashion of their forefathers, were still without the most trivial improvement. Their houses were of a conical form, about six or seven feet in diameter at their base (which is the ground) and are constructed by a number of stakes, chiefly of the willow tribe, which are driven erect into the earth in a circular manner, the upper ends of which being small and pliable are brought nearly to join at the top, in the centre of the circle; and these being securely fastened, give the upper part or roof somewhat of a flattish appearance. Thinner twigs of the like species are horizontally interwoven between the uprights, forming a piece of basket work about ten or twelve feet high; at the top a small aperture is left, which allows the smoke of the fire made in the centre of the hut to escape,[1] and admits most of the light they receive: the entrance is by a small hole close to the ground, through which with difficulty one person at a time can gain admittance. The whole is covered over with a thick thatch of dried grass and rushes.

These miserable habitations, each of which was allotted for the residence of a whole family, were erected with some degree of uniformity, about three or four feet asunder, in straight rows, leaving lanes or passages at right angles between them; but these were so abominably infested with every kind of filth and nastiness, as to be rendered not less offensive than degrading to the human species.

[1] Menzies' account differs somewhat: 'Their Habitations or Wigwams were aptly compared to a crowded cluster of Bee-hives...The Fire is placd in the middle of the Wigwam & as no particular aperture is left at the top for the smoke to go out at, it was observd oozing through the Thatch.' – 18 November.

Close by stood the church, which for its magnitude, architecture, and internal decorations, did great credit to the constructors of it; and presented a striking contrast between the exertions of genius and such as bare necessity is capable of suggesting.[1] The raising and decorating this edifice appeared to have greatly attracted the attention of the fathers; and the comforts they might have provided in their own humble habitations, seemed to have been totally sacrified to the accomplishment of this favorite object. Even their garden, an object of such material importance, had not yet acquired any great degree of cultivation, though its soil was a rich black mould, and promised an ample return for any labour that might be bestowed upon it. The whole contained about four acres, was tolerably well fenced in, and produced some fig, peach, apple, and other fruit-trees, but afforded a very scanty supply of useful vegetables; the principal part lying waste and over-run with weeds.

On our return to the convent, we found a most excellent and abundant repast provided of beef, mutton, fish, fowls, and such vegetables as their garden afforded. The attentive and hospitable behaviour of our new friends amply compensated for the homely manner in which the dinner was served; and would certainly have precluded my noticing the distressing inconvenience these valuable people labour under, in the want of almost all the common and most necessary utensils of life, had I not been taught to expect, that this colony was in a very different stage of improvement, and that its inhabitants were infinitely more comfortably circumstanced.

After dinner we were engaged in an entertaining conversation, in which, by the assistance of Mr. Dobson our interpreter, we were each able to bear a part. Amongst other things I understood that this mission was established in the year 1775, and the Presidio of St. Francisco in 1778,[2] and that they were the *northernmost settlements, of any description, formed by the court of Spain on the continental shore of North-West America, or the islands adjacent,* exclusive of Nootka, which I did not consider as coming under that description any more than the temporary establishment which, in the preceding spring had been formed by Senʳ Quadra near Cape Flattery, at the entrance of the straits of Juan De Fuca; and which has been already stated to be entirely evacuated. The excursions of the Spaniards seemed to be confined to the neighbourhood of their immediate place of residence, and the direct line of country betwen one station and another; as they have no vessels for embarkation excepting the native canoe, and an old rotten wooden one, which was lying near our landing place. Had they proper boats on this spacious sheet of water, their journies would not only be much facilitated, but it would afford a very agreeable variety in their manner of life, and help to pass away many of the solitary and wearisome hours which they must unavoidably experience. I understand that

[1] This church, a massive stone building, which is still in existence, replaced a first temporary structure. Construction began in 1782 and it was dedicated in 1791, only a year before Vancouver's visit.

[2] Vancouver was misinformed. As already noted, both were established in 1776.

the opposite side of the port had been visited by some soldiers on horseback, who obtained but little information; some converted Indians were found living amongst the natives of the northern and western parts of the port, who were esteemed by the Spaniards to be a docile, and in general a well-disposed people; though little communication took place between them and the inhabitants of this side. The missionaries found no difficulty in subjecting these people to their authority. It is mild and charitable, teaches them the cultivation of the soil, and introduces amongst them such of the useful arts as are most essential to the comforts of human nature and social life. It is much to be wished, that these benevolent exertions may succeed, though there is every appearance that their progress will be very slow; yet they will probably lay a foundation, on which the posterity of the present race may secure to themselves the enjoyment of civil society.

The next establishment of this nature, and the only one within our reach from our present station, was that of Sta Clara, lying to the south-eastward, at the distance of about eighteen leagues, and considered as one day's journey. As there was no probability of our wood and water being completely on board in less than three or four days, I accepted the offer of Senr Sal and the reverend fathers, who undertook to provide us horses for an expedition to Sta Clara the following morning. At the decline of day we took our leave, and concluded a visit that had been highly interesting and entertaining to us, and had appeared to be equally grateful to our hospitable friends.

On my return to the Presidio, I was favored with a polite reply from Senr Quadra; in which he informed me, that neither the Chatham nor the Dædalus had yet arrived at Monterrey, but that on their reaching that port, I might rely on their receiving every assistance and service in his power to bestow; and trusted it would not be long ere the Discovery would rejoin them at Monterrey.

During the night, the wind from the S.W. blew a strong gale, and continued with much rain until Tuesday morning the 20th; when the weather being serene and pleasant, we undertook our journey to Sta Clara.[1] We called in our way on our friends at the Presidio and mission, with whose company we were to have been favored; but in consequence of some dispatches received by Senr Sal which required his immediate attention, and of the indisposition of one of the fathers, they begged leave to decline the engagement; we therefore, agreeably with the fashion of the country, sat out, attended by a drove of spare horses, more than double the number of our party, under the guidance of the serjeant of the Presidio, who was accompanied by six stout

---

[1] 'Capt. Vancouver Lts. Puget, Baker & Johnstone Messrs Orchard Stewart & Dobson went on Shore early in the morning mounted their Horses on the Beach & set out for Sta. Clara. The state of my health at this time for bade my undergoing much fatigue, otherwise I should willingly have accompanied them on this journey.' – Menzies, 20 November. Menzies afterwards borrowed Johnstone's journal and copied much of his account of the visit to Santa Clara into his own journal.

active soldiers, fully accoutered for our protection and for affording us such assistance as we might require.[1]

We considered our route to be parallel with the sea coast; between which and our path, the ridge of mountains before-mentioned extended to the south-eastward; and as we advanced, their sides and summits exhibited a high degree of luxuriant fertility, interspersed with copses of various forms and magnitude, verdant open spaces, and enriched with stately forest trees of different descriptions. The plain on which we rode stretched from the base of these mountains to the shores of the port, and gradually improved as we proceeded. The holly-leaved oak, maple horse-chestnut, and willow, were increased from dwarf shrubs to trees of tolerable size, having some of the common English dwarf oak scattered amongst them.

Our journey was estimated at 18 leagues, in which distance the country afforded no house, hut, nor any place of shelter excepting such as the spreading trees presented. About noon, having then advanced about twenty-three miles, we arrived at a very pleasant and enchanting lawn, situated amidst a grove of trees at the foot of a small hill, by which flowed a very fine stream of excellent water. This delightful pasture was nearly inclosed on every side, and afforded sufficient space for resting ourselves and baiting our cavalry.[2] The bank which overhung the murmuring brook was well adapted for taking the refreshment which our provident friends had supplied: and with some grog we had brought from the ship, (spirits and wine being scarce articles in this country) we all made a most excellent meal; but it required some resolution to quit so lively a scene, the beauty of which was greatly heightened by the delightful serenity of the weather. To this, however, after resting about an hour, we were obliged to submit, when a fresh supply of cavalry being selected from the drove of horses, we mounted and pursued our journey.[3]

[1] The party had an escort of 'a Serjeant & four soldiers to guard guide & attend them with about forty horses that were drove after them to change or relieve them that might be tired.' Menzies, 22 November, basing his remarks on Johnstone's account. Puget agrees that there were four soldiers, not six. Manby (who was not one of the party but no doubt had seen the soldiers) describes their equipment: 'the travelling Regimentals of these Men, consists of a Coat of Mail made of Moose Deerskin, the Breast of the Horse is guarded with the same, which effectually turn an Arrow, Skirmishes often take place, with wandering Tribes, but as the Spaniards, are most excellent horsemen, and each Armed with a Musquet, a pair of Pistols, Sword and Lance, they destroy without Mercy, and are in general Victorious.' – Manby, Letters, November.

[2] i.e., giving food and water to the horses.

[3] The ride was much longer than expected; Johnstone, amongst others, had understood that the distance was 18 miles, not 18 leagues, and the unaccustomed form of exercise took its toll of the sailors. 'By Dismounting all were tired, some sore, but good humour prevaild in the highest degree, those who limpd the most laughd at their own pains & gave mirth to the rest.' After the luncheon break the party set off at a gallop, mounted on fresh horses, but 'from the stiffness & attitudes of some of the Riders it was evident that their bodies wishd for a more moderate pace, but this could not be allowd, for they were scarcely half way.' When the party finally arrived at Santa Clara 'Mr. Baker & Mr. Johnstone were so ill, that they were immediately obligd to go to bed...' – Menzies, 22 November.

We had not proceeded far from this delightful spot, when we entered a country I little expected to find in these regions. For about twenty miles it could only be compared to a park, which had originally been closely planted with the true old English oak; the underwood, that had probably attended its early growth, had the appearance of having been cleared away, and had left the stately lords of the forest in complete possession of the soil, which was covered with luxuriant herbage, and beautifully diversified with pleasing eminences and vallies; which, with the range of lofty rugged mountains that bounded the prospect, required only to be adorned with the neat habitations of an industrious people, to produce a scene not inferior to the most studied effect of taste in the disposal of grounds; especially when seen from the port or its confines, the waters of which extend some distance by the side of this country; and though they were not visible to us, I was inclined to believe they approached within about a league of the road we pursued. Our riding was attended with some inconvenience, on account of the fox earths, and burrows of rabbits, squirrels, rats, and other animals;[1] but our sure-footed horses avoided every danger, notwithstanding we rode at a brisk rate. Having passed through this imaginary park, we advanced a few miles in an open clear meadow, and arrived in a low swampy country; through which our progress was very slow, the horses being nearly knee-deep in mud and water for about six miles. The badness of our road rendered this part of our journey somewhat unpleasant. About dark we reached better ground, and soon after the night closed in, we arrived at the mission of Sta Clara, which according to my estimation is about forty geographical miles from St. Francisco. Our journey, excepting that part of it through the morass, had been very pleasant and entertaining; and our reception at Sta Clara by the hospitable fathers of the mission, was such as excited in every breast the most lively sensations of gratitude and regard. Father Thomas de la Pena[2] appeared to be the principal of the missionaries. The anxious solicitude of this gentleman, and that of his colleague Father Joseph Sanchez,[3] to anticipate all our wishes, unequivocally manifested the principles by which their conduct was regulated. Our evening passed very pleasantly, and after a most excellent breakfast next morning, the 21st, on tea and chocolate, we took a view of the establishment and the adjacent country.

[1] This is the only reference Vancouver makes to wild life, but Manby, interested in hunting, secured other details from members of the party: 'Foxes were so numerous, that scarce an hour past without seeing dozens, and the air was oftened [sic] darkened by the large flocks of Wild Geese; not being accustomed to be molested, they suffered themselves to be approached within half a dozen yards, before they rose, numbers of Deer were seen, and the Soldiers report Bears innumerable, inhabit the Woods and Mountains.' – Manby, Letters, November.

[2] Father Tomás de la Peña. Menzies, following Johnstone, describes him as being 'a very corpulent man, far advanced in Years & of a most venerable appearance, yet he trudgd about in the most lively manner to administer every comfort to his guests.' – 22 November.

[3] Father José Sanchez, a man of great ability; later president of the California missions.

The buildings and offices of this mission, like those of St. Francisco, form a square, but not an entire inclosure. It is situated in an extensive fertile plain, the soil of which, as also that of the surrounding country, is a rich black productive mould, superior to any I had before seen in America. The particular spot which had been selected by the reverend fathers, for their establishment, did not appear so suitable to their purpose as many other parts of the plain within a little distance of their present buildings, which are erected in a low marshy situation for the sake of being near a run of fine water; notwithstanding that within a few hundred yards they might have built their houses on dry and comfortable eminences.

The stream of water passes close by the walls of the fathers apartments, which are upon the same plan with those of St. Francisco; built near, and communicating with the church, but appearing to be more extensive, and to possess in some degree more comforts, or rather less inconveniences, than those already described. The church was long and lofty, and as well built as the rude materials of which it is composed would allow; and when compared with the unimproved state of the country, infinitely more decorated than might have been reasonably expected.

Apartments within the square in which the priests resided, were appropriated to a number of young female Indians; and the like reasons were given as at St. Francisco for their being so selected and educated. Their occupations were the same, though some of their woollen manufactures surpassed those we had before seen, and wanted only the operation of fulling, with which the fathers were unacquainted, to make them very decent blankets. The upper story of their interior oblong square, which might be about one hundred and seventy feet long, and one hundred feet broad, were made use of as granaries, as were some of the lower rooms; all of which were well stored with corn and pulse of different sorts; and besides these, in case of fire, there were two spacious warehouses for the reception of grain detached from each other, and the rest of the buildings, erected at a convenient distance from the mission. These had been recently finished, contained some stores, and were to be kept constantly full, as a reserve in the event of such a misfortune.[1]

They cultivate wheat, maize, peas and beans; the latter are produced in great variety, and the whole in greater abundance than their necessities require. Of these several sorts they had many thousand bushels in store, of very excellent quality, which had been obtained with little labour, and without manure. By the help of a very mean, and ill contrived plough drawn by oxen, the earth is once slightly turned over, and smoothed down by a harrow; in the month

---

[1] Menzies gives some additional details, based on Johnstone's account: 'There were a number of other houses adjacent to the Mission for Artificers, & twelve or fifteen Soldiers with their Families under the Command of an Alferez or Ensign & a corporal., which are deem'd necessary for the protection of the Mission, but it is further protected by its vicinity to the Town of St. Joseph [San José] which is but a short distance to the Southward and Eastward of it & contains about four hundred Spaniards, chiefly old Soldiers & their Families...' – 22 November.

of November or December, the wheat is sown in drills, or broad cast on the even surface, and scratched in with the harrow; this is the whole of their system of husbandry, which uniformly produces them in July or August an abundant harvest. The maize, peas, and beans, are produced with as little labour; these are sown in the spring months, and succeed extremely well, as do hemp and flax, or linseed. The wheat affords in general from twenty-five to thirty for one according to the seasons, twenty-five for one being the least return they have ever yet deposited in their granaries from the field; notwithstanding the enormous waste occasioned by their rude method of threshing, which is always performed in the open air by the treading of cattle. The product of the other grains and pulse bears a similar proportion to that of the wheat. I was much surprised to find that neither barley nor oats were cultivated; on enquiry I was given to understand, that as the superior kinds of grain could be plentifully obtained with the same labour that the inferior ones would require, they had some time ago declined the cultivation of them. The labours of the field are performed under the immediate inspection of the fathers, by the natives who are instructed in the Roman Catholic faith, and taught the art of husbandry. The annual produce is taken under the care of these worthy pastors, who distribute it in such quantities to the several persons as completely answers all the useful and necessary purposes.

Besides a few acres of arable land, which we saw under cultivation near the mission, was a small spot of garden ground, producing several sorts of vegetables in great perfection and abundance. The extent of it, however, like the garden at St. Francisco, appeared unequal to the consumption of the European residents; the priests, and their guard consisting of a corporal and six soldiers. Here were planted peaches, apricots, apples, pears, figs, and vines, all of which excepting the latter promised to succeed very well. The failure of the vines here, as well as at St. Francisco, is ascribed to a want of knowledge in their culture; the soil and climate being well adapted to most sorts of fruit.[1] Of this we had many evidences in the excellence of its natural unassisted productions. In this country the oak, as timber, appears to take the lead. A tree of this description near the establishment measured fifteen feet in girth, and was high in proportion, but was not considered by the fathers as of an extraordinary size; and I am convinced, that on our journey we passed several oaks of greater magnitude. The timber of these trees is reputed to be equal in quality to any produced in Europe. The elm, ash, beech, birch, and some variety of pines, grew in the interior and more elevated parts of the country in the greatest luxuriance and abundance.

Our attention was next called to the village of the Indians near the mission. The habitations were not so regularly disposed, nor did it contain so many, as the village at St. Francisco; yet the same horrid state of uncleanliness and laziness seemed to pervade the whole. A sentiment of compassion involuntarily

[1] The flourishing wine industry now existing in California proves the truth of this opinion.

obtruded on the mind in contemplating the natural or habitual apathy to all kind of exertion in this humble race. There was scarcely any sign in their general deportment of their being at all benefited, or of having added one single ray of comfort to their own wretched condition, by the precepts and laborious exertions of their religious instructors; whose lives are sacrificed to their welfare, and who seem entirely devoted to the benevolent office of rendering them a better and a happier people. They appeared totally insensible to the benefits with which they were provided, excepting in the article of food; this they now find ready at hand, without the labour of procuring it, or being first reduced by cold and hunger nearly to a state of famine, and then being obliged to expose themselves to great inconvenience in quest of a precarious, and often scanty means of subsistence. Not only grain, but the domestic animals have been introduced with success amongst them; many of the natives have, by the unremitted labour of the fathers, been taught to manufacture very useful and comforable garments from the wool of their sheep; for the introduction of this animal they ought to be highly grateful, since by the mildness of the climate, and the fertility of the soil, they are easily propagated and reared; and while they provide them with comfortable clothing, afford them also nourishing and delicate food. These advantages however seemed to have operated as yet to little purpose on the minds of these untaught children of nature, who appeared to be a compound of stupidity and innocence; their passions are calm; and regardless of reputation as men, or renown as a people, they are stimulated neither to the obtaining of consequence amongst themselves by any peaceful arts, nor superiority over their neighbours by warlike achievements, so common amongst the generality of the Indian tribes. All the operations and functions both of body and mind, appeared to be carried on with a mechanical, lifeless, careless indifference; and as the Spaniards assert they found them in the same state of inactivity and ignorance on their earliest visits, this disposition is probably inherited from their forefathers.

Further efforts are now making at this mission, to break through the gloomy cloud of insensibility in which at present these people are inveloped, by giving them new habitations; an indulgence that will most probably be followed by others, as their minds appear capable of receiving them. A certain number of the most intelligent, tractable, and industrious persons, were selected from the group, and were employed in a pleasant and well-adapted spot of land facing the mission, under the direction and instruction of the fathers, in building for themselves a range of small, but comparatively speaking comfortable and convenient habitations. The walls, though not so thick, are constructed in the same manner with those described in the square at St. Francisco, and the houses are formed after the European fashion, each consisting of two commodious rooms below, with garrets over them. At the back of each house a space of ground is inclosed, sufficient for cultivating a large quantity of vegetables, for rearing poultry, and for other useful and domestic purposes. The buildings were in a state of forwardness, and when finished, each house was designed to accommodate one distinct family only; and it is greatly to be wished, for the credit of the rational part of the creation, that this supine race of our fellow creatures may not long remain insensible to, and unconvinced of, the superior advantages they may derive, or the new comforts they may possess, by this alteration in their mode of living. It is by no means improbable, that by this circumstance alone they may be roused from their natural lethargic indifference, and be induced to keep themselves clean, and to exert themselves in obtaining other blessings consequent on civilized society. This once effected, the laborious task of their worthy and charitable benefactors will wear the appearance of being accomplished; and should it be hereafter attended with a grateful sense of the obligations conferred, it is not possible to conceive how much these excellent men will feel rewarded, in having been the cause of meliorating the comfortless condition of these wretched humble creatures.

Our conversation admitted of no pause with these seemingly happy and benevolent priests; whilst we acquired much information we were highly entertained; and the day was far advanced by the time our curiosity was thus far gratified.

In compliment to our visit, the fathers ordered a feast for the Indians of the village. The principal part of the entertainment was beef, furnished from a certain number of black cattle, which were presented on the occasion to the villagers. These animals propagate very fast, and being suffered to live in large herds on the fertile plains of Sta Clara, in a sort of wild state, some skill and adroitness is required to take them. This office was at first intended to have been performed by the natives, but it was overruled by Senr Paries an ensign in the Spanish army, who, with one of the priests of Senr Quadra's vessel, had joined our party from a mission at some little distance called Sta Cruz. This gentleman conceived the business of taking the cattle would be better performed by the soldiers, who are occasionally cavalry, and are undoubtedly very good horsemen. We mounted, and accompanied them to the field, to be spectators of their exploits. Each of the soldiers was provided with a strong line, made of horsehair, or of thongs of leather, or rather hide, with a long running noose; this is thrown with great dexterity whilst at full speed, and nearly with a certainty, over the horns of the animal, by two men, one on each side of the ox, at the same instant of time; and having a strong high-peaked pummel to their saddles, each takes a turn round it with the end of the line, and by that means the animal is kept completely at bay, and effectually prevented from doing either the men or horses any injury, which they would be very liable to, from the wildness and ferocity of the cattle. In this situation the beast is led to the place of slaughter, where a third person, with equal dexterity, whilst the animal is kicking and plunging between the horses, entangles its hind legs by a rope, and throws it down, on which its throat is immediately cut. Twenty-two bullocks, each weighing from four to six hundred weight, were killed on this occasion; eighteen were given to the

inhabitants of the village, and the rest were appropriated to the use of the
soldiers, and the mission, in addition to their regular weekly allowance of
twenty-four oxen, which are killed for their service every Saturday: hence
it is evident, as the whole of their stock has sprung from fifteen head of
breeding cattle, which were distributed between this and two other missions,
established about the year 1778;[1] that these animals must be very prolific to
allow of such an abundant supply. Their great increase in so short a time is
to be ascribed to the rigid œconomy of the fathers, who would not allow
any to be killed, until they had so multiplied as to render their extirpation
not easy to be effected. The same wise management has been observed with
their sheep, and their horses have increased nearly at the same rate.

Although this village did not appear so populous as that at St. Francisco,
I was given to understand that there were nearly double the number of
inhabitants belonging to it; and that in consquence of the many unconverted
natives in the neighbourhood of Sta Clara, several of the Christian Indians of
good character were dispersed amongst their countrymen, for the purpose of
inducing them to partake of the advantages held out to them, in which they
had not been altogether unsuccessful. All who have offered themselves as
converts have been admitted and adopted, nothwithstanding the artifices of
several, who have remained in and about the mission until they have acquired
a stock of food and clothing, with which they have decamped. This improper
conduct has, however, had no sort of effect on the benevolent minds of the
fathers, who have not only uniformly supplied their wants on a second visit,
but also those of many wandering tribes that would be at the trouble of asking
their assistance.

Thus concluded our morning's entertainment, and we retired to dinner. In
the convent a most excellent and abundant repast of the productions of the
country was provided, which were in the greatest perfection. The day passed
to the mutual satisfaction of all parties, and we found ourselves under some
difficulty the next morning, Thursday 22d, to excuse ourselves from accepting
the pressing solicitations of these good people, to prolong our stay at Sta Clara;
this, however, necessity and not inclination obliged us to decline. We took
our leave at an early hour, highly gratified by our reception and entertainment
which had amply compensated for the fatigue or inconvenience attending so
long a journey, performed in a way to which we were so little accustomed.

The mission of Sta Clara is situated at the extremity of the S.E. branch of
port St. Francisco, which terminates in a shallow rivulet extending some
distance into the country,[2] from whence, and the confines of the port in its
vicinity, Sta Clara is well supplied with a variety of excellent fish.

To the eastward at the distance of about five leagues, near the sea coast,
or rather on the borders of the bay of Monterrey, is the mission of Sta Cruz,

[1] Presumably San Francisco de Asís and San Juan Capistrano, both founded in 1776.
[2] Santa Clara is on the Guadalupe River, a few miles S of the S end of San Francisco
Bay.

very recently established;[1] and like those before described governed by three fathers of the order of St. Francisco, and protected by a corporal and six soldiers. As this establishment was in its infancy I much wished to have seen it, but as my leisure would not admit of extending our excursion, we lost no time in proceeding to the ships. Our road back was over a more elevated country than that of the morass, leading through a continuation of the forest of oaks, but greatly inconvenienced by the many holes in the ground before noticed; and our good friend and guide the sergeant, apprehending that the approach of night might make us liable to accident, was induced to conduct us through a lower country, which he did not suspect to be so wet and unpleasant as we afterwards found it. We were, however, very fortunate in point of weather, which during our three days excursion was very mild, serene, and pleasant; and on our arrival at the ship in the evening, I had the pleasure to find the Chatham near us at anchor.[2]

Friday 23d. From Mr. Broughton I had the additional happiness of understanding that all were well on board; and that during the time of our separation he had been employed in prosecuting the examination of the river Columbia, which was found to extend further than we had supposed. The particulars of this survey, together with those of Mr. Whidbey's examination, whom we expected to meet at Monterrey, and such information respecting a cluster of islands seen by the late Lieutenant Hergest as could be gained from his log-book and papers, I shall postpone for future consideration and recital.

The arrival of the Chatham in some measure hastened our departure. Having by a very tedious process completed our stock of water, and taken on board a small quantity of fire wood, every thing was received from the shore, and the vessels unmoored the next morning in order to put to sea; but the wind and tide proving unfavourable we remained at anchor during the day. I therefore employed this interval in noticing the following circumstances, which occurred after our return from Sta Clara.

The average price of the large cattle at this port on my arrival, I understood to be six Spanish dollars each; the sheep, in proportion. Having receiving as many of these as were wanted for the use of both vessels, with some vegetables, poultry, &c. I presented Senr Sal with the amount of their value, as our supply had been principally procured from him. Much to my surprize, he declined accepting the money, in payment; and at length acquainted me, that he had been strictly enjoined by Senr Quadra, on no pretence whatever to accept any pecuniary recompence from me; as every thing of that nature would be settled by himself on our meeting at Monterrey. These injunctions from Senr Quadra

[1] The Santa Cruz Mission was on the sea coast, at the N end of Monterey Bay. It was about 30 miles SE of Santa Clara, not 15 miles, as Vancouver states.

[2] The Chatham had arrived on the afternoon of 22 November. 'The next morning the 23rd we were supplied with Fresh Beef & Greens for the Ships Company, for the first time since leaving the Cape of Good Hope, a matter that gave the Jacks no small Satisfaction.' – Bell, November.

removed my difficulties, as I should ill have known how to have requited such generosity, or to have accepted such obligation, from persons who, in every respect excepting that of food, had the appearance of poverty, and of being much pressed for the most common conveniencies of life.

My late excursion into the country had convinced me, that although its production, in its present state, afforded the inhabitants an abundant supply of every essential requisite for human subsistence, yet the people were nearly destitute of those articles which alone can render the essentials of life capable of being relished or enjoyed. On this occasion I experienced no small gratification, in being able to relieve their wants by the distribution of a few necessary articles and implements, culinary and table utensils, some bar iron, with a few ornaments for the decoration of their churches; to which I added one hogshead of wine, and another of rum; and consigned the whole to the care of Senr Sal, with a request that an equal distribution should be made between the Presidio and the missions of St. Francisco and Sta Clara. This was punctually attended to, and I had the satisfaction of finding the several articles were received as very acceptable presents.

The inclemency of the weather, and the short stay I purposed to make on our arrival in this port, prevented my erecting the observatory on shore; sufficient observations were however procured for ascertaining its latitude to be 37° 48′ 30″, and its longitude 237° 52′ 30″.[1] The variation of the compass, by six sets of azimuths, varying from 12° 2′ to 13° 32′, gave the mean of 12° 48′ eastwardly.

The morning of Sunday the 25th brought a fresh breeze against us from the N.W.; but being prepared to depart, and having a strong ebb tide in our favor, we turned out of the port[2] against a very disagreeable irregular sea, produced by the opposing elements. After entering the channel leading out, soundings could not be gained with the hand-line until we were about two miles to the south-westward of the S.E. point of entrance, when we suddenly arrived in 10, 7, and 6 fathoms water. In this situation we were about two miles to the south of our former track, when going into the port: where in five fathoms water the same disagreeable agitation of the sea was experienced: hence I concluded that it was occasioned by a bank, or bar, at the distance of near four miles from the port, extending right across its entrance.[3] This bar we soon passed over, and again lost soundings with the handline. At noon our observed latitude was 36° 53′; the outer points of the entrance into the port of St. Francisco bore by compass N. 10 E. and N. 28 E.; and the extremes of the coast in sight, from N.W. to S. 28 E.; along which our course was directed southerly at a little distance from the shore, towards Monterrey.

[1] Vancouver's lat. was very near the correct reading, but the long. was probably about 122° 27′ W (237° 33′ E).

[2] The commandant at Santa Clara accompanied Vancouver when he returned to San Francisco 'to take passage on board the Discovery to Monterrey.' Menzies, 23 November.

[3] The San Francisco Bar, which extends from about 3 miles S of Point Lobos to within about half a mile of Point Bonita.

Thus we quitted St. Francisco, highly indebted to our hospitable reception, and the excellent refreshments, which in a few days had entirely eradicated every apparent symptom of the scurvy.

My engagements in the country on my first arrival, and my haste to depart from St. Francisco, on the arrival of the Chatham, prevented me from obtaining any precise information respecting the port; every thing, however, that we were able to notice, tended to confirm the original opinion, that it was as fine a port as the world affords; failing only in the convenience of obtaining wood and water. It is however probable, that, on due examination, these essential articles might be obtained with less difficulty than we experienced. So far as we became acquainted with its soundings, they appeared regular and good; the bottom excellent holding ground; and though we passed over some that was hard, in going from our first anchorage to the other, it was not in a situation where vessels are likely to remain stationary; nor do I consider the bank or bar without, as any detriment to the port, though an unpleasant sensation is frequently occasioned in passing over it.[1] I have however been given to understand, that the port is not much in repute with the maritime Spaniards, on account of the strength of its tides; this disapprobation is easily accounted for, when the manner of securing their vessels is considered. This is done invariably by mooring them head and stern, with many anchors and cables; never less than four, and seldom less than six; a very injudicious method when under the influence of rapid and irregular tides. The tides, however, at St. Francisco, to persons unaccustomed to navigate in tidesways, may be an objection; but to those who know how to benefit by their stream they are amongst its greatest advantages, since the prevailing winds are from the westward, frequently continue many days together, and blow directly into the port, which would render its egress difficult at those times without the assistance of the ebb tide; which, in the stream of the port, takes, I believe, a regular course with the flood, nearly six hours each way, and is high water about 11h 24' after the moon passes the meridian: though in the place where we anchored, and particularly at the last, the tides were very irregular; nor could we form any true judgment of their rise and fall, which appeared to be very inconsiderable. Our first place of anchorage possesses many advantages, superior to those we found at the second. The tides are there infinitely the most regular, and notwithstanding the bank of mud prevented our landing in some places, it does not extend all round the cove; for its south-western part is a steep shore, and might easily be made commodious for obtaining fuel and water; the latter is very good, and there is an abundance of the former immediately in its vicinity. The anchorage is more secure, by being completely land-locked, and further removed from the ocean. Independently of these places of safety, there is every reason to

---

[1] Potatopatch Shoal, on the N part of the bar, is said to have been so named because 'schooners from Bodega Bay frequently lost their deck load of potatoes while crossing the shoal.' – *U.S. Coast Pilot* 7, p. 174.

conclude that the northern parts of this extensive port would afford many situations preferable to either.

With a fresh gale from the N.W. we made great progress to the southward along the sea-coast; having the range of mountains which were to the right of us in our journey to Sta Clara, now on our left hand, and presenting us a very different aspect. Their western side, exposed to all the violence and changes of an oceanic climate, was nearly destitute of wood or verdure; some grovelling shrubs were scattered in the vallies, and some dwarf solitary trees were seen on the sides of the mountains, which had in general a very naked and barren appearance.

Wishing to delineate the coast, which we found to extend nearly S. 14 E., from the entrance of St. Francisco, we plied during the night; and the next morning shewed our situation to be off the entrance of the bay of Monterrey, where we were becalmed until noon, when a pleasant breeze from the westward allowed us to steer for the center or bottom of the bay, whose shores were chiefly composed of low compact land; but in this point of view, the more southern and western parts of them seemed to be very much elevated, and bore the appearance of being insular. As we steered along, I was in constant expectation of finding a proper place of anchorage, which was not discovered until four in the afternoon, by making the signal I had settled with Senr Quadra, which was immediately answered from the Presidio. Our anchorage was directed to be nearly under the high land before mentioned, on the southern side of the bay. About seven in the evening Mr. Whidbey came on board from the Dædalus, which vessel had arrived, all well, on the 22d, after having completed the service on which she had been employed. Soon after we were met by some Spanish boats, sent by Senr Quadra to our assistance; and in about an hour we were safely moored with our anchors to the N.W. and S.E.; the latter lying in nine fathoms water, good holding ground. Our distance from the nearest or S.W. shore about a quarter of a mile; the points of the bay bore by compass N. 45 W. and N. 52 W.; the former point, Anno Nuevo, distant seven or eight leagues; the latter, called Point Pinos, was about a mile off.[1]

On our arrival we found here at anchor, besides the Dædalus, the following vessels belonging to the crown of Spain; the brig Active, on board of which was Senr Quadra's broad pendant, the Aransasu, and a schooner.[2]

[1] The ships anchored in the S end of Monterey Bay, an open roadstead about 20 miles wide, extending from Point Pinos in the S to Point Santa Cruz in the N. Both in his text and on his chart Vancouver places Point Ano Nuevo in the position of Point Santa Cruz. The point now called Point Ano Nuevo is 18 miles NW of Point Santa Cruz.

[2] 'a Schooner which lately came from San Blas.' – Menzies, 26 November.

CHAPTER II.

Transactions at Monterrey—Description of the Mission of St. Carlos—Departure of the Dædalus for Port Jackson—Situation and Description of Monterrey Bay—Account of the Presidio—Generous Conduct of Senr Quadra—Astronomical and Nautical Observations.

HAVING arrived in the famous port of Monterrey (so distinguished by the Spaniards)[1] on Tuesday the 26th, I waited on Senr Quadra, who had taken up his residence at the governor's house in the Presidio. After the usual compliments had passed, and I had received repeated assurances of friendship and hospitality, I returned on board, and at sun-rise the next morning, Wednesday the 27th, the Presidio was saluted with thirteen guns; which being equally returned, the topsails were hoisted, and Sen[r] Quadra's broad pendant saluted with the same number. After receiving the return of this compliment, Sen[r] Quadra, accompanied by the acting governor Sen[r] Arguello,[2] with Sen[r] Caamano, and several Spanish officers, returned my visit, all of whom were received on board the Discovery and Chatham with such marks of respect and ceremony as were due to their rank and situation. When these formalities were over, I accompanied Sen[r] Quadra on shore to partake the entertainment of his hospitable table.

In the course of conversation Sen[r] Quadra informed me, that on his arrival in this port from Nootka, he found orders directing him to capture vessels he would find engaged in commercial pursuits on this coast, from these Presidios northward, to the extent where the general traffic is carried on; excepting the vessels belonging to the people of Great Britain, who were to proceed without the least interruption or molestation. These orders from the court of Spain induced us both to believe that our respective sovereigns had

---

[1] Monterey is the modern spelling.

[2] José Dario Argüello. Bell states that Quadra had usurped Arguello's authority and had taken command of the province improperly as 'his power extended not so far, he was Governor of San Blas and Toupic only and commander in chief of the Naval forces of San Blas & on the Coast of California.' But Bell hastens to add: 'This usurpation however sprung not from haughty ambition, or ostentatious pride, or from any motives that could throw the slightest taint on Mr. Quadra's character as a private Man, it was readily allowed he err'd only from want of knowledge, and that his principal motive was the having it in his power by this means to behave to us in the generous and hospitable manner which he afterwards did, and which he could not have answered for in Lieutn. Arguello had he suffered him to remain Commanding Officer.' – November.

adjusted, and finally concluded, every arrangement with respect to the territories at Nootka.

This information appeared to me of a very important nature, and in the event of my being able to procure a passage to England for an officer through New Spain, would induce me to relinquish the design I had meditated of sending the Chatham home this season, for the purpose of conveying such intelligence as I had now the power of communicating.[1] Although I might have been materially incommoded by the absence of our little consort in the further prosecution of my voyage, yet the informing of government how far I had been able at this time to carry His Majesty's commands into execution, appeared to me so absolutely indispensable, that I had determined to submit to any inconvenience rather than omit so essential a part of my duty; especially, as in addition to our own exertions during the preceding summer, I had obtained the possession of all the charts of the Spanish discoveries to the northward of our own researches.

These surveys, together with an account of our transactions at Nootka, and other information I had acquired respecting these countries, I considered of a nature too important to withhold; as it was only by such a communication that any just or reasonable conclusion could be drawn, either in respect of the national advantages which were likely to result from a further prosecution of commercial pursuits in these regions, or of the most proper situations for the purpose of forming permanent establishments on the coast, to protect and facilitate the trade if carried further into execution. This intelligence, on which the accomplishment of one of the principal objects of our voyage might depend, together with my other dispatches, I proposed to intrust to the care of Lieutenant Broughton the commander of the Chatham, who had been privy to the whole of my transactions with Senr Quadra at Nootka; and whose abilities and observations would enable him, on his arrival in England, to satisfy the Board of Admiralty on many point of inquiry, for which it was impossible I could provide in my dispatches. On this occasion I requested of Senr Quadra, if it were compatible with his inclination and the disposition of the Spanish court, that Mr. Broughton should be permitted to take his passage by the way of New Spain to England. To this Senr Quadra without the least hesitation, and in the most friendly manner replied, that Mr. Broughton might accompany him to St. Blas, where he would supply him with money, and every other requisite in his power, which could contribute to render his laborious journey across the continent of America as pleasant as could be expected from the nature of the undertaking. At so obliging and generous an offer I testified every sentiment I was capable of expressing; and used my

---

[1] 'This was a disappointment to many [in the Chatham], who from the pleasing anticipation of enjoying the amusements of London in about 7 or 8 months time, were now to anticipate the horrors of the dreary unhospitable Coast of America, for two years at the least before they could realize the pleasure of their native Country.' – Bell, November.

utmost endeavours that no time should be lost in preparing for Mr. Broughton's departure, since on that depended not only the sailing of ourselves, but the departure of Senr Quadra and the vessels under his orders.

After having obtained permission, the observatories and tents were sent on shore; and on Wednesday the 28th I began to make the observations which were necessarily required.

The decks of the Discovery, in consequence of the late inclement weather, were found to be excessively leaky, and to require caulking; many of the sails wanted material repair: these, with various other services, were put in a train of execution.[1] On board the Chatham all were busily employed, particularly in recruiting their stock of provisions; as, in consequence of my former intention, no more had been received on board than would be absolutely necessary for her passage home; it now, however, became requisite that both vessels should receive from the Dædalus as large a portion of stores, provisions, &c. as each was capable of stowing.

Having given proper directions for carrying these several services into effect, on Sunday the 2d of December, in consequence of a very polite invitation, I paid my respects to the Mission of St. Carlos,[2] accompanied by Senr Quadra, Senr Arguello, Senr Caamano, Mr. Broughton, and several other English and Spanish officers.

This establishment is situated about a league to the south-eastward of the Presidio of Monterrey. The road between them lies over some steep hills and hollow vallies, interspersed with many trees; the surface was covered over with an agreeable verdure; the general character of the country was lively, and our journey altogether was very pleasant.

Our reception at the mission could not fail to convince us of the joy and satisfaction we communicated to the worthy and reverend fathers, who in return made the most hospitable offers of every refreshment their homely abode afforded. On our arrival at the entrance of the Mission the bells were rung, and the Rev. Fermin Francisco de Lausen, father president of the missionaries of the order of St. Francisco[3] in New Albion, together with the fathers of this mission,[4] came out to meet us, and conduct us to the principal residence of the father president. This personage was about seventy-two years of age, whose gentle manners, united to a most venerable and placid countenance, indicated that tranquillized state of mind, that fitted him in an eminent degree for presiding over so benevolent an institution.

[1] Spanish caulkers helped with the work, as they had done at Nootka. Humphrys' log includes the note: 'paid the Caulkers for their work both there [at Monterey] and at Nootka.' – 30 December.

[2] The San Carlos Borromeo or Carmelo Mission, founded in 1770. The latter name derives from the Rio Carmelo, now the Carmel River.

[3] One of the leading figures in the history of the California missions.

[4] Identified by Marguerite Eyer Wilbur in *Vancouver in California 1792–1794* (Los Angeles, 1954) as Fathers Pascual de Arenaza, José de Paula, Miguel Sanchez and Francisco Señan.

The usual ceremonies on introduction being over, our time was pleasantly engaged in the society of the father president and his two companions, the priests regularly belonging to the mission of St. Carlos, who attended us over their premises. These seemed to differ but little from those at St. Francisco, or Sᵗᵃ Clara; excepting that the buildings were smaller, the plan, architecture, and materials exactly corresponding.

In their granaries were deposited a pretty large quantity of the different kinds of grain before noticed at the other establishments, to which was added some barley, but the whole was of an inferior quality, and the return from the soil by no means equal to that produced at Sᵗᵃ Clara. Here also was a small garden on the same confined scale, and cultivated in the same manner as observed at the other stations.

An Indian village is also in the neighbourhood; it appeared to us but small, yet the number of its inhabitants under the immediate direction of this mission was said to amount to eight hundred, governed by the same charitable principles as those we had before visited. Notwithstanding these people are taught and employed from time to time in many of the occupations most useful to civil society, they had not made themselves any more comfortable habitations than those of their forefathers; nor did they seem in any respect to have benefited by the instruction they had received. Some of them were at this time engaged under the direction of the fathers, in building a church with stone and mortar.[1] The former material appeared to be of a very tender friable nature, scarcely more hard than indurated clay; but I was told, that on its being exposed to the air, it soon becomes hardened, and is an excellent stone for the purpose of building. It is of a light straw colour, and presents a rich and elegant appearance, in proportion to the labour that is bestowed upon it. It is found in abundance at no great depth from the surface of the earth; the quarries are easily worked, and it is I believe the only stone the Spaniards have hitherto made use of in building. At Sᵗᵃ Clara I was shewn a ponderous black stone, that Father Thomas said was intended to be so appropriated as soon as persons capable of working it could be procured. The lime they use is made from sea shells, principally from the ear-shell, which is of a large size and in great numbers on the shores; not having as yet found any calcareous earth that would answer this essential purpose. The heavy black stone is supposed to be applicable to grinding, and should it be found so to answer, it will be a matter of great importance to their comfort, since their only method of reducing their corn to flour is by two small stones placed in an inclined position on the ground; on the lower one the corn is laid, and

---

[1] 'They shewed us their Church which was small & neatly ornamented, but they were at this time employd in building another upon a much larger scale.' – Menzies, 2 December. The Chapel of San Carlos de Borromeo had been damaged by fire in 1789 and was being rebuilt. It was rededicated in 1795. About this time, partly because of the poor quality of the soil, it was decided to move the mission to the valley of the Carmel River. Construction of a new church there began in 1793.

ground by hand by rubbing the other stone nearly of the same surface over it. The flour produced by this rude and laborious process makes very white and well tasted, though heavy bread, but this defect is said by the Spaniards to be greatly remedied when mixed with an equal proportion of flour properly ground.

After we had satisfied our curiosity in these particulars we rode round the neighbourhood of the mission. It was pleasantly situated, and the country, agreeably broken by hills and vallies, had a verdant appearance, and was adorned like that in the vicinity of Monterrey, with many clumps and single trees, mostly of the pine tribe, holly-leaved oak and willows; with a few trees of the poplar and maple, and some variety of shrubs, that rather incommoded our travelling, which was chiefly confined to one of the vallies, and within sight of the buildings. Through this valley a small brook of water about knee-deep, called by the Spaniards Rio Carmelo,[1] takes its course, passes the buildings of the Mission, and immediately empties itself into the sea.

In this valley, near the sides of the Carmelo, a few acres of land exhibited a tolerably good plant of wheat; but as the soil here, as well as at Monterrey, is of a light sandy nature, its productions are consequently inferior to the other two missions I had visited; yet I was given to understand, that the interior country here, like that at St. Francisco, improves in point of fertility, as it retires from the ocean.

On our return to the convent, we found a most excellent repast served with great neatness, in a pleasant bower constructed for that purpose in the garden of the mission. After dinner we were entertained with the methods practised by the Indians in taking deer, and other animals, by imitating them. They equip themselves in a dress consisting of the head and hide of the creature they mean to take; with this, when properly put on and adjusted, they resort to the place where the game is expected, and there walk about on their hands and feet, counterfeiting all the actions of the animal they are in quest of; these they perform remarkably well, particularly in the watchfulness and the manner in which deer feed. By this means they can, nearly to a certainty, get within two or three yards of the deer, when they take an opportunity of its attention being directed to some other object, and discharge their arrows from their secreted bow, which is done in a very stooping attitude; and the first or second seldom fails to be fatal. The whole was so extremely well contrived and executed, that I am convinced a stranger would not easily have discovered the deception.

In the evening I returned on board,[2] and was on Monday the third

---

[1] Now the Carmel River.

[2] Vancouver omits all mention of an entertainment offered at the Presidio which Menzies describes in some detail: 'We returnd in the evening to the Presidio where we were invited to a dance at the Governor's house, it was to begin at seven, but the Ladies had such unusual preparations to make that they could not be got together till near ten, & as they enterd they seated themselves on Cushions placed on a Carpet spread out at one

honoured with the company of most of the party to dinner; including Sen^ra Arguella the governor's wife, and some other ladies of the Presidio; but the motion of the ship, though very inconsiderable, greatly to my disappointment obliged the ladies, and indeed some of the gentlemen, very soon to retire.

The various employments which constantly engaged my time when on board, joined to my attendance on the observatory on shore, left me but little leisure to indulge either in exercise, or social entertainment; nor was it without much difficulty, that I now and then snatched a few hours of relaxation, to partake of the society of our attentive and hospitable friends.[1]

It was not until Sunday the 9th that my arrangements permitted me to make another short excursion with Senr Quadra and our numerous friends, to dine at the garden of the Presidio. This spot might contain about four acres of land, situated in a valley about a league to the eastward of the Presidio. Its soil, like the generality in this neighbourhood, when compared with that of Sta Clara, could be considered only as indifferently good; it is however greatly benefitted by a fine stream of water that runs close past it, and enables the gardener to keep it properly moist in dry weather, and in the rainy season of December, January and February, prevents its being flooded. With these advantages it generally produces a great abundance of the several kitchen vegetables with some fruit; but in consequence of the many vessels, that have been employed on the coast of North West America this season, resorting hither for refreshments, both on their passage from and on their return to St. Blas, the productions of this and the only other garden at St. Carlos were nearly exhausted. Were a little labour however bestowed on the cultivation of an

end of the room: They were variously dressed, but most of them had their Hair in long queues reaching down to their waist, with a tassel of ribands appendant to its extremity. They danced some country dances, but even in this remote region they seemd most attachd to the Spanish exhilerating dance the *Fandango*, a performance which requires no little elasticity of limbs as well as nimbleness of capers & gestures. It is performd by two persons of different sex who dance either to the Guittar alone or accompanied with the voice; they traverse the room with such nimble evolutions, wheeling about, changing sides & smacking with their fingers at every motion; sometimes they dance close to each other, then retire, then approach again, with such wanton attitudes & motions, such leering looks, sparkling eyes & trembling limbs, as would decompose the gravity of a Stoic. The two Sandwich Island women at the request of Captain Vancouver exhibited their manner of singing & dancing, which did not appear to afford much entertainment to the Spanish Ladies, indeed I believe they thought this crude performance was introduced by way of ridiculing their favourite dance the Fandango, as they soon after departed.' – 2 December.
[1] Vancouver was engrossed in the task of preparing the despatches and charts that Broughton was to carry to London, but Manby seems to have had a great deal of free time. One entertainment of which he disapproved was the bull fight which seems to have been an almost daily occurrence: 'after dinner, a Bull is dragged into the Presidio square, and there cruelly tormented for an hour, till the poor Animal becomes perfectly mad, all Spaniards expressed a partiality for this barberous sport, Men on horseback attack the outrageous Beast with Lances.' Quadra organized an elaborate bear hunt, but no bear was found. 'As the Horses are good we had our Races, and many other diversions. The Foxes afforded us excellent sport, as in the extensive plains, they gave us a Chase of great length...' – Manby, letters, December.

additional space for this essential purpose, a scarcity would not be likely to happen; as the soil seems well adapted to horticulture, and the climate produces a perpetual spring. Of this we had a manifest proof, by seeing peas, beans, lettuces, cabbages, and various other esculent plants, some springing from the ground, and some in perfection, whilst others had produced their seed or were fallen to decay.

This garden, though situated at a pleasant distance for an excursion, was not provided with any fixed accommodation for visitors. The only places of shelter near it (for they could scarcely be called houses) were a few miserable mud huts, the residence of the gardener, and a few soldiers who are stationed there for its protection. This deficiency afforded to Senr Paries a second opportunity of exercising his genius, in the construction of another temporary bower for our reception, similar to that which he had erected in the garden of the mission at St. Carlos. In both he had succeeded much to the approbation of all his friends, who had greatly profited by his kind solicitude for their comfort and happiness.

Few objects or circumstances occurred in the course of this excursion worthy of notice. The surrounding country consisted chiefly of a sandy heath, overgrown with a naturally impassable thicket of shrubs about four or five feet high, which afforded an excellent cover for deer, foxes, hares, rabbits, quails, &c. some of which we saw in passing along the roads cut through it.

The late inconvenience experienced by some of my visitors, in consequence of the ship's motion, became a subject of our conversation; and as this was impossible to be provided against, I solicited the honour of my Spanish friends company at our encampment on shore. This accordingly took place the following day, Monday the 10th, when I was gratified with the presence of most of the ladies, as well as the gentlemen, at dinner. A display of fire-works was exhibited in the evening. These, still remaining in excellent preservation, afforded a very high degree of satisfaction, not only to our visitors, but their dependents of every description; the whole of whom in the neighbourhood, with a greater number of Indians, were assembled on this occasion, and most probably partook of an entertainment to which most of them were before intire strangers. This evening concluded by a dance and supper, which was not ended until a late hour.

The Dædalus having delivered such provisions and stores as could be taken on board the Discovery and Chatham, on Wednesday the 12th, her hold was restowed, and our carpenters were employed in fitting up commodious stalls on board of her, for the reception of live cattle; Senr Quadra with his accustomed politeness and liberality, offered me any number of those animals, with such other productions of the country as I might judge to be necessary, for the service of His Majesty's infant colony in New South Wales. Twelve cows, with six bulls, and the like number of ewes and rams, were received on board the Dædalus[1] on the 24th; but the ship was detained until a sufficient

[1] Both Bell and Manby state that there were about 30 sheep.

quantity of provender for their maintenance could be procured. The country, at this season affording but a scanty supply, furnished employment for almost all our people in cutting it wherever it could be found.[1] Water also was not very easily obtained, since it could only be had in small quantities at a time, from a number of shallow wells dug by ourselves. It was however extremely good, and might have been procured in any quantity with little labour, by sinking wells of a proper construction to a moderate depth; notwithstanding this, the Spaniards are content to take on board for their common use at sea, water of a very inferior quality, because it is procured without any trouble. That which is drunk at the table of the officers is, however, very fine water, and is brought in carts from the river Carmelo. But to return, these several employments prevented the sailing of the Dædalus until Saturday the 29th, when she departed with the cattle in very high condition.[2]

On this occasion Lieutenant James Hanson received from me his orders to proceed to New South Wales,[3] to call at Hergest's islands,[4] in his way thither, for a supply of water and food for the cattle, and any refreshments for the crew that could be procured: passing thence to the North of all the low islands,

---

[1] 'as there was no Hay to be procurd in this Country for feeding them on the passage, parties were employd on shore from each Vessel in cutting Grass for that purpose, but it was so dry & shrivelld by long exposure to the weather, that it was not at all likely to afford sufficient nourishment for their support, & this was found to be fatally verified by most of them dying on the passage.' – Menzies, 18 December. (One of several entries that show that the text of Menzies' journal that has come down to us is a narrative revised after the event.)

[2] Vancouver was later to note that only one cow, three ewes and a ram survived the journey and were landed in New South Wales. (See p. 1081.) Warren Cook states, without providing any evidence (*Flood Tide of Empire*, p. 388) that Vancouver 'cancelled plans for sending the *Daedalus* to the penal colony at Australia's Botany Bay to obtain colonists for Nootka' and adds that the ship was sent instead 'to New South Wales for provisions to supply the *Discovery* and *Chatham* until further orders came from London.' The latter assumption is incorrect; the *Daedalus* had been chartered specifically to act as a supply ship for the expedition, and the voyage to Australia was being made according to plan. As noted in the introduction, the possibility of partly manning a British post on the Northwest Coast with discharged convicts had been proposed before Vancouver left England, but neither his narrative, not two letters he wrote to Governor Phillip of New South Wales (which are printed in the appendix) contain any suggestion that the scheme should be revived. However, a letter written by Whidbey at Monterey to an unidentified correspondent (also printed in the appendix) shows that the establishment of a colony on the coast was being discussed. As Whidbey had been 'informed a Settlement is going to be made on this side of America,' he wrote, 'I beg leave to offer my opinion on the subject.' He then proceeded to recommend sites for trading posts, etc., and to suggest that Botany Bay 'Convicts who have served their time of punishment...instead of returning to England to become a fresh prey on the Public' should 'be sent to this Country and settled at the Head of Fuca Straights – where there is a country equal to any in the world.' – 2 January 1793. Original in the Huntington Library, California.

[3] Dated 'on board his Majesty's sloop Discovery, in Monterrey Bay', 31 December 1792. Printed in *Historical Records of New South Wales*, Series I, Vol. I (Sydney, 1914), pp. 681–3.

[4] In the group now known as the Marquesas.

to proceed to Otaheite; from Otaheite to New Zealand, and from thence to port Jackson, where I was particularly anxious the Dædalus should arrive as soon as possible, because the cattle, sheep, &c. in the event of their being preserved, could not fail to be a very valuable acquisition to that country. Beside these, it was by no means improbable that Mr. Hanson might be enabled to procure a considerable number of hogs and fowls, at the several islands he might touch at: these I also conceived would be highly acceptable at Port Jackson, and he had my directions to use his discretion in thus appropriating such articles of traffic consigned to me, as yet remained on board the Dædalus.

His visit to Otaheite had another object beside that of procuring refreshments, which was to receive on board twenty-one English seamen who had been cast away in the ship Matilda, of London, on the 25th of February, 1792, on a ledge of rocks, not within sight of any land, and said to be situated in latitude 22° south, and longitude 138° 30′ west.[1] After this unfortunate accident the crew returned in their boats to Otaheite; from whence, six days before, they had departed in the ship. From Otaheite the second mate and two of the sailors had, in one of the open whale boats, proceeded towards New South Wales. The rest of the crew remained on the island, excepting Mr. Matthew Weatherhead the commander of the vessel, who, with two men and two boys, had taken their passage from Otaheite on board the Jenny of Bristol;[2] and on their arrival at Nootka, Senʳ Quadra not only provided Mr. Weatherhead with a passage toward England through New Spain, but benevolently furnished him with a sum of money to defray his expences through a country where the inhabitants would necessarily be strangers to himself and all his connections.

The misfortune of this shipwreck appeared to have been attended with very unpleasant consequences to our friends at Otaheite. The few valuable articles which these unfortunate people had been able to save from the wreck, instead of having been secured and properly taken care of, had been indiscriminately dispersed, or left to the disposal of the natives. This had produced a jealousy between the chiefs of Matavai and those of Oparre, and on their disagreement concerning the division of the spoil, some of the Englishmen had sided with the chiefs of the one party, whilst others had taken up the cause of the other. A war was the necessary consequence between the two districts, which had

[1] The Matilda was 'one of the Botany Bay Transports who left England about the same time we did, & having deliverd his Cargo at Port Jackson in New South Wales, he [Captain Weatherhead] left that place to proceed on the Southern Whale Fishery, & on his way touchd at Otaheite to refresh his people, but about six days after leaving that place he lost his Ship on a rocky Shoal'. – Menzies, 29 August 1792.

[2] Bell states that 'the very confined size of his Vessel [78 tons], and the large crew he had, together with his not being provided with a Superfluity of Provisions' made it impracticable for Captain Baker of the Jenny to take more than this number on board. – Bell, 30 August 1792. The Jenny arrived at Nootka on 7 October 1792. Bell gives the name of the captain as Wetherell.

terminated very disastrously for Matavai. Nearly the whole of that beautiful district had been laid waste, their houses burnt down, and their fruit trees torn up by the roots, and otherwise destroyed. This was the sum of what I was able to learn; but the very confused and incoherent detail that was given me of all these transactions, prevented my acquiring any satisfactory information on this melancholy event.[1]

Having now positively determined on the mode to be pursued in the execution of the remaining objects of our voyage, I requested Commodore Phillips would, at Port Jackson, complete the cargo of the Dædalus to a year's provisions of all species, and such stores as I judged would be necessary for the Discovery and Chatham; and to forward them by this vessel to me at Nootka, where her commander should find sufficient instructions for the regulation of his conduct, should he arrive there in my absence.

I communicated to Commodore Phillips the few discoveries we had made in the South Pacific Ocean, and transmitted him a copy of my survey of that part of the south-west coast of New Holland, which we had visited.[2]

We had, by this time, procured such observations as were necessary for determining the situation of this place, as likewise for ascertaining the rate of the chronometers, and for correcting my survey of the Coast of New Albion, southward, from Cape Mendocino to this bay. These several matters, owing to the very unfavourable passage we had had from Nootka, not being yet intirely completed, produced a longer delay at Monterrey than I could have wished; not only because I was anxious that our time should be otherways employed, but also that Senr Quadra's departure should not be postponed on our account. I was, however, in some degree reconciled to his detention, by the repeated friendly assurances he gave me, that his time was mine, earnestly requesting that I would not hesitate so to employ it, as to make my dispatches as complete as I might on the present occasion deem it expedient.

Every hour was therefore dedicated to this purpose, which necessarily precluded me from making more than a few cursory remarks on Monterrey. These, with the astronomical and nautical observations that were made on shore at the observatory, will conclude this chapter.

This famous bay is situated between point Pinos and point Anno Nuevo, lying from each other N. 72 W. and S. 27 E. 22 miles apart.[3] Between these points, this spacious but very open bay is formed, by the coast falling back from the line of the two points, nearly four leagues. The only part of it that

---

[1] For a contemporary account of the Pare-Matavai war see Oliver, *Ancient Tahitian Society* (Honolulu, 1974), III, 1281–4. Captain Bligh was in Tahiti April 7–July 18, 1792, and Oliver quotes extensively from his 'Journal of the Voyage of H.M.S. Providence' (P.R.O., Adm. 55/152). The *Jenny* sailed for Nootka a week before Bligh arrived.

[2] Vancouver's letter to Phillip was dated 'Discovery, at sea, 15th Oct'r, 1792'. Both this letter and a second letter to Phillip written at Monterey on 29 December 1792 are printed in the appendix.

[3] As already noted, Vancouver places Point Ano Nuevo in the position of Point Santa Cruz.

is at all eligible for anchoring, is near its south extremity, about a league south-eastward from point Pinos; where the shores form a sort of cove, that affords clear good riding, with tolerable shelter for a few vessels. These, for their necessary protection from the sea, must lie at no very great distance from the south-west shore; where, either at night or in the morning, the prevailing wind from the land admits the sailing of vessels out of the bay, which otherways would be a tedious task, by the opposition of the winds along the coast, which generally blow between the N.W. and N.N.W. To these points of the compass this anchorage is wholly exposed; but as the oceanic swell is broken by the land of point Pinos, and as these winds, which prevail only in the day time, seldom blow stronger than a moderate gale, the anchorage is rendered tolerably safe and convenient; and notwithstanding these north-westerly winds are common throughout most part of the year, I have not heard of an instance of their being so violent as to affect the safety of vessels tolerably well found with anchors and cables. The soundings are regular from 30 to four fathoms; the bottom, a mixture of sand and mud; and the shores are sufficiently steep for all the purposes of navigation, without shoals or other impediments. Near point Anno Nuevo are some small rocks, detached from the coast at a very little distance; the shores of point Pinos are also rocky, and have some detached rocks lying at a small distance from them, but which do not extend so far into the ocean as to be dangerous. The rocky shores of point Pinos terminate just to the south of the anchoring place, where a fine sandy beach commences, which extends, I believe, all round the bay to point Anno Nuevo. In a direction N. 42 E. at the distance of four leagues from point Pinos, is what the Spaniards call Monterrey river;[1] which, like the river Carmelo, is no more than a very shallow brook of fresh water, that empties into that part of the bay. Here a small guard of Spanish soldiers are generally posted, who reside on the spot in miserably wretched huts. Near point Anno Nuevo is another of these rivers,[2] something less than the other, in whose neighbourhood the mission of Sta Cruz is planted. Such are the rivulets to which the Spaniards in their representation of this country, as well by their writings as their charts, have given the appellation of *rivers*, and delineated them as spacious and extensive.

The anchorage already described, is the only situation in the bay where vessels can ride with any degree of safety or convenience. In its neighbourhood is the Spanish establishment. The Presidio is about three quarters of a mile to the southward of the spot, where the sandy beach before mentioned commences. This is the landing place, where they have erected a most wretched kind of house, and for the reception of a guard of soldiers generally posted there.[3]

[1] Now the Salinas River. Named Rio de Monterey by the Spaniards in 1776, and known as the Monterey River as late as 1850.   [2] The San Lorenzo River.

[3] In the first edition the sentence concludes: 'a most wretched kind of house, which they call a store-house, serving for that purpose, and for the reception of a guard of soldiers generally posted there.'

The Presidio, like that of St. Francisco, is situated in an open clear plain, a little elevated above the level of the sea; the space, between the Presidio and the landing place, is very low swampy ground. The former does not appear to be much benefitted by its vicinity to fresh water, since in the dry season it must be brought from a considerable distance, as the Spaniards had not been at the pains of sinking wells to insure a permanent supply. There were many delightful situations in the immediate neighbourhood of the Presidio, with great diversity in the ground to favour the taste of the ingenious, and a soil that would amply reward the labour of the industrious, in which our Spanish friends might with equal ease have sat themselves down; more comfortable, more convenient, and I should conceive more salutary than their present residence appeared to be.

The most important of all blessings, health, is here treated with great indifference; since not only the climate of Monterrey, but the whole of the surrounding country, has the reputation of being as healthy as any part of the known world.[1] Other objects of a secondary nature, such as the place of their abode, convenience, or comfort, have no greater influence on their consideration, as the present Presidio is the identical one that was built on the first establishment of this port in the year 1770, without having undergone the least improvement or alteration since that period. The buildings of the Presidio form a parallelogram, comprehending an area of about three hundred yards long, by two hundred and fifty yards wide, making one intire inclosure. The external wall is of the same magnitude, and built with the same materials; and except that the officers apartments are covered in with a sort of red tile made in the neighbourhood, the whole presents the same lonely uninteresting appearance, as that already described at St. Francisco. Like that establishment, the several buildings for the use of the officers, soldiers, &c. and for the protection of stores and provisions, are erected along the walls on the inside of the inclosure, which admits of but one entrance for carriages or persons on horseback; this, as at St. Francisco, is on the side of the square fronting the church, which was rebuilding with stone, like that at St. Carlos. Besides the principal gateway, they have small doors that communicate with the country, nearly in the middle of the side walls, to the right and left of the

---

[1] Menzies did not share this opinion; he and others found the Monterey climate very trying, partly because of the changes in temperature, which might be 90° F in the daytime and 30° at night: 'These great & sudden changes...affected every one more or less with rheumatic pains and catarrhous complaints, particularly the Spaniards who were accustomd to tropical regions, but none sufferd more from it than the Indians that happend to be brought from other places on board the Shipping in the Bay, whose constitutions were not habituated to such changes. An Indian Boy whom the Spaniards brought from Charlotte Islands in the ship Aranzaza, though from a much colder climate died here after a short & severe illness. The Sandwich Islanders were likewise all very ill with Colds, particularly the two women, whose complaints were the severest & most tedious & remaind long in a doubtful state of recovery, yet they Bore their ailments with a degree of patience & resignation that would reflect honor on a more enlightened tribe.' – 13 January 1793.

entrance. One of these, on the right hand, is through the apartments of the commanding officer. These are much more extensive than those at St. Francisco, as they consist of five or six spacious rooms with boarded floors, but under the same disadvantage of wanting glass, or any substitute for it. The window places are open, and only on the side of the houses which looks into the area; as no apertures, I believe, are allowed to be made in the grand wall of the inclosure, excepting for the doors; which are those already mentioned; with one at each of the officer's houses contiguous to the governor's, and one other on the opposite side. These are all the apertures in the wall, which when seen at a distance has the appearance of a place of confinement. At each corner of the square is a small kind of block house, raised a little above the top of the wall, where swivels might be mounted for its protection. On the outside, before the entrance into the Presidio, which fronts the shores of the bay, are placed seven canon, four nine and three three-pounders, mounted; these, with those noticed at St. Francisco, one two-pounder at Santa Clara, and four nine-pounders dismounted, form the whole of their artillery. These guns are planted on the open plain ground, without any breast work or other screen for those employed in working them, or the least cover or protection from the weather. Such, I was informed, was also the defenceless state of all the new settlements on the coast, not excepting St. Diego, which from its situation should seem to be a post of no small importance.

The four dismounted cannon, together with those placed at the entrance into the Presidio, are intended for a fort to be built on a small eminence that commands the anchorage. A large quantity of timber is at present in readiness for carrying that design into execution; which, when completed, might certainly be capable of annoying vessels lying in that part of the bay which affords the greatest security, but could not be of any importance after a landing was accomplished, as the hills behind it might be easily gained, from whence the assailing party would soon oblige the fort to surrender; nor do I consider Monterrey to be a very tenable port without an extensive line of works.

The Presidio is the residence of the governor of the province, whose command extends from St. Francisco, southward, along the exterior shore, to cape St. Lucas;[1] and on the eastern side of the peninsula of California, up that gulf to the bay of St. Louis.[2] The rank in the Spanish service, required as a qualification to hold this extensive command, is that of lieutenant colonel. Whether the governor interfered in the common garrison duty I know not. A lieutenant and ensign, sergeant, corporals, &c. resided also in the Presidio; the establishment of which I understood was similar to all the rest in the province, but was then incomplete in consequence of the recent death of the late commandant. By this event, Lieutenant Arguello, properly the commander at St. Francisco, as being the senior officer, had taken upon him the

[1] Cabo San Lucas, the S tip of Lower California.
[2] The Bahia San Luis Gonzaga, on the E side of the Lower California peninsula.

government, and had sent the alferez, or ensign, Senr Sal, to command at St. Francisco; which posts we understood they were severally to retain, until another lieutenant colonel should be appointed to the government.

By what I was able to learn, I did not consider the number of soldiers who composed the garrison as exceeding one hundred, including the non-commissioned officers.[1] From this body detachments are drawn for the protection of the neighbouring missions; the remainder, with their wives and families, reside within the walls of the Presidio, without seeming to have the least desire for a more rural habitation; where garden ground and many other comforts may easily be procured, at no great distance from the seat of the establishment. This seemed to be composed intirely of military people, at least we did not see amongst them those of any other description. The few most necessary mechanical employments were carried on in an indifferent manner by some of the soldiers, under permission of the commanding officer.

I must now for the present quit the interesting subject of these establishments; in which we unexpectedly not only found an asylum, and pleasant retreat from the vicissitudes and labours of our voyage, but the gratification of social intercourse with a set of liberal-minded, generous people, each of whom endeavoured to surpass the other in manifesting an interest for our welfare, and expressing on every occasion the happiness they felt, in relieving our wants or rendering us any kind of service. Their friendly and hospitable behaviour daily proved the sincerity of their professions, by making our residence whilst among them, as comfortable and agreeable as their circumstances would permit.

With the most grateful recollection of the attentive civilities, disinterested kindnesses, and benevolent assistance received at the hands of intire strangers, I should very insufficiently requite their goodness, or comply with the dictates of my heart, were I to omit the opportunity which now presents itself of

---

[1] Menzies noted that the Spaniards had outposts to keep watch on the Indians and 'give timely intimation to the Garrison in case of any hostile appearances', a precaution that was 'extremely necessary as there did not appear to be above three hundred soldiers for the defence of the two Garrisons [San Francisco and Monterey] and the four adjacent Missions.' But the soldiers were 'generally Stout Men capable of bearing great fatigue, & without any exaggeration the most dextrous & nimble Horsemen we ever saw...' He described their accoutrements: 'when Mounted they carry a Target with which they parry off the missile Weapons of the Indians; Their Body is defended by a quilted buff coat of several folds of leather without sleeves, which is impenetrable to Arrows; They have a kind of Apron of thick leather fastend to the pummel of the Saddle & falling back on each side covers the Legs & Thighs & affords considerable defence either in passing through thorny brush woods with which the Country abounds, or from such Weapons as the Indians generally make use of. Their offensive Weapons are a Musket, a broad sword & a pair of large Pistols all of which are generally carried in leather cases securd to the Saddle; they also carry a Lance in their hand which they manage with great dexterity. Thus equippd & with a large cloak thrown over his Shoulders to keep himself & his accoutrements dry, a Californian soldier makes a formidable & curious appearance.' – 13 January.

making this record, of the weighty obligations conferred upon us on this occasion.[1]

The well-known generosity of my other Spanish friends, will, I trust, pardon the warmth of expression with which I must ever advert to the conduct of Senr Quadra; who, regardless of the difference in opinion that had arisen between us in our diplomatic capacities at Nootka, had uniformly maintained towards us a character infinitely beyond the reach of my powers of encomium to describe. His benevolence was not confined to the common rights of hospitality, but was extended to all occasions, and was exercised in every instance, where His Majesty's service, combined with my commission, was in the least concerned.

To Senr Quadra we were greatly indebted, for waiting our arrival at Monterrey, for the friendly and hospitable reception we experienced, and afterwards for remaining there for the sole purpose of affording me an opportunity of transmitting through the medium of his kind offices, my dispatches to England; when his time, no doubt, would have passed infinitely more to his satisfaction at the town of Tepic, the place of his residence in the vicinity of St. Blas. Such sacrifices did not however fill the measure of Senr Quadra's liberality; for, on my requesting an account of the expences incurred for the refreshments, with which the three vessels under my command had been so amply supplied, here and at St. Francisco, together with the charges attendant on the cattle, sheep, corn, &c. &c. put on board the Dædalus for His Majesty's infant colony in New South Wales, he not only revolted at the idea of receiving any payment, but gave strict orders that no account whatever should be rendered; nor would he accept of the most common voucher, or other acknowledgment, for the very liberal supply we had received, of such essential importance, not only to our health and comfort at the time, but to our subsequent welfare.

On my first arrival at Monterrey I had questioned Senr Quadra, as to the supply of refreshments, and the price of the different species we should require. To the first he assured me, that every thing the country afforded was at our service; and as to the last, he said that could be easily settled on our departure. On this ground I now strongly urged his compliance with his former promise, especially as the account between us was of a public nature; but all my remonstrances were to no effect; he insisted that he had fulfilled his promise, since the only *settlement* in which he could possibly engage, was that of seeing we were accommodated to the extent of our wishes, with every supply the country could bestow; adding, that repayment would most amply be made, by the promised success attending every creature and production, that we had received either for our own use, or for other purposes. And as it was probable

---

[1] In the first edition the sentence concludes: 'of making this, though rude and unpolished, yet grateful record, of the weighty obligations I shall for ever feel to have been conferred upon us on this occasion.' Presumably John Vancouver felt that this was too fulsome a declaration.

our respective courts would become acquainted with our several transactions, he should submit all further acknowledgment to their determination.[1]

The venerable and respectable father president of the Franciscan missionaries, with all the excellent and worthy members of that religious order, together with Sen[rs] Caamano, Arguello, Sal, and the whole of the Spanish officers with whom we had the honour of being acquainted, demand from us the highest sentiments of esteem and gratitude. Even the common people were intitled to our good opinion and respect, as they uniformly subscribed to the exemplary conduct of their superiors, by a behaviour that was very orderly and obliging.

To the reverence, esteem, and regard, that was shewn Sen[r] Quadra by all persons and on all occasions, I must attribute some portion of the respect and friendship we received; and consider the general disposition in our favour to have acquired no little energy, by the noble example of that distinguished character.

Captain King, when speaking in his pleasing language of our benevolent friend Major Behm, at Kamschatka,[2] pourtrays with justice the character of Sen[r] Quadra, whose general conduct seems to have been actuated by the same motives of benevolence, and governed by principles of similar magnanimity.

The parting from a society for which we had justly conceived a very sincere regard, could not take place without sensations of much regret. My concern on this occasion was increased by my powers of administering to their comfort by a supply of the necessary utensils which they needed, being so much limited. Such articles however as I could possibly spare, or make shift without, I consigned to their use, and having selected an assortment of the most necessary kind, I had the satisfaction to understand that they were highly valued and thankfully received.[3]

[1] It appears that Quadra made himself personally liable for the supplies provided for Vancouver's ships. When the *Discovery* returned to Nootka Sound in May 1793, letters were received that Broughton had written in Mexico, on his way to England. 'From Mr. Broughton's letters we also understand that Sr Quadra gave the Governor of Monterrey Bonds to the amount of 1800 dollars for the refreshments which our Vessels received while we staid in California & this without giving us the least intimation of the Sum to which his public spirited generosity had thus made him liable for he positively refusd accepting of a receipt or the least indemnification from Capt Vancouver at parting for the liberal supplies we receivd by his orders in that Country.' – Menzies, 20 May 1793.

[2] Major Magnus von Behm, Governor of Kamchatka when Cook's third expedition, under the command of Captain Clerke, visited the region in 1779. In the course of a long euology, Captain James King wrote in his journal: 'The whole of his disinterested'd conduct could not fail of making us regret the parting with a man who we had little prospect of ever seeing again. If every country that the stranger may be driven to, had a Behm to preside over their affairs, what honour would redound to their Sovereigns, & to their Country, & what credit would it be to human Nature...' Cook, *Journals*, III, p. 673.

[3] Vancouver seems not to have known that disagreements arose regarding the way in which the gifts were distributed. Menzies tells the story. The articles selected were sent 'to the Governor, to be divided between the Garrison & the surrounding Missions in whatever manner he thought it might be most beneficial to the Country in general. But

The following are the results of such observations as were made for ascertaining the situation of the observatory on shore at Monterrey. Whence it appeared that Mr. Kendall's chronometer on the 28th of November, allowing the Nootka rate, shewed the longitude to be 238° 36′ 15″

Mr. Earnshaw's pocket watch: 238 27

Mr. Arnold's pocket watches:

(No. 82) 238 30 15

(No. 14) 238 9 45

(No. 176) 238 30

Longitude of the observatory at Monterrey by lunar observations taken there.

		sets of distances				
Dec. 5,	Myself,	eight	moon and sun	238°	17′	25″
—	Mr. Whidbey,	eight		238	33	20
7,	Mr. Whidbey,	seventeen		238	42	52
—	Myself,	twelve		238	30	54
8,	Myself,	twelve		238	29	40
—	Mr. Whidbey,	twelve		238	45	29
—	Mr. Whidbey,	three	moon and regulus	237	54	25
—	Myself,	three		238	11	10
9,	Myself,	four	moon and sun	238	31	26
—	Mr. Whidbey,	twelve		238	42	
10,	Mr. Whidbey,	twelve		238	40	54
—	Myself,	eight		238	32	9
18,	Myself,	sixteen		238	19	50
—	Mr. Whidbey,	sixteen		238	8	14
19,	Mr. Whidbey,	two		238	23	37
—	Myself,	two		238	31	45
20,	Myself,	sixteen		238	10	45
—	Mr. Whidbey,	sixteen		238	8	32
21,	Mr. Whidbey,	eight		238	16	16
—	Myself,	eight		238	13	56
—	Mr. Whidbey,	four	moon and aldeberan	238	52	56

The mean of the whole, *collectively* taken, being one hundred and ten sets by Mr. Whidbey, and eighty-nine by myself, amounting in all to one hundred and nintety-nine sets of lunar distances; each set as usual containing, six observations;[1]

on the 16th we found that this manner of sharing out these donations had excited a good deal of discontentment. The Fathers in particular complained of their not having received so liberal a share as those at St Francisco & Sta. Clara.' – December 16.

[1] The error on Vancouver's longitudes, which almost always placed positions too far to the E, has been discussed in the introduction (pp. 52–54). Cook placed Cape Flattery 13′ too far to W, but the relatively few determinations of longitude he made on the Northwest Coast were usually very near the true location, sometimes within a minute or two. One

shewed the longitude to be   238 25 45.[1]

The longitude of Monterrey, deduced from the above authority, was found to differ 10′ 30″ from that shewn by Mr. Kendall's chronometer on our arrival. On the belief that this difference arose from an error in the chronometer, commencing from the change of climate about the time we passed cape Mendocino, it has been allowed and corrected, both in the foregoing journal and in my chart of the coast of New Albion, south-eastward from that cape to this station.

The longitude, thus ascertained, is found to differ likewise from that assigned to it by Senr Melaspina, who places Monterrey in 237° 51′, and who also places the north promontory of cape Mendocino, 26′, and point de los Reys, 33′, further to the westward of their situations shewn by our observations. By these calculations, the whole of the coast of North West America that we have yet visited, is uniformly removed to the eastward of the longitude assigned to it by Captain Cook and Senr Melaspina; authorities no doubt that demand the greatest respect and confidence; yet, from the uninterrupted serenity of the weather that prevailed at the time our observations were made, I have been induced to adopt the meridian obtained from the result of our own observations, which, at noon on the 29th of December, shewed Kendall's chronometer to be fast of mean time at Greenwich,

$$1^h\ 32'\ 32''\ 14'''$$

And to be gaining per day on mean time at the rate of   18 25

Mr. Earnshaw's pocket watch, fast of mean time at Greenwich,   1 14 1 14

And gaining per day,   4 27

can surmise, however, that he would not have been unduly critical of Vancouver's errors, as he had made kindred mistakes himself. Beaglehole points out that his justly famous chart of New Zealand, based on his 1770 survey, 'one of the very remarkable things in the history of cartography', had one major defect: 'It was a matter of longitude. The greater part of the North Island is 40′ too far east, and the greater part of the South Island, 30′.' – *The Life of Captain James Cook* (London, Hakluyt Society, 1974), p. 223. Cook was unaware of this until he returned to New Zealand in 1773, on his second voyage, when it was revealed by the 'multitude of observations' made by William Wales, the expedition's remarkable astronomer. 'I mention these errors,' Cook commented, 'not from a supposition that they will much effect either Navigation or Geography, but because I have no doubt of their existance.' – Cook, *Journals*, II, 580. The important thing was that features of the New Zealand coast were placed accurately in relation to one another. The same was true of Vancouver's chart of the Northwest Coast. Malaspina's longitudes were calculated as from Cadiz; Wagner tabulated a series extending from Cabo Corrientes to Cape Hinchinbrook and converted them to readings W of Greenwich. – *The Cartography of the Northwest Coast of America* (Berkeley, 1937), I, 230. A check of nine of these, all known to Vancouver, shows that in five instances the error was one to four minutes; in the other four it varied from 6 to 9 minutes. Six of the locations were too far W; the other four were too far E.

[1] The position of Point Pinos light, some distance W of Vancouver's anchorage, is lat. 36° 38′ N, long. 121° 56′ W (238° 04′ E).

Mr. Arnold's No. 82, fast of mean time at
Greenwich   4 25 41 14
And gaining per day,   25 6
Mr. Arnold's No. 14, fast of mean time at
Greenwich,   1 6 15 14
And gaining per day,   19 33
Mr. Arnold's No. 176, fast of mean time at
Greenwich,   3 3 32 14
And gaining per day,   34 45

The latitude, deduced from twenty-two meridional altitudes, taken on both sides of the arch of Mr.
Ramsden's new circular instrument, varying
between 36° 35' 27", and 36° 36' 50", shewed the
mean collectively taken   36° 36' 20"

This most excellent instrument was used, both at Nootka and at this place,
for the purposes it is intended to answer, in making such observations as we
required; in doing which its excellence was fully proved, and Mr. Ramsden
is deserving of great commendation for its accuracy, and the ease with which
it is managed and kept in its adjustments.

The variation of the magnetic needle in thirty sets of azimuths by three
compasses, differing from 9 to 15 degrees, gave the mean result 12° 22',
eastwardly.

The vertical inclination of the magnetic needle was found to be
Marked end
    North face East,   62° 48'
    North face West,   63 47
Marked end
    South face East,   62 48
    South face West,   62 39
                                            _____

    Mean inclination of the marine dipping needle   63 0 30

The tides appeared to be irregular and of little elevation; by their general
motion, they seemed to flow but once in twenty-four hours, and it was high
water about seven hours and a half after the moon passed the meridian; the
rise and fall was about six feet at the spring, and four feet at the neap tides.

Thus conclude the transactions of the voyage, appertaining particularly to
the Discovery, to the end of the year 1792. The two following chapters will
contain the services performed, and the information acquired, by the officers
under my command during the time of our separation.

CHAPTER III.

Lieutenant Broughton's Account of Columbia River.

ON reference to the preceding part of this narrative it will be found, that on the 21st of October we stood to sea at the commencement of a heavy gale of wind, from off the entrance of Columbia river; leaving the Chatham there at anchor, in full confidence that her commander, Mr. Broughton, would, prior to his departure, endeavour to gain all possible information respecting the navigable extent of that inlet, and such other useful knowledge of the country as circumstances would admit of. The implicit reliance I had on Mr. Broughton's zeal and exertions, will be found to have been worthily placed, by the perusal of the following narrative of that officer's transactions.[1]

The situation the Chatham had gained in the entrance of Columbia river was by no means comfortable at low water, when the depth did not exceed four fathoms, and the sea broke very heavily about a cable's length within the vessel, on a bank of two and a half fathoms, which obtained the name of SPIT BANK.[2] The place of their anchorage was, by observation, in latitude 46° 18'; bearing S. 50 E. about a mile and a quarter from the inner part of cape Disappointment,[3] from whence to the opposite shore, across the channel leading to sea, the breakers formed nearly one connected chain, admitting only of one very narrow passage, which lies in a direction about W. by N. from a point Mr. Broughton called Village Point,[4] there being in its vicinity a large deserted village.

[1] Broughton's original narrative has disappeared. Edward Bell's journal is the only other surviving account that chronicles the exploration of the river in any detail. The text of this portion of the journal, edited by J. N. Barry, was published in the *Oregon Historical Quarterly*, XXXIII (1932), pp. 31–42, 143–55.

[2] Now Sandy Island and its extensions eastward, which have altered greatly in size and shape since 1792. The *Chatham* was anchored S of the W end of the spit.

[3] Bell mentions that 'when we clear'd the inner point of Cape Disappointment, we observed the Jenny Schooner lying at Anchor in a Bay [Baker Bay] under the Cape, and Mr. Baker the Master came off to us.' – 20 October. Broughton does not mention the *Jenny* until his return from exploring upstream.

[4] Bell notes that the village was 'call'd in Mr. Gray's Sketch Chenooke', but there are no place names on the copy of Gray's chart in C.O. 5/187. It is named 'Village Chenoke' on Broughton's chart, which places it near the present site of MacGowan, Washington, W of Point Ellis. This had been a village of the Chinook Indians, who occupied the N bank of the Columbia from its mouth to Grays Bay. They gave their name to the Chinookian family of Indians, consisting of a dozen main tribes, who inhabited the valley

747

The Discovery having put to sea without making any signal to the Chatham, Mr. Broughton very judiciously concluded that I was desirous he should explore and examine this opening on the coast; and in order that no time should be lost in carrying this service into execution, he proceeded at two in the afternoon, with the first of the flood and a strong gale at S.W. up the inlet, keeping the Village point, which lies S. 70 E. five miles from cape Disappointment, well open with a remarkable projecting point, that obtained the name of TONGUE POINT,[1] on the southern shore, appearing like an island. The depth of water here was not less than four fathoms, and as they approached the deserted village the depth increased to six, seven, and eight fathoms. The wind by this time obliged them to bring to, for the purpose of double reefing the topsails; and whilst thus engaged, the rapidity of the flood tide impelled them into three fathoms water, before sufficient sail could be made on the vessel to render her governable. By this means she was driven on a bank of sand, where the strength of the stream, preventing an anchor being carried into deep water, she remained aground until high tide; when they hove into ten fathoms with the greatest ease, and there rested for the night.[2] Mr. Broughton had, for his guidance thus far up the inlet, a chart by Mr. Gray, who had commanded the American ship Columbia; but it did not much resemble what it purported to represent.[3] This shoal, which is an extensive one lying in mid-channel, having completely escaped his attention.

The next day, being the 22d of October,[4] the wind blew strong from the eastward, and there was little probability from the appearance of the weather

of the Columbia from its mouth to The Dalles, well beyond the point reached by Broughton in his exploration. The Clatsop tribe lived along the S side of the river near its mouth, and as Broughton worked his way upstream he encountered several other tribes, including the Cathlamet Indians, whose territory extended along the N bank from Grays Bay to a little beyond Abernathy Creek (and on the S bank from Tongue Point to Puget Island), and the Skilloots, who lived above and below the mouth of the Cowlitz River. The tribes all seem to have been on good terms with one another, as the large gatherings Broughton met with obviously included groups from several tribes.

[1] The name has been retained.

[2] Manby, perhaps exaggerating, makes this mishap more serious than this account suggests: the Chatham had 'the misfortune to run on a sand bank, a rapid Tide lay us on a dangerous heel, and it was with the utmost difficulty she was kept from upsetting. An hour passed, in this critical state, before we were cleared, from the perils of Shipwreck, the Decks being eased of many weighty articles, and by the assistance of the Stream Anchor carried out, our Bark again floated, a good deal damaged in her bottom.' – Letters, December.

[3] Presumably the chart a copy of which Vancouver sent to London. It extends only as far as Harrington Point, the E point of Grays Bay. Gray entered the river in the Columbia on May 11 and left it on May 20, 1792. For the fragment of the ship's log describing the visit see F. W. Howay (ed.), Voyages of the 'Columbia' to the Northwest Coast (Boston, 1941), pp. 435–8; and for John Boit's account, pp. 396–9.

[4] When copying or paraphrasing Broughton's narrative, Vancouver converted the dates to local time, one day earlier than the time still being used by the expedition in 1792. Thus in Bell's journal the corresponding entries are dated one day later – in this instance 23 October.

Plate 35. Reduced facsimile of Broughton's 'Plan of the River Oregan [the Columbia], from an Actual Survey.'

of soon being able, with any degree of safety, to remove the vessel further up the inlet. That intention being laid aside, Mr. Broughton proceeded with the cutter and launch to examine the shores of its southern side. He first landed at the deserted village,[1] on the northern shore, and on the eastern side of Village point; which he found a good leading mark for clearing the shoals that lie between it and cape Disappointment, carrying regular soundings of four fathoms. From this point he passed over to point Adams,[2] the starboard or S.E. point of entrance into this inlet; and in this way crossed a shoal bank, supposed to be a continuation of that on which the Chatham had grounded. The least water found upon it was two and a half fathoms, and the sea was observed to break at intervals in several places. Point Adams is a low, narrow, sandy, spit of land, projecting northerly into the ocean, and lies from cape Disappointment, S. 44 E. about four miles distant. From this point the coast takes a sudden turn to the south, and the shores within the inlet take a direction S. 74 E. four miles to another point, which obtained the name of POINT GEORGE.[3] From point Adams the breakers stretched into the ocean, first N. 68 W. about a league, then S. 83 W. about four miles, from whence they took a rounding course to the southward, extending along the coast at the distance of two leagues and upwards.

These form the south side of the channel leading into this inlet, which is about half a league wide. The northern side is also formed by the breakers extending two miles and a half from cape Disappointment. In this point of view, the breakers were so shut in with each other, as to present one entire line of heavy broken water, from side to side across the channel.

At this place was found the remains of a deserted Indian village,[4] and near it three large canoes supported from the ground, each containing dead human bodies. These canoe coffins were decorated at the head and stern with rude carved work, and from their decayed state seemed to have been thus appropriated for a great length of time. Another sepulchre was discovered, bearing some affinity to our mode of burial. The body was rolled up in deer skins, and after these with mats, and then laid at full length in a wooden box, which exactly fitted it. The flesh of the body was preserved quite firm. After the party had satisfied their curiosity, every thing that had been displaced by their examination was restored to its original situation.

The shoal on which the Chatham had grounded, was found to extend within half a mile of the eastern side of point Adams. The space between the shoal and the land formed a shallow channel over a kind of bar, on which was found

[1] Others who went ashore underwent an ordeal similar to that already suffered in Toba Inlet: 'some of the people and one of the young gentlemen also landed, and went up to look at this Village, but when they got up to it, they were surrounded with swarms of Fleas, that soon settled in quantities on their Cloathes, and they were all obliged to run into the Water to rid themselves of their unpleasant companions.' – Bell, 23 October.

[2] Named by Gray in May 1792.

[3] Now Smith Point, site of the city of Astoria.

[4] At Tansy Point. This had been a Clatsop village.

little more than three fathoms water, into a Bay that lies between point Adams and point George;[1] whither Mr. Broughton directed his course, and found on each side of the bar, the soundings regular from three to seven fathoms. The shores of this Bay were low land, and the water again shoaled as he advanced to three and two and a half fathoms. Near the shores on either side the sea broke very high, and on the water were seen many pelicans. As the party approached the centre, or rather the S.E. corner of the Bay, they discovered a small river, whose entrance was about two cables length in width, and the depth of water five fathoms, gradually diminishing to two fathoms. By the shores it appeared to be high water, yet the stream attended them up the river, which now took a south easterly direction, in a winding form, and branched off into several creeks. After advancing about seven miles the width decreased to 19 fathoms, and it being then high water, any further examination was deemed unnecessary. The evening at this time having nearly closed in, the party returned about a mile, and took up their residence for the night on the back of the river, which, after Sir George Young of the royal navy, Mr. Broughton distinguished by the name of YOUNG'S RIVER;[2] whose termination was supposed to have been seen by some of the party, but Mr. Broughton was of opinion, from the strength of the tide, that its source was at some distance. The night was windy, and it rained without ceasing until day-light the next morning, which was very pleasant, and greatly inriched the prospect of the beautiful, surrounding country. From the banks of the river a low meadow, interspersed with scattered trees and shrubs, extended to the more elevated land. This was of easy ascent, and was agreeably variegated with clumps and copses of pine, maple, alder, birch, poplar, and several other trees, besides a considerable number of shrubs, greatly diversifying the landscape by the several tints of their autumnal foliage. The marshy edges of the river afforded shelter to wild geese, which flew about in very large flocks; ducks were in abundance, as were the large brown cranes before noticed in the more northern parts of New Georgia.

On leaving the river, as they proceeded to point George, they found the greatest depth of water at about two thirds flood neap tides, was $2\frac{1}{2}$ fathoms; this continuing intirely across the entrance of Young's river, renders it navigable for small vessels only. From hence the launch was sent on board, with orders to sound in direct line to the Chatham, then at anchor off the deserted village. The continuation of the shoal in this passage was found to be a great obstacle to the navigation of the inlet.

Mr. Broughton proceeded in the cutter at a moderate distance from the shore, with soundings of 3, 4, 5, 6, and 7 fathoms to Tongue point. On the eastern side of this point the shores first fall to the southward, and then stretch nearly E.N.E. From this point was seen the centre of a deep bay, lying at the distance of seven miles, N. 26 E. This bay terminated the researches of Mr. Gray; and to commemorate his discovery it was named after him GRAY'S

---

[1] Youngs Bay.　　　　　　　　　　　　[2] Now Youngs River.

BAY.[1] Mr. Broughton now returned on board, in the hope of being able to proceed the next flood tide higher up the inlet. In the afternoon he reached the Chatham, finding in his way thither a continuation of the same shoal on which she had grounded, with a narrow channel on each side, between it and the shores of the inlet; on this middle ground the depth of water was in overfalls from three fathoms to four feet. Mr. Broughton got the Chatham immediately under weigh, with a boat a-head to direct her course. His progress was greatly retarded by the shallowness of the water. A channel was found close to the northern shore, where, about dark, he anchored for the night in seven fathoms water, about two miles from the former place of anchorage.[2] Before day-break the next morning (October 24th) the vessel, in tending to the tide, tailed on a bank; this however was of no consequence, as on heaving short she was soon afloat again. At day-light Mr. Manby was sent to sound the channel up to Gray's bay, where in Mr. Gray's sketch, an anchor is placed; but on Mr. Manby's return he reported the channel to be very intricate, and the depth of water in general very shallow. This induced Mr. Broughton to give up the idea of removing the Chatham further up the inlet, the examination of which he determined to pursue in the boats. After ascertaining the vessel's station to be in latitude 46° 17', longitude 236° 17½',[3] he departed with the cutter and launch, with a week's provisions, to carry his determination into effect. A strong easterly gale attended with squalls was against them, but the flood tide favoured their progress until six in the evening, when, on the ebb making, they took up their abode for the night on the western side of Gray's bay. They rowed across the bay the next morning, in squally unpleasant weather, with regular soundings of 4, 5, 6, 7, and 8 fathoms. The depth of water within the bay was not more than two fathoms, interspersed near the bottom of the bay with frequent overfals of four fathoms. After passing Gray's bay, the continental shores became high and rocky. About a mile S.W. by W. from the east point of the bay,[4] which lies from its west point N. 78 E. at the distance of four miles,[5] commences a range of five small low sandy islets, partly covered with wood, and extending about five miles to the eastward. The easternmost, which was also the largest, was nearly at the extremity of the shallow space they had thus examined.[6] Between the ocean and that which should properly be considered the entrance of the river, is a

[1] Now Grays Bay; spelled Grey's Bay on Broughton's chart.

[2] The chart shows that the anchorage was on the E side of point Ellis, near the present site of Megler, Washington.

[3] The correct position would be about lat. 46° 15' N, long. 123° 51' W (236° 09' E).

[4] Harrington Point.

[5] Broughton evidently considered Rocky Point, which is within the bay, to be its W point. The bay is now considered to extend W to Grays Point, which is about 6 miles W of Harrington Point.

[6] There are now about a dozen marshy islands in this area, but they have undoubtedly changed greatly in size and shape since Broughton's day; it is impossible to identify his five islands. Presumably the island named Termination Island on his chart was meant to represent the largest of the five.

space from three to seven miles wide, intricate to navigate on account of the shoals that extend nearly from side to side; and ought rather to be considered as a sound, than as constituting a part of the river, since the entrance into the river, which they reached about dark, was found not to be more than half a mile wide, formed by the contracting shores of the sound. Between the points of entrance, lying from each other N. 50 E. and S. 50 W. there were seven fathoms water. The northernmost point[1] is situated in latitude 46° 18½', longitude 236° 34½', from whence the river takes a direction about S. 45 E. From the east point of Gray's bay to this station, the shore is nearly straight and compact, and lies in a direction S. 87 W. They stopped to dine about three miles from the east point of the bay, on the side of a high steep hill, on the northern shore, facing one of the above low islets; from whence extended a long, sandy, shallow spit, down the channel, inclining towards the opposite or southern shore, which was low, and appeared also very shoal. From this steep hill a remarkable pillar rock[2] lies S. 79 W. about a mile from the shore, on the starboard or southern side of entrance into the river. Not only within, but without this rock, the water is very shallow, with overfals from 2½ to six fathoms; but by keeping the northern shore on board from Gray's bay, a sufficient depth of water will be found. The two points of entrance into the river are formed by low marshy land, the southernmost seemed to be an island; and to the N.W. of the most northern, a branch took a northerly direction, which was named ORCHARD'S RIVER;[3] in one of these the party passed a very uncomfortable night, owing to the dampness of their situation.

At day-light the next morning, 26th October, with the first of the flood, Mr. Broughton proceeded up the river, whose width was nearly half a mile. The shores on either side were low and marshy; on the N.E. they were from 8 to 10 fathoms, but on the opposite shore the depth of water did not exceed four fathoms, one third of the channel over. After advancing about two leagues the land became high and rocky on both sides; here a well wooded island, about a league and a half long, divided the stream, and afforded a good passage on each side of it; the deepest is on the N.E. side,[4] in which was found 10 and 12 fathoms water. About a league past the S.E. point of this island, which received the name of PUGET'S ISLAND,[5] the river continued its direction to latitude 46° 10', longitude 236° 50'; where it took a short turn N. 56 E. for about a league;[6] at this turn a small river presented itself, which Mr.

---

[1] Broughton's chart shows that he considered the N point of the entrance to the river to be just E of the mouth of Skamokawa Creek. This would be about 28 miles from Cape Disappointment.

[2] Now named Pillar Rock Island.

[3] Now Skamokawa Creek. Broughton named it after H. M. Orchard, clerk of the *Discovery*.

[4] Cathlamet Channel. The main navigation channel is now S of the island.

[5] Now Puget Island.

[6] The river changes direction at Cape Horn, which is in lat. 46° 09' N, long. 123° 17' W (236° 43' E).

Broughton named SWAINE'S RIVER.[1] In this neighbourhood they were joined
by some of the natives in four canoes. Their clothing was chiefly deer skins,
though a few had garments made of sea otter skins. These good people sold
the party a few fish, and then took their leave. Their language was so totally
different from that of the other American Indians, that not a single word could
be understood. The shores abounded with fine timbers, the pine predominated
on the higher lands, but near the banks of the river grew ash, poplar, elder,
maple, and several other trees unknown to the party. The ebb tide rendered
their progress very slow, and it was evening before they arrived at the end
of the above-mentioned north-eastwardly reach. On the northern shore was
seen a village of the natives,[2] who evidently solicited the landing of the party;
but choosing to wave their civility, they proceeded up the river, which took
a direction S. 62 E. from the village passing some islands lying in the middle
of it; these occupy about two miles; their easternmost point is about a league
from the above village, and after the second lieutenant of the Discovery, they
were named BAKER'S ISLANDS.[3] The bold northern shore now became low
near the banks of the river, and rose high again, at a distance, in a gradual
ascent. Mr. Broughton crossed over half a mile to the eastward of Baker's
islands, to a high bluff point named by him POINT SHERIFF,[4] where good shelter
for the night was found on a sandy beach. At this time they had gained only
22 miles after rowing twelve hours. The river here was about half a mile
wide, and the best channel from point Sheriff was found along the southern
shore.

Nine canoes, with a number of Indians, took up their lodging in a small
creek at a little distance from the party. This circumference served to convince
Mr. Broughton, that the further he proceeded the more the country was
inhabited. At first their warlike appearance produced some small degree of
caution; but this was afterwards, by their orderly behaviour, proved to have
been unnecessary. From ten in the morning, when it appeared by the shore
to be high water, the party had rowed against the stream to their landing place,
where, although the tide continued to rise until midnight, the stream had run
up only two hours.

At seven the next morning (October 27,) with the stream still running down

[1] On Broughton's chart Swaine's River is shown W of Manby's River (which was
named later), but when describing the return journey Broughton reversed this order. The
two supposed rivers were the W and E entrances to Wallace Slough, which lies behind
Wallace Island, on the S side of the Columbia. Bell's Point (not mentioned in the text)
is shown on the N shore opposite the E end of Puget Island; the present Nassa Point would
seem to be the most likely identification. At the time, Spelman Swaine was 3rd lieut. of
the Discovery, Thomas Manby master of the Chatham, and Edward Bell her clerk. All three
names have been superseded.

[2] On the W side of Abernathy Creek.

[3] The present Crims Island, and the smaller islands near it, which probably had different
shapes and sizes in 1792. Joseph Baker was 2nd lieut. of the Discovery.

[4] Now Green Point. The name is correctly spelled Sherriff on Broughton's chart. John
Sherriff was master's mate of the Chatham.

very rapidly, they proceeded in their examination, passing to the north of a small woody island, which, after the surgeon of the Chatham, was named WALKER'S ISLAND.[1] The soundings were from four to seven fathoms. About ten o'clock the tide was flowing fast according to the appearance of the shore, and, for about two hours, the stream favoured their progress; after this, great delay and much fatigue was endured, by a strong ebb tide and a fresh easterly wind. The nine canoes attended them, and as they passed some small creeks and openings on the sides of the river their numbers kept increasing.

Eastward from Walker's island and nearly into mid-channel a bank partly dry extends for two or three miles, but admits of a clear passage on either side; the passage to the south, being the widest and deepest, has five or six fathoms water. After passing this bank, the channel continued on the southern side, with soundings from six to ten fathoms. They now again approached high land, and on the northern shore was a remarkable mount, about which were placed several canoes, containing dead bodies; to this was given the name of MOUNT COFFIN.[2] About a mile to the eastward of mount Coffin, their Indian attendants stopped at a single hut,[3] but Mr. Broughton continued rowing until three in the afternoon; when, having increased their distance only nine miles from point Sheriff, the party stopped to dine on the southern shore. This was high and rocky, and terminated the direction of this reach, in latitude 46° 5′, longitude 237° 11′, from whence the river ran S. 18 E.[4] and the same depth of water continued. The northern shore, instead of being the steepest, now consisted of low, flat, sandy, shores, through which, nearly opposite to their dinner station, where the river was about half a mile wide, two other streams fell into it. The westernmost was named RIVER POOLE, and the easternmost KNIGHT'S RIVER; this last is the largest of the two;[5] its entrance indicated its being extensive, and by the signs of the natives, they were given to understand, the people up that river possessed an abundance of sea-otter skins. After dinner the party proceeded up the reach, extending S. 18 E. passing a low sandy island[6] at its entrance against a very strong stream; and having advanced about four miles, they took up their residence for the night. Several of their friendly Indian attendants, as usual, lodged at a small distance; it was low water at half past ten at night, and high water about two in the morning.

About six o'clock on Sunday morning, (October 28) Mr. Broughton continued to proceed against the stream, and soon passed a small rocky islet,

[1] The name Walker Island has been retained.
[2] This name has also survived.
[3] Presumably the hut was near a creek that is shown on Broughton's chart as Hut Creek.
[4] Broughton must have been on or very near the site of the town of Rainier, Oregon. Its position is lat. 46° 05′ 30″ N, long. 122° 56′ W (237° 04′ E).
[5] Now the Cowlitz River. Captain John (afterwards Admiral Sir John) Knight served with Broughton in the American Revolutionary War. The important port of Longview, Washington, has grown up at the mouth of the river. The River Poole, little more than a slough, has been diverted to serve logging industries.
[6] Cottonwood Island.

about twenty feet above the surface of the water. Several canoes covered the top of this islet, in which dead bodies were deposited.[1] About two miles from hence is a low sandy island,[2] having a spit stretching from each end to some distance. On each side, the channel is clear, the south side is the deepest, having three or four fathoms water. From this island the reach takes a more eastwardly course about four miles, to a point on the north shore, in latitude 45° 56', longitude 237° 18'.[3] The soundings to this point, which is high and rocky, were from four to seven fathoms; the shores of the opposite or southern side of the river are low, and produce many willow-trees; the high and rocky banks were covered with pine-trees down to the water's edge. From hence, with little variation, the river's direction is about S. 5 E. the channel is narrow, and on the eastern shore the depth of water was from four to six fathoms.

Here were three openings stretching in an easterly direction, formed by two small woody islands, on one of which was a grove tall and strait poplars. These were distinguished by the name of URRY'S ISLANDS.[4] Abreast of these is a shoal that joins the south side of the river, and renders the passage close to their shores very narrow; beyond them the river, now about a quarter of a mile wide, is free from obstruction, and the general depth five and six fathoms to another point, about four miles to the south of the above mentioned high one, where, for the first time in this river, some oak-trees were seen, one of which measured thirteen feet in girth; this, therefore, obtained the name of OAK POINT. Close to the south of it was a small brook that ran to the eastward,[5] off which a bank of sand diverted the channel to the western shore, where soundings were found from five to eight fathoms. About three miles and a half from Oak point Mr. Broughton arrived at another, which he called POINT WARRIOR, in conseqence of being there surrounded by twenty-three canoes, carrying from three to twelve persons each, all attired in their war garments, and in every other respect prepared for combat.[6] On these strangers

---

[1] Coffin Rock. Named Burial Head on Broughton's chart.

[2] Sandy Island. From the Cowlitz River to the Willamette River the course of the Columbia is almost directly S. Broughton's chart shows a Hartwell's River flowing in from the W near the S end of Sandy Island. This would be the outlet of the long narrow slough behind Deer Island; its other outlet is about 6 miles upstream.

[3] Martin Bluff, in lat. 45° 58' N, long. 122° 49' W (237° 11' E). On the other side of the channel Point Scott, now Deer Island Point, is marked. Presumably it was named after James W. Scott, a midshipman in the *Chatham*.

[4] Martin Island and Burke Island. Named Urry's Isles on Broughton's chart.

[5] Goerig Slough. Oak Point was evidently a short distance downstream from the slough. J. N. Barry identified it as the site of Columbia City, a town on the opposite side of the river, but Broughton's chart places it on the same side as the slough.

[6] Warrior Point, at the tip of Sauvie Island, which lies between the Columbia River and Multnomah Channel. 'In case of a sudden attack from this powerful fleet, we had regulated every thing in the best manner for our defence, the Swivel was primed, and a Match kept burning, all the Muskets & Pistols in the two Boats were loaded with Ball, and every man had his Cartouch Box buckled on him, with his Musket by his side, together with Cutlass, Pistols, &c. Mr. Broughton by way of shewing them that our Arms were loaded and in good order, fired a Musket with a Ball in it into the Water, which at first

discoursing with the friendly Indians who had attended our party, they soon took off their war dress, and with great civility disposed of their arms and other articles for such valuables as were presented to them, but would neither part with their copper swords, nor a kind of battle-axe made of iron. [1]

At point Warrior the river is divided into three branches; the middle one was the largest, about a quarter of a mile wide, and was considered as the main branch; the next most capacious took an easterly direction, and seemed extensive, to this the name of RUSHLEIGH'S RIVER was given; and the other that stretched to the S.S.W. was distinguished by the name of CALL'S RIVER. [2]

On the banks of Rushleigh's river was seen a very large Indian village, and such of the strangers as seemed to belong to it strongly solicited the party to proceed thither; and, to enforce their request, very unequivocally represented, that if the party persisted in going to the southward they would have their heads cut off. The same intreaties, urged by similar warnings, had before been experienced by Mr. Broughton during his excursion, but having found them to be unnecessary cautions, he proceeded up that which he considered to be the main branch of the river, until eight in the evening; when, under the shelter of some willows, they took up their lodging for the night on a low sandy point, [3] accompanied by twelve of the natives in a canoe, who fixed their abode very near to them. During the whole of this day little assistance had been derived from the flood tide, the ebb had slackened for about two hours, but no current upwards during that time was perceptible.

The next morning, (October 29) they again proceeded up the river, and had a distant view of mount St. Helens, lying N. 42 E. In sounding across the river, whose width was here about a quarter of a mile, from three to twelve fathoms water was found. Owing to the rapidity of the stream against them they were under the necessity of stopping to dine at not more than four or five miles from their resting place; here it was low water at noon, and though the water of the river evidently rose afterwards, yet the stream continued to run rapidly down. The greatest perpendicular rise and fall appeared to be about three feet. In this situation the latitude was observed to be 45° 41′, longitude

seem'd to terrify the Chief, and all the Indians, for they immediately hid their heads below the Gunwhales of the Canoes, and it was some time before they could be persuaded to hold them up again. Soon after this perceiving that our intentions were as peaceable, as their own, they took off all their War Garments, and every man seem'd eager to dispose of his Bows and Arrows for old Buttons, Beads, &c. nor was the Chief the least eager among them.' – Bell, 28 October.

[1] Bell added a sketch of this weapon to his description. It was probably received in trade from Sioux Indians in the Dakotas. See J. N. Barry, 'Columbia River Exploration, 1792', *Oregon Historical Quarterly*, XXXIII (1932), p. 153.

[2] The largest (middle) channel was the Columbia River. Rushleigh's River is now the Lewis River; the derivation of Broughton's name for it is not known. Call's River is now Multnomah Channel. It was named after Sir John Call, the military engineer, for whom Broughton had already named Call Inlet.

[3] Probably Willow Point, on Sauvie Island; named by Broughton on his return journey down the river.

237° 20';[1] when mount St. Helens was seen lying from hence N. 38 E. our distance from point Warrior being about eight miles.

In their way hither they had passed two Indian villages on the west side of the river,[2] and had been joined by an hundred and fifty of the natives in twenty-five canoes. To avoid any surprize they dined in their boats; this precaution was however unnecessary, for on some trivial presents being made, a trade immediately commenced, in which the Indians conducted themselves with the utmost decorum. No attempts were made to pass the line drawn on the beach, excepting by two who appeared to be the principal chiefs, and who were permitted to join the party. These seemed to be very well disposed, and inclined to communicate every information; but, unfortunately for our gentlemen, a total ignorance of the Indians' language precluded their profiting by these friendly intentions.

At one o'clock they quitted their dinner station, and after rowing about five miles, still in the direction of the river S. 5 E. they passed on the western side a small river leading to the south-westward;[3] and half a mile further on the same shore came to a larger one, that took a more southerly course. In the entrance of the latter, about a quarter of a mile in width, are two small woody islets; the soundings across it from two to five fathoms. The adjacent country, extending from its banks, presented a most beautiful appearance. This river Mr. Broughton distinguished by the name of RIVER MUNNINGS.—[4] Its southern point of entrance, situated in latitude 45° 39', longitude 237° 21', commanded a most delightful prospect of the surrounding region, and obtained the name of BELLE VUE POINT;[5] from whence the branch of the river, at least that which was so considered, took a direction about S. 57 E. for a league and a half. A very distant high snowy mountain now appeared rising beautifully conspicuous in the midst of an extensive tract of low, or moderately elevated, land, lying S. 67 E. and seemed to announce a termination to the river.[6] From Belle Vue point they proceeded in the above direction, passing a small wooded island, about three miles in extent, situated in the middle of the stream. Their route was between this island and the southern shore, which is low; the soundings between its northwest point and the main land were three fathoms, increasing to four, five, and six, off its southeast point; from whence the river took its course S. 75 E. This obtained the name of MENZIES'

---

[1] Marked 'Observation Station' on the chart. It was in the vicinity of Reeder Point.

[2] These are marked on Broughton's chart.

[3] This small river has been obliterated by the extensive dredging and filling that has taken place in this area.

[4] River Mannings in the first edition, but River Munnings on Broughton's chart, which is probably correct. This is now the Willamette River; the large city of Portland is on its banks a few miles from its mouth.

[5] Belle View Point on Broughton's chart; now Kelley Point. The lat. is correct, but the long. should be 122° 46' W (237° 14' E). The name Belle Vue Point survives, but it has migrated across the Willamette to the N point of entrance.

[6] Mount Hood (11,235 ft.), the highest point in Oregon.

ISLAND;[1] near the east end of which is a small sandy woody island that was covered with wild geese.[2] From Belle Vue point, a small stream of flood had attended them to this station; but here a rapid downward current was met, though it was by no means high water.

At the several creeks and branches they had passed they lost successively most of their Indian companions, excepting one elderly chief, who, in the most civil and friendly manner had accompanied them from the first, and had a village still farther up the river.[3] Having received many presents he had become much attached to the party, and, to manifest his gratitude, he now went forward to provide them with lodgings, and whatever acceptable refreshments his village might afford. About seven in the evening they reached his habitation, where he much wished them to remain; but preferring a more secluded resting place, they resorted to a shallow creek a mile further up the river, and about eight miles from Belle Vue point,[4] where they passed the night. Here it was low water about two, and high water at half past five o'clock the next morning. At seven they again departed, but were obliged to retire some distance to clear a shoaly spit that lies off this creek; after this they proceeded to the northern shore. This shore was well wooded, composed of stony beaches, and the soundings were regular from two to seven fathoms. The southern shore, though low and sandy, was also well clothed with wood; the breadth of the river was about a quarter of a mile, and its direction was the same as before-mentioned.

The wind blew fresh from the eastward, which, with the stream against them, rendered their journey very slow and tedious. They passed a small rocky opening that had a rock in its centre, about twelve feet above the surface of the water; on this were lodged several large trees that must have been left there by an unusually high tide.[5] From thence a large river bore S. 5 E. which was afterwards seen to take a south-westwardly direction, and was named

[1] Hayden Island. The city of Vancouver, Washington, successor to Fort Vancouver, the Hudson's Bay Company trading post established here in 1825, has grown up on the N bank of the river. NW of the city is Vancouver Lake, a large shallow pond two miles or more in diameter.

[2] Tomahawk Island.

[3] This was Chief Soto, whose friendliness was still the subject of comment 20 years later. Franchère relates that when travelling up the Columbia in 1811 he 'came to a fisherman's cabin where we were regaled on fresh salmon. Here we found an old blind man who received us most kindly and who our guide told us was a white man. His name was Soto and the only information I could gather about him was that he was the son of a Spaniard who had been shipwrecked at the entrance to the river and had escaped with part of the crew. Some of them were killed by the Clatsops. Four others remained among the Indians and married native women.' – W. Kaye Lamb (ed.), *The Journal of Gabriel Franchère* (Toronto, The Champlain Society, 1969), p. 71. See also J. Neilson Barry, 'Spaniards in Early Oregon', *Washington Historical Quarterly*, XXIII (1932), 25–34.

[4] Presumably the shallow channel S of Lemon Island and the much larger Government Island. The entrance is about 10 miles from Kelley Point.

[5] Broughton should have realized that he had reached a point where the influence of the tides was very limited; high water at the time of the freshet had deposited the trees.

BARING'S RIVER;[1] between it and the shoal creek is another opening;[2] and here that in which they had rested stretched to the E.N.E. and had several small rocks in it. Into this creek the friendly old chief who had attended them went to procure some salmon, and they pursued their way against the stream, which was now become so rapid that they were able to make but little progress. At half past two they stopped on the northern shore to dine, opposite to the entrance of Baring's river. Ten canoes with the natives now attended them, and their friendly old chief soon returned and brought them an abundance of very fine salmon. He had gone through the rocky passage, and had returned above the party, making the land on which they were at dinner an island. This was afterwards found to be about three miles long, and after the lieutenant of the Chatham, was named JOHNSTONE'S ISLAND.[3] The west point of Baring's river is situated in latitude 45° 28',[4] longitude 237° 41'; from whence the main branch takes rather an irregular course, about N. 82 E.; it is near half a mile wide, and in crossing it the depth was from six to three fathoms. The southern shore is low and woody, and contracts the river by means of a low sandy flat that extends from it, on which were lodged several large dead trees. The best passage is close to Johnstone's island; this has a rocky bold shore, but Mr. Broughton pursued the channel on the opposite side, where he met with some scattered rocks; these however admitted of a good passage between them and the main land; along which he continued until towards evening, making little progress against the stream. 'Having now passed the sand bank,' says Mr. Broughton, 'I landed for the purpose of taking our last bearings; a sandy point on the opposite shore bore S. 80 E. distant about two miles; this point terminating our view of the river, I named it after Captain Vancouver; it is situated in latitude 45° 27', longitude 237° 50'.'[5] The same remarkable mountain that had been seen from Belle Vue point, again presented itself, bearing at this station S. 67 E.; and though the party were now nearer to it by seven leagues, yet its lofty summit was scarcely more distinct across

[1] Over the years the freshets have so altered the configuration of the low islands, sand bars and southern shore of this part of the river that it is impossible to identify some of the features mentioned. To add to the difficulties, Broughton's description of this part of his journey is often difficult to follow. Baring's River was probably what is now the Sandy River.

[2] Camas Slough, behind Lady (Johnstone's) Island.

[3] Now Lady Island.

[4] The lat. must have been about 45° 33' N.

[5] The location of the feature that Broughton named Point Vancouver was long a subject of controversy. The matter seems to have been settled by a special investigation by Capt. R. S. Patton, Director of the US Coast and Geodetic Survey; the text of his report was published in the *Oregon Historical Quarterly*, xxxv (1934), pp. 31–8. In a decision dated 8 December 1932 the Board ruled that Point Vancouver was on the N shore of the Columbia River 'in approx. lat. 45° 33·1' N., long. 122° 16·3' W [237° 43·7' E]' and defined it as 'The easternmost extremity or tangent of the north shore...as seen by Lieut. W. R. Broughton... from the landing place two miles down stream at which he terminated his exploratory journey up the river.'

the intervening land which was more than moderately elevated. Mr. Broughton honoured it with Lord Hood's name;[1] its appearance was magnificent; and it was clothed in snow from its summit, as low down as the high land, by which it was intercepted, permitted it to be visible. Mr. Broughton lamented that he could not acquire sufficient authority to ascertain its positive situation, but imagined it could not be less than 20 leagues from their then station.[2]

Round point Vancouver the river seemed to take a more northerly direction; its southern shores became very hilly,[3] with bare spots of a reddish colour on the sides of the hills, and their tops were thinly covered with pine trees. The opposite shore was low, well wooded, and mostly composed of stony beaches. The breadth of the river here was a quarter of a mile; it afforded a clear good channel on the northern shore, with soundings across from six to two fathoms, shoaling gradually to the bed of sand that stretches from the opposite side. During this day, they had constantly rowed against the stream, having increased their distance only twelve miles up the river; and notwithstanding there had been a sensible regular rise and fall of the water, it had not in the least degree affected the stream, which had run constantly down with great rapidity.

Mr. Broughton at this time calculated the distance, from what he considered the entrance of the river, to be 84, and from the Chatham, 100 miles.[4] To reach this station had now occupied their time, with very hard labour, seven days; this was to the full extent for which their provisions had been furnished; and their remaining supplies could not with all possible frugality last more than two or three days longer. And as it was impossible under the most favourable circumstances, they should reach the vessels in a less space of time, Mr. Broughton gave up the idea of any further examination, and was reconciled to this measure, because even thus far the river could hardly be considered as navigable for shipping.[5] Previously to his departure, however, he formally

[1] At this time a Vice-Admiral and a member of the Board of Admiralty. Vancouver had already named the Hood Canal in his honour.

[2] It is less than 40 miles distant.

[3] Broughton was seeing the beginning of the great gorge that the Columbia River has worn through the Cascade Range. The Bonneville hydroelectric power dam is about 18 miles upstream from Point Vancouver.

[4] The distance from Skamokawa was approximately 93 statute miles (81 nautical miles) and from the *Chatham* about 114 miles (99 nautical miles). The total distance from Cape Disappointment was about 127 statute miles (or 110 nautical miles).

[5] Bell realized that it was necessasry to turn back, but he regretted the decision: 'I am inclined to think that its [the river's] Source or termination is as distant from this Sandy point, as that is from the entrance. Perhaps it might be deemed by some very sagacious people, an idle conjecture, was I to say that this River *might* communicate with some of the Lakes at the opposite side of the Continent, but such a thing is not impossible, nor do I conceive altogether improbable. We find the Hudsons Bay Company are extending their factory's upon the Inland navigation farther every year, and why a River on this side of America shou'd not run up so high, as one on the opposite side, I leave to those, to give the reason, who dispute it, however from all this I only mean to say that in my opinion,

took possession of the river, and the country in its vicinity, in His Britannic Majesty's name, having every reason to believe, that the subjects of no other civilized nation or state had ever entered this river before;[1] in this opinion he was confirmed by Mr. Gray's sketch, in which it does not appear that Mr. Gray either saw, or was ever within five leagues of, its entrance.[2]

The friendly old chief, who still remained of their party, assisted at the ceremony, and drank His Majesty's health on the occasion; from him they endeavoured to acquire some further information of the country. The little that could be understood was, that higher up the river they would be prevented passing by falls. This was explained, by taking up water in his hands, and imitating the manner of its falling from rocks, pointing, at the same time, to the place where the sun rises; indicating, that its source in that direction would be found at a great distance.

By the time these ceremonies and inquiries were finished, the night had closed in; notwithstanding this, Mr. Broughton re-imbarked, and with the stream in his favour sat out on his return. All the Indians now very civilly took their leave, excepting the old chief and his people, who, their route being the same way, still bore them company. Little opportunity had been afforded, especially at the latter part of their journey up the river, to ascertain the depth of the channels: to supply this deficiency, the two boats spread, and sounded regularly all the way down. By this means a bank was found extending intirely across Baring's river, and from thence across the main branch, which they had navigated, to the rocky passage at the west end of Johnstone's island; the greatest depth having been only three fathoms, Mr. Broughton was confirmed in the opinion he had previously formed, that any further examination of this branch would be useless.

After passing to the west of the rocky passage, the best channel is on the southern shore, but even that is intricate, and the greatest depth of its water is only four fathoms. They took up their abode for the night about half a mile from their preceding night's lodging; having returned in three hours the same distance that had taken them twelve hours to ascend.

In the morning of the 31st of October it was low water at four, and high water at six o'clock; the rise and fall of the water did not appear generally to exceed two feet, and the stream constantly ran down. Mr. Broughton departed early, and off the village of their friendly old chief was joined by him and his whole tribe. Soundings were pretty regular, until the party were

any place of such extent, and that admits a doubt, shou'd certainly be explored as high as practicable.' – 29 October. Bell's remarks are interesting, for within twenty years the Columbia was to become a regular travel route for fur traders coming from E of the mountains.

[1] Broughton named Possession Point to commemorate the ceremony. It was on the S bank of the Columbia; his chart suggests that it was at the bend in the river E of the mouth of the Sandy River.

[2] Neither Gray's chart nor the log of the *Columbia* suggests that Gray went farther up the river than Grays Bay.

abreast of some barren land, off which is an extensive bank. On this there were only three feet water; this depth continued nearly to the east point of the islet, that was observed before to be covered with wild geese, and obtained the name of GOOSE ISLAND.[1] The channel here is on the southern shore, until the passage between Menzies island and the north shore is well open; this is good and clear with regular soundings from three to seven fathoms, quite to Belle Vue point, where a spit lies out at some small distance. The land in the neighbourhood of this reach, extending about five leagues to Baring's river, is on the southern side low, sandy, and well wooded. On the north side the country rises beyond the banks of the river with a pleasing degree of elevation, agreeably adorned with several clumps of trees; and towards the eastern part of the reach, it finishes at the water's edge in romantic rocky projecting precipices.

The good old chief here took his leave of the party. In commemoration of his friendly behaviour, and his residence being in the neighbourhood, this part of the river obtained the name of FRIENDLY REACH,[2] and a point on the northern shore, bearing from Belle Vue point S. 67 E., PARTING POINT.[3] From this place to the station where Mr. Broughton observed the latitude on the 29th, the soundings were from six to ten fathoms; from whence a bank of sand extended along the western shore about a league, reaching over two-thirds of the channel, leaving a very narrow passage of the depth of ten to twelve fathoms. This bank terminates at Willow Point, from whence the soundings decreased from nine to six fathoms. About three miles from this point, on the opposite or eastern side of the river, an opening or arm was passed, leading to the N.E. This was named by Mr. Broughton, after the master of the Discovery, WHIDBEY'S RIVER.[4] The western point was flat, and produced some grass and willow trees. The opposite shore still continued more elevated, and from Whidbey's river was covered with pine trees. At the entrance into this river the depth of water was six or seven fathoms; but on approaching point Warrior for about two miles, it decreased to three and four fathoms, and again increased to ten and twelve fathoms off that point; from thence to Oak point the depth was from ten to five fathoms, here the party rested for the night, and perceived it to be low water at half past three, and high water at five in the morning of the 1st of November. In this situation they had before seen many of the natives, but the night most probably now prevented their appearance. The weather had the preceding day been gloomy, attended with fog and rain; this morning it was fair and pleasant, with a favourable eastwardly breeze. In passing from Urry's islands, the soundings were first from seven to three, then from four to nine fathoms; the depth again decreased as the low sandy island was approached, to six, three, and four fathoms; this

[1] Tomahawk Island.
[2] Broughton's chart indicates that he intended this name to apply to the river between Government Island and Hayden Island.
[3] Now Mathews Point.   [4] Now Bachelor Island Slough.

latter depth continued between the island and the northern shore, which is the best channel, passing close to the main land. From this island, where the water all round it is shoal, a spit extends some distance to the westward, on which there was no more than three fathoms; but from thence to the rocky islet where the canoes with the dead bodies were deposited, [1] it increases to seven and twelve fathoms; about a mile above this rock, a bank extends to the eastern shore nearly into mid-channel, where the depth of water did not exceed two fathoms and an half, all the way to Knight's river. [2] The shores on this side are low, flat, and sandy; on the western side high and woody, and affording a clear though narrow channel, with soundings from five to eight fathoms.

Knight's river is about the eighth of a mile in width; and from its entrance, where its depth is four fathoms, it takes a direction S. 51 E. Leaving Knight's river, the soundings increased from seven to twelve fathoms, until mount Coffin was reached, where the depth of water was only six fathoms; and passing between the northern shore, and the dry sand bank, from three to five fathoms only were found; but the soundings increased from six to ten fathoms as the party advanced towards Walker's island. On the western point of this island they made a late dinner, and had an opportunity of observing, that during the rising of the water the stream did not run up, the surface of the water being still and stationary; it was high water at five in the afternoon. From this point the depth continued from five to seven fathoms, until Baker's islands were approached. A shoal spit extends from the longest and largest of these islands, or that which was so considered, to the eastward; on this was found only two and a half or three fathoms water. To the north of this apparently large island are three smaller ones, which admit a clear though narrow passage between them and the northern shore. On one of these, under the shelter of a grove of fine poplars, Mr. Broughton rested for the night. At day-light the next morning their journey was resumed, and in passing Swaine's river, [3] which takes a south-westerly direction, no bottom could be found with fifteen fathoms of line; but towards its western point soundings were had of three and four fathoms. About a league to the westward of this is Manby's river, [4] taking a course S.S.W.; from hence the depth of water was from seven to nine fathoms, until they approached near the east point of Puget's island; from whence a shoal extends about a mile nearly into mid-channel; on this there were only two fathoms, but on crossing over to the southern shore, it deepened to seven fathoms. Mount St. Helen's was here very distinctly seen lying S. 81 E. Puget's island was passed on the south, and observed to produce on that side only a few pine trees of inferior size; but it afforded a good channel of

---

[1] Coffin Rock.
[2] The Cowlitz River.   [3] The E entrance to Wallace Slough.
[4] The W entrance to Wallace Slough. This is the first mention of Manby's River by name. As already noted, the names of Swaine's River and Manby's River have been transposed on Broughton's chart.

seven, ten, and thirteen fathoms of water: the latter depth was off its western extremity, which is a low marshy point covered with reeds. Soon after passing this point, another branch of the river was opened,[1] which appeared, by the high land on the southern side, to lead into the sound in a direction N. 56 W. But as in its entrance the depth of water was only two fathoms and an half, Mr. Broughton was induced to give up his intention of examining it, and pursued his former course, keeping near the southern shore, consisting apparently of a cluster of marshy islands. The north westernmost of these forms the south point of the entrance into the river; and on the west, or sound side of this point, the low marshy land takes a south-westerly direction, whose other openings appeared to communicate with the last mentioned. Before these openings lie the shoals already noticed. On the northern shore, immediately without the entrance into the river, is an Indian village;[2] a part of it only was occupied by the natives, who supplied our friends very liberally with salmon, and promised to follow them with more to the vessel. From hence they steered for a low sandy island, partly covered with trees, in the eastern part of the sound, with soundings from seven to five fathoms, until they drew very near to it, when the water became so shallow that they were obliged to haul off. Towards its north-west part two fathoms and an half were found close to it. Mr. Broughton had no opportunity of examining whether there was any passage in this situation towards the southern shore, as it was at this time dark; but. by its former appearance from the elevated land on the northern shore, he was of opinion there was not. A bank nearly dry continued all the way from this island to point Adams. He however passed some distance along the north edge of the bank, towards Tongue point, in three fathoms water, until nearly a-breast of Gray's bay; here they came to overfalls from three to seven fathoms, and found themselves within, or to the south of, a dry bank, which obliged them to pull back in order to clear it; after which they had regular soundings in crossing Gray's bay from four to six fathoms water.

At nine in the evening the party arrived on board the Chatham; having employed exactly half the time in returning, that had been occupied in going up this river, in consequence of the general rapidity of the stream downwards, and of being assisted sometimes by a favourable wind.

Mr. Broughton had now lost sight of the Discovery twelve days, and though he had received no orders for the investigation he had undertaken, yet he was convinced, that in so doing he would act agreeably to my wishes; and having obtained so much information, he deemed it expedient to join the Discovery with all possible dispatch.

Much to his satisfaction, he found the Chatham ready in every respect for

---

[1] Clifton Channel, separated from the northern channel that Broughton followed by Tenasillahe Island and a series of low marshy islands.

[2] Marked on Broughton's chart, to the W of Skamokawa Creek (Orchard's River).

sea;[1] the next morning she was unmoored; but the wind from the east shifting suddenly to the southward, and blowing in squalls very hard, attended with a heavy rain, they remained at their anchorage until the next day, when the weather being more moderate they got under weigh; but they had scarcely filled their sails when the wind, as on the preceding day, came round, and as they had a very narrow space to work in between the northern shore and the shoals, they again anchored in eight fathoms water, to wait a more favourable opportunity. This presented itself in the afternoon; but by the time they had reached the large deserted village, it again became stormy, with a heavy rain from the westward, which compelled them again to stop in six fathoms water, a little below the deserted village called by the natives Chenoke. Cape Disappointment bore by compass N. 84 W., Tongue point N. 64 E., one mile distant; point Adams S. 51 W., and the nearest shore north, at the distance of a quarter of a mile.

The same unpleasant weather continued until the next morning, November 6, when, with the wind at E.N.E. they stood towards cape Disappointment. The launch sounded the channel before the vessel, and the surf was soon seen to break across the passage leading to sea with great violence, and in such a manner as to leave no apparent opening. The wind at this time also veering to the south, induced Mr. Broughton to bear away for a bay that is situated immediately within, and on the eastern side of cape Disappointment;[2] the south-east end of that promontory forms its west point of entrance; its east point being formed by the west extremity of the spit bank, lying from each other E.S.E. and W.N.W. about three quarters of a mile asunder. In passing the channel a sufficient depth of water was found, until bordering too much on the spit bank they came into three fathoms, with a very confused sea that broke violently on the bank. At ten in the forenoon they anchored in five fathoms water; point Adams, by compass, bearing S. 46 E. Chenoke point S. 86 E. the inner part of cape Disappointment forming the west point of entrance into the bay S. 4 E. half a mile distant; and the southernmost part of the coast in sight S. 36 E.

Here was found the Jenny of Bristol, the same vessel that had been passed by the Chatham on her first arrival. Mr. Broughton was informed by the master of this vessel, Mr. Baker, that a constant succession of bad weather had prevented his putting to sea; that he had made several attempts, but from the violence of the surf and its breaking intirely across the entrance, he had not been able to effect that purpose. In the afternoon, Mr. Broughton went

---

[1] This was due to Manby, who had been left in charge of the ship. 'The first favourable moment I moored the Vessel close to the Shore, and [as Broughton had taken both the ship's boats] purchased a large canoe from the Indians, which fully answered my purpose.' Wood was secured from an unexpected source: 'a great deal of drift Wood was at all times floating with the tide, and served our purpose to complete our stock of Fire Wood without much trouble.' – Manby, letters, October.

[2] Baker Bay.

on shore in order to view from the hills the state of the channel into the ocean. This presented one intire range of heavy breakers, reaching across from side to side.

Fresh gales with squally weather from the S.E. on the 7th. The Chatham, with half a cable only, rode very easy; and the Jenny lying within her, in three fathoms water, at low tide, with the cape bearing by compass S.E. was intirely becalmed under its high land. The afternoon being more moderate the seine was hauled, but with little success. The weather still continuing unfavourable, the next day was employed in replenishing their stock of wood and water, and Mr. Broughton in person sounded the bay, and part of the channel. The depth of water between the Chatham and Jenny, and within the spit bank, towards a small river in the northern part of this bay,[1] was from 5 to 3, 4, 5, 6, 7, and then overfalls of 2 and 3 fathoms, to the spit bank; where the water broke very heavily. From the Chatham across to the breakers off point Adams, were found not less than $4\frac{1}{2}$ fathoms, but the sea broke so violently that he was prevented sounding through the channel, which was not distinguishable in any direction.

Mr. Manby and some others of the gentlemen, who with Mr. Baker had been up the small river, returned in the evening with eighteen geese, besides a great number of ducks, and some smaller birds.

The morning of the 9th brought fair and pleasant weather, with the wind at S.E. Mr. Broughton again visited the hills of the cape to take some angles; the sea was too much agitated by the breakers to allow the appearance of any opening through them towards the ocean. In his walk he killed a fine deer. The weather being more moderate than it had been for many days, induced a number of the inhabitants to visit the Chatham; these brought a large supply of fish, and moose-deer sufficient for the crew. Amongst the Indians were several who had followed them up the river, and who now brought their various commodities for sale, in the same friendly manner they had done before. The latitude observed this day was 46° 19'. In the afternoon Mr. Sheriff was sent to sound, and view the channel out to sea. On his return it was reported to be clear, smooth, and no where less than four fathoms water.

The next morning, with a moderate breeze at E.N.E. the Chatham weighed at half ebb from Baker's bay, so named by Mr. Broughton after the commander of the Jenny, whose track he followed; Mr. Baker having obligingly offered, as his was the smallest vessel, to lead out,[2] and having been here in the earlier part of the year, he was better acquainted than Mr. Broughton with the course of the channel. After making two short trips, the Chatham just weathered the cape, and the breakers that lie off it. The

[1] Named James's River on Broughton's chart, no doubt after James Baker, master of the *Jenny*. Now the Wallacut River.

[2] 'Mr. Baker had very civilly offered to lead out in the Jenny, as she only drew 8 feet of Water, whilst our heavy tub drew upwards of 12...' – Bell, 10 November. The *Columbia* had drawn between 6 and 8 feet.

soundings were from 6 to 9 and 11 fathoms, the sea extremely irregular and confused. On standing over towards point Adams, the depth decreased to 6, 5, and $4\frac{1}{2}$ fathoms. Their course was now directed W. $\frac{1}{2}$ S. close to the southern side of the channel. Here the heavy breakers rolled with impetuous force against the wind and tide, and greatly retarded their progress. For, notwithstanding the fresh favourable breeze that blew right aft, there was much difficulty to keep the vessel's head the right way, owing to the violence of the sea, that made her pitch so incessantly as to shake the wind out of her sails.

The Jenny appeared to get out without shipping any water; the Chatham followed her track, but the sea broke several times over her from stem to stern; due precautions however having been taken, none of the water got below. In this unpleasant situation little progress was made. Mr. Broughton suspecting they might have occasion for the boats, had kept them both out in readiness for any emergency. Unfortunately one of these tremendous surges stove the launch, which filled, and by the violence of the jerk broke the tow-rope. One of their marines was unhappily the boat keeper, and it was impossible at the moment to afford him any other assistance than that of veering a buoy a-stern; this expedient however failed, and they had every reason to fear that the poor fellow would be drowned. After contending with three other such violent billows, the wind and tide carried the vessel out with great velocity; and on their arriving in smoother water, the cutter was instantly dispatched to the assistance of the marine, who was perceived amidst those violent agitations of the water, still holding fast of the launch; which, having been more sensibly operated upon than the vessel by the strength of the tide, had drifted clear out; and those on board the Chatham had the inexpressible happiness of seeing the cutter bring both their ship-mate and the launch safely alongside, with the loss only of the furniture that she had contained.[1] Both boats were immediately hoisted in, and the Chatham made sail to the S.S.E. with a fine breeze at N.W. in company with the Jenny.

Soon after the Chatham was out a ship was seen in that quarter, which Mr. Broughton would have concluded to be the Dædalus store ship, had not Mr. Baker informed him that she had joined the Discovery off the entrance, the day after he went up the river; the sequel however shewed that he was not mistaken, this vessel proving to be the Dædalus, which had been detained by the inclemency of the weather in Gray's harbour, until within a few hours of her being seen by the Chatham.

Thus the Chatham quitted Columbia river; the rest of the time, till she joined the Discovery, was employed in performing a very boisterous and unpleasant passage, until she passed cape Mendocino, exactly similar to that

---

[1] The rescue was accomplished with remarkable speed: 'in less than ten minutes, the Cutter was mann'd and sent after the Launch...the man was safe, [but] every thing belonging to her, Oars, Masts, Sails was lost and her side was stove in...' – Bell, 10 November.

which we had experienced.[1] I shall conclude this account of Columbia river, by a few short remarks that Mr. Broughton made in the course of its survey, in his own words:

'The discovery of this river we were given to understand is claimed by the Spaniards, who call it Entrada de Ceta, after the commander of the vessel, who is said to be its first discoverer, but who never entered it;[2] he places it in 46°, north latitude. It is the same opening that Mr. Gray stated to us in the spring, he had been nine days off the former year, but could not get in, in consequence of the out-setting current. That in the course of the late summer he had however entered the river, or rather the sound, and had named it after the ship he then commanded. The extent Mr. Gray became acquainted with on that occasion is no further than what I have called Gray's bay, not more than 15 miles from cape Disappointment, though according to Mr. Gray's sketch it measures 36 miles.[3] By his calculation its entrance lies in latitude 46° 10', longitude 237° 18', differing materially in these respects from our observations.[4]

'The entrance, as already stated, lies between the breakers extending from cape Disappointment on the north side, and those on the south side from point Adams, over a sort of bar, or more properly speaking, over an extensive flat, on which was found no less depth of water than four and a half fathoms. The best leading mark is to bring the Tongue point, which looks like an island near the southern shore, to bear by compass about E. by N. and then steer for it; this was observed in the passages of the Chatham in and out, though on the latter occasion, circumstances were too unpleasant to allow of great precision.

'From the information and experience derived by this visit, it appears to be highly adviseable, that no vessel should attempt entering this port, but when the water is perfectly smooth; a passage may then be effected with safety, but ought even then to be undertaken with caution: bordering on the breakers

---

[1] Vancouver does not mention that the *Chatham* twice encountered the *Jenny* on her voyage southward: 'In the afternoon [of 14 November] we Spoke the Jenny, who had parted from us the first night, she seem'd to have suffered much in her Sails by the late bad weather.' On the 17th 'The Jenny once more join'd us, and Mr. Baker came on board with a very piteous Tale, that the late bad Weather had done his Sails & rigging so much damage that he was in great distress, particularly for Rope and Sewing twine, of which articles as we had plenty Mr. B. supplied him a Coil of 2 inch rope & a Bale of Twine.' On the 19th 'the Jenny now parted from us in her passage to England...' – Bell, 14, 17 and 19 November.

[2] Bruno de Hezeta discovered the mouth of the Columbia in August 1775 and named it Ensenada de la Nuestra Señora de Asuncion. Wagner notes that it usually appeared on Spanish maps as Entrada de Ezeta.

[3] The scale on the copy of Gray's chart in C.O. 5/187 is in leagues, and by this scale the distance from Cape Disappointment to the middle of Grays Bay is about 13 leagues or 39 miles. The actual distance is about 20 miles.

[4] Cape Disappointment light, on the SE point of the cape, is in lat. 46° 16·6' N, long. 124° 03·1' W (235° 56·9' E).

off point Adams, and keeping the Tongue point well open, with Chenoke, or Village point, will avoid the Spit bank, and give a clear channel up to Chenoke; but in case of failure in the wind or tide, it will then be most adviseable to anchor in Baker's bay, bringing its entrance to bear north, and keeping close round the Cape breakers, where the depth of water is from eleven to nine and six fathoms, close to the Cape shore. Within the Cape are three rocky islets in the bay, the middle one being the largest; just on with the Cape is the line of direction going in, or out; leading along the southern side of the spit bank in deep water, and near this islet, bringing the Cape to bear between S. and S.E. is good anchorage, in five fathoms water. The latitude is 46° 19', longitude 236° 7', and the variation of the compass 20° eastwardly. The greatest rise and fall of the tide in this bay observed by Mr. Baker was twelve feet; high water at full and change at half past one o'clock. Mr. Manby's observations on board the Chatham confirmed those of Mr. Baker, as to the time of high water; but the rise and fall of the tide with him did not exceed six feet, and the greatest strength of the tide was about four knots.[1]

'This bay, beside affording good and secure anchorage, is convenient for procuring wood and water; and, by keeping upon good terms with the natives, who seemed much inclined to be friendly, a supply of fish, and other refreshments, may easily be obtained. The heavy and confused swell that in bad weather constantly rolls in from the sea over its shallow entrance, and breaks in three fathoms water, renders the space between Baker's bay and Chenoke point a very indifferent roadstead. Cape Disappointment is formed by high steep precipices, covered with coarse grass, the sides and tops of the hills with pine trees. Point Adams being the south-east point of entrance is low and sandy, from whence the country rises with a gradual ascent, and produces pine and other trees. Any further nautical information that may be required will be better obtained by reference to the sketch.

'With respect to its natural productions, and other interesting matter; the weather experienced on board the vessel having uniformly been similar to that afterwards encountered at sea, precluded any competent knowledge being acquired. The trees principally composing the forest, were pines of different kinds, growing to a large size, but were unequal to those of Nootka. Near the water-side were found maple, alder, and ash, and at some distance up the river, beside these, the oak, poplar, and oriental strawberry tree were produced, with many other forest trees, unknown to the gentlemen, who made a short excursion into the country, and who were only able to judge of the indigenous quadrupeds or animals, by the skins the natives wore or brought to barter; these were similar to those found on others parts of the coast. The birds that were procured were large brown cranes, white swans, white and brown geese, ducks, partridges, and snipes; a variety of others were seen that could not be

---

[1] 'Mean ranges of tides on the Columbia River range from 6·7 feet at Youngs Bay [opposite Baker Bay]...to 3·3 feet at Longview, Wash. [at the mouth of the Cowlitz River], to 1·3 feet at Vancouver, Wash. [opposite Hayden Island].' U.S. Coast Pilot 7, p. 238.

taken. All that were brought on board, excepting the brown cranes, proved excellent at table. The river seemed to abound with fish, from the supply the natives provided, consisting of two sorts of salmon, both very good; sturgeon of a large size and very fine flavor, with silver bream, herrings, flat fish, and soirdinias; of these four last sorts some were caught in the seine. The skirts of the woods afforded a most excellent green vegetable, resembling in appearance and taste the turnip-top when young. A bulbous root, about the size, and not unlike the crocus, that ate much like mealy potatoe, wild mint, ground ivy, and wild lavender, all these the natives make great use of, together with berries of various kinds, particularly the cranberry, of a most excellent flavor, and the first we had seen on this coast.

'The natives[1] differed in nothing very materially from those we had visited during the summer, but in the decoration of their persons; in this respect, they surpassed all the other tribes with paints of different colours, feathers, and other ornaments. Their houses seemed to be more comfortable than those at Nootka, the roof having a greater inclination, and the planking being thatched over with the bark of trees. The entrance is through a hole, in a broad plank, covered in such a manner as to resemble the face of a man, the mouth serving the purpose of a door-way. The fire-place is sunk into the earth, and confined from spreading above by a wooden frame. The inhabitants are universally addicted to smoking. Their pipe is similar to ours in shape; the bowl is made of very hard wood, and is externally ornamented with carvings; the tube, about two feet long, is made of a small branch of the elder. In this they smoke an herb, which the country produces, of a very mild nature, and by no means unpleasant; they however took great pleasure in smoking our tobacco; hence it is natural to conclude, it might become a valuable article of traffic amongst them. In most other respects they resemble their neighbours, as to their manners and mode of living, being equally filthy and uncleanly.

'The soil of the low ground was mostly a stiff, rich clay, capable to all appearance of being made very productive; that on the high land amongst the pine trees, a black mould, seemingly composed of decayed vegetables.'

Having now concluded Mr. Broughton's very interesting account of the river Columbia, and the adjacent country; I shall in the next chapter proceed with the transactions of the Dædalus; and, in the first place, notice Mr. Whidbey's account of Gray's harbour; where, although he was longer detained from us, he had not an opportunity of employing his time to so much advantage in geographical pursuits as Mr. Broughton; the regions allotted to his examination having been found of very limited extent.

[1] The various tribes of the Chinookian family.

CHAPTER IV.

Mr. Whidbey's Account of Gray's Harbour—Transactions of the Dædalus at the Marquesas, and at some newly-discovered Islands—Murder of Lieutenant Hergest at Woahoo—Arrival of the Dædalus at Nootka.

A T sun set, on the 18th of October, the Dædalus anchored before the entrance of Gray's harbour,[1] in seven fathoms water, about half a mile from the reef that extends from the north point of entrance; a boat was sent to examine the passage into this harbour, but returned with little more information than that of its being very intricate, and that it would require much time to become acquainted with it. At day-light the next morning, a boat was again sent for the same purpose, and afterwards the ship was got under weigh, in order to be in readiness; but the boat not returning, another was dispatched at noon, and at three o'clock both returned; the first having been detained by the strength of the flood tide. From their report the ship immediately bore away, and passed a bar in 18 feet water. The bar extends directly across the entrance into the harbour, which is about a mile wide; from whence they proceeded up the channel, formed by two reefs about three quarters of a mile asunder, extending into the ocean from the points of land which form the entrance into this harbour. Here the depth of water regularly increased from four to eleven fathoms, but the ebb tide made so strong, that although the ship went nearly at the rate of five knots, little progress was made; this compelled them to anchor about seven o'clock in the latter depth, having a clear sandy bottom. The outer breakers on the reef, forming the northern side of the passage, bore by compass S. 58 W. distant two miles; a dry sand bank N. 81 W. half a mile distant; the inner breakers on the same side N. 34 E. at the like distance; the outer breakers on the southern side S. 32 W. distant two miles; and the inner breakers on that side, N. 65 E. these form the channel within the bar: there is also a breaker on the bar about a quarter of a mile from the S.W. point of the northernmost ledge of breakers, which bore S. 50 W.

On the morning of the 20th the wind blowing a strong gale from the N.E. prevented the ship moving; but whilst the flood tide lasted, the boats were

---

[1] The *Columbia* entered Grays Harbor (as the name is now spelled) on 7 May 1792 and Gray named it Bulfinch Harbor after Charles Bulfinch, part owner of his ship. The name is used in the surviving fragment of the ship's log, but Boit refers to Gray's Harbor in his log. Vancouver adopted the latter name.

profitably employed in the further examination of the channel. The observed latitude was found to be 46° 58½'.

Fair weather attended the N.E. gale, which continued until the next morning, when the wind veered to the S.E. the Dædalus than stood into the harbour, and was moored about noon in 4 fathoms water, off the north point of entrance.

This is a rounding point, bearing by compass from N. 34 W. to N. 68 W. the former distant half a mile; the south point of entrance bore S. 20 W. and the intermediate space was shut in from the sea by the reefs. This anchorage was found to be a very snug and safe situation, and it was a fortunate retreat, as a hard gale of wind set in from the S.E. with a great deal of rain, which continued until the next morning, when Mr. Whidbey began his examination of the harbour. It seemed to be of no great extent, as the land appeared to be closely connected on every side; the operation however proved to be very tedious, in consequence of the very bad weather, and the difficulty of approaching the several parts of the shore on which it was necessary to land. This survey was not finished so far as the boats could proceed, until the morning of the 26th. The north point of entrance, named by Mr. Whidbey after Captain Brown, now Rear Admiral, is situated in latitude 47°, longitude 236° 7';[1] the variation of the compass 18 easterly. From hence its southern point of entrance, which obtained the name of Point Hanson[2] after Lieutenant Hanson who commanded the Dædalus, lies S. 10 E. distant about two miles and a quarter from the former: the breakers of the north side of the channel stretch first S. 33 W. for half a league, and then S. 72 W. two miles and three quarters further, where they terminate on that side. Those on the southern side extend first N. 59 W. for a mile, and then S. 61 W. two miles and three quarters further, where these also terminate. From these terminations of the reefs, the bar stretches across from point to point, on which at high neap tides there is only twenty feet water; having on it the breaker before noticed, contracting the width of the passage, which can only be considered to lie between it and the southern reef. After passing the bar the channel appeared to be uninterrupted, the northern side being the deepest, with regular soundings from four to fourteen fathoms; the latter depth was found in the narrowest part, not more than half a mile wide, between the two first mentioned projecting points of the reef, from the points of the habour. Thence in the line of mid-channel the depth decreases to six fathoms between the points of the harbour, and to four and three fathoms towards the southern side, which is the shallowest; it however increases to ten and decreases again to six and three fathoms near point Brown: this is the boldest shore, and affords a space of near two miles in extent to the N.E. east and S.E. of it, where may be found good and secure anchorage; with regular soundings from ten to four fathoms; to the north is excellent anchorage also in four to six fathom water,

[1] Point Brown. Its position is lat. 46° 56' N, long. 124° 10' W (235° 50' E).
[2] Now Point Chehalis.

though this is more confined by the shoals. From point Brown, to a point up the harbour, lying from it N. 65 E. at the distance of four miles and a quarter, which obtained the name of POINT NEW[1] after the master of the store ship, the northern shore forms a deep bay, falling back near a league and a half from the line of the two points. This bay is occupied by shoals and overfalls commencing about a mile to the north of point Brown, stretching nearly in an eastern direction, and passing, about a mile to the southward of point New, up to the navigable extent of the harbour, which terminates in an eastern direction about two leagues from point Brown, though the shore on each side retires about half a league further back; but the intermediate space, consisting of a shallow flat, (where was the appearance of a small rivulet) prevented the head of the harbour from being approached. From this station the shoals on its southern side take a direction nearly S. 73 W. until they reach within about one mile and three quarters of point Brown, lying from that point S. 45 E.; there, a point is formed that stretches to the southward, and admits of a narrow channel of about four and five fathoms water, between them and the shoal that lies on the eastern side of point Hanson, into a small cove, lying from that point S. 50 E. two miles distant. These shoals, extending intirely round the harbour, are in some parts, particularly on its south side, dry at low water, and on them are lodged great numbers of dead trees and logs of drift timber. There are also two other shoals situated at the distance of two miles to the eastward of point Brown, lying nearly in a north and south direction. The easternmost, which is the largest, and partly a dry sand, nearly connects the two shoal banks, admitting a narrow passage to the north of it with five fathoms, and another to the south of it in which there is only three fathoms water. The rise and fall of the tide was here found to be about ten feet, and it is high water about 50' after the moon passes the meridian. The only leading marks for sailing into this harbour, are two small red cliffy islets lying to the N.W. of point New; the outermost of these, having the resemblance of a flower pot, in a line with point Brown, leads over the centre of the bar; as also, over part of the northern reef, which is easily avoided by keeping in the depth of water already mentioned, after crossing the bar. Any further nautical information that may be required, will be found by reference to the sketch of this survey.[2]

This port appears to be of little importance in its present state, as it affords but two or three situations where the boats could approach sufficiently near the shores to effect a landing; the most commodious place was at point Brown; another near point Hanson; and one in the cove or creek to the S.E. of that point. The shallowness of the water on the bar also renders it by no means a desirable port. To pass this is impracticable unless near high water, even with vessels of a very moderate size, and it should then be attempted with the utmost

---

[1] The name has been retained, but it does not appear on Whidbey's chart.

[2] Whidbey's chart is an inset on the engraved chart of the Northwest Coast from lat. 46° 30' N, to 52° 15' N. The 'red cliffy islets' are now Neds Rock.

caution; since Mr. Whidbey had great reason to believe that it is a shifting bar; there being a very apparent difference in the channel on their arrival, and at their departure, when it seemed to have become much wider but less deep. A dry sand bank which lay near their anchorage the first evening on the north side of the channel, was now intirely washed away by the violence of the sea, which had incessantly broke upon the shoals and bar.

Wood and water are at too great a distance to be easily procured, particularly the latter, which is found in small springs only, running through the sand near point Hanson, at the distance of a mile from the landing place, over a very heavy sand.

The surrounding shores are low and apparently swampy, with salt marshes; the soil is a thin mixture of red and white sand, over a bed of stones and pebbles. At a small distance from the water side the country is covered with wood, principally pines of an inferior stunted growth.

Both the Dædalus and Chatham had greatly the advantage of the Discovery, by being detained in port during the boisterous weather that we contended with. There they procured a most abundant supply of excellent fish, and wild fowl; the productions of Gray's harbour being similar to those found in and about Columbia river. Salmon, sturgeon, and other fish, were plentifully obtained from the natives, and geese, ducks, and other wild fowl, shot by themselves in such numbers, as sometimes to serve the whole of their crews. The best sporting ground in Gray's harbour was found to be on its south side.

Mr. Whidbey estimated the number of Indians inhabiting this place at about one hundred; they spoke the Nootka language, but it did not appear to be their native tongue; and they seemed to vary in little or no respect from those people we had occasionally seen during the summer. Their behaviour was uniformly civil, courteous, and friendly. In Mr. Whidbey's excursion to the head of the harbour he was visited by nineteen of them, who, having satisfied their curiosity and received some trivial presents, were about to depart, when the boat in endeavouring to approach a small rivulet became entangled amongst shoals, sunken logs of wood, and stumps of trees; on which there being some sea occasioned the boat frequently to strike, and rendered its situation very disagreeable; the friendly Indians, perceiving their embarrassment, very kindly by signs, and other means, afforded them such assistance as soon conducted them into deep water, when they took their leave and departed.[1]

[1] By contrast, in May Gray had felt it necessary to fire on the Indians. The day after the *Columbia* arrived, Boit's log records, 'they brought a great many furs which we purchas'd cheap for Blankets and Iron'. In the evening they 'heard the hooting of Indians, all hands was immediately under arms, severall canoes was seen passing near the Ship, but was dispers'd by firing a few Musketts over their heads.' Later 'a large Canoe with at least 20 Men in her got within 1/2 pistol shot of the quarter, and with a Nine pounder, loaded with langerege [langrage] and about 10 Musketts, loaded with Buck shot, we dash'd her to pieces, and no doubt kill'd every soul in her. The rest soon made a retreat.' In spite of this, many canoes 'brought plenty of Skins' the next day. – *Voyages of the 'Columbia'*, p. 395.

Mr. Whidbey considered them to be rather a more slender race than we had been accustomed to see, and that, contrary to the generality of the men we had become acquainted with on the coast of North West America, these did not appear to be jealous of their women, but allowed them to repair on board the vessel, where they remained many hours at a time much to their satisfaction. They appeared to be divided into three distinct tribes, or parties, each having one or two chiefs. When enquiries were made of any one part respecting the other two, they would reply that the others were bad people, and that the party questioned were the only good Indians in the harbour. Hence may be inferred that they were at this time at variance, and that their interests were totally separate from each other.[1] Some of their war canoes were seen: these had a piece of wood rudely carved, perforated, and placed at each end, three feet above the gunwale; through these holes they are able to discharge their arrows, without exposing their persons to their adversaries, either in advancing or retreating.[2] Each canoe held twenty people or upwards; little difference appeared in their bows or arrows from those generally met with; the former were somewhat more circular, and the latter were pointed with iron, copper, or shells, some of which were barbed; these seemed to be their most favourite weapon, and were managed with great dexterity. One of the Indians desired the mate of the Dædalus to shoot a pelican sitting on the water about fifty yards off. The mate fired twice with single ball without hurting the bird, which kept its station. The Indian missed it with the first arrow, but with the second he pierced through the wing and body of the pelican, to the great exultation of all the natives present. They are well versed in commercial pursuits, and dealt very fairly and honestly. For sea-otter skins they sometimes required iron in exchange, but in general sold them for copper and woollen cloth. About thirty or forty good sea-otter skins, with many of inferior quality, were thus purchased; for their less valuable commodities they were partial to pale blue beads, two of which would buy a large salmon. They appeared to be a hardy people, and inured to the inclemency of the weather; which, when at the worst, did not deter them from visiting the ship, though the sea frequently broke intirely over them. On such occasions they bale their canoe, and paddle on, without the least apparent concern.

This is the substance of the information acquired by Mr. Whidbey in his visit to Gray's harbour; and, as the observations made on the passage of the Dædalus from thence to Monterrey, would, like those of the Chatham, be only a repetition of what has been already related, I shall now proceed to state some interesting intelligence collected from letters written off Owyhyee by the late Lieutenant Hergest, agent to the Dædalus transport, respecting his

[1] Two Salishan tribes inhabited Grays Harbor: the Chehalis, who had villages on the S shore, and in the lower valley of the Chehalis River, and the Humptulips, who had villages on the N shore and others in the valley of the Humptulips River. The Indians Broughton saw may also have included some Chinook visitors from the Columbia River.
[2] Boit noted that 'Their Canoes was from the Logs rudely cut out, with upright ends', but makes no mention of loopholes. *Voyages of the 'Columbia'*, p. 395.

transactions at the Marquesas, and the discovery of some islands to the N.W. of them, with an extract from his log-book on the same subjects; together with the account given by Mr. Thomas New, the master, of the unfortunate death of that officer, and of the late Mr. Gooch the astronomer. As the preceding part of Mr. Hergest's voyage appeared by the journals on board to contain no very interesting intelligence, the narrative will commence on the arrival of the Dædalus at the Marquesas.

The length of the passage from Falkland's islands into this ocean, rendered it necessary that Mr. Hergest should embrace the earliest opportunity to recruit his water, and procure refreshments, especially as the character, that had been lately published in England of the inhabitants on the Sandwich islands, made it uncertain that any supplies would be procured from that quarter. Having made the Marquesas, Lieutenant Hergest directed his course for Resolution bay in the island of Ohetahoo;[1] where the Dædalus anchored on the evening of the 22d of March, 1792, in 22 fathoms water, sandy bottom; having worked into the bay against very heavy squalls and gusts of wind, which came down with great fury from the hills that overlook the shores.

In one of these heavy squalls, about four o'clock the next morning, they parted from their anchor and drove out of the bay. The vessel was scarcely clear of the points when Mr. Hergest discovered the ship to be on fire. They had all been prevented sleeping during the night by the ship having been full of smoke; those who had the watch on deck attributed this circumstance to the smoke having come from the shore; and this opinion, very inconsiderately and without reflection had been generally adopted, until Mr. Hergest, after the ship had cleared the points of the bay, in going into the cabin was convinced that the smoke originated from a nearer and more alarming cause. On lifting up the gun room scuttle, there immediately issued an immense column of smoke, which left no doubt of their perilous situation, as the fire was close to the magazine. Not a moment was lost in getting out the powder, and putting it into a boat alongside, but this was no easy task to perform; as the gun-room was extremely hot and full of smoke, and the powder, very injudiciously, had been promiscuously stowed amongst the ship's provisions. On this occasion there appears to have been no exertion wanting in the crew of the Dædalus, to whose credit Mr. Hergest observes, that in that trying moment every man stood firm to his duty, without suffering fear or panic to swerve them from its execution; although on some other occasions they had given him much trouble and serious concern. At first the fire was supposed to have been occasioned by some oakum, stowed in the forepart of the gun-room, taking fire, by accidentally getting wet; since no light had ever

---

[1] Hergest's spelling of Vaitahu. In May 1774, on his second voyage, Cook in the *Resolution* anchored in Resolution Bay (now Vaitahu Bay). The island then still retained its Spanish name, Santa Christina; it is now Tahu Ata. Hergest was a midshipman in the *Adventure* on the second voyage, but she was not in company with the *Resolution* when Cook visited the Marquesas.

been near it. After a large quantity of provisions had been hoisted up to get out the powder, the smoke was still found to ascend from below; this circumstance, with that of the deck being so hot as not to allow the people keeping their hands upon some lead that was laid upon it, convinced them that the fire must be in the lazaretto below, where some pursers beds were now recollected to have been *very improperly* stowed; and from the seas they had shipped during the tempestuous weather which they had experienced in their passage round cape Horn, no doubt was entertained that these beds had got wet and had taken fire. Every minute confirming Mr. Hergest in this opinion, care was immediately taken to stop every avenue and crevice about the after hatch-way, to prevent any communication of air before they ventured to scuttle the deck for the purpose of extinguishing the fire by pouring water over it. Happily they had day-light for executing this; and were soon convinced that the fire had originated as they had last conjectured, from the appearance of the ascending smoke, on scuttling the deck, as also of the good effect of their judicious labours. Other holes were now bored immediately over the beds, and after pouring down large quantities of water, they soon had reason to be gratefully thankful to Divine Providence for so timely and critical a preservation. Some of the beds were entirely consumed; a case on which they were laid, as also the deck over them, were burnt some way into the wood to a black cinder. Little else was stowed with these beds but rum and oil; so that had the fire once broke out into a blaze, the extinguishing it, or preventing its communication with these inflammable substances, would have been morally impossible, and their destruction would have been inevitable.[1]

The fire thus providentially discovered and happily extinguished, all the bedding, being either burnt or rotten, was got up and thrown overboard. Fearful of drifting too far to leeward, they were obliged to make sail in order to work into the bay, although the decks at this time were very much encumbered. Many of the natives were about the ship, employed in picking up the rotten bedding that had been thrown into the sea. At eleven in the forenoon they anchored near their former station. The natives had taken away the buoy, but had fastened a piece of wood to the buoy-rope, which answered all the purposes of recovering their anchor; this was soon effected, and the ship steadied with the kedge anchor to the southward; the south point of the bay bearing by compass S.W., the north point N.W., and the watering-place E. by N. one mile distant. The village in the south cove being the nearest shore, was at the distance of about a quarter of a mile.

In the afternoon Mr. Hergest in the cutter, attended by the second mate

---

[1] This passage prompted a comment, signed 'L', in the *Naval Chronicle*: 'It has been my constant practice, to order all straw to be thrown overboard, when unpacked. I forbad any bottles being packed in straw, or hay; but allowed them to be packed in oakum: – there not being a sufficient quantity, I procured saw-dust; in which some bottled porter burst, and mixing with the saw-dust, heated so much, that if, according to custom, the saw-dust had not been often examined, it would in the space of an hour have taken fire.' – II (1799), p. 513.

in the long boat, went to procure water, and landed with the mate and three men, though not without much difficulty on account of the surf. This did not permit them to put more than two casks on shore. Many of the natives were assembled, and in consequence of there being no chief amongst them were soon found to be very troublesome, as they stole every thing they could make off with, so that not a bucket was left them to fill the casks with water. Mr. Hergest, finding that his party on shore would require considerable reinforcement to effect his purpose, was about to embark, when one of his people claimed his attention. The natives had amused themselves by pulling the hair of a young man, and other waggish tricks, whilst his endeavours to prevent this rudeness afforded the rest of the Indians as high an entertainment as it would have done an English rabble. These indignities were so galling to the poor fellow, that no longer able to endure them, and not being in a situation to resent the insults he received, he burst into a flood of tears. On Mr. Hergest reproaching him in rather harsh terms for exposing so great a proof of his weakness, he found himself suddenly turned round by the natives who were behind him, and his fowling piece forcibly wrenched out of his hand. On the impulse of the moment he called to the mate to fire and bring down the thief, but fortunately, 'I say fortunately,' repeated Mr. Hergest, 'his piece was not cocked, and I had time to recollect that his musket was then the only one on shore; and there is no saying what consequences might have followed had the thief been shot.'[1] Mr. Hergest and his party very prudently retired immediately to their boats, which they effected without any opposition; but on re-embarking, it was found that some of the Indians had dived under water and cut the long boat's grapnel-rope, by which means they lost the grapnel.

These unprovoked injuries and indignities were not easily to be put up with; and Mr. Hergest very properly reflected, that passing by such insults and depredations would only encourage the islanders to persevere in these unwarrantable practices. In order, therefore, to awe them into better behaviour, he rowed close to the beach, and discharged a volley of musketoons and small arms over their heads. This measure had the good effect of driving them all, excepting one man, from the beach among the trees; this fellow was bold enough to remain, and throw stones with his sling at the boats. Mr. Hergest however took no notice of him, being determined to shew them the effect of their great guns, four of which were fired over the village on his return to the Dædalus. These produced such consternation, that the natives were seen making the best of their way in every direction towards the mountains.

The clearing the ship's decks and putting her to rights employed all hands

[1] In very similar circumstances a native had been shot accidentally and killed at the time of Cook's visit; and, Cook relates, although 'they afterwards stood in great dread of the Musquet, nevertheless they would often exercize their tallant of thieving upon us, which I thought necessary to put up with as our stay was likely to be but short among them.' – *Journals*, II, p. 366.

till nearly dark, when one of the natives swam off with their usual ensigns of peace, a green bough, wrapped up in white cloth; this he threw into the ship, and immediately returned to the shore. By this act of humiliation on the part of the natives, Mr. Hergest had great reason to expect that he should be enabled to carry into execution the service they had to perform on shore, without further molestation; and to hope that none of the Indians were killed or materially hurt, as his intention was only to frighten them, and by the superiority of his powers to shew them, that such improper behaviour should not long remain unchastised. In these expectations, the next morning (October [March] 24th)[1] he met with no disappointment, though it was not possible to restrain intirely the exercise of their thievish faculties, even on board the ship. The astronomer's theodolite, in its case, happening to be on deck, one of them contrived to convey it away, but being discovered swimming with it to his canoe, a musket was discharged by the chief mate, and it had the good effect of making the Indian abandon his prize, which was recovered, the case being sufficient to keep it afloat. After this the natives supplied them with bread fruit, together with a large quantity of other vegetables, and a few small pigs.

On Mr. Hergest's return to the shore, with a guard well armed, for the purpose of procuring water, no inconvenience arose from the natives; on the contrary, they cheerfully assisted in swimming off to the boats, filling and rolling down the water casks, and in other services, for which they were liberally rewarded with such trivial articles as they most highly esteemed.

One person only had been seen bearing the appearance of a chief, whose name was *Tu-ow*, and who had been amongst their first visitors on their arrival. In the afternoon he brought as a present some vegetables, with a small pig or two, for which he received a suitable reward; and was also presented by Mr. Hergest with the only English sow he had left, for the purpose of improving the breed of those animals in that country. Their operations were now carried on in a very amicable manner, but the number of visitors greatly impeded their business; to obviate this inconvenience the colours were hoisted, in order to signify that the ship was *tabooed*. This had the desired effect with respect to the men; but the women, who probably had more incitements than bare curiosity, were not to be so easily restrained. They still continued to swim from the shore in such numbers, that they were obliged, frequently, to fire muskets over their heads to deter them from advancing.

A tolerable supply of vegetables was obtained, but so few hogs, that it was noon on the 26th before a sufficient number were procured to serve the ship's company at the rate of one pound and a half per man; and these were purchased with twelve inches of bar iron for each small pig.

Two chiefs, who visited the ship on the 27th, restored the grapnel that had been stolen, and promised to bring back Mr. Hergest's fowling-piece. In the

[1] Here and twice in succeeding paragraphs October is mistakenly printed for March in both the first and second editions.

afternoon Mr. Hergest was employed in surveying and sounding the bay, the depth of water was found to be regular from 30 fathoms at its entrance to nine fathoms towards the shore, admitting of good anchorage within that space. Round the shores of the bay, at a very small distance, the depth of water was from seven to five and four fathoms.

Having completed their supply of water on the 29th of October [March], and having finished all the business they were here desirous of executing, just as they were preparing to sail the two chiefs who had returned the grapnel revisited the ship, and repeated their promise that the fowling piece should be restored. In consequence of their former good behaviour they had received many valuable presents; and as they were now in Mr. Hergest's power, and as he was well assured that they could obtain the restitution of his gun, he informed one of the chiefs that the ship was immediately going to sea, and that if the fowling piece was not instantly sent on board he should be carried away from his island. To these threats he paid little attention, until an armed centinel was placed to guard him in the cabin; when his apprehensions became visible, and were not a little augmented by the alarm of the Indians on board, most of whom quitted the ship. Mr. Hergest, perceiving his agitation, used every means to assure him, that he should not be hurt, but yet if the gun was withheld, that he would on a certainty proceed with him to sea. This conversation had the desired effect; a message was sent to the chief in whose possession the piece was, and in about half an hour a canoe was seen coming towards the ship displaying the usual emblems of peace, in which was a chief who had brought back the gun, and to whom Mr. Hergest delivered up the prisoner unhurt. The tears, eager salutation, and the fond delight expressed by the chief who had been detained on again embracing his countrymen, plainly discovered the terror of his mind under the apprehension of seeing them no more. They now parted very good friends, and both the prisoner and the other chief seemed perfectly reconciled on receiving some useful presents.

Thus the Dædalus quitted the island and its inhabitants with whom they seemed to be continually on the eve of a quarrel, in consequence of their repeated and daring thefts. Mr. Hergest very humanely concludes the account of his transactions at the Marquesas, by expressing much happiness that he had not been driven to the melancholy necessity of putting any of the natives to death, for the security of their property; and, excepting one man who was detected in stealing a bucket, and who was suffered to reach his canoe before a musket was fired, with the intention to frighten him by passing the ball through his canoe, but which unintentionally passed through the calf of his leg, no other person appeared to have received the least injury. This was a very fortunate circumstance, as the shot fired from the great guns went far up the valley, where were many of their habitations; and their escaping unhurt on that occasion was more than could well have been expected. It is, however, very probable they may not fare so well on the future arrival of other vessels, since their inordinate propensity to thieving seems beyond all restraint or controul; and there did not appear to be any chief amongst them, who possessed either inclination or authority sufficient to deter them from such practices.

In the evening, about five o'clock, they weighed and steered to the northward. At day-light the next morning (30th October [March]) they came within sight of some islands, which appeared to Mr. Hergest to be new discoveries.[1] Those first seen were three in number, one bearing by compass N. by E. the other N. by W. and the third S.W. by S. They fetched the S.W. part of the easternmost, where a good bay was found with a sandy beach.[2] Some rocky islets lie to the S.E. of it, and from a gully in the N.W. part of the bay, there was an appearance of procuring a supply of water. To the east of the south point there appeared another good bay; and along the western shore, shallow broken water. But, on rounding that point, and hauling to the north along the west side, the broken water was found to extend not more than a quarter of a mile from the shore. On this side there is neither cove nor inlet, only a rocky shore, with two small rocky islets off its N.W. point. This island is about six leagues in circuit, and is in latitude 8° 50' south; longitude 220° 51' east.[3] It is inhabited by a tribe of seemingly friendly Indians, some of whom visited the ship in their canoes. In the vallies were a great number of cocoa nut and plantain trees, and the whole island presented an infinitely more verdant and fertile appearance than those they had just quitted. From hence they stood over to the southernmost island[4] which appears at a distance like a remarkably high rock, with three peaked rocks close to it; these are about the middle of the island. The night was spent in keeping their station near it, and in the morning their course was directed towards its S.W. point. As the shore was approached, the land was seen to be well cultivated and numerously inhabited. More than one hundred Indians were soon assembled round the ship in their canoes, disposing of cocoa nuts, plantains, &c. for beads and other trifles, and behaving in a very friendly manner. At the S.W. end of this island is a very good bay, with a sandy beach in its eastern part.[5] Along the southern side are other bays; one in particular appeared to retire deeply in towards the south east end of the island, having an islet lying off it, not unlike in shape to a cathedral; and other rocks and islets. From the west point of this island, forming also the west point of the finest and deepest bay it affords, its shores trend round to the N.E. and, like the west side of the island they

---

[1] Hergest was approaching the northern group of the Marquesas. Unknown to him they had been discovered by Joseph Ingraham, in the American trading ship *Hope* in April 1791. For Ingraham's own account see 'An Account of a recent discovery of seven Islands in the South Pacific, by Joseph Ingraham,' *Collections*, Massachusetts Historical Society, 1st series, II (1793), pp. 20–4.

[2] Ua Huka was the island; the bay is named Friendly Bay on Hergest's chart. It is now Baie d'Hane (France took possession of the islands in 1842).

[3] The correct position is lat. 8° 55' S, long. 139° 33' W (220° 27' E).

[4] Ua Pou.

[5] This bay is also named Friendly Bay on Hergest's chart. Now Baie de Vaiehu.

were at the preceding day, (which received the name of RIOU'S ISLAND) [1] are rocky, and bear rather a sterile appearance. This island obtained the name of TREVENEN'S ISLAND; [2] it is situated in latitude 9° 14′ south, longitude 220° 21′ east.

In the forenoon of the 1st of April, the south side of the third island was passed, which was named SIR HENRY MARTIN'S ISLAND; [3] immediately to the west of its S.E. point, called point Martin, is a deep well-sheltered bay bounded by sandy beaches, this obtained the name of COMPTROLLER'S BAY; [4] it was not examined, but on passing had the appearance of a safe and commodious port. At its head was a break in the shores, supposed by some to be the mouth of a rivulet, but as it appeared too large for so small an island to afford, Mr. Hergest was rather inclined to believe it only a deep cove.

They were here visited by many of the natives paddling and sailing in their canoes; who behaved in a very civil and friendly manner. About two leagues to the westward of point Martin is a very fine harbour, extending deep into the island, and bounded by a most delightful and fertile country. Mr. Hergest, accompanied by Mr. Gooch, went with the cutter to take a sketch, and to examine the port, which he called PORT ANNA MARIA. [5] It was found to be very easy of access and egress, without any shoals or rocks that are not sufficiently conspicuous to be avoided; the depth at its entrance 24 fathoms, gradually decreasing to seven fathoms, within a quarter of a mile of its shores; the bottom a fine sand, and the surrounding land affording most perfect security against the winds and sea in all directions. An excellent run of fine water flows into the harbour, which possesses every advantage that could be desired.

The country seemed to be highly cultivated, and was fully inhabited by a civil and friendly race of people, readily inclined to supply whatever refreshments their country afforded. Our people were induced to entertain this opinion from the hospitable reception they experienced on landing, from the chiefs and upwards of fifteen hundred of the natives who were assembled on the shores of the harbour. On their return to the ship they found the same harmony subsisting there with the Indians, who had carried off and sold a supply of vegetables and some pigs. They renewed their route along the south side of the island to its S.W. point, when they hauled their wind along the western side. This is a rocky iron bound shore without cove or bay. It had a verdant appearance, but no great sign of fertility, nor were any habitations or natives perceived. About sun-set they discovered what appeared like a large rock to the north-westward, about six or seven leagues distant, and during the night they remained near Sir Henry Martin's island; but in the morning not being able to fetch its N.E. point they quitted it; its N.W. side appeared

[1] Now Ua Huka. Named Washington Island by Ingraham.

[2] Now Ua Pou. Named Federal Island by Ingraham.

[3] Now Nuku Hiva, the largest island of the group. Ingraham had named it Franklin Island.

[4] Now Baie du Controleur.   [5] Now Baie de Taiohae.

to contain some small bays, and towards its N.E. extremity the land turned, apparently, short round, forming a bay something similar to, but not so deep as Comptroller's bay. Another rock just above water now shewed its head to the eastward,[1] and to the northward of that before mentioned. These Mr. Hergest represents to be dangerous; they lie nearly W. by N. about six leagues from the western side of Sir Henry Martin's island, which is about sixteen leagues in circuit. Its centre is situated in south latitude 8° 51′, longitude 220° 19′, east.

After leaving this island, two others were discovered to the northward of them. On the morning of the 3d of April they bore up to the southward, along the east side of the south-westernmost. This is the largest of the two, its shores are rocky, without any coves or landing places, and though its surface was green it produced no trees, yet a few shrubs and bushes were thinly scattered over the face of the rocks; nor did it seem to be otherwise inhabited than by the tropical oceanic birds. These were in great numbers about it, and it seemed to be a place of their general resort. The N.W. side, however, had a more favourable aspect, and though its shores were also rocky a number of trees were produced, as well on the sides of the hills, as in the vallies. This side afforded some coves where there is good landing, particularly in one near the middle; this, from the appearance of its northern side, was called BATTERY COVE.[2] A little more than a mile to the north of this cove is a bay, which Mr. Hergest and Mr. Gooch examined. Good anchorage and regular soundings were found from eighteen to five fathoms water; the bottom a fine clear sand. An excellent run of fresh water discharged itself into the bay near a grove of cocoa-nut trees; here they landed, and found a place of interment, and a hut near half a mile from it by the side of a hill; but there were no people, nor the appearance of any having been recently there; although it was manifest that they did, on some occasions, resort to the island. This induced Mr. Hergest to forbear cutting down any of the cocoa-nut trees as he had at first intended to do; and he procured by other means as many of the fruit as served the whole crew, with five to each person.[3]

The landing was but indifferent on account of the surf; but water is easily obtained.

After ascertaining the last mentioned island to be eight miles long and two miles broad, and to be situated in south latitude 7° 53′, longitude 219° 47′ east, they took leave of these islands the next morning; and to the N.E. of the last, at the distance of about a league, they discovered another, nearly round and much smaller, with two islets lying off its S.W. point; to this was given the name of ROBERTS'S ISLAND.[4]

---

[1] This should read 'westward'.
[2] Not marked on Hergest's chart.
[3] Cocoa Nut Bay on Hergest's chart.
[4] On Hergest's chart the name Roberts's Isles is applied to both the larger and the smaller islands just described. They are now named Eiao and Hatutaa respectively. Ingraham had named them Knox and Hancock islands.

Mr. Hergest states, that during the time he was amongst these islands and at the Marquesas, they were subject to frequent heavy squalls and much rain. He compares the inhabitants of this group to those of the Marquesas, [1] in colour and in size: but in manners, behaviour, dress, and ornaments, excepting that of their being less punctured, they more resembled the people of Otaheite and the Society islands.

On the first information of the Dædalus having visited these islands, I concluded they had not been seen before, and to commemorate the discovery of a very worthy though unfortunate friend and fellow traveller in my more early periods of navigating these seas, I distinguished the whole group by the name of HERGEST'S ISLANDS. But I have since been informed, that these islands had been discovered and landed upon by some of the American traders, [2] and that in fine weather the southernmost is visible from Hood's island, the most northern of the Marquesas. Hence they are considered by some as properly appertaining to that group, although neither the Spanish navigator, [3] nor captain Cook who visited the Marquesas after him, had any knowledge of such islands existing.

This is the amount of all the information I have been able to collect from Mr. Hergest's papers respecting his voyage thus far; the imperfect arrangement of which offers an additional cause, if an additional cause could be wanting, to lament the untimely and melancholy fate of that valuable officer; who, in several interesting particulars in his observations on these islands, refers to documents which I have never seen, and which would of course have enabled me to illustrate many points and descriptions which, for that reason, I have not been able to insert.

The unfortunate, as well as the successful adventures of persons employed on services of a public nature, being generally objects of minute inquiry, I shall conclude this chapter with the account delivered to me by Mr. New, the master of the Dædalus transport, of the melancholy fate that attended Lieutenant Hergest her commander, Mr. Gooch the astronomer, and the unfortunate seaman who was murdered with them.

In their passage from Hergest's to the Sandwich islands there did not appear any thing worthy of remark except a strong current that set at the rate of 30 miles a day, and obliged them to stand to the eastward lest they should fall to leeward of those islands. The Dædalus by this means arrived off Owhyhee, and Mr. Hergest received the orders I had left there. [4] From thence he proceeded to the N.W. side of Woahoo, not having any expectation of finding the Discovery at that time on the south side of the island, as I had appointed. This unfortunate determination, though contrary to the orders I had given, appeared to him at the time to be right, in order to insure the most expeditious passage towards Nootka.

[1] Meaning the southern group of the Marquesas.
[2] Joseph Ingraham, in 1791, as already noted.
[3] Alvaro de Mendana, who discovered the islands in 1595.
[4] The letter had been left with Rowbottom in March 1792.

In the morning of the 7th of May, the Dædalus arrived in that bay where the Resolution and Discovery had anchored in 1779,[1] but Mr. Hergest declined anchoring there, as he considered the inhabitants of that neighbourhood to be the most savage and deceitful of any amongst those islands. For this reason he lay to, and purchased from the natives some hogs, vegetables, and a few gourds of water. In the evening he stood off shore, and desired that the inhabitants would bring a further supply of water and refreshments the next morning; but it falling calm, and the current setting the ship to the westward, it was near noon on the 11th before they regained the shore, when Mr. Hergest receded from his former wise determination, and unhappily for himself and those who fell with him, ordered the ship to be anchored. The cutter was hoisted out and veered astern for the better convenience of purchasing water from the natives, but before three casks were filled, which was soon done, he ordered the cutter alongside, the full casks to be taken out and replaced by empty ones; and then, accompanied as usual by Mr. Gooch, he went on shore, and another boat was hoisted out for the purpose of obtaining water; while those on board continued making purchases until near dark. At this time the cutter returned, with only five persons instead of the eight who had gone on shore in her, from whom was learned the distressing intelligence, that Mr. Hergest, Mr. Gooch, and two of the boat's crew having landed unarmed with two of the water casks to fill, their defenceless situation was perceived by the natives, who immediately attacked them, killed one of the people, and carried off the commander and the astronomer. The other being a very stout active man made his escape through a great number of these savages, fled to the boat, and with two others landed again, with two muskets, and with the intention to rescue their officers, and to recover the body of their mess-mate. They soon perceived that both Mr. Hergest and Mr. Gooch were yet alive amongst a vast concourse of the inhabitants, who were stripping them, and forcing them up the hills behind the village: they endeavoured to get near the multitude, but were so assailed by stones from the crowd, who had now gained the surrounding hills, that they were under the painful necessity of retiring; and as night was fast approaching, they thought it most advisable to return on board, that more effectual means might be resorted to on this unfortunate occasion.

Mr. New immediately assembled all the officers, to consult with them what was best to be done. It was agreed to stand off and on with the ship during the night, and in the morning to send the cutter well manned and armed on shore, and if possible to recover their unfortunate commander and shipmates. An old chief belonging to Attowai,[2] who had been on board since the Dædalus entered the bay, and had been promised by Mr. Hergest a passage to his native island, went also in the boat, to assist as an interpreter, and to employ his good offices. He was first landed, and went towards the natives, of whom he demanded the absent gentlemen; on which he was informed they

---

[1] Waimea Bay. Clerke's journal shows that the Resolution and the Discovery anchored there on 28 February 1779, a fortnight after Cook's death.   [2] Kauai.

were both killed the preceding night. Having delivered this message, he was sent back to demand their bodies; but was told in reply, that they had both been cut in pieces, and divided amongst seven different chiefs; at least it was so understood by those in the boat from the language and signs which the chief made use of.[1]

After this conversation the savages came in great numbers towards the sea side, and threw stones at the party in the boat, who fired several times and at length obliged them to retire. Finding their errand to be completely fruitless, the boat returned on board, in which the old chief re-embarked, and the vessel bore away to land him agreeably to a former promise at Attowai; but when they were about five or six leagues to leeward of Woahoo, about five in the evening, the old chief made a sudden spring overboard, and swam from the ship, which was instantly brought to, but on finding that he still continued to swim from them, without the least inclination of returning on board, they filled their sails, and having then no business at Attowai, they made the best of their way towards Nootka, agreeably to my directions.

On the 13th of June they made the American coast; the wind having been constantly in the N.W. quarter, they were not able to fetch higher up than the latitude of 41° 30', from whence they beat to windward the rest of the way to Nootka, where they arrived on the 4th of July. In compliance with a letter of instructions left by the late commander of the Dædalus in his bureau, addressed to Mr. Thomas New in case of his death, Mr. New opened the dispatches addressed to me from the Lords of the Admiralty, and agreeably with the directions they contained, he delivered to Senr Quadra, the commanding officer at that port, the letter therein inclosed, and addressed to him from the Spanish minister.

Thus conclude all the matters and transactions of our voyage up to the end of the year 1792. In the following chapter I shall resume the narrative of our proceedings at Monterrey.

[1] For Vancouver's account of his inquiry into the murders, and the apprehension, trial and execution of three men deemed to have been implicated, see pp. 875–81.